Scandinavians in the State House

• • •

Scandinavians
in the State House

How Nordic Immigrants Shaped Minnesota Politics

Klas Bergman

MINNESOTA
HISTORICAL
SOCIETY PRESS

The publication of this book was supported though a generous grant from the Dale S. and Elizabeth D. Hanson Fund for Swedish American History.

Unless otherwise indicated, all images are from Minnesota Historical Society collections.

www.mnhspress.org

The Minnesota Historical Society Press is a member of the Association of American University Presses.

Manufactured in the United States of America

10 9 8 7 6 5 4 3 2 1

∞ The paper used in this publication meets the minimum requirements of the American National Standard for Information Sciences—Permanence for Printed Library Materials, ANSI Z39.48–1984.

International Standard Book Number
ISBN: 978-1-68134-030-2 (paper)
ISBN: 978-1-68134-031-9 (e-book)

Library of Congress Cataloging-in-Publication Data

Names: Bergman, Klas, 1942– author.
Title: Scandinavians in the state house : how Nordic immigrants shaped Minnesota politics / Klas Bergman.
Description: St. Paul, MN : Minnesota Historical Society Press, 2017. | Includes bibliographical references and index.
Identifiers: LCCN 2016058992 | ISBN 9781681340302 (pbk. : alk. paper) | ISBN 9781681340319 (ebook)
Subjects: LCSH: Scandinavians—Minnesota—Politics and government. | Scandinavians—Minnesota—History. | Scandinavian Americans—Minnesota—Politics and government. | Scandinavian Americans—Minnesota—History. | Immigrants—Minnesota—History.
Classification: LCC F615.S18 B47 2017 | DDC 977.6/004395—dc23
LC record available at https://lccn.loc.gov/2016058992

This and other Minnesota Historical Society Press books are available from popular e-book vendors.

TO MARGA

• • •

Contents

Preface

THIS IS THE STORY OF IMMIGRATION and politics, or more precisely the story of Scandinavian immigrants in Minnesota and their role, impact, and legacy in Minnesota politics.

Hundreds of thousands of immigrants from the five Nordic countries in northern Europe settled in Minnesota between 1850 and 1930: Norwegians, Swedes, Finns, Danes, and Icelanders. They threw themselves into politics quickly after arriving in the new country, often more quickly than other immigrant groups. Over time, they came to dominate and shape Minnesota's politics, starting at the local level as town clerks, treasurers, auditors, school board members, and sheriffs, before eventually broadening their sights and ambitions and entering state and national politics as governors, state senators and house members, US senators and representatives, and ultimately vice presidents of the United States.

Since 1892, Minnesota has had twenty governors of Nordic descent; between 1915 and 1976, a span of more than fifty years, every Minnesota governor was of either Swedish or Norwegian descent, except for a Finland-Swede and one Dane. Two of them were talked about as possible candidates for the highest office in the land but died young. Two others, who served as vice presidents, did run for the highest office, but lost. They are just a part of a remarkable political legacy that has profoundly shaped Minnesota politics and made Minnesota different from other states in ways that have influenced American politics well beyond its borders.

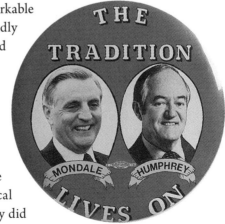

Many Nordic immigrants came to America for political reasons, blacklisted in their home countries because of their radical politics. Once in Minnesota, they did not let up. They were trade unionists, founders of cooperatives, strike leaders in the mines on the Iron Range, socialists, Wobblies (members of the radical Industrial Workers of the World, or IWW), and communists. One rose to become head of the American Communist Party. Some were sentenced to prison and some were deported to their home countries. Others became emigrants again, leaving Minnesota and the United States for the Soviet Union to help build the new communist state.

Over time, Minnesota has become the most Scandinavian of all the states. As of 2016, one-third of its 5.4 million inhabitants are of Scandinavian descent. For a visitor, the state feels Scandinavian, with its lakes, forests, summer meadows, and bitter winters and the prevalence of Scandinavian traditions in summer as well as winter. But the state is also changing, with new and different immigrant groups arriving—Somalis, Hmong, Hispanics—many of whom are now entering Minnesota politics. The three latest governors have not been Scandinavian, and the question is what, if anything, remains of Minnesota's Scandinavian political legacy? Will it survive in the new Minnesota?

Large segments of American voters think that government doesn't work. Minnesota has charted its own course, founded in its Scandinavian heritage of a sensible and open-minded approach that values compromise and results. This pragmatism has resulted in Minnesota's image as the state that works. When the United States looks for ways to make its politics and government work, it could do worse than to look to Minnesota and its success, just as Europe, or for that matter America, could do worse than to look to northern Europe, where five small nations have become among the most successful countries in the world as measured by standard of living, quality of life, work/life balance, business innovation, and even happiness, according to numerous international comparisons and rankings.

1

The Beginnings

Outside of the Nordic countries, no other part of the world has been so influenced by Scandinavian activities and ambitions as Minnesota.

Professor Sten Carlsson, Uppsala University, Sweden, 1970

THE FALL OF 2014 IN MINNESOTA was gloriously sunny and unusually warm. But as many of the leading candidates from Minnesota's Democratic Party, known as the Democratic-Farmer-Labor (DFL) Party, gathered one morning in front of the State Capitol in St. Paul in the days before the November elections, the weather had turned cold, and one could feel the Minnesota winter approaching.

They had gathered for a final, frenetic "Get Out the Vote" statewide bus tour culminating in the Twin Cities with a Midnight Madness event, a last-minute attempt to get people to the polls to cast their votes. Governor Mark Dayton and US senator Al Franken, both seeking reelection, were there; so were Lori Swanson and Rebecca Otto, also up for reelection as attorney general and state auditor, respectively, and Steve Simon, seeking the voters' support in his first run for secretary of state. Others were Amy Klobuchar, Minnesota's second US senator; mayors Chris Coleman and Betsy Hodges from St. Paul and Minneapolis; US congressman Keith Ellison; state speaker of the house Paul Thissen—all lending their support to bring home a DFL victory on November 4.

In an election year and with a strong political headwind, it was an uphill battle for the Minnesota Democrats, and they knew it. But the wind had blown hard in Governor Dayton's face before, not the least in 2010, when he faced a Republican stampede for lower taxes and smaller government by vowing a tax increase, promising greater investments in education, and touting the importance of government. He won narrowly, and with the backing of DFL majorities in both the state senate and house, Dayton got a $2.1 billion tax increase, mostly on the wealthy and on cigarettes, signed a bill legalizing gay marriage in Minnesota, and created free, statewide, all-day kindergarten.

In the 2014 elections, Dayton was running on that record. Standing in front of the DFL bus with the slogan, "On the Road to a Better Minnesota," he and the other Democrats spoke about the importance of the next few days and the importance of voting. Steve Simon, candidate for secretary of state, an office that supervises elections, underlined how Minnesota had the highest voter turnout of any state in the country, nine elections in a row. That, he said, is part of the Minnesota culture—to make it as easy as possible for everyone to vote.

None of the DFL speakers that day alluded to the fact that they stood in the shadows of giants in Minnesota politics, on hallowed Scandinavian American political ground. Right behind them, in front of the impressive State Capitol designed by architect Cass Gilbert, stood the statues of Norwegian-born former governor and US senator Knute Nelson and three-time governor John Albert Johnson, the son of Swedish immigrants and the first Minnesota-born governor.

The inscriptions on the statues read:

> Knute Nelson, February 2, 1843–April 28, 1923. Three years a soldier in the Civil War. Three times a member of Congress. Twice Governor of Minnesota. Five times our United States Senator. A brave son of Norway. A true patriot devoted in his allegiance to America. A wise statesman uncompromising in support of the principles in which he believed. A distinguished citizen of Minnesota.

> John Albert Johnson, July 26, 1861–Sept 21, 1909. Three times Governor of Minnesota. A poor boy. A country editor. A natural leader. Cut off in his prime. The nation mourns his loss. His life was gentle and the elements so mixed in him that nature might stand up and say to all the world, this was a man. This monument is raised by one hundred thousand of his friends.

Elsewhere on the capitol grounds is the statue of yet another former Scandinavian American governor, Floyd Bjornstjerne Olson, born of a Norwegian father and Swedish mother, who, as the leader of the Minnesota Farmer-Labor Party in the 1930s, paved the way for the creation, in 1944, of the DFL.

Statue of Knute Nelson in front of the Minnesota State Capitol in St. Paul. Photo from Wikimedia Commons

Both John A. Johnson and Floyd B. Olson died young, when they stood on the doorstep of national political prominence. Johnson had been tagged as a possible presidential candidate in 1912, and Olson was a potential vice presidential running mate to Franklin Delano Roosevelt in 1940. In a sense, they were forerunners to two other Scandinavian American politicians from Minnesota who did make it to the highest echelons of American national politics: Hubert H. Humphrey and Walter F. Mondale, both US senators, both vice presidents of the United States, and both Norwegian Americans.

Mondale is not, at least not yet, honored with a memorial at the State Capitol. But Humphrey is, and the inscription on his statue is a quotation from a speech he gave in 1977: "It was once said that the moral test of Government is how that Government treats those who are in the dawn of life, children; those who are in the twilight of life, the elderly; and those who are in the shadows of life, the sick, the needy and the handicapped."

Close to Humphrey is the statue of a legendary aviator, Swedish American Charles A. Lindbergh Jr., the first man to fly solo across the Atlantic. He played no political role in Minnesota, but his Swedish-born father, Charles August Lindbergh Sr., did. A longtime Republican member of the US House of Representatives and a leading voice against American involvement in World War I, Lindbergh Sr. ran for governor as a populist Republican in 1918 but lost narrowly in the primary to another Swedish American, Joseph A. A. Burnquist, who would go on to oversee a notorious era of suppression of dissent in Minnesota.

And on the other side of the capitol, overlooking them all, stands the memorial statue of the Viking who came to America long before any of them, Leif Erikson.

The involvement of Scandinavian immigrants in Minnesota politics goes far beyond these few political luminaries, however, and indeed began even before Minnesota became a state in 1858. The first Scandinavian was elected to political office in the Minnesota Territory in 1856, when Ole Knudsen, from Hedemarken in Norway, was voted in as county commissioner in Houston County. The delegation to Minnesota's constitutional convention in October 1857 included two Norwegian immigrants, John A. Anderson and Charles Hanson, and one Swedish immigrant, Peter (Pehr) A. Cederstam. The final document was sent to the people of Minnesota, who, on October 13, 1857, overwhelmingly voted for its approval, 30,055 to 571. On May 11, 1858, Minnesota was admitted to the Union as the thirty-second state of the United States of America.

The new state constitution encouraged political participation by immigrants by granting (men only) very liberal voting rights, including to noncitizens if they had filed a declaration of intent to become citizens and had lived in the United States for a year, four months in Minnesota, and ten days in the voter precinct. (Eventually, starting in 1896, the voting rules were slightly tightened, requiring citizenship for three months together with five years of residency in the United States and one year in Minnesota.) The new immigrants from northern Europe took advantage of these liberal voting laws and seemed almost in a hurry to take part in the affairs of their new home country. This is reflected in the speech given by Norwegian immigrant journalist Paul Hjelm-Hansen in the town of Alexandria in 1869:

> Be agreed among yourselves, you Swedish, Norwegian, and Danish men and women, help and support one another.... I do not wish to say that the Scandinavians should form a power all of themselves or be a state within a state.... On the contrary, it is the sacred duty of the emigrants who wish to make this country their ... home ... to become assimilated ... to learn the English language and to ... uphold the spirit and institutions of the Republic. The sooner this comes about the better.

Hjelm-Hansen was born in Bergen on Norway's Atlantic coast in 1810. He studied law but eventually became a journalist and author. He did not arrive in America until 1867, already fifty-seven years old. Two years later, he was appointed by the governor of Minnesota to act as an agent of the State Board of Immigration and was sent out to gather information about the United States for prospective immigrants. He traveled extensively in the Upper Midwest, particularly in the Red River Valley on the border between Minnesota and the Dakotas. Hjelm-Hansen wrote about his travels for the Norwegian papers *Faedrelandet og Emigranten* and *Nordisk Folkeblad* in Minneapolis, which published, in all, sixteen of his articles between April 1868 and February 1870. By the time of his speech in Alexandria, he had become a leading spokesman for Norwegian emigration to America, and to Minnesota in particular. Later, Hjelm-Hansen became involved in numerous journalistic endeavors in Minnesota, among them helping to found *Budstikken,* a leading Norwegian-language paper in Minneapolis. He died in 1881 and is buried underneath a headstone whose inscription today is practically illegible, in the Aspelund Emmanuel Lutheran Church cemetery in Wanamingo, in southern Minnesota, a long way from Bergen.

The same year that Hjelm-Hansen gave his speech in Alexandria, a man named Hans Mattson was elected as Minnesota's secretary of state, the first Scandinavian to win a statewide political office in Minnesota. In those years, Minnesota needed immigrants so the state could continue to grow, and immigration was strongly encouraged by the political and business leaders and by the railroads. Mattson also became a leading promoter of Scandinavian immigration to Minnesota, and his speech at the Republican Party's convention in St. Paul in 1869 echoed the sentiments of Hjelm-Hansen. He said, "It is true that we have left our beloved home country—and left the last flowers on our ancestors' graves—and have come here to stay. We are not a people of isolated clans, and we do not wish to create a Scandinavian nationality in the midst of all of you.... Yes, we love this great land of liberty and we wish to be and remain Americans."

Born in 1832 in the village of Önnestad near the town of Kristianstad in Skåne in southern Sweden, Mattson had arrived in America in 1851, at the age of nineteen. His stirring appeal in 1861 to Minnesota's Scandinavians to join the Union army and fight for liberty had made him well known in the state. The appeal, originally printed in the Swedish-language paper *Hemlandet,* was reprinted in a Minneapolis paper in January 1918, as it was "applicable" to World War I:

> It is high time for us, as a people, to rise with sword in hand and fight for our adopted country and for liberty.... This land we, as strangers, have made our home, has received us with friendship and hospitality. We enjoy equal privileges with the native born. The path to honor and fortune is alike open to us and them. The law protects and befriends us all alike. We have also sworn allegiance to the same.... Countrymen, arise to arms, our adopted country calls. Let us prove ourselves worthy of that land and of those heroes from whom we descend. Let us place ourselves on the side of liberty and truth, not only with words but with strong arms—with our lives.

The appeal was part of the overwhelming support in Minnesota for President Abraham Lincoln and the Union, and the young state became the first to offer troops to the Union army. In all, about 22,000 Minnesotans fought for the Union. At least three thousand Swedish immigrants fought for the Union, and another several hundred served in the Union navy—a high percentage when the total number of Swedish immigrants in America, according to the 1860 US census, was 18,625.

Hans Mattson became Colonel Hans Mattson as head of the Third Minnesota Regiment, which had gathered at Fort Snelling immediately south of Minneapolis with 790 Swedes and 30 Norwegians from Red Wing, Vasa, Chisago Lake, Stillwater, Albert Lea, and other small Minnesota towns after the appeal. The war launched Mattson's political career, as it did many

others', underlining Swedish American scholar O. Fritiof Ander's contention that participation in the Civil War was "almost a requisite" for success
in politics. Mattson's Danish friend F. Sneedorff Christensen, editor of *Nordisk Folkeblad* in Rochester, had urged Mattson to run and proposed him
for secretary of state on the Republican ticket. Christensen, according to
Norwegian American scholar Odd S. Lovoll, was probably the first person
in Minnesota who openly urged Scandinavian immigrants to get involved
in politics.

Mattson was elected secretary of state three times and remained a "sincere and consistent Republican" all his life, never swerving from his allegiance to Lincoln's party.

Swedish immigrant Tufve Nilsson (T. N.) Hasselquist, a Lutheran
pastor and journalist, had issued a similar call to action as the Civil War
approached. Born in the village of Osby in Skåne in 1816, not far from
Mattson's birthplace, Hasselquist had come to America in 1852 and settled
in Galesburg, Illinois. A few years later, in 1855, he founded *Hemlandet, Det
Gamla och Det Nya* (The Homeland, Old and New), a newspaper that was
both political and religious. It became one of the most influential of all the
Swedish American newspapers. Through his paper, Hasselquist was "greatly
responsible for the shaping of Swedish American political opinion," writes
Ander in his biography of the clergyman, journalist, and educator. Hasselquist took a "definite stand" on slavery as the most important issue of the
day, and he "gradually and cautiously led his readers into the ranks" of the
Republican Party, which had been formed in 1855 with the primary goal of
preventing the extension of slavery as the United States expanded into new
territories. Slavery, said Hasselquist, could not be defended; it was contrary
to the spirit of the Bible.

In the election of 1856, in which the new Republican Party swept every
state in the North, Hasselquist pleaded with the Swedish immigrants to cast
their votes for the Republican Party as "the only true anti-slavery party,"
adding, "May not the immigrated Norseman dishonor himself, his countrymen, his home, his forefathers, his ancient liberty, by giving his vote for
slavery." With time and the ascent of Lincoln, he became more and more
openly partisan, describing the Democratic Party as "catholic, Irish, law-
less, disorderly" as well as corrupt and dishonest. During the presidential
election of 1860, the new state of Minnesota with its Scandinavian immigrants joined the northern tier of voters in support of Lincoln, and every
reader of *Hemlandet* received a photo of the new president; when he died,

the paper came out with black borders. In both 1860 and 1864, the voters of Minnesota supported Lincoln for president, not the least in Swedish and Norwegian counties such as Chisago, Goodhue, Fillmore, and Hennepin, which includes the city of Minneapolis.

Hasselquist urged Swedes in America to become citizens and vote. He was "largely responsible" for the Swedish immigrants changing their political alliance, and according to Ander, "his influence in shaping the political opinion of his countrymen was permanent." The Swedish Americans, who in the early 1850s typically voted for the Democratic Party, were by the end of the 1800s over 90 percent Republican.

The same could be said of Minnesota's Norwegian immigrants. In a 1909 speech at the Norwegian Society of Minneapolis, prominent Norwegian American journalist Luth Jaeger called the Scandinavians' faithfulness to the Republican Party "slavish" and "practically part and parcel of the religious creed of the Norwegians." He added, "To be branded a Democrat was little better than to be branded an atheist or infidel." For the Norwegians, the Republican Party "represented Protestantism, high moral ideals, and prohibition, as well as free land under the Homestead Act." Anti-Catholicism was prevalent among the Norwegians as well as the Swedes, which further distanced them from the Democratic Party, which was supported by Catholic Germans and Irish.

A Norwegian newspaper also played an important role in persuading Norwegian immigrants to switch their vote to Lincoln and the Republican Party. *Emigranten,* founded in 1852, started out as an independent Democratic paper but switched political course in 1857 under Carl Fredrik Solberg's leadership. Solberg saw the Republican Party as the champion of the distribution of free land, so important to the immigrants, and he adopted "No slavery for either black or white" as the paper's slogan. Solberg, who had been born in Christiania (Oslo), Norway, in 1833, came to America with his family at the age of twenty. After a stopover in Pennsylvania, the family moved to Wisconsin, where Solberg got a job with *Emigranten.* During the Civil War, he traveled as a correspondent for the paper with what was known as the Norwegian Regiment. The Norwegians fought for the Union in the Civil War in even greater numbers than the Swedes, at least eight hundred from Minnesota and three thousand from Wisconsin. In Wisconsin, Hans Christian Heg, born in Lierbyen in Norway in 1829 and arriving in America at the age of eleven, organized the Norwegian Wisconsin Fifteenth Regiment, of which 90 percent were Norwegians and the rest Danes and Swedes. Heg died at the Battle of Chickamauga in 1863.

In 1872 Solberg founded another Norwegian paper, *Minnesota,* in Minneapolis. He died in 1924 at the age of ninety-one.

Former Minnesota governor Al Quie talked in an interview about his grandfather, Halvor Quie, an immigrant from Norway: "My grandfather read *Uncle Tom's Cabin* when it came out in 1852—we still have the first edition—and he became so opposed to slavery that when Lincoln called for volunteers, he signed up and recruited others." He was shot in the leg at Antietam as a member of the First Minnesota Sharpshooters. "And so," Quie added, "eventually I came out for civil rights."

For the Scandinavian immigrants, according to Lovoll, the Civil War "marked a decisive phase in the immigrants' process of adjustment," and "the enormous conflict created a new patriotism, a sense of having earned a legitimate place in America."

BEFORE THE CIVIL WAR, there were not many Scandinavian immigrants in Minnesota. Jacob Fahlstrom (Swedish: Fahlström), born in Stockholm in 1793, was the first Swedish settler, arriving in 1823. He became a fur trader and mail carrier, and later in life a Methodist preacher. Fahlstrom lived among the local Indian tribes and turned guide and interpreter. He was known to the local Native Americans as "Yellow Head" for his blond hair, and as the "Swede Indian" to the white settlers. Fahlstrom married Margaret Bongo, whose father was the son of a freed African slave and whose mother was Ojibwe. They had many children and farmed around the town of Afton, east of St. Paul, on the western bank of the St. Croix River. Fahlstrom died in 1859 and his wife in 1880. They are buried in a small, almost forgotten cemetery named after him on land that was part of their Valley Creek farm and is now surrounded by private homes in a suburban enclave just outside Afton. Their graves are unmarked, but a plaque erected in 1964 by the United Methodist Historical Society of Minnesota tells their story.

Nils Nilsen from Modum was among the first permanent Norwegian residents in Minnesota. He arrived in St. Paul in 1849 and later went west to farm in Otter Tail County. Ingeborg Levorsdatter Langeberg was the first woman settler. She came from Nes in Hallingdal in 1850 and became a maid in the home of the territorial governor Alexander Ramsey.

By 1860, just before the outbreak of the Civil War, the new state had 175,000 non-Indian residents, mostly Yankees who had moved west from New England, the mid-Atlantic states, Pennsylvania, and Ohio. There were also 58,700 foreign-born residents in Minnesota, or 29 percent of the total population: 18,400 Germans, 12,800 Irish, 8,400 Norwegians, and 3,100

Swedes, all part of a population boom in the 1850s, when the number of residents in Minnesota jumped by 2,831 percent.

Although the Civil War and the US–Dakota War of 1862 in Minnesota put a temporary halt to European immigration, the passage of the Homestead Act in 1862 became an irresistible incentive for land-hungry, and hungry, Scandinavians hoping to take advantage of the offer of 160 acres of land, granted free after five years if the land was improved. Arriving in Minnesota in ever greater numbers, these Scandinavians "were the peasant foot soldiers of economic development in Minnesota." Reflecting on his own ancestors' decision to leave their Norwegian homeland, former Minnesota house speaker Steve Sviggum took a boat ride through the beautiful fjords of Norway and asked the boat captain why his relatives would ever leave this place. The captain simply replied, "They were starving."

From 1840 to 1930, the height of mass emigration to the United States, a total of more than 2.7 million people left the five Nordic countries for America: 1.25 million Swedes, 875,000 Norwegians, 300,000 Danes, 300,000 Finns, and a few thousand Icelanders. Only Ireland saw a greater percentage of its population leave for America than Norway, Iceland, and Sweden. By 1880, 71 percent of all Minnesota residents were first- and second-generation Europeans. Of these, the German-born were the most numerous (67,000), but collectively there were more Scandinavians: 107,000. Ten years later, the numbers of Norwegian- and Swedish-born Minnesotans had increased to about 100,000 each, and about 14,000 Danes. By 1905, the Swedes had overtaken the Germans as the largest single foreign-born group in Minnesota. That year, the Swedes numbered 126,280, compared to 119,860 Germans and, in third place, 111,600 Norwegians. The three remaining Nordic groups—the Finns at 19,840, the Danes at 16,100, and the Icelanders at 386—were far behind.

For many, emigration meant survival. Migration scholars talk about push and pull factors to describe the complex interaction of reasons people emigrate and immigrate. For the Europeans who went to America by the millions, the primary push factor was poverty—caused by overpopulation, economic crises, joblessness, crop failure, and lack of available land in their home countries. Other driving factors were religious intolerance, a rigid social hierarchy with undemocratic practices, and more personal reasons such as the widespread blacklisting for radical political or labor activities, resistance to military service, and the tradition that only the oldest son in a family was eligible to inherit the parents' farm holdings, which left the rest of the siblings landless. And they were pulled to America by earlier emigrants who wrote home about available land on the American frontier, new economic opportunities, and higher wages, religious openness, and social mobility and equality.

And why Minnesota?

It's often said that the immigrants from northern Europe came to Minnesota because it looked like home, with its forests and lakes and rolling landscape and a climate with four different seasons. And it is true that parts of Minnesota, especially around Chisago Lake and Red Wing, bear an uncanny resemblance to parts of Sweden, and this is where the first Swedes in Minnesota settled. Northern Minnesota, in its grandness and its forests and lakes, looks very much like northern Scandinavia. However, much of Minnesota does not look like Scandinavia at all—there is no Baltic Sea or Atlantic Ocean, no fjords, no mountains, no archipelago, and the vast, treeless prairie is completely alien to Scandinavia. The Scandinavians, especially the Norwegians from their mountains and fjord valleys, were hesitant at first about moving there. They needed the trees to build their homes, or so they thought. But in the end, they could not resist the free land in the Red River Valley of western Minnesota.

So, to the question of why Minnesota, the answer is land—plenty of available free land. By 1860, only 15 percent of the land in Minnesota had been occupied by American and European migrants. The Minnesota frontier opened up just as the mass emigration from Scandinavia started in earnest. Historian John G. Rice calls this the "coincidence of the timing," when "land and employment presented themselves just when the immigrants needed them." Most immigrants were pushed and pulled from the Nordic countries just when their skills most matched Minnesota's opportunities.

From the 1880s until the early 1920s, with steadily less Minnesota land available, the immigrant families were replaced by single and poorer Scandinavians, mostly men, some with labor movement experience. Many went to northern Minnesota to work as lumberjacks, miners, farmers, and fishermen. But many—including young, single men and women—settled in Minnesota's cities, drawn by stories in letters and newspapers and by returnees, to work as domestics, factory hands, tradespeople, and entrepreneurs. World War I brought new immigration restrictions, but immigration took an upward turn again in the 1920s, when economic conditions in the five Nordic nations were still difficult for many.

John G. Rice writes about five waves of Swedish immigration. During the first, from 1845 to 1854, which Rice calls the "pioneer period," only 14,500 Swedes left for America. For them, the "pull" opportunity in America—the possibility for poor and land-hungry farm families to obtain land—was greater than the "push" of discontent in Sweden. This created what has been called "folk migration," the emigration of whole farm families, from the Scandinavian countryside. They came via Illinois and Chicago, which became a mecca for Swedish immigrants. From there, they spread out over the Upper Midwest.

The second wave, between 1863 and 1877, is what Rice calls the "flight from hunger," when the "push" factors were stronger. Nearly 135,000 Swedes left for America, driven away by severe crop failures and widespread hunger. Many were single and poor but still looking for land. The third wave, from 1880 to 1893, was the time of mass migration, when almost 475,000 Swedes left for America. Primarily characterized by young and single adult immigrants, this third wave was more governed by "pull" rather than "push" factors, and the migration became more urban, with almost half of the new immigrants to Minnesota settling in the Twin Cities of Minneapolis and St. Paul. These new immigrants no longer sought land but rather jobs, which were largely found in the factories and flour mills of the cities. For the Swedes, the top year for immigration was 1887, when 46,264 Swedes settled in Minnesota.

Rice calls the fourth and fifth waves of Swedish emigration to America the "fortune seekers" period, during the years 1900 to 1913, when 280,000 Swedes left for America, and the "end of an era," between 1920 and 1930, when only 100,000 Swedes arrived in America. The peak years for Minnesota during these waves were in 1910, when 24,184 Swedes settled here, and 1923, when 26,370 arrived. The immigrants in the fourth wave were overwhelmingly young and single, attracted by the strong "pull" of higher pay in the American labor market. And they came to the cities of America. By 1905, the Twin Cities, with 38,000 Swedes making up 7.5 percent of the city's population, had the largest concentration of Swedes of all cities in the United States after Chicago.

Five years later, an estimated 61 percent of the Swedish-born immigrants in America lived in cities, a much higher percentage of urbanization than the other Nordic immigrants. In Minnesota as a whole, 12 percent of the population was Swedish American—much higher than in any other state. In "Swedish" counties such as Chisago and Isanti, the Swedish immigrants were 59 and 66 percent, respectively, of the county's entire population.

Minnesota was truly the most "Swedish" of all the states in America.

The Norwegians also came in waves after an initial phase starting in 1825, when fifty-two immigrants left Stavanger for America on the ship *Restauration*. It was not until the 1860s that the number of immigrants dramatically increased, and by 1930 a total of 875,000 Norwegians had left for America. They came in three great waves, according to Norwegian immigration scholar Ingrid Semmingsen. The first was from the 1860s to the early 1870s, the second from 1879 to 1893, when 250,000 Norwegians left for America, and the third from 1900 to World War I. The peak year of immigration was 1882, when 28,804 Norwegians settled in Minnesota, followed by 26,784 in 1903 and 18,912 in 1910. The situation for the Norwegians was somewhat different than for the Swedes. Between 1815 and 1865, Norway experienced a doubling of its population that coincided with food shortages, farm closures, and even starvation. When new land opened up in the Midwest, the farmers of Norway saw a "new opportunity for themselves and their children to continue their lives as farmers," to preserve their way of life in America. "They preferred this to the alternative of urbanization," writes Semmingsen. "One might say that paradoxically rural conservatism prompted them to make a radical decision" to go to America.

In the town of Muskego, a few miles southwest of Milwaukee, Wisconsin, eighty Norwegian immigrants signed and published the Muskego Manifesto on January 6, 1845. Its purpose was to defend their decisions to leave Norway for America: "We harbor no hopes of acquiring wealth, but we live under a liberal government in a fertile land, where freedom and equality prevail in religious as well as civil affairs, and without any special permission we can enter almost any profession and make an honest living; this we consider to be more wonderful than riches, for by diligence and industry we can look forward to an adequate income, and we thus have no reason to regret our decision to move here."

And so they kept coming, seemingly constantly looking for new land, even after they had arrived and settled in America, first in states like Illinois and Wisconsin and then onward, to Minnesota and the Dakotas. They "leap-frogged" already inhabited areas into the wilderness. In Minnesota the Norwegians continued to farm, first in the southeastern corner of the state, in counties such as Houston, Fillmore, and Goodhue, and then, as land opened up farther west, in the Red River Valley along the border between Minnesota and North and South Dakota, in counties like Otter Tail, Polk, Norman, Yellow Medicine, Clay, Swift, and Lac qui Parle. Major settlements in the Red River Valley got their start in 1871. By 1875, 50 percent of the settlers in some counties in western Minnesota were born in Norway, and by 1890, more than half of all of Minnesota's Norwegian population had settled in the Red River Valley. There they clung to traditions and a way of life that provided continuity with life in Norway. The parish Lutheran church remained a central institution, and some of those immigrants who had been active participants in Norway's social reforms "quickly became involved in the Minnesota political scene."

The Norwegian immigrants stayed more rural than any other ethnic group in America, and the second generation produced even more farmers than the first. In 1900, only one-fourth of the 336,000 Norwegians born in America lived in towns with more than 25,000 inhabitants, and as late as 1940, over half of all Norwegian Americans in the Midwest lived outside of centers with more than 25,000 inhabitants. In 1920, over half of those born in Norway and 65 percent of their descendants lived in rural areas in the United States.

Eventually, the Norwegian settlers looked around in the many little villages and towns and saw only fellow Norwegians and realized that they had to get involved in their community, in its civic affairs—in local politics. Having been ruled for so long by the Danes (from 1537 to 1814) and the Swedes (from 1814 to 1905), the Norwegian immigrants were more nationalistic, refusing to be lumped together with other Scandinavians. They also proved adept at politics, "perhaps," writes historian Steven J. Keillor, "because immigrants from a land ruled by others simply wanted political power more than others."

In contrast to other ethnic groups coming to Minnesota, the Norwegians not only settled among fellow Norwegians, they also sought out people from the same region and valley, the same *bygd*, or countryside, from which they, themselves, had come, and they formed *bygdelag*, Norwegian local societies. "Intense nationalism toward outsiders co-existed with intense localism toward each other," writes Keillor.

The Danes came to America in much smaller numbers, 309,000 in total, and Minnesota was not the primary destination. More Danes settled in Iowa and Wisconsin. Most of the Danes came after the Civil War, and the top year of Danish immigration to Minnesota was 1882, when 2,769 arrived and settled in the state. Lutheran immigrants moved to religious colonies at Tyler, in southwestern Minnesota, and at Askov in the northeastern part of the state, which were established by the Danish Evangelical Lutheran Church and the Dansk Folkesamfund (Danish Folk Society). But the Danes were less exclusively Lutheran than the Norwegians and Swedes and more of them were Mormons, Baptists, Methodists, and Seventh-Day Adventists.

Most of the Danish immigrants, about 70 percent overall, came from Denmark's rural areas. They brought the idea of cooperatives, especially dairy cooperatives, from the old country, and in 1890, the Clarks Grove Cooperative Creamery Association was founded in Freeborn County in southern Minnesota. Its success inspired cooperatives in other areas of the economy, and by 1918, there were 630 cooperative creameries in Minnesota. Land O'Lakes was founded in 1921 in St. Paul by 320 dairy farmers who joined together to form the Minnesota Cooperative Creameries Association. Today the company is one of the largest producers of butter and cheese in America.

The Icelandic immigrants in Minnesota congregated far from the ocean and their traditional hot springs, in three counties on the western edge of the state: Lyon, Lincoln, and Yellow Medicine. The little town of Minneota, out on the treeless prairie, became the center of the Icelandic immigrant community. At its height in 1925, the first- and second-generation Icelanders in the Minneota Colony numbered around one thousand people. The Icelanders started coming in 1870, with a top year in 1887, when 1,978 arrived. In pure numbers, they were far fewer than the immigrants from the other four Nordic countries. Still, Icelandic emigration to America was larger per capita than any other European country except Ireland and Norway.

Minnesota's first Icelanders were led by Gunnlaugur Petursson and his family, who arrived in July 1875 and claimed land a few miles northeast of what was to become the town of Minneota. The Icelandic settlers were successful farmers and, like the Danes, they formed cooperatives. The Verslunarfjelag Islendinga, or the Icelandic Mercantile Company, was formed as a cooperative in 1886 and in 1901 became a retail store, called the Big Store— "the glory of mercantile Minneota . . . Harrods, Macy's, Marshall Field, and Dayton's rolled into one," writes Bill Holm, the award-winning Icelandic American writer from Minneota. The Opera Hall on the second floor was rented out for dances and performances and served as a general community center. The Big Store closed in 1972.

The Icelandic immigrants brought with them a rich literary tradition. The *Minneota Mascot* became an important English-language newspaper. It was owned and operated for many years by the Bjornson family, first by Gunnar B. Bjornson, who was born in Iceland, and then by his sons. Gunnar and his son Valdimir were also prominent politicians. In addition, *Vinland*, the only Icelandic language newspaper ever printed in America, was published for a few years out of Minneota, as was a monthly literary magazine with the same name. The Icelandic immigrants formed a reading society and everyone had libraries in accordance with the rich Icelandic literary tradition. One writer said it was considered a disgrace if an Icelandic child could not read before first grade.

The Finns also came to Minnesota in waves, but their peak years were later than the other Nordic groups. The first wave came in 1864 and 1865 to Franklin in Renville County and to Cokato in Wright County, both rural areas west of the Twin Cities. By 1880, Cokato was the largest Finnish rural settlement in America, and it is the oldest continuous Finnish settlement in Minnesota. In the 1870s, the second wave of immigrants made their homes around New York Mills in Otter Tail County, in northwest Minnesota. Finally, a third and much larger wave of immigrants arrived around the turn of the century. By this time, there was no more free land for homesteaders, so the Finns settled on the Iron Range in northeastern Minnesota and found jobs as lumberjacks and in the iron mines. Nearly 3,500 Finns came to America in 1898, and the numbers more than tripled in one year, to 12,990 in 1899. The top year for Finnish immigration was in 1902, when 23,152 arrived in Minnesota; 19,007 arrived in 1910 and 20,057 in 1913. About 40 percent of all Finnish immigrants settled in Minnesota and Michigan. By the peak year of 1920, some 29,100 foreign-born Finns lived in Minnesota, out of a total of 149,824 in the whole country.

The Finns who came to America left a country that hadn't been independent for hundreds of years, ruled first by the Swedes until 1809 and then by the Russians from 1809 to 1917. It was a poor and overpopulated country. Turbulent times in the homeland during the early 1900s helped to spark the third and largest wave of Finnish immigration. Increased political oppression during Russian rule added to the urgency. Czar Nicholas II's Russification program in 1899 put an end to Finland's special and long-held autonomous status, which it had enjoyed under both the Swedes and the Russians. Nicholas II made Russian the official language of Finland and decreed that all Finnish men must serve in the Russian army. This caused an emigration explosion. While only 61,000 Finns left for America between 1874 and 1893, 270,000 emigrated between 1894 and 1914. "It was unique, they came all at once," said immigration scholar K. Marianne Wargelin, who is also the honorary consul of Finland in Minneapolis. "They needed work and they came for political reasons. They did not want to serve in the Russian army."

The Finnish immigrants in the third wave were mostly young common laborers; two-thirds of them were men. Many were political refugees, victims of deportation, dissident intellectuals, socialist activists, draft dodgers. Finnish women came to America at slightly lower rates than their Scandinavian counterparts. They had gained the right to vote in Finland already in 1906 and played active roles, once in America, in politics, the unions, and the cooperatives.

Between 20 and 25 percent of all Finnish immigrants to the United States were Finland-Swedes, part of the Swedish-speaking minority in Finland. The Finland-Swedes lived, and still live, mainly on the Finnish west coast along the Baltic Sea. Because of its historic links with and geographic proximity to Sweden, Finland is still officially a bilingual Finnish/Swedish country, although the Swedish-speaking population is only about 5.5 percent.

The immigrants from the five Nordic countries brought with them parts of their culture and traditions, foremost of which was their Lutheran religion. One of the first things immigrants did when settling in Minnesota was to build a church, followed by a school. "The church was the first, the most important and the most significant institution that the immigrants established," writes historian Marcus Lee Hansen. He further argues that the clergy was keen on getting involved in politics and the immigrant church had "a great influence on determining how the naturalized citizen would cast his vote." This was particularly true in the early decades of Scandinavian immigration, when the church was politically aligned with the majority of Scandinavian Americans in its support of the Republican Party. This changed, starting in the 1890s, as many Scandinavian immigrants started to lean toward reform-oriented movements such as populism or progressivism, while the immigrant church remained a conservative force, loyal to the Republicans. The church lagged behind the immigrant community in general in the process of Americanization, and as Minnesota's political landscape diversified, the role and influence of the churches decreased.

In Scandinavia, the church was the center of the community and life, the place where everyone met. The pastor was a servant of the state, and up to 1866, the clergy as an estate were represented in a separate chamber in parliament. The new constitution of Sweden in 1809 granted religious liberty, but, in fact, all the way up to 1858, someone practicing a dissenting religion could be exiled, fined, or even imprisoned.

"It is by no means purely accidental that the confluence of various forms of dissatisfaction with the state church coincided with the beginnings of emigration from Sweden," writes immigration historian George M. Stephenson. He saw a line of progression, from dissent to persecution to indignation to agitation to reforms and, finally, to emigration. "One cannot escape the conclusion that religion played an important role in stimulating the desire to emigrate." The religious revivals shook the state church but also the political and social institutions, since the church and the state were so connected. In fact, "it is impossible to draw a sharp line of demarcation between religious and political persecution, so closely were the church and the state knit together."

Once in America, the Lutheran church among the Norwegian immigrants became "plagued by disharmony and divisiveness," which led to the foundation of fourteen Lutheran synods between 1846 and 1900. The infighting was often vicious, many times far worse than in the political arena. In this regard they differed from the Swedes, who had only one Lutheran synod, the Augustana Synod, founded as the Scandinavian Evangelical Lutheran Augustana Synod in 1860 with both Swedish and Norwegian members. By 1926, the Swedish Augustana Synod had over 311,000 members and it was a united church, mainly, perhaps, because if you did not agree with it, you simply left—for an alternate church such as the Mission Covenant Church with 30,000 members, Swedish Methodists with 21,000, or the Baptists with 31,000. The Norwegians left the Augustana Synod in 1870 and formed the Norwegian Augustana, only to split again a short time later. A new unity among the Norwegian Lutherans did not come about until 1917, when a great merger occurred and the Norwegian Lutheran Church of America (Den norsk lutherske kirke i Amerika) was formed with almost half a million members in over three thousand congregations and one thousand pastors.

The Danes and the Finns fought similar religious battles. The Danish Evangelical Lutheran Church in America from 1872 contained two major factions: the happy Danes and the holy Danes, or Grundtvigians and Inner Mission. In the 1890s they split into two churches, both rejecting the state church back in Denmark. The "happy Danes" promoted education and culture through folk schools, while the "holy Danes" were more pietistic, and more numerous. The Finns organized Lutheran congregations wherever they settled, although only one in four Finnish immigrants chose to belong to a church once they arrived in America. There were at least three main factions of the old Lutheran Church of Finland: the Apostolic Lutheran Church, known as Laestadians after pastor Lars Levi Laestadius, who led a pietistic revival in the 1850s in northern Sweden; the Suomi Synod, which most closely resembled the Church of Finland; and the Finnish American National Evangelical Lutheran Church. In Cokato in 1876, the followers of Laestadius built the first Finnish church in Minnesota. In addition, like the other Nordic immigrants, the Finns became Methodists, Baptists, Mission Friends, and Mormons.

The immigrants from Norway, Sweden, and Finland also brought with them their temperance societies. Among the Finns on the Iron Range, such temperance societies often came about even before a church was built. Drinking was a problem in the old countries. In the 1800s, Sweden had the highest per capita consumption of liquor in Europe. Workers and farmhands were often paid with a bottle of *brännvin*, aquavit, at the end of the week. By the mid-1800s, the use of aquavit had become so universal, Stephenson writes, that "it must bear a portion of the blame for the poverty, misery, crime and economic depression" in Sweden in those days. But the Swedish clergy at the time took little or no interest in the temperance movement. In fact, they saw it as a kind of competitor to them and to the church. The result was the creation of a close relationship between the temperance movement and the religious revival movement, which opposed the power and influence of the state church, particularly among the new immigrant communities in America.

In Norway, too, alcohol abuse was considered one of the great evils of the 1800s, although drunkenness was probably greater among Norwegian Americans than in their home country, and "no issue concerned the Norwegian American authors more than the temperance cause." In the 1880s, temperance societies and Good Templars lodges were founded all over America, and by 1914, the International Order of Good Templars had more than fifty Norwegian lodges. That same year, the Minnesota Total Abstinence Society, "Minnesota Totalafholdsselskab," which was organized in 1885, had 125 local groups. Leading Norwegian American publicist Waldemar Ager wrote in 1914 in the Temperance People's Celebratory Publication, "Avholdsfolkets Festskrift," that "in relation to their numbers, the Norwegian immigrants had made a greater contribution to the temperance cause" than any other immigrant group in America. The most prominent example of this is the ill-fated National Prohibition Act, also known as the Volstead Act, of 1920, which introduced prohibition in America. It is named after Andrew J. Volstead, son of Norwegian immigrants, from Kenyon, Minnesota, and a Republican member of the US House of Representatives between

1903 and 1923. Opponents of the National Prohibition Act, repealed in 1933, called it the "Norwegian law."

While the temperance movement had existed in Finland since the 1830s, it did not really take off until the Friends of Temperance was founded in 1884. Many saw the need to stop drinking as a necessary step in creating an independent nation. Some 34,000 people had joined by 1905. After coming to the United States, many Finns joined temperance societies founded by the Swedes and Norwegians before they started their own group in 1886 in the Iron Range towns of Tower-Soudan. They named it Pohjan Leimu (Northern Light). The following year, Toivon Tähti (Star of Hope) was started in Duluth. In 1903, almost one third of the 1,200 adult Finns in the mining town of Virginia belonged to the local temperance society Valon-tuote (Product of Light). In 1908, the Finnish temperance movement in America reached a high point with 13,000 members in 245 local societies. These were associated with both the socialist organizations and the members of the Church of Finland (the main church group around the Suomi Synod). In fact, radicals often used the temperance halls for their activities.

The temperance halls in America became hubs of activity, including dances, music, drama groups, festivals, and summer schools for the children, all part of an effort to help the immigrants adjust to life in America and to promote self-organization. They played a role in the Americanization of the immigrants by teaching them administration and how to conduct meetings, "advancing their skills in the participatory politics of American democratic society." The temperance push among newly arrived Finns was peculiarly American, argues John I. Kolehmainen, who sees the temperance societies both as a social movement and a crusading institution that "took the Finns beyond the temperance halls into other activities, like politics."

In Norway, the temperance movement was associated with greater political consciousness, and the activists in the temperance movement in America gave Norwegian American politicians an edge as a result of that political activism. "They gained experience in democratic procedure," Lovoll told me. "That shows the influence of the temperance movement." Activity in the temperance movement became a sort of training ground for political activism and often paved the way for political careers. Lovoll also notes that the Norwegians and Swedes stuck together and cooperated on this issue, and many of them were elected as a result of their allegiance to the temperance cause, which had broad support in both immigrant communities. Scandinavian candidates promised to keep alcohol out of the counties if they were elected.

Finnish Lutheran congregation in front of the Finnish Temperance Hall at Mountain Iron, Minnesota, 1896

Lovoll also sees a connection between the temperance societies and women's right to vote, which was not established in Minnesota until 1920, when the necessary two-thirds of the states had ratified the Nineteenth Amendment. Lovoll ventured to say that it probably took this long for Minnesota's women to get the right to vote because the women put so much into the temperance movement.

In the story of Minnesota politics, it is important to point out not only the large and influential role the Scandinavians came to play, but also the lack of political influence of the German immigrants, in spite of their large numbers as the dominant immigrant group in Minnesota. As of 2016, there has been no German governor in Minnesota, although Harold Stassen, Republican governor between 1939 and 1943, had a mixed ethnic background, including German. The list of German Americans representing Minnesota in the US House of Representatives is very short, and it was not until 1978 that a Minnesota German was elected to the US Senate. That year, in fact, there were two: David Durenberger and Rudy Boschwitz, both Republicans.

Uppsala University professor Sten Carlsson contrasted German "underrepresentation" in Minnesota politics with Scandinavian "overrepresentation," writing that the latter's political dominance "exceeded their numerical share of the population." He argued that the political traditions of Sweden and Norway play a role here, but more important, the German underrepresentation reflected the "religious diversity" between Catholic and Protestant Germans and "their lack of political unity and of succinct constitutional traditions." This German underrepresentation in Minnesota politics was evident from the very beginning of Minnesota as a state, when the early German immigrants were Democrats and supported immigration and Catholic rights and opposed the temperance movement. And even though many Germans fought for the Union in the Civil War, the war increased their alienation from the state's Republican government. According to historian Kathleen Neils Conzen, the German immigrants felt that the government had failed to protect them from the Indians in the war of 1862, and then sought to draft them into the Union army, rounding up any resisters. World War I put an end to any ambitions among German immigrants to win leading political positions in Minnesota, and World War II and the Holocaust further underlined this reality.

"The German story has been submerged . . . so the Scandinavian story got to be more dominant," said Margaret Anderson Kelliher, former speaker of the state house. Her father was Swedish and her mother German, and she grew up in the small town of Judson in Blue Earth County in southern Minnesota, where there were both Swedes and Germans. "The influence of the Scandinavians focused a lot on the civic culture, how people connect to each other, how people care for each other, and the Germans brought this highly ordered civic society."

"The Germans were mainly interested in preserving their cultural heritage, their language, their church affiliation," said historian Hyman Berman. "They did not really look to move out of the German community. They remained insular. They were forced out in World War I but forced out in a very negative way and it did not lead to any positive results."

The failed German revolution of 1848 brought both political and religious refugees to America, including the freethinkers. In Minnesota, these immigrants settled in different regions of the state. New Ulm, the leading German town in Minnesota, was initially the center for the freethinking, anticlerical Turners before both the Catholics and the Lutherans flocked to the town, and in Stearns County, another center of German settlement, the Catholics totally dominated. In addition, the Lutherans were divided into several competing synods while others joined the Methodists and Baptists. Minnesota's Germans created self-contained ethnic enclaves with highly concentrated populations. Church services were in German; schools taught religion, and classes were taught in German by teachers trained in seminaries and supervised by a priest. Children did not go to college or university, as it "was seen as useless for farm families." And while the Scandinavians embraced public education, the Germans preferred parochial schools. All this helped maintain the German language, but it also prevented or, at a minimum, slowed down the assimilation of the German immigrants into Minnesota's politics and culture.

In contrast, the Swedish immigrants never organized such self-contained ethnic enclaves, and Swedish pastors never tried to organize the local economy "to protect Swedish religious ways." Still, "faith and language were preserved in 'Swedeland' but it was more open to outside influence, for its individuals pursued economic gain apart from the group." And as for the Norwegians, the fact that they split into so many Lutheran synods "prevented the clergy from centering a community's economic and social life officially in the church." Their support for public education over parochial schools further hastened the assimilation of Scandinavian immigrants, especially compared to the Germans of Stearns County.

The result of all this was that "unlike Minnesota's Scandinavians or the Irish in St. Paul, Germans were never able to translate their numbers, early arrival, and associational habits into group political power. . . . They were too divided by religion, class and cultural values to form a reliable voting bloc capable of exerting statewide political influence." This lack of German unity, together with the Yankee/Scandinavian alliance within the dominant Republican Party, sidelined the Germans politically and culturally in the nineteenth century, and this continued into the twentieth century. In Republican Minnesota, the fact that the Germans were mostly Democrats made them a political minority despite their large numbers. And many of their strongly held views, such as their opposition to prohibition and the temperance movement, further limited their statewide political power, although there were exceptions in local politics in counties with large German populations.

In contrast to the Germans, but similar to the Scandinavians, the Irish favored public schools for their children, in part as a path to assimilation. St. Paul's legendary Irish archbishop John Ireland wanted his countrymen to become Americans as quickly as possible, and he feared that separate parochial schools would delay integration into the American mainstream. And so the Irish, despite also being Catholics and not as numerous as the Germans, came to play a much more active role in Minnesota politics, particularly in the capital, St. Paul, where they captured the mayor's office time and time again (including Chris Coleman, elected and reelected since 2005 and the son of legendary Irish American Nick Coleman, the first Democratic majority leader in the state senate). Statewide, however, Irish success has been limited. The fact that the Irish were Catholics caused tension and rivalries with the Yankees and the Scandinavians, even outright discrimination. Minnesota has had no Irish governor, although it did have a lieutenant governor between 1860 and 1863 by the name of Ignatius Donnelly, who would become one of Minnesota's most famous politicians.

From its beginning, both as a territory and as a state, Minnesota had numerous "old stock" Americans, or Yankees, from New England, New York, Pennsylvania, Ohio, and Michigan, who came to hold political power in the first decades of Minnesota's existence. They "built farms, started towns, opened business places, invested money, speculated, pioneered professions, launched newspapers, schools and churches, engaged in politics and government, and left the imprints of their leadership on numerous institutions." They also laid the foundation for the school system, free and open to everyone. Those same Yankees argued that the "New England of the West" needed a university, and in 1851 the University of Minnesota's charter was signed by the territorial governor, Alexander Ramsey. The Yankees also brought to the new state their religious, educational, cultural, and political antislavery, antiliquor, and anti-illiteracy beliefs. Seven of the state's first ten governors were New Englanders, including Henry Sibley, Alexander Ramsey, John Pillsbury, and Lucius Hubbard. They were also all Republicans, except Sibley.

As Norwegian American historian Theodore C. Blegen puts it, the twin goals of the Republican Party—ending slavery and liquor reform—greatly appealed to the Scandinavian immigrants, who were "as staunchly antiliquor and antislavery as the New Englanders." The result was that the two groups became powerful political allies in Minnesota. Education was another area of key interest to both groups. After the University of Minnesota was founded, the Scandinavians quickly followed suit by founding colleges of their own— the Swedes with Gustavus Adolphus College in St. Peter and Bethel University in St. Paul, and the Norwegians with St. Olaf College in Northfield, Augsburg College in Minneapolis, and Concordia College in Moorhead.

Don Ostrom, professor emeritus at Gustavus Adolphus College, whose ancestors all emigrated from Sweden, said the wealthy Yankees of Minnesota—the Pillsburys, the Daytons—saw themselves as stewards of their wealth, which was not to be used for ostentatious display. The goal was to build a better community for everyone, and "if it took a lot of money to build a Guthrie Theater or a Minnesota Orchestra, well, that is what you did. But, also, if it took raising taxes to get a baseball or a football stadium, or to get a great university or a good pre-K through high school system, that's what you also did."

Lori Sturdevant, political columnist with the *Minneapolis Star Tribune*, described Minnesota as a New England state, founded by New Englanders with their Puritan heritage, which had a lot in common with the Scandinavians and their heritage. In a way, she said, "the Scandinavians fit hand in glove with the New Englanders"—antislavery, hard work, education. Former Minnesota supreme court justice Paul Anderson put it this way: "Yes, you can't discard the Yankees, but what I think the Scandinavians said to the Yankees was, 'I call and raise you one.' The Scandinavian vision of community was broader than the Yankees' vision."

THE HUNDREDS OF THOUSANDS of Nordic immigrants who made Minnesota the most Scandinavian of all the states came to America to escape crop failures, hunger, and religious intolerance, and those who came first mainly came for land, free land, to farm. Those who came later came in search of jobs, in the flour mills, iron mines, and lumber industry. They came in waves, but not in great numbers until after the Civil War, and they helped shape the new state of Minnesota, playing a crucial role in forming the state's political culture. Aided by almost universal literacy, these immigrants put prime importance on education, which coincided with the values of Minnesota's first immigrants, Yankees from New England. The potent Yankee-Scandinavian political alliance, embraced within the Republican Party, served to exclude the state's largest immigrant group, the Germans, who were mainly Democrats.

The Scandinavians were eager to assimilate. When the Civil War broke out, thousands joined the Union army, ready to fight for their state and their new home country. They learned English and attended public schools, and they became civically involved soon after their arrival in Minnesota. After their political breakthrough toward the end of the nineteenth century, Scandinavian immigrants and their descendants were an integral part of every phase of Minnesota's political history, among both the rural conservatives and the urban progressives. In many ways, they came to form a new political class in Minnesota, following the years of Yankee domination, and their brand of politics set a political legacy that helped build the modern state of Minnesota.

2

Four Pioneers

I was in every sense an American and not a "Swede" Governor.

Adolph Olson Eberhart, Minnesota Governor, 1909–15

MAYBE ONE COULD HAVE seen it coming, first in 1882, when Norwegian-born Knute Nelson was elected to the US House of Representatives, and then in 1886, when Swedish-born John Lind followed him into that same political body. Their victories signaled that important changes were underway in Minnesota politics, which led to the stunning breakthrough in 1892 when Nelson was elected as Minnesota's first Scandinavian governor.

These victories illustrated that a new and, eventually, powerful bloc of voters had arrived on Minnesota's political scene. Up until then, the state's governors had all been so-called Yankees—three from New York, three from Pennsylvania, and one each from Connecticut, Ohio, Michigan, Missouri, and New Hampshire.

But now, Knute Nelson—from Voss in Norway.

His victory marked a new era in Minnesota politics as Scandinavians started to replace New Englanders as the state's political elite. Nelson's victory was followed by more firsts in Minnesota gubernatorial politics. John Lind, who in 1886 became the first Swedish-born member of the US Congress, was elected as the first Swedish-born governor of Minnesota in 1898. In addition, Lind was Minnesota's first non-Republican governor since the state's first governor, Henry Sibley, in 1858. In 1904, John A. Johnson, also a Democrat and the son of Swedish immigrants, became the first Minnesota-born governor, and he, in turn, was followed from 1909 to 1915 by another Swedish-born immigrant, his lieutenant governor Adolph Olson Eberhart, a Republican. Johnson and Eberhart, although from different parties, formed Minnesota's first Scandinavian American leadership duo. More were to follow.

Where they were born and where they came from mattered in these early years in Minnesota politics. During the twenty-three years from 1892 to 1915, the series of Scandinavian governors was interrupted only twice, by men with the last names Clough and Van Sant. Following a one-year turn by New England–born Winfield Hammond in 1915 came another remarkable series of Scandinavian governors that lasted through the 1930s: Swedish Joseph A. A. Burnquist, Norwegian J. A. O. Preus, Norwegian Theodore Christianson, Norwegian/Swedish Floyd B. Olson, Danish Hjalmar Petersen, and Norwegian Elmer Benson. Petersen, born in 1890 in the small village of Eskildstrup on the island of Fyn in Denmark, was the twentieth century's last foreign-born Minnesota governor.

At this time, it was often jokingly said that Minnesotans did not care what the governor's national background was, as long as he was Scandinavian. Or, in a more modern version, "If your name is Anderson, you're probably governor." And even when the long string of Scandinavian governors was briefly interrupted, the lieutenant governor was often Scandinavian: Norwegian A. E. Rice, Swedish Gottfrid T. Lindsten, the Danes Hjalmar Petersen and Ancher Nelsen, Swedish Alec G. Olson, and Swedish Marlene Johnson, who, in 1983, became the first female lieutenant governor of Minnesota.

In 1939, Harold Stassen, of German/Czech/Norwegian descent, was elected governor and led Minnesota until 1943, when he was succeeded by yet another series of Scandinavian governors: Norwegian Edward J. Thye (1943–47), Swedish Luther W. Youngdahl (1947–51), Finland-Swede C. Elmer Anderson (1951–55), Swedish/Norwegian Orville Freeman (1955–61), Norwegian/Swedish Elmer L. Andersen (1961–63), Norwegian Karl Rolvaag (1963–67), Swedish Harold LeVander (1967–71), Swedish Wendell Anderson (1971–76), followed by Norwegian Albert Quie (1979–83), and Swedish Arne Carlson (1991–99).

From 1893 to 1999, for more than one hundred years of Minnesota's political history, all but five of twenty-six governors were Scandinavian. They represented all political parties—twelve Republicans, one Democrat/Populist, one Democrat, three Farmer-Labor, and three Democratic-Farmer-Labor (DFL). Of the twenty-one Scandinavians, eight were Swedish, seven Norwegian, three Norwegian/Swedish, one a Finland-Swede, one a Dane, and one with German/Czech/Norwegian roots.

Nelson, Lind, Johnson, and Eberhart, Minnesota's first four Scandinavian governors—the four pioneers—laid the foundation for Minnesota's Scandinavian political legacy at the statewide level. Of the four, only Johnson was born in Minnesota. For Nelson and Lind, the fact that they were born abroad was more a liability than an asset, although being a

Scandinavian became more of an asset with time. Lind was aware of this "dubious advantage" as a Swedish-born politician, writing, "though person of foreign birth may be ever so competent, still people are inclined to doubt it, or at least they have suspicions until they can actually see him and ascertain for themselves."

The Scandinavian immigrants who came to have a political career in Minnesota generally arrived in the country at a young age, or at the latest in their twenties, and it usually took fifteen to twenty years to make their political debut. None of them were rich, including American-born John A. Johnson, who grew up poor in the town of St. Peter.

KNUTE NELSON, BORN IN Evanger in the Norwegian district of Voss in 1843, arrived in America when he was six years old, accompanied only by his mother, who had borrowed $45 to pay the fare to America. Nelson had been born out of wedlock, and the identity of his biological father remained a mystery throughout his life. His mother, Ingebjørg Haldorsdatter Kvilekval, born in 1814, portrayed herself as a widow with a child once the two arrived in America. He was baptized Knud Evanger.

After almost two years in Chicago, Knud's mother married Nils Olson Grotland, a farmer, also from the Voss district, and they moved to the Norwegian American communities of Skoponong and Koshkonong in southern Wisconsin. Knud Evanger changed his name to Knute Nelson to honor his stepfather. There were no Norwegian schools where they settled, and young Knute came under the strict tutelage of an Irish Catholic schoolteacher named Mary Blackwell Dillon. The Americanization of Knute Nelson began. It continued during his years at the Albion Academy, a "monument to New Englanders' strong desire to educate and Christianize the frontier West," and where the Scandinavian students were less than ten percent of the two to three hundred students.

Shortly after the outbreak of the Civil War, Knute Nelson enlisted in the Union army, eventually ending up in the Fourth Wisconsin infantry regiment, an overwhelmingly "American" regiment, in contrast to the all-Scandinavian Fifteenth Wisconsin under the leadership of the Norwegian immigrant Colonel Hans Christian Heg. Nelson's war experience further Americanized him, and he was critical of what he perceived to be a lack of support for the Union, a lack of patriotism, among his fellow Norwegian Americans. The bitter debate about slavery among the Norwegian Lutheran clergy also "distanced him from his Norwegian-American roots." Nelson could not stand the Copperheads, a faction of Northerners within the Democratic Party who sympathized with the Confederacy, and by the time he mustered out of the Union army in 1864 and became an American citizen in 1866, his political affiliation had changed, from an antislavery, pro-Union Democrat to a Lincoln Republican. Like the president a frontier politician, Nelson was described as doing only three things: "he read, he worked, and chewed tobacco."

Nelson was also described as "salty, gruff, independent, schooled politically by local and regional political battles." And his political battles were many, beginning with his two terms in the Wisconsin State Assembly and followed by his service in the Minnesota Senate, to which he was elected after he had moved to Alexandria, Minnesota, in 1871 to set up his law practice. The 1882 congressional election to decide who was going to represent northern Minnesota's new Fifth Congressional District, where approximately 50 percent of the population was Scandinavian American, proved to be particularly contentious. Nelson actively sought support from the Scandinavians, having declared, "I feel that in this district we are entitled to a Norwegian." The Fifth District was frontier territory and the campaign was tough and dirty, with massive voter fraud. But in the end, Nelson proved as tough if not tougher than his opponent, Charles Kindred, a fellow Republican, and defeated him by almost five thousand votes in the primary, and then clobbered the Democratic candidate, Edward P. Barnum, in the general election.

Nelson's election to the House of Representatives as the first Norwegian-born member of Congress launched his political career. Two easy reelection victories followed. He ran for governor of Minnesota and became the state's twelfth governor and Minnesota's first Scandinavian and first foreign-born governor in 1892. He was reelected two years later only to resign in early 1895 to run for the US Senate. At that time, the Minnesota state senate elected the US senators, and Nelson proved again his tough political instincts, at times

Governor Knute Nelson, circa 1895

furiously demanding that his fellow Scandinavians support him. "I am a Norwegian," he once told a Swedish state senator. "If I were a Swede, you would vote for me in a minute. That is the way with you Swedes, but I will show you yet who is master here." Nelson won. He remained in the Senate, reelected three times by the Minnesota state senate and once by popular vote, until his death in 1923.

Nelson's success cannot be understood without considering the agrarian crusades of the 1870s and 1880s and the subsequent rise of the Farmers' Alliance—an agrarian reform movement—as a statewide phenomenon with "formidable political mobilization." In 1890, the Farmers' Alliance promoted its own gubernatorial candidate, Sidney M. Owen, under the banner of the People's/Populist Party. Owen lost, but the year marked the end of "unchallenged Republican supremacy" and the "emergence of third-party protest on a large scale." Together, the candidates of the Democratic, Farmers' Alliance, and Prohibition parties tallied almost twice as many votes as the winning Republican candidate, William Rush Merriam. Behind these figures was the agrarian disaffection, centered in the western part of Minnesota, among Scandinavian, and especially Norwegian, farmers. The goal of the Republican Party in 1892 was to "rescue" Minnesota from the newly formed Populist or People's Party, which was dominated by the Farmers' Alliance and its many Scandinavian American supporters. Knute Nelson was called on to recapture the Scandinavian vote for the Republican Party. Being both a farmer and a Scandinavian was "a practically unbeatable combination in Minnesota," and Nelson was unanimously nominated.

Just as in his other campaigns, Nelson fought hard. One encounter in the town of Elbow Lake produced headlines in both the American and Scandinavian-language press. When heckled fiercely at a meeting, Nelson stormed down off the podium, shouting "I will fix him," and grabbed Norwegian American Populist leader Tobias Sauby by the neck and forced him to sit down. The two men were eventually separated and Nelson resumed his speech, but when he arrived in the town of Dalton a couple of days later, he was arrested for assault and battery. The charge was later dropped. For the anti-Republican Minneapolis publication *Svenska Amerikanska Posten*, the leading Swedish American newspaper in the state, this lack of self-restraint by "Stryparen Knute"—Knute the Choker—was yet further proof that Nelson did not deserve the support of the Scandinavian voters. Other papers, however, expressed the opinion that the confrontation would gain Nelson votes. For some, the Elbow Lake incident typified the 1890s battles between Republican Party elites and Populist farmers.

Søren Listoe, the Danish-born newspaper editor of the Norwegian-language paper in St. Paul, *Nordvesten,* was a friend and close ally of Nelson. In October 1892, just before the gubernatorial election, Listoe, who made little distinction between Norwegians and Swedes—in politics they were all Scandinavians—made a direct ethnic appeal to Minnesota's Scandinavians to vote for Nelson: "This time we have power in our own hands, if we only can stand together and not let liars confuse our Norwegian heads.... Scandinavians who despise Knute Nelson also despise their own home country, Norway. So, [you] Scandinavians, wake up to fight!" Still, *Svenska Amerikanska Posten*—an outlier of sorts in the Scandinavian immigrant community for its staunchly Democratic sentiments—vigorously opposed Nelson's candidature, showing that party affiliation was at times more important than national heritage. Nelson was not a Democrat, and that was more important for the paper than that he was a fellow Scandinavian.

The "Little Norwegian," as he was called, eventually had to rely on Scandinavian American votes, primarily Norwegian but also some Swedish, to win the election. He captured 109,220 votes, or 42.7 percent, overall, compared to 37 percent for the Democrat, Daniel Lawler, and 15.6 percent for the People's/Populist Party candidate, Ignatius Donnelly. Nelson won in some heavily Norwegian counties like Fillmore, Houston, and Otter Tail but lost to Donnelly in counties like Kittson, Marshall, and Polk, also with substantial Norwegian populations. He also won in the heavily Swedish, traditionally Republican, counties Chisago, Isanti, and Washington. The fact that he headed the Republican ticket saved the party from going down, for without Nelson drawing Scandinavian votes, Minnesota likely would have gone Democrat. "Let's see in two years, if the Republicans can fool the voters one more time," *Svenska Amerikanska Posten* wrote.

Nelson was now the "rising sun" of Minnesota politics. He was the "ultimate success story" and the "object of great ethnic pride." Nelson's support, founded in ethnic appeals, broadened as he nourished a role as a broker, both between the Scandinavian immigrants and the "old stock" population and between farmers and landowners and the Empire Builder James J. Hill and his railroad. It was a role he came to refine during his long political career.

When Nelson ran for governor again in 1894, he was easily reelected, capturing 147,943 votes, beating the Populist Party's Sidney Owen by more than 60,000 votes. The Republicans won all seven of the state's congressional seats and an overwhelming majority in the state legislature. Under Nelson's leadership, the "Republican elites had clearly beaten back the assault" of the populist People's Party and the Farmers' Alliance in Minnesota, and

Nelson was ready to move on to the US Senate, where he would enjoy an almost thirty-year career.

At the time of his death, Knute Nelson had become a political legend in Minnesota, a source of immense pride among Norwegians, both in America and in Norway. However, as historian Carl H. Chrislock writes, "nearly all Norwegian Americans admired Knute Nelson, but many of them rejected his politics." His political career was founded in his Norwegian background and based on support from Scandinavian American voters, but moved beyond ethnicity so that, in the end, he became a truly American politician.

JOHN LIND WAS BORN on the Persgård farm in Kånna parish in Småland, southern Sweden, in 1854 and came with his family to America in 1868, a particularly harsh year for farmers in Sweden. His parents, Gustaf Jonasson and Katrina Jonasdotter, changed their name to Lind once in America, taking the name from his Swedish family farm, Lindbacken—the Lind Hill. The family settled in Goodhue County, Minnesota, not far from the little town of Vasa. These were hard years, and young John had to have his left hand amputated following a hunting accident.

That never seemed to hamper him later in life, however, as illustrated in a story when John Lind left the old capitol after his last day as Minnesota governor, on January 9, 1901. According to his biographer George Stephenson, Lind put on his coat and started walking. Pedestrians in St. Paul "might have seen the tall, one-armed man, wearing a determined look, glancing neither to the left nor the right until he reached the office of Harry Black, the managing editor of the *St. Paul Dispatch*. Upon entering Black's office the former governor informed the managing editor that he was now a private citizen and demanded to know if a retraction was now forthcoming. When Black refused to comply with the demand, the governor's good right arm shot out and avenged the insult, whereupon Lind calmly left the office." The "insult," which Lind himself later called "the vilest that could be uttered against a citizen," regarded a cartoon stigmatizing Lind as a "traitor." Lind's right hook was met with approval from many quarters, although Lind later said he regretted having resorted to violence. Two days after the confrontation, the other St. Paul paper, the *Pioneer Press*, ran a cartoon showing Lind with a boxing glove on his right hand and a tag on his coat that read, "John Lind. Private Citizen at Large." Another paper called out, "Bravo, John Lind." An already popular former governor became even more popular. Clearly, Lind, like Nelson before him, was ready to play hardball, if so required.

In his youth, Lind was a good student at the Central Schoolhouse in Red Wing and, eventually, he became both a teacher and a lawyer. He settled in New Ulm, which had a large German population. Lind learned German and he quickly became involved in local affairs and active in the Republican Party. He was superintendent of schools in Brown County for a couple of years before he decided to run for US Congress. He was victorious in his first attempt in 1886 and was reelected twice before deciding not to run again.

He served part of his six years in the House of Representatives together with Knute Nelson. The personal relations between Minnesota's two most "distinguished Scandinavians" appeared to be harmonious. Lind called them "pleasant." In 1892, Lind supported Nelson for governor after declaring in a letter to Nelson that "we cannot afford to stand in each other's way" and making clear that he thought it important for the Scandinavians in Minnesota to stick together. But they also never became close friends, as Nelson was "jealous" of his rights and "suspicious" of others' motives, according to Stephenson. Fundamentally, the two men were different; Lind was open and direct, while Nelson "was the shrewd politician with a finesse that Lind never acquired."

Although the two were political rivals, the big election battle between the "Little Giant" and "Honest John," as Nelson and Lind were called, never materialized. With time, their relations grew cooler, as Lind moved away from the Republican Party. In early 1896, when he was practicing law in New Ulm, Lind broke with the Republicans, principally over the issue of the gold standard, which to Lind and other Silver Republicans meant the "obliteration" of the middle class and the "division" of people into very rich and very poor. They favored "bimetallism," and that fall Lind ran for governor as the so-called Fusion candidate of the Democrats/Populists/Free Silver Republicans, to Nelson's great consternation. In a speech, Nelson said that electing Lind would give Minnesota the "blackest eye it ever had" and the East would regard it "as the abode of wild, long-haired Populists." Lind lost by 3,500 votes, thanks in part to conservative Scandinavian voters, who stayed loyal to the Republican Party.

In 1898, Lind ran again as a Fusion candidate—or as a "political orphan," as he liked to describe himself. His strongest assets were his Swedish nationality but more so his integrity and honesty. This time he also ran as a veteran first lieutenant of the Spanish-American War after having enlisted and served in that conflict. He won easily following a campaign run by a young Swedish compatriot and immigrant from Malmö named Leonard August

Governor John Lind seated in his office in the State Capitol, circa 1900

Rosing. The victory as Minnesota's first non-Republican governor since Sibley, and as its first Democrat/Populist governor, heralded the start of the Progressive Era in the state's politics. "Without him, the Populist elements would not have succeeded in holding their forces together," writes A. E. Strand. "He presented an undaunted front and gallantly led his variegated and mosaic army against a strong array of Republican leaders, skilled in all the tactics of political warfare, and this, too, with all the great newspapers of the state in hostility against him. He was not able to organize a new permanent party out of the Populist elements, but he did succeed in leading most of those elements into the Democratic Party." Lind's victory was helped by the Scandinavian vote, but not exclusively so, for he was never a purely ethnic candidate, capturing 35 percent of the Swedish vote, 20 percent of the Norwegian vote, and ten percent of the German vote.

In 1900, Lind narrowly lost his reelection bid, largely because many thousands of ballots were declared invalid on a clever maneuver orchestrated by a Republican operator named Tams Bixby. Lind's biographer calls it a "trick," one that caused between 15,000 and 20,000 votes for Lind to be invalidated because their ballots were marked both for Lind as a "People's-Democrat" and for Thomas H. Lucas as a "Social-Democrat." Apparently, these voters voted for every candidate designated as a "Democrat," as Bixby had hoped would happen. Lind lost the election to Republican Samuel Van Sant by 2,254 votes.

With the exception of another two-year term in the US House of Representatives a few years later, John Lind never ran for political office again. However, his political involvement and career continued outside of elective politics, as a member of the Board of Regents of the University of Minnesota and, maybe foremost, as an international diplomat, most prominently serving as President Woodrow Wilson's personal representative to Mexico in 1913.

His biographer George M. Stephenson called John Lind "an oracle of progressive and independent thought" and a "man with an old world background who became intensely American." Lind died in Minneapolis in 1930.

SAMUEL VAN SANT, born in Rock Island, Illinois, succeeded John Lind as governor, but only two years later the Scandinavians returned to power, this time electing John Albert Johnson. In addition, Swedish-born Republican Adolph Olson Eberhart was elected lieutenant governor. In those days, the governor and lieutenant governor ran on separate tickets.

John Albert Johnson was born in 1861 just outside the town of St. Peter, the home of Gustavus Adolphus College, founded by Swedes a few years after his birth. Johnson never studied there. In fact, he never even finished high school, going to work at thirteen to support the family. He was the son of Gustav Jönsson and Caroline Hedén, born in the Swedish provinces of Småland and Östergötland, respectively. At the age of thirty-three, his father seemed more or less to have been put on the boat to America by relatives after squandering his inheritance, while his mother became an orphan during a cholera epidemic upon arrival in America. They met and married in the new country. But the father, a blacksmith, drank himself to death and the mother became a washerwoman to support the family. Young John started working in a drugstore, where he stayed until his mid-twenties, when an opportunity opened up to edit the city's paper, the *St. Peter Herald*. He took the job and rose quickly in the ranks of local journalism, becoming the president of the Minnesota Editorial Association in 1893, at the age of thirty-two.

Five years later, Johnson was elected to the Minnesota state senate after one previous failed attempt. He served only one four-year term before losing his reelection bid. Then, in 1904, he won the Minnesota governorship, running as a progressive Democrat. "The rise of American boys from obscure poverty to high positions has plenty of examples. John A. Johnson is one of them," writes historian William Watts Folwell. What followed was a highly successful political career, during which Johnson was twice reelected comfortably in a state that was overwhelmingly Republican. Folwell calls Johnson's victory in 1906, in which he won 61 percent of the vote, the "greatest personal triumph ever witnessed in Minnesota politics," as the Republicans won everything else. Johnson captured 50 percent of the Swedish and Norwegian vote, a remarkably high figure considering the Scandinavians' faithfulness to the Republican Party.

Johnson enjoyed broad popular support and was considered a man of the people, described by his biographer Winifred Helmes as "more like an Irishman than a Swede," a man with a sunny disposition, a ladies' man who loved baseball and loved to dance and play poker, although never for high stakes. Photos of him show a tall, handsome man whose looks are reminiscent of President John F. Kennedy.

John A. Johnson and John Lind were political contemporaries and colleagues, and "the most widely known men of Swedish extraction in the state." When Knute Nelson publicly spoke out against Johnson in the 1904 election for governor and urged the Scandinavians to vote Republican, Lind was the "only recognized political leader in Minnesota who spoke up for Johnson." After Johnson's victory, Nelson wrote his friend Søren Listoe that "there will be no easy matter to find a man who can beat Governor Johnson." He was right. No one ever did. Johnson's speech at the Gridiron Club in Washington, DC, in December 1907 in front of 250 prominent guests, including President Teddy Roosevelt, was "like a Western breeze rolling over the jaded East." He became a national figure and, instantly, a possible candidate for president. The next year, however, the Democratic Party chose William Jennings Bryan as its candidate. Johnson immediately proclaimed his support.

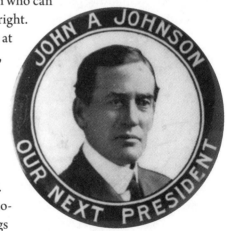

Presidential campaign button for Governor John A. Johnson, 1908

John A. Johnson's life was cut short by cancer. After four years and nine months as Minnesota's governor, he died in 1909, only forty-eight years old, on the brink of a national career. His death has "hardly been equaled by the mourning of any other citizen except Abraham Lincoln." On September 22, 1909, 75,000 people paid their respects at the rotunda of the State Capitol in St. Paul to this "Lincoln of the Northwest" and "Swedish-America's until now most prominent son."

UPON HIS DEATH, Johnson was succeeded by his lieutenant governor, Adolph Olson Eberhart, who would go on to serve as Minnesota's governor from 1909 to 1915. In the Scandinavian world of Minnesota at the time, Johnson and Eberhart knew each other, of course, but it was more than that. As Eberhart writes in his unpublished memoir, which he dictated from his sick bed at the age of seventy-three, the two had a "great friendship." That friendship was helpful, Eberhart writes, and he received Democratic support because of it.

Born Olaf Adolf Olson in Kil, Sweden, in 1870, he traveled alone to America at the age of eleven to join his parents and siblings, who had left him behind as they were unable to pay his ticket to America. After his arrival, young Olaf worked on farms and cattle ranches in Nebraska and southern Minnesota for many years, partially to help his parents, who did not seem to be very successful farmers. He was twenty-one before he had a chance to study full-time. Once at Gustavus Adolphus College in St. Peter, he wasted no time, completing seven years of studies in four. It was during his university studies that he changed his name and came to be known as Adolph O. Eberhart, or A. O. Eberhart, because Olson was such a common name. Three years of law studies in Mankato followed, whereupon he launched his law and business career. In 1902, he was elected as the youngest member of the Minnesota Senate. For Eberhart, school reform was the principal reason for entering politics, and he had pledged reforms to the schoolteachers. He writes later, "I had only one political ambition and that was to redeem that pledge," which would mean "the complete transformation of rural life" in the state.

Eberhart was reelected in 1905 and then elected lieutenant governor in 1906, before becoming governor in 1909 following Johnson's death. In 1910, he was elected governor in his own right and was then reelected in 1912. According to Strand, Eberhart's success "was partly luck, partly the result of his careful judgment and another part due to that fact that he was a Scandinavian." His run for another term in 1914 came to an end in the Republican primary, when he was defeated by another Swedish American, Joseph A. A. Burnquist. Eberhart's attempt to win a seat in the US Senate in 1916 also failed, and he left politics. He ended his days in a rest home in Savage, Minnesota, where he wrote his memoir and died in 1944. It was a life dedicated to all striving for success, he writes: "There is in the truest sense no such thing as failure."

THESE FOUR SCANDINAVIAN political pioneers were very different in appearance and temperament, in addition to their politics. Knute Nelson, bearded, short, and gruff; John Lind, taut, serious, cerebral, and, like Nelson, humorless; and John A. Johnson was "simply irresistible." A. O. Eberhart looked like a bureaucrat, stiff and serious.

After the 1892 breakthrough by Nelson and with Eberhart as the state's top political officer two decades later, historian Sten Carlsson concludes that the role of the Scandinavian voters in the two major political parties had by this time been accepted without reservations. It had become less urgent to underline ethnic points of view or emphasize Scandinavian demands for reasonable representation. The Americanization of Minnesota's Scandinavian immigrant politicians was complete.

The four pioneers knew, of course, that they were Scandinavians and were proud of it. As "pioneers in the settlement of the great Northwest, the Scandinavians have become foremost in the splendid citizenship which makes the North Star State so proud of its own position in the constellation," said Governor John A. Johnson in a speech on Norway's National Day, Syttende Mai, in 1905. He and the three others undoubtedly utilized their heritage politically, as when Johnson proudly declared that Scandinavians "have not only fought their way to success, but in their fairness of their fighting have won the respect and regard of all people, and tonight, as a son of Scandinavian immigrants, I am before you as a governor of the state."

At the same time, in their many inaugural addresses through the years, none of the four governors talked about their Scandinavian backgrounds or made any comparisons between the old and new home countries. They were aware of their political power as Scandinavians but were carful not to flaunt it. In a speech to the Scandinavian Club at the University of Minnesota titled "Scandinavians could boss state politics," then lieutenant governor Adolph O. Eberhart said, "If our people bound themselves together into a firm organization, they could control the politics of the state. But they are not clannish and show no inclination to do so. They are as open-minded a people politically as there is." Lind never campaigned openly for the Scandinavian vote, and many Swedes did not support him, instead siding with the conservative Republican Swedish Lutheran clergy who opposed the Democrat/Populist.

It was a balancing act to be a "hyphenated" American, a Norwegian-American or a Swedish-American, as Knute Nelson learned from his visit to the World's Fair in Chicago in 1893. There, on Syttende Mai, Nelson gave an almost hour-long speech, entirely in English, about Norway's history. It was well received by the large Norwegian audience, but Nelson failed to visit the Minnesota Building at the fair, and people came to wonder which land the governor loved best: Norway or America. "Governor Nelson seems to have persuaded himself that he has been elected governor of Norway and Sweden instead of Minnesota," the *Northwestern Chronicle* of St. Paul wrote. For Minnesota's first foreign-born governor to prefer to honor the success of Norwegians and Norwegian Americans over that of Minnesota was "unforgivable" to some.

All four governors spoke the languages of their parents, even Johnson, who never visited Sweden but who spoke Swedish at home growing up. But he never used it publicly, even when he spoke to Scandinavian audiences. Neither did the other three. The four all strove hard to be American. About Lind, Stephenson writes, one could almost feel how torn he was between his country of birth and his new home country as World War I was approaching. Lind, an anti-imperialist who did not want America to go to war but who supported the war effort once it did, was "deeply grieved" that Sweden might appear to be an ally of Germany. In a speech in 1917, Lind said that the Swedes are "our friends in peace, aye, more than friends, for they are kindred. But in war, if such should come . . . they are enemies." And, "unless they choose to have a government in harmony with the aspirations of the free peoples of the earth they must suffer the consequences of the actions of their rulers."

While Lind never forgot his Swedish heritage, he did not identify himself with the Swedish Americans as a group. As he grew older, he became more interested in his native country and its history. He was an avid reader of the Swedish American newspapers, and every year he sent Christmas presents to his Swedish relatives and wrote letters to them in excellent Swedish. In 1928, when Lind was seventy-four years old and after only one visit to Sweden in all that time, he even wrote a letter in the provincial dialect of his childhood province of Småland.

A. O. Eberhart performed a balancing act similar to his predecessors Nelson and Lind. In his memoir he writes, "I was in every sense an American and not a 'Swede Governor' and had every reason to be proud of my American citizenship, although it was not my fortune to be a direct descendant of the Mayflower party." While addressing a patriotic rally in New York during World War I, the ex-governor said: "Sometimes I have been introduced as the 'Swedish governor of Minnesota.' No reflection could possibly be intended thereby. But let there be no occasion even for a misunderstanding. I am an American not only by right, but by choice, and I am trying to deserve that greatest of all distinctions."

That did not stop Eberhart from politically exploiting his Scandinavian background, as evidenced, for example, in the days before the 1910 election, when a photo of his five young children dressed in traditional Swedish national costumes dominated *Svenska Amerikanska Posten*'s front page with a text that underscored that Eberhart was as good an American as anyone else, but that he also, in his heart and soul, was Swedish.

After his years as governor, in 1920, he visited Sweden and Lake Fryken close to his old home in his boyhood's Värmland. He was then fifty years old. The visit seemed to have been an inspirational experience, judging from his unpublished memoir, for he writes about nice churches and red houses with white trimmings, about law and order—there was no crime or graft—about total literacy, and about a fully organized society with modern insurance and pension. He also writes about the Swedish cooperatives, children's playgrounds, nurseries, and hospitals, and concludes: "It seems to me that it is the duty of every American to study the other nations of the world as to know them better."

Like Lind and Eberhart, Knute Nelson also visited his home country only once, in 1899. The visit lasted three months and included Norway, Sweden, and Denmark. In his home village of Evanger in the Voss district, Nelson gave his first official speech ever in Norwegian, at the celebrations welcoming the village's most famous son. He even switched into the Vossing dialect at times. As he left Norway, Nelson bid an emotional farewell to "dear Mother Norway," saying, "we did not leave you, beloved countrymen, like emigrants from other countries, with hate and resentment. No, hard times, which were not our mother country's fault, and the Viking spirit drove us across the ocean." And once in America, he continued, we have tried "to be good, useful, trustworthy fellow citizens," partly to bring honor to Norway.

Governor A. O. Eberhart arriving by car in Cokato, 1910

At the time of Nelson's trip, tension was rising between Norway and Sweden over the future of their 1814 union. Nelson pleaded with his old countrymen to keep the peace, urging reconciliation between Norwegians and Swedes. In May 1905, as negotiations between Norway and Sweden were close to collapse, Nelson, speaking at the Swedish-Norwegian Odin Club in Minneapolis, urged Norway to remain in the union. A few days earlier, on Syttende Mai, Governor Johnson had expressed similar sentiments, urging the two sides to "bind up their wounds, heal their differences, grow into a closer union and build up a united nation." He talked about Norwegian and Swedish immigrants working on a common cause to the glory of America. Swedish and Norwegian Americans, he said, regret the differences in the Fatherland, and "they find no harbor or anchorage among their sons and brethren in this new home."

Nelson's and Johnson's speeches clearly reflected the fact that relations between Norwegians and Swedes in Minnesota were better than those between the two peoples in the home countries. Their conciliatory tones likely also had political reasons, in that they sought to avoid offending either Scandinavian voting group in the state. Nelson's speech met harsh criticism from many Norwegians, and despite urgings by the most prominent Norwegian Americans all over America, he refused to lobby for US recognition of an independent Norway. He had both Norwegian and Swedish constituents, and to demand that he back Norway in this conflict "was to draw a line in the sand" and he refused to do so. At this point, however, it all also seemed too late. The dissolution of the union progressed speedily, and Norway reached full independence later that year.

THE YEARS UNDER THE first four Scandinavian governors, from 1892 to 1915, were years of change for Minnesota, as the Republican Party's monopoly on power ended during the Populist and then the Progressive eras. The agrarian protest and reform movement gained widespread support, not the least among Scandinavian immigrants. Adolph O. Eberhart writes in his memoir that it was "only natural that a large number of Scandinavians should jump on the bandwagon and ride with the Democrats," as they had "failed for almost two generations to gain any great considerable amount of political influence although they constituted a fairly large majority in the Republican Party." He also laments what he describes as "illogical and unfair discrimination" when it comes to the question of American citizenship, where the Scandinavians were considered foreigners but the Irish, not least because of their knowledge of the English language, were Americans. Although Scandinavians had firmly established themselves in Minnesota politics by the time of Eberhart's governorship, many, particularly among the Swedes, felt they were being taken for granted by the Republican Party leadership—treated like "voting cattle"—which partly explains their drift to the Populists and, eventually, to the Democratic Party.

Republican Knute Nelson's gubernatorial victory in 1893 meant a big change for Nelson, as he went from being one of hundreds of members of the US House of Representatives to governor of Minnesota. It was, write Gieske and Keillor, "a risky office for a cautious politician like Nelson," particularly during these years of agrarian protests and demands for reforms. Sounding like a "frugal Scandinavian American farmer" in his inaugural address, Nelson emphasized education and called for cost cutting in government, but he also attempted to answer the Populists' demands for farm reforms. Having a Republican majority in the state legislature was, of course, advantageous for Nelson, particularly since that majority feared the Populist winds blowing over Minnesota, and so, in the end, it passed most of Nelson's proposals, including a state-owned grain elevator in Duluth, a bill for free textbooks, an occupational safety act, and a workers' antidiscrimination law. Nelson also approved a bill to build a new capitol in St. Paul. Nelson was not a Populist, but as a Scandinavian, he was familiar with the widespread political sentiments among Scandinavian farmers, and he understood that he needed, somehow, to respond to these reform demands. His modest reforms served to undermine Populist protests. The reward of his fellow Republicans in the legislature, who eventually supported his program, was Nelson's convincing reelection victory in 1894. He had "survived the risks of being a governor."

The victories by Democrats Lind in 1898 and Johnson in 1904 did not change the overall political balance of power in Minnesota. The Republicans were still firmly in control of the state legislature. Lind, who heralded the Progressive Era, was unable to realize any large reforms during his term in office. However, his inaugural address came to serve as a "blueprint for reform" that influenced his successors. He urged tax reforms, increased taxes for the railroads, improvement in care for the mentally ill, and support for education and forestry, and voiced approval of direct democratic control of the state government by the people in the form of the direct primary, initiative, referendum, and recall. As Lind saw it, the state's greatness was to be found in just laws, enlightened public interest, and a fair sharing of its wealth by the people. Most of this did not meet the approval of the legislature, and so, as he left office after failing in his reelection bid, he stressed again in his final address the need for tax reform, income and inheritance tax, and taxes on both domestic and foreign corporations.

Lind's tenure in office gave reform "added impetus and respectability," and "it became a norm, a point of reference for the policy-making of succeeding administrations." His influence was particularly lasting in two matters. One was his "cavalier attitude" toward party affiliation, which encouraged the independent voting ethic so important among Minnesota progressives, and the other was his suspicion of imperialism, a view also held by many in the Midwest. He succeeded by having good relations with the populists as well as keeping the confidence of the middle class. As Lind left office, and in spite of his lack of success as a Fusion governor in a state dominated by the Republicans, he was widely regarded as "one of the ablest and most popular" governors that Minnesota had ever had, one who had shown "courage, ability, and good judgment." Although Lind "accomplished none of his major goals," historian William E. Lass writes that Minnesota was "profoundly affected by the tone he set" during the first decade of the twentieth century.

Many historians rank John A. Johnson as an "outstanding progressive," who built on the ideas of reform that Lind had initiated. He was a "conciliator who avoided going beyond the consensus of his time," as he "did not dedicate his political career to a series of crusades for righteous causes."

Johnson favored tax reform, public utilities, lower freight rates on the railroads, direct election of US senators, and woman suffrage, and although the Republicans held a majority in the state legislature, he manage to obtain bipartisan support on a number of issues, such as regulating insurance companies and timber sales on public lands and tightening inheritance laws. He also instituted a new state board of immigration to boost immigration to Minnesota.

In July 1907, his leadership skills were put to a severe test when the first massive strike broke out among the mine workers on the Iron Range in northern Minnesota. At the time, the mines shipped millions of tons of iron ore every year to the steel mills in Pittsburgh and other big cities. Thousands of miners left their jobs in protest against poor pay, working conditions, and working hours and for the right to organize. The mining company and local law enforcement pleaded with Governor Johnson to send in troops to maintain order. He refused. Instead, he traveled to the Range, to the towns of Hibbing, Eveleth, and Virginia, to talk to both sides. He warned against violence and issued a proclamation: strikers had a right to assemble in their own halls; marching was prohibited; there was to be no disturbing of the peace and no trespassing on private property; no one should be prevented from going to work; and there should be no action by public officers. The governor demonstrated that the law applied to both sides. The miners went back to work shortly after his visit. There was no violence. Peace was kept.

Johnson was also devoted to conservation, which had become an issue already as early as 1876, when many Minnesotans saw the need for regulating how the state's big forests should be used and the Minnesota State Forestry Association was founded. Christopher Columbus Andrews, a Massachusetts lawyer who had moved to Minnesota before the Civil War, was a leader in this movement. While serving as US minister (ambassador) to Sweden and Norway, Andrews had become impressed with Sweden's reforestation projects, and he thought Minnesota needed something similar. After returning from Scandinavia, Andrews became involved in the management of Minnesota's forests, serving as the state's chief fire warden and forestry commissioner for over a dozen years, becoming "more influential than any other Minnesotan in advocating forest planning."

By the time Adolph O. Eberhart became governor in September 1909, the winds of reform were blowing hard in the state. His reelection in 1912 was not ensured, and late in his term, perhaps to strengthen his reelection bid, Eberhart called the Minnesota legislature into special session to enact a series of reforms that would assert his progressive credentials. The results were impressive: a new statewide direct primary election law; an anticorruption law that limited the use of money in elections; a new law restricting child labor; higher railroad taxes; workmen's compensation; mothers' pensions; and the elimination of partisan political designations for state legislative candidates. In addition, the special session ratified two US constitutional amendments, one about federal income tax and the other clearing the way for the direct election of US senators. His maneuver was called an "artful coup." In only thirteen days, the legislature "completely revolutionized the state's present political system." Eberhart went on to defeat his opponents in the Republican primary, although his victory was not overly convincing. His 62,400 votes were far short of a majority of the total 164,000 votes cast. In the general election, he again failed to capture a majority, but he won because his opposition was split among Democrats, Prohibitionists, Progressives, and Socialists. While Eberhart won almost 130,000 votes, the four other candidates together captured 189,000 votes.

A. O. Eberhart is regarded as an "experienced and skilled" politician who came to adjust well to the changing times and who was not afraid to use his veto power. Eberhart was not really a reformer but more of a traditional conservative Republican. In 1912, for example, both he and US Senator Knute Nelson supported the Republican Party's candidate William Taft over Teddy Roosevelt, the candidate of the Progressive, or Bull Moose, Party. They were on the losing side, for Taft went down in a clear defeat in Minnesota to Roosevelt, who captured over twice as many votes. Even the Democrat Woodrow Wilson secured more votes than Taft, and the Socialist candidate Eugene V. Debs claimed 27,500 votes. The numbers show that the progressive tide in 1912 was overwhelming, concludes historian Carl Chrislock.

One major ripple in that progressive tide was a reform movement in which Scandinavian politicians—led by governors John A. Johnson and A. O. Eberhart and several Norwegian-born state legislators—played leading roles: the abolition of the death penalty. The death penalty had existed in Minnesota since statehood in 1858, but between 1906 and 1911, governors Johnson and then Eberhart commuted all death sentences to life imprisonment. In 1911, Eberhart abolished the death penalty altogether in the state.

Johnson had long been an opponent of the death penalty, and he declared it publicly after the scandalously botched hanging in February 1906 of William Williams, who had been sentenced to death for a double homicide. At the execution, it took more than fourteen minutes before the condemned man was pronounced dead. The death penalty, said Johnson, was a "relic of the past," and the sooner it was done away with the better. To a friend, Johnson confided that he would rather resign than, as governor, personally aid in the execution of a condemned man.

Bills to abolish the death penalty had been introduced in the Minnesota legislature as early as 1891, and often by Scandinavian representatives such as Hans Bjorge of Otter Tail County, John Knuteson of Polk County, and Jens Kristian Grondahl of Goodhue County. All three of them were born in Norway, where the last execution in peacetime occurred in 1876, although the death penalty was not formally abolished there until 1905. The bill that finally met with success in the Minnesota legislature was introduced by George MacKenzie, a Republican state representative of Scottish/Canadian origin and a longtime death penalty opponent. It happened during the thirty-seventh session of the legislature, following Eberhart's inaugural address in January 1911 in which he stated his opposition to the death penalty and called for its abolition. He believed that "the interests of justice and humanity demand the repeal of the law," and he predicted that crime would be reduced by the abolition of "this antiquated practice in criminal procedure."

While the legislature debated the future of the death penalty, Eberhart refused to set execution dates for two convicted killers, telling the press that "I have always been opposed to capital punishment." Finally, on April 22, 1911, the last day of the legislative session, the bill abolishing the death penalty in Minnesota passed. Eberhart signed it into law two days later. He had stepped forward in spite of his reputation for evading controversial issues, writes law professor John Bessler.

Minnesota was one of nine states that abolished the death penalty during the Progressive Era, but Minnesota and North Dakota were the only states to refuse to reinstate it during the 1930s.

THE YEARS FROM 1892, when Knute Nelson was first elected governor, to 1915, when A. O. Eberhart left office, were, indeed, breakthrough years for Minnesota's Scandinavian immigrants and their participation in the state's political life, laying the foundation for the future.

These were years of great political change, when the long-standing Republican monopoly on power was broken, including the election of the first non-Republican governor (John Lind) since the state's very first governor. And even though the state's more traditional political dynamic returned following Eberhart's governorship, with the Republican Party again coming to dominate, the Populist and Progressive eras had made a deep impact on the policies and political landscape of Minnesota.

All four of these political pioneers depended on the Scandinavian vote to win elections, although that dependency varied. They sought the Scandinavian vote, but they were also careful about how they positioned themselves, and none ran for office with an overtly ethnic message; they were not ethnic candidates. They strove to be Norwegian Americans or Swedish Americans, with the emphasis on *Americans,* as Governor Eberhart once proclaimed.

Nonetheless, Nelson, Lind, Johnson, and Eberhart were the pride of Minnesota's Scandinavian communities, and their success encouraged other Scandinavians to get involved in politics. The result was not only continuing success for Scandinavian Americans seeking high political office in Minnesota, but thousands of local and lower-level political officials taking part in shaping the state's political and social identity. They were involved in the community, in civic life as a whole, and as the *Minnesota Compendium of History and Biography* in 1904 pointed out in glowing terms: "No people in the United States have shown a greater patriotism nor a more profound sense of the duties of citizenship in a free republic than have the native born of the great Scandinavian Peninsula."

Soon There Were Thousands

There are enough of Scandinavian officials to govern a fair-sized kingdom in Europe.

O. N. Nelson, 1893

THE FIRST FOUR SCANDINAVIAN American governors—the four pioneers—were just the top of the iceberg. Underneath, new Scandinavians settlers threw themselves into the state's politics, and soon these immigrant politicians numbered in the thousands.

"What has always struck me is how political the Scandinavians were and how quickly they moved into politics," said David Lanegran, professor emeritus at Macalester College. "Whether this was something particular for the frontier, where the communities were forming very quickly and there was a need, I don't know, but they moved into what I would call, for lack of a better word, a 'political vacuum.'" Also, Lanegran added, since there were not enough Yankees in Minnesota, the Scandinavian immigrants sort of filled in and settled in homogeneous areas where the township system demanded that the people living there also run them. "There was no sheriff or priest that would come and run things. So in part, it might have been because the separation of church and state forced them into politics. . . . All of a sudden, they could do what they liked, freed from the Church of Sweden. . . . There was a need for a community to be run." Swedish historian Sten Carlsson also sees a pattern. On the one hand, he writes, it is "surprising" that the Scandinavian immigrants entered Minnesota politics so quickly—they were a factor in the state's politics already in the 1880s—but, in fact, the breakthrough that came around the turn of the century was the result of "long and purposeful preparations."

Often little is known about these early immigrant politicians beyond basic information. Some of them were well educated, some were descendants of prominent families in the old countries. Many came to America as children with their parents, and although they often spoke Swedish or

Norwegian at home, they quickly became Americanized. Some came to America with barely a few years of schooling. Still, almost all of them were literate as a result of the strong educational traditions in Scandinavia— universal elementary education had been adopted in Denmark in 1814, in Sweden in 1842, and in Norway in 1848. In addition, Scandinavia had a long-standing literary tradition going back to the Icelandic sagas, and the Lutheran churches strongly encouraged reading. A commitment to education became central for the Scandinavian immigrants once in Minnesota, and the public schools and higher public education were important means of integration into American society. Many of the Scandinavian politicians in Minnesota were second-generation immigrants, following their fathers' footsteps into politics. They had come to the United States as young children or were born in the new country. Many achieved the college education their parents lacked. For them, the fact that they were Norwegian or Swedish or Danish was not that important.

The second-generation immigrants inhabited two worlds simultaneously, and they often wanted to forget everything about their homelands— language, religion, family customs—according to immigration scholar Marcus Lee Hansen. However, the third generation was different, he adds. They were all born in America, and they were a new force. There was no reason for feelings of inferiority, and they had a "spontaneous, almost irresistible impulse" that focused on "the thoughts on heritage—the heritage of blood." To Hansen, the Scandinavian immigrants were "inveterate joiners," a "habit which was without question the result of a feeling of lonesomeness." Immigration scholar Lawrence Fuchs, quoted by Swedish immigration historian Dag Blanck, opines that American nationalism allowed for "voluntary pluralism" for immigrants like the Scandinavians. This made it possible for them to maintain ancestral cultures while being loyal to American political philosophy. Thus, writes Blanck, by becoming Swedish American, they also became Americans—a building block in the construction of their American national identity.

With time, as their Americanization continued, their ethnic backgrounds became less and less important. By 1905, for example, the official *Minnesota Legislative Manual*, the so-called Blue Book, no longer shows the birthplace of the legislators. They were now Americans, and that brought greater political success.

The Norwegians led the way. The first was Ole Knudsen, from Hedemarken, who was elected county commissioner in Houston County in 1856.

Then followed Torbjørn G. Fladeland and Hans Hansen Holten, from Telemarken, both members of the first Minnesota Territorial Legislature. In 1859, Lars K. Aaker became the first Norwegian member in the Minnesota State Legislature, followed by the first Swede, Lars Johan Stark, in 1864, the first Dane, Søren Listoe, in 1874, the first Finn, John Saari, in 1904, and the first Icelander, Gunnar B. Bjornson, in 1912.

More breakthroughs came during the late nineteenth century. In 1872, Albert E. Rice, from Vinje in Telemarken, was elected to the Minnesota Senate, where he served until 1886, when he was elected lieutenant governor; that same year, Swede Hans Mattson was elected secretary of state, marking a first: two Scandinavians holding major statewide offices at the same time.

Another Norwegian immigrant, Charles Kittelson, was elected state treasurer in 1879, and still another, Adolph Biermann, became state auditor in 1890. Biermann was also the first Democrat to win a statewide political office in Minnesota, which Sten Carlsson sees as the Democratic Party's breakthrough in Minnesota politics. Biermann was born in Christiania (Oslo) in 1842, and twenty years later, after emigrating to America, he enlisted in the Union army and fought in the Civil War.

Between 1847 and 1905, there were, in total, 3,044 Norwegians elected to political offices in the United States. Of these, 1,220—more than one-third of the total—were elected in Minnesota. During the last four decades of the 1800s, the state legislature had one hundred seventy Norwegian, eighty Swedish, and five Danish members. In 1917 alone, there were twenty-one Norwegians, ten Swedes, and two Danes. In addition, the Norwegians occupied five of Minnesota's ten seats in the US House of Representatives and one of two seats in the US Senate. By 1917, the Norwegian Americans had become an "impressive political bloc . . . a force to be reckoned with in the politics of the American Middle West," writes Norwegian American historian Jon Wefald.

The fact that the Norwegian Americans were much more politically active in the young state of Minnesota than the other Scandinavian immigrants made them more resemble the politically active Irish Americans than the Swedish Americans, writes Danish scholar Jørn Brøndal. He argues that the Swedish immigrants arrived with less democratic experience than the Norwegians or the Danes, because the democratic political institutions came later in Sweden (1866) than in Norway and Denmark, although the

Minnesota Danes, in contrast to those in neighboring Wisconsin, never played a prominent role in state politics. In addition, the Norwegians came to America earlier than the Swedes, which affected the timing of the growth of ethnic institutions like the church and the press as well as their political mobilization. By 1880, the Swedish-language press had started to insist that the Swedish immigrants assert themselves more in Minnesota's politics. However, few Swedes had the required qualifications for a political career. Few had mastered English and few had legal training. The Swedish American colleges trained ministers, steeped in Swedish traditions, which "fostered an exclusiveness which did not develop successful politicians." They also did not offer legal training, often necessary for a political career. In view of all this, "one is amazed to find even prior to 1900 a large number of Swedes" appointed or elected to political offices.

In contrast, the Norwegians arrived in America with both knowledge of and experience in local affairs in their homeland, largely because an 1836 law applied democratic principles from the 1814 Norwegian constitution (at the time the second most democratic constitution in the world after the US Constitution) to local self-government such as parish councils. Norway also instituted universal male suffrage earlier than Sweden, 1898 compared to 1907. Thus, upon arrival, the Norwegian immigrants had more practical political experience than the Swedes.

The first years in America were often harsh, and there was time for little besides trying to survive. The settlers also had to overcome the "handicap of nationality," as well as the fact that native-born Americans were "jealous of their Anglo-Saxon institutions" and did not "quickly step aside." But, once the Norwegians entered the political arena, they were "no novices," and it would "be wrong to view them as ignorant peasants."

The Norwegian American officeholders were particularly dominant in counties with a heavy Norwegian immigrant presence, not the least because they were often the only people living there. Of all the major immigrant groups in Minnesota, the Norwegians were the most rural, living in areas sparsely populated by other European immigrants. In some of these counties, such as Otter Tail—the "banner county of the farmers' movement"—the Norwegians amounted to 25 to 30 percent of the total population around 1890.

As they started to get involved in the local affairs of their communities, an isolated ethnicity was created. The fact that many immigrants came from isolated rural communities "encouraged an extreme localism and a sense of kinship with others from the same area," and they "recreated the rural Norwegian community to an astounding degree."

The Norwegian immigrants were particularly drawn to four county offices: treasurer, registrar of deeds, sheriff, and auditor. They were less interested in running for coroner or surveyor or superintendent of schools, probably because those positions required professional training and English fluency. As their political apprenticeship progressed, as their knowledge of the English language improved, their ambitions grew, and by the beginning of the 1890s, as the townships were organized and the Norwegian settlements matured, they started to set their eyes on both statewide and national offices.

Historian Jon Wefald argues that Norwegian immigrants' politics from the 1890s to World War I were "unrelentingly progressive, frequently radical" and that they were "one of the most consistently reform-minded ethnic groups in America." Scholars have different theories on why so many Norwegian immigrants sympathized with the agrarian protest movements, particularly in the northwestern counties of Minnesota. Much can be explained by the economic conditions among these wheat farmers of western Minnesota, which were different from farmers in other regions: the population was sparser, the conditions were harsher, and farmers were more dependent on a single crop. Wefald traces the reform-mindedness back to what he calls Norwegian "folk culture," founded in social cohesion and communalism, which, in turn, stressed economic self-sufficiency and cooperation. In the end, this led to a "common goal for the Norwegians—the goal of a cooperative commonwealth." In their compact settlements in western Minnesota, where they often lived and worked with people from the same valley in Norway, from the same *bygd* (countryside), they were "hostile to competitive capitalism" and wanted to avoid sharp competition between their neighbors. They were also suspicious of middlemen and of corporate businesses: "They preferred communal and family self-sufficiency and desired a highly cohesive and socially harmonious community."

Swedish scholars Harald Runblom and Hans Norman, although not outright refuting Wefald, argue that the issue is more complex and that influences from Norway "were not alone in shaping Norwegian radicalism." Carlton C. Qualey, another Norwegian American scholar, also finds Wefald's argument "not wholly convincing." He argues that local issues were decisive and that it was not until the economic conditions for these immigrant farmers became "intolerable" during the Populist and Progressive eras that their old allegiance to the Republican Party was broken. He writes, "It is not at all demonstrated, that they carried over from Norway an ingrained suspicion of officialdom. . . . It is far more evident that American conditions and circumstances governed their political behavior."

In historian Carl H. Chrislock's view, the Norwegian immigrants came with a sense of community and responsibility for its welfare along with a suspicion of the elites after hundreds of years under first Danish and then Swedish rule. But domestic American impulses also interacted with each other to produce a mixed Norwegian American political orientation with a "left-of-center tilt." For Chrislock, the Norwegian farmers' involvement in the agrarian protest movements of the Upper Midwest and in the Nonpartisan League's radical political program advocating state ownership could find its justification in their "ancestral heritage"—poor farmers from Norway could not be "easily persuaded that state-owned enterprises were inherently evil." They were rooted in a rural culture with a peasant class-consciousness, a dislike for the government, and a suspicion of towns.

Odd S. Lovoll also underscores that the Norwegians in Minnesota "played a part in the formulation of several aspects of the political culture" there, and once the Progressive Era had run its course the conservative business philosophy of the Republican Party prevailed. James Youngdale sees a link between the new and the old country, writing that "these rebellions were fertilized and given character by the old country traditions."

Clearly, Norwegian American voters were not unified. In fact, as Peter Grepperud puts it, "diversity rather than cohesion characterized the Norwegian American political experience in northwestern Minnesota." They were a house divided as the agrarian protest movements rolled in over Minnesota, and third-party radicalism became an ever-more-present alternative to the traditional Republicanism of the Norwegian/Scandinavian voters. Historian Lowell J. Soike writes about realignment, caused not so much by voters switching parties as by new, inactive voters, "with weak party attachments," who were drawn to agrarian party movements or alternatives. And the divisions were further amplified by pushback from businesses and from parts of the Norwegian community in North Dakota, led by the influential Norwegian-language paper *Normanden* in Grand Forks.

US Senator Knute Nelson, a member of the Republican establishment and himself a farmer from western Minnesota, also opposed the agrarian protest movements and in particular the Nonpartisan League, writing in a letter in 1920, "The truth is, there is no use disguising it, the Norwegians are at the bottom of our political troubles in the NW [Northwest]. The Norwegians put the Nonpartisan League into power in North Dakota and they are at the bottom of our troubles in Minnesota." When Nelson won reelection to the US Senate in 1918, he failed to win his home county of Douglas, where the League was strong.

The Democratic Party was never a serious alternative for the Norwegian American farmers in western Minnesota, largely because of one thing they all shared: anti-Catholicism that transcended state boundaries and crossed generations. To be a Catholic was to be a Democrat, and the Democratic Party was the party of the Pope. This anti-Catholicism was fomented by organizations such as the American Protective Association (APA), founded in neighboring Iowa. In the Twin Cities, one of APA's leaders was Norwegian American Ole Byorum. In addition, temperance was an important issue among the Scandinavian immigrants. The Germans and Irish, who were both Catholic and "wet," voted Democrat—another reason for staying away from the Democratic Party. There were some exceptions during these years, such as when the two Swedish American Democrats, John Lind and John A. Johnson, were elected governors. Still, the Republican Party continued to rule the Minnesota legislature. Only in 1916, when Woodrow Wilson ran for president, did the Democratic Party attract a "sizeable," or 31 percent, presidential vote from Minnesota's Norwegian American community. Between 1880 and 1924, only an average of 16 percent of the Norwegian American votes went to the Democratic presidential candidates.

The Norwegian and Swedish immigrants generally got on well with each other in their new home country, and they collaborated in Minnesota politics, particularly in the early years. At that time, of course, Sweden and Norway were still joined in their union, and there was lots of movement of people between the two countries, both for work and for studies. They often also personally knew each other and worked together. This was particularly true in the Scandinavian community in the Twin Cities. In his post-gubernatorial career, for example, John Lind started a law practice with the prominent Norwegian lawyer Andreas Ueland, and both Lind and later Governor Joseph A. A. Burnquist chose as their close aides fellow Swedish Americans, who went on to become chairs of Minnesota's Republican and Democratic parties, respectively.

Leonard August Rosing, an immigrant from Malmö, Sweden, engineered Lind's victory in 1898. He had arrived in America in 1869, at the age of eight, with his parents, settling on a farm in Goodhue County, south of Minneapolis. Starting out as a Republican, he switched to the Democratic Party in 1890 over the tariff issue and rose quickly in its ranks. In 1896, he became chairman of the Democratic State Central Committee. Two years later, he ran Lind's campaign for governor and became part of Lind's cabinet. When Rosing himself ran for governor in 1902, Lind strongly supported him, stating that he was educated, capable, and well informed, progressive while at the same time conservative, a man of willpower who makes important decisions. Rosing lost the election but continued to be active in the Democratic Party until his death at forty-seven.

Gustav Lindquist was the close confidant of Burnquist during his time as governor from 1915 to 1921. Born in Sweden in 1882, Lindquist left for America at nineteen and went straight to St. Paul. By 1915, he had developed an extensive business network around the state and a reputation as a "genius for organization." Burnquist appointed the ardent Republican Lindquist deputy state insurance commissioner and then asked him to be his private secretary because he "needed a patriotic American of tact and ability." Shortly thereafter, Lindquist was also made chairman of the Republican State Central Committee. In 1918, Lindquist was the man behind Governor Burnquist's election victory in that year's bitter election. In 1920, Burnquist promoted Lindquist to Minnesota's insurance commissioner, and the next governor, J. A. O. Preus, reappointed him.

THE SCANDINAVIAN IMMIGRANTS initially made their mark on statewide politics through the office of secretary of state, Minnesota's chief election officer. Beginning in 1869, when the Swedish immigrant and Civil War veteran Hans Mattson first captured the office, it became something of a Scandinavian entitlement, or gateway, into Minnesota politics, as Mattson was followed by Norwegians and Swedes with names like Johannes Irgens, Frederick Brown, Albert Berg, Peter Hanson, and Mike Holm. Irgens and Brown were both grandsons of former bishops in the town of Bergen, Norway—Ole Irgens and Johan Nordahl Brun—and Brown's brother was Johannes Brun, a prominent stage actor in Norway.

In 1869, Scandinavians within the Republican Party gathered for a Scandinavian Republican convention and nominated Mattson to be their candidate for secretary of state. The Norwegian Lars K. Aaker presided at the boisterous convention banquet, which featured twelve toasts for America,

Scandinavia, and the Republican Party. At the convention, Mattson declared that "there should be no distinction between Norwegians, Swedes, and Danes, and that's been the spirit of this convention." Unity among Scandinavians was strong in the early years of their political involvement, but with time, the rivalries grew, and pan-Scandinavian groups split up into national groups. The Swedes, in particular, began to resent the Norwegians' sizable and long-standing lead among political officeholders, and many intense political battles across nationalities followed—not the least for the office of secretary of state. There was much talk in the Swedish American press about fairness and about the Republican Party treating the Swedes as "voting cattle" and as "stepchildren." Still, the Norwegians and the Swedes preferred each other to any non-Scandinavians, and they voted for each other with few exceptions, urged by the Scandinavian press to vote for *vår landsman*—our countryman—in openly ethnic appeals.

When Hans Mattson lost his reelection bid for secretary of state in 1890 to the Norwegian Frederick P. Brown, it greatly upset the Swedes, and two years later the Democrat Peter Nelson—who was born in Småland in 1843 and came to America in 1866—was nominated to run against Brown. By then, Brown was called "cunning" and "crafty" by *Svenska Amerikanska Posten,* which reported that the Republican convention succeeded in stealing the nomination from the Swedes while Brown, in his role of secretary of state, brought "dishonor" to his office and "deserves the public's contempt" after he had manipulated the ballots in the interest of the Republican Party. "We must show the Irish and the Norwegians," the paper commented, "that you cannot ignore the Swedes."

The Nelson-Brown fight in 1892 illustrates the ever-present conflict between ethnic loyalties and party loyalties. The Swedish-language paper *Skaffaren* in the Twin Cities, usually staunchly Republican, endorsed the Swede, Nelson, even though he was a Democrat. Here, clearly, the ethnic factor played the deciding role. However, Brown won again, and by the time he ran for reelection in 1894, the Swedes apparently had had enough and put up three Swedes against the incumbent Norwegian. Albert Berg, born in Center City, Minnesota, "the jovial Swede" from Chisago County, won. Berg was reelected twice, first in 1896 and then 1898, the same year that John Lind was elected governor. The victory led the usually faithful Republican paper *Minnesota Stats Tidning* to proclaim proudly on its front page with big photos of Lind and Berg: "For the first time in our country and in our state's history, two Swedish Americans have captured the state's two highest offices, and that this has occurred in Minnesota is completely as it should be, since Minnesota is America's Sweden." Berg was, in turn, succeeded by another Swede, Peter E. Hanson from Skåne, who was, in turn, reelected twice, in 1902 and 1904.

The Scandinavians continued their long and firm grip on the position of secretary of state for decades, first through Mike Holm and then through Joan Anderson Growe. Mike Holm, a Republican, was secretary of state from 1921 to 1952, reelected every two years regardless of which party the governor represented. Born Mikael Hanson in Ringvattnet in the northern Swedish province of Jämtland in 1876, Holm was seven years old when he arrived in America with his parents, who settled in Marshall County in western Minnesota before moving to Roseau County near the Canadian border. *Svenska Amerikanska Posten* called him a "self-made man" who had been on his own since he was twelve years old. He served for many years as a probate judge in Roseau County, a "friend of the widows and the orphans," before being elected secretary of state. In the Swedish American press of the time, Holm is described as polite, helpful, and hard-working, a "gentleman" in the best sense of the word. Although he was a Republican, he had support and credibility among Democrats. Holm's political longevity made his career unique. And after his death, he was succeeded by his third wife, Virginia Holm, elected in November 1952 to serve out her husband's term as well as her own two-year term. She failed to win reelection in 1954.

Mike Holm's remarkable thirty-one years as Minnesota's secretary of state was almost duplicated in more modern times by Joan Ruth Anderson. Launching her political career under her married name, Joan Anderson Growe, and representing the Democratic-Farmer-Labor Party (DFL), she served as secretary of state from 1975 to 1999.

Called "the legendary Joan Growe" when she was introduced to thunderous applause at the DFL convention in Duluth in 2014, Joan Ruth Anderson was born in Minneapolis in 1935 but grew up in the town of Buffalo, Minnesota. Her father, whose parents came from Linköping, Sweden, and who never spoke English until he started school, owned a hardware store in town and served as mayor from 1954 to 1963. The essence of Minnesota, Joan Anderson Growe told me, is "community—you are responsible for each other and . . . people look out for each other." Here, "it's ingrained in us to do good and not only achieve political power—public service is an honorable calling."

She became a teacher, married and had four children, divorced, and became politically active, opposing the Vietnam War and joining the League of Women Voters. Then, in 1972, "all of a sudden, I ran for the state legislature," she said. "I was endorsed unanimously and then ignored. I did not know what to do. A core group of about thirty women got together and this became the thing to do in the Eden Prairie/Minnetonka district. It was knock and talk, every day. The party chairman lived in my district but I never saw him. One time someone from the party knocked on my door and offered to help and I had him watch my four kids since my nanny was not feeling well. We won, with 55 percent of the vote. I was in shock. When I went to the party headquarters that night, I met Martin Sabo for the first time. He just said, 'Joan Growe won.'"

To have a last name ending with 'son' on the ballot "was really good," she said. "There were always a lot of Scandinavians in Minnesota—we were never a real minority." Two years later, Joan Anderson Growe ran for secretary of state and won, beating the incumbent Arlen Ingolf Erdahl, a Norwegian American Republican, who opposed the voter reforms passed by the DFL-controlled legislature. She set about implementing the reforms. She was met with skepticism among her staff at first, but "I worked well with the county auditors and hired a male election director, a sort of an old boy.... We computerized the whole thing as the first state in the country and people came to study our system. We worked very aggressively on turnout and instituted same-day voter registration."

Later, she helped ensure passage of a motor vehicle/voter registration law, which became national law in 1993. Growe's efforts have been "largely responsible for changes that have established Minnesota as a state with the highest voter registration and turnout in the country."

In 1984, Joan Anderson Growe ran for the US Senate but lost to the incumbent Republican, Rudy Boschwitz. It was the year when Walter Mondale and the first woman vice presidential candidate, Geraldine Ferraro, were crushed by Ronald Reagan. Afterward, Anderson Growe said, talking about Ferraro and herself, "although we did not win, we opened doors that will never be closed again.... I hope I have provided some leadership for these women."

Joan Anderson Growe continued in her role as Minnesota secretary of state for another fifteen years while at the same time becoming active as an international election observer. She continues to speak out on matters dear to her heart, such as women's issues and voters' rights.

Secretary of State Joan Anderson Growe with a group of children encouraging people to vote, 1976

AS WITH THE ABOLITION of the death penalty in Minnesota earlier in the twentieth century, Scandinavians came to play leading roles in two other major reform movements of the time: woman suffrage and prohibition. Norwegian immigrant Ole O. Sageng became a kind of "progressive folk hero" and the suffragists' "most enduring friend" in the Minnesota legislature. He was dubbed "The Napoleon of Woman Suffrage," and he fought harder for women's right to vote "than any other man in Minnesota."

Like many of his Norwegian American contemporaries, Sageng grew up on a small farm on the prairie in western Minnesota. Born in Østerdalen, Norway, he came to America with his family in 1878 at the age of seven and settled near the town of Dalton in Otter Tail County in northwestern Minnesota. One of seven children, he graduated from high school in Fergus Falls, attended Augsburg College in Minneapolis, and became a teacher and a farmer. He also became active in politics. After a couple of failed attempts, he was elected to the Minnesota House of Representatives in 1900 representing the Populist Party. The victory led to a long political career serving his district in both the Minnesota house and senate, and for several terms as the legislature's only Populist. Eventually, he switched to the Republican Party and became a leading spokesman for its progressive wing. In 1924, he ran for the US Senate as a progressive Republican but lost in the primary. Many years later, in 1950, he returned to the state legislature a final time as a member of the Minnesota Senate. It was a "remarkable political comeback at the age of seventy-eight," according to his biographer Cecil M. Johnson, who himself grew up in Dalton. He described Sageng as a consummate politician, an excellent legislator, completely honest, but also a most unsuccessful farmer—he was poor all his life.

Sageng's political career during the first two decades of the twentieth century was marked by the two big issues of the day: woman suffrage and temperance, or prohibition. He came out early for the right of women to vote, more than two and half decades before the Nineteenth Amendment finally made that possible. Brenda Ueland, daughter of Clara Hampson Ueland, Minnesota's suffrage leader, once said that Sageng "was symbolic of everything wonderful in Minnesota—sturdy and spare and good and self-taught, one of those countless obscure but great men." Writes Barbara Stuhler, "the suffragists adored Sageng."

As Johnson tells it, Sageng was interested in the issue of woman suffrage already as a high school student. In 1893, he wrote an essay called "Woman Suffrage," in which he forcefully argued for the right of women to vote, deeming it one of the most important issues of the time. Still, once in the state senate, Sageng did not become fully engaged in the issue for a few sessions; in fact, according to one account, it was not until a fellow senator said that if men in Minnesota continued to be complacent in this matter, "we would wake up one day and find the Turkish women voting before the Minnesotans." A startled Sageng "consented to espouse our cause, with most vigorous earnestness and has done so ever since."

During the following years and legislative sessions, Sageng presented numerous bills that would extend to women their full voting rights, but was narrowly defeated again and again, once by only one vote. His efforts were finally superseded by the Nineteenth Amendment to the US Constitution that gave women the right to vote. In a special legislative session in Minnesota in September 1919, the amendment was ratified in less than thirty minutes, in the senate by 60 votes to 5, and in the house by 120 votes to 6. Minnesota was the fifteenth state to ratify.

How did a poor Norwegian-born farmer from a little town in northwestern Minnesota come to be the leading male proponent of woman suffrage? Sageng seems never to have answered that question himself during his lifetime. His daughter, Mathilda, answered it many years later, saying simply, "His mother. His mother." Her father, she said, always thought his mother was so intelligent and that it was a shame that she could not vote. One of his biggest disappointments was that Minnesota became a "suffrage follower rather than a leader."

Scandinavian women played a major part in this fight for the right to vote, which had been going on in Minnesota since 1881, when fourteen women founded the Minnesota Woman Suffrage Association (MWSA). The Scandinavian Woman Suffrage Association (SWSA), founded in 1907, was the leading organization for the Nordic activists. By then, the women of Finland had already obtained the right to vote, while Norway followed in 1913, Denmark in 1915, and Sweden in 1919. As a result, "members of the SWSA saw themselves as having 'a peculiar prestige' among suffrage clubs." Their ranks included working women and single women, but mainly women with small children. The average age was thirty-two. When SWSA was founded, the great majority of members were Norwegian Americans and Swedish Americans, with a couple of Danish Americans and one Finnish American. Most of them were first-generation immigrants; some were members of prominent immigrant families. By 1919, some thirty thousand women in Minnesota belonged to a local suffrage group.

These were no "gentle warriors," as Barbara Stuhler calls her book on Minnesota's suffrage movement. They fought hard. Many of them were, if not Scandinavian immigrants themselves, married to Scandinavian immigrants, such as Clara Hampson Ueland, Julia Bullard Nelson, and Anna Dickie Olesen. Ueland was married to the prominent Norwegian immigrant and lawyer Andreas Ueland. "My parents were political idealists, feminists, democrats," their daughter Brenda Ueland later wrote. Her father, born at Heskestad in Norway in 1853, was the son of Ole Gabriel Ueland, at one time president of the Norwegian parliament, Stortinget.

In 1914, Clara Ueland became president of the Minnesota Woman Suffrage Association and led a procession of almost two thousand suffrage supporters in Minneapolis. She then joined the Scandinavian women's organization and also became the first president of the Minnesota League of Women Voters. She died in a traffic accident in 1927, sixty-six years old.

Swedish American Nanny Mattson Jaeger was one of the first presidents

Scandinavian women in national costumes and carrying flags during a suffrage parade in Minneapolis, 1914

of the Scandinavian Woman Suffrage Association. The daughter of Colonel Hans Mattson, the former secretary of state and a leading member of Minnesota's Scandinavian community, she was married to Luth Jaeger, a prominent Norwegian American journalist and strong supporter of woman suffrage. Nanny Mattson Jaeger believed that international connections would make for an international solidarity of women. Born in Red Wing, south of the Twin Cities, she attended school in Sweden for five years, between 1871 and 1876. After her return to Minnesota, she became the first woman to enter the University of Minnesota, in 1877. With time, she became a link with Scandinavia on the issue of woman suffrage.

Brenda Ueland has described Nanny Mattson Jaeger as a "rather formidable" woman, "piercing and ironically intelligent," who was proud of the woman suffrage record in Scandinavia. She also strongly believed in assimilation, and she linked woman suffrage to the process of Americanization. "Ethnicity was a means to achieve enfranchisement," according to historian Anna Peterson, who also writes that the Scandinavian Woman Suffrage Association "imparted a distinctly Scandinavian flair to American suffrage goals," with traditional folk costumes and folk dancing and Norwegian, Swedish, and Danish flags, to help draw the crowds for fund raisers. At one point, in 1914, over a thousand people gathered for a festival in St. Paul. As assimilation demands grew, the Scandinavian suffragists debated changing their organization's name to avoid ethnic identification, but in the end they kept their name.

Nanny Mattson Jaeger is one of twenty-five of Minnesota's leading suffragists honored at the Minnesota Woman Suffrage Memorial next to the State Capitol in St. Paul. So is another Swedish American, Bertha Berglin Moller, born in Hällesjö in the province of Jämtland in northern Sweden in 1888, where her father was a tenant farmer. Her Swedish name was Brita Kristina. At five years old, she came to America with her parents, Magnus Persson Berglin and Brita Greta Ersdotter, and her six siblings. Two of her uncles, Magnus Ericson and Anders Olof Fränden, were members of the Swedish parliament (Riksdag) and authors of legislation for women's rights.

Bertha Berglin grew up in Rush City, Minnesota. After high school, she attended Duluth Normal School and became a teacher. She married Charles Moller in 1910 and in 1916 became involved in the suffrage movement after meeting Clara Ueland. She joined both the Minnesota suffrage movement and the Scandinavian Woman Suffrage Association. However, Berglin Moller soon turned to a more radical suffrage group, the National Woman's Party (NWP), for which she became secretary in Minnesota. She staged suffrage ballots in various cities around Minnesota and she participated in picketing and demonstrations in Washington, DC, in front of both the White House and the US Capitol, in late 1918. At the protests, police poured down on the marchers and Berglin Moller, who led them, was arrested eleven times, more than any other Minnesota woman, and she served two short jail sentences for her activities. Afterward, she said that "even those who did not defend the pickets are now indignant at the brutality of the government methods."

The issue of picketing had been contentious among the women in Minnesota, and at the Minnesota Woman Suffrage Association's convention in November 1917, the Scandinavians, who largely supported picketing as a strategy, marched out in protest when the convention did not endorse these tactics. During World War I, some thought picketing unpatriotic, but others, like Nanny Mattson Jaeger, supported it as it made the whole struggle more visible. It was shortly after the convention that Bertha Berglin Moller announced that she was joining the National Woman's Party and the protests in Washington, DC.

After women won the right to vote, Bertha Berglin Moller worked on issues such as child labor and the peace movement. In 1923, she and her husband moved to Chicago, and in 1925, she graduated with a bachelor's of law from Northwestern University. In 1930, she divorced Moller and married Peter Delin, whose name she took. Press reports say that Bertha Delin was a Democrat and an active member in Chicago's women's organizations, including the National Woman's Party. In 1929, she represented the party at an international industrial conference in Berlin, Germany. She worked as a lawyer in Chicago's Sanitary District, where she managed personal injury claims. Later, she was appointed prosecutor for the Women's Court of Cook County. In the 1940s, she worked for the labor board in Washington, DC. Bertha Berglin Moller Delin died on October 13, 1951, in San Francisco, sixty-three years old, but she is buried in the Scandinavian Cemetery in Forest Lake, Minnesota, under her American maiden name, Bertha C. Berglin.

The Minnesota Woman Suffrage Association had male members and developed strong alliances with the state's Scandinavian politicians. When Clara Ueland once took stock of the Scandinavians in the 1917 Minnesota congressional delegation, she described Senator Knute Nelson as firmly pro-suffrage and as someone who had been "so long a friend." US congressmen Sydney Anderson, Ernest Lundeen, Halvor Steenerson, Carl Van Dyke, and Andrew Volstead—all Scandinavian Americans—were also for woman suffrage. The fact was, writes Anna Peterson, "more Scandinavian-American men voted in favor of enfranchising women than did any other ethnic group in the Midwest." And when it mattered most, when the US Congress voted on woman suffrage in May and June of 1919, the whole Minnesota delegation, including Senator Nelson and all four Scandinavians in the House of Representatives, all voted yes.

By 1920, two-thirds of the states had ratified the Nineteenth Amendment, and in 1922, four women were elected to the Minnesota legislature, the first women members of that body. But it was not until 1954 that the first woman from Minnesota was elected to the US Congress. Cornelia "Coya" Gjesdal Knutson was the daughter of Christian and Christine (Anderson) Gjesdal, Norwegian immigrants who farmed in Edmore, North Dakota. Her father had been active in the Nonpartisan League. She graduated from Concordia College in Moorhead, Minnesota, and became a teacher. She served two terms in the House of Representatives, from 1955 to 1959, representing northwestern Minnesota as a member of the DFL Party. Seeking a third term, she was defeated after the infamous "Coya, come home" letter from her husband, Andy, an alcoholic whom she later divorced. In the letter, which had actually been written by her enemies in the party, Andy urged her not to run for reelection and instead return to their home. The letter was followed by a press release in which Andy pleaded for a return to the "happy home life" from before Coya ran for office. She was not persuaded. She ran again, but lost to another Norwegian American, Republican Odin

Langen, whose campaign slogan was "A big man for a man-sized job." Coya Knutson ran for Congress again, several times, but without success. She was a maverick, often challenging the DFL leadership by running in the primaries against endorsed candidates. In 1960, the whole party leadership— including Senator Hubert Humphrey, Governor Orville Freeman, and Lieutenant Governor Karl Rolvaag—campaigned against her when she challenged the endorsed DFL candidate, Roy E. Wiseth, for a seat in the state senate. Coya Knutson died in 1996, eighty-two years old.

Minnesota's voters did not send another woman to the US House of Representatives until 2000, when Betty McCollum, DFL, was elected. In 2006, Amy Klobuchar, also DFL, became the state's first female US senator. Two decades earlier, in 1983, Minnesota had elected its first female lieutenant governor, Swedish American Marlene Johnson, DFL, and the next six lieutenant governors were also women. In 1977, Governor Rudy Perpich appointed the first female member of the state's supreme court, Rosalie Wahl, and by 1991, Minnesota's highest court had a female majority, a first in the nation. Norwegian American Lorie Skjerven Gildea was appointed chief justice of the court in 2010.

A Scandinavian American woman also served as speaker of the Minnesota house from 2007 to 2011: Margaret Anderson Kelliher. A Democrat, she ran for governor in 2010 but lost. Swedish on her father's side and largely German on her mother's, she grew up on a farm in Blue Earth County in southern Minnesota and became involved in politics as a teenager during the farm crisis in the 1980s. "One night at dinner," she recalled, "my father put his head down and started to cry. I was pretty certain I had never seen him cry before, but he wouldn't talk and went out. So I started getting involved in politics. I wanted to know what was going on."

She aligned with the Democrats although, she said, she is pretty sure she came from a long line of Republicans, but her parents were very private and never talked about politics. She distinctly remembers watching Humphrey's funeral on television. She later met Walter Mondale, who also came from southern Minnesota. "Yes, there is a Scandinavian trait to Minnesota politics," she said: "Self-deprecating, sense of humor, modesty, the collective, strong communal aspects, very humble." She was selected to portray Santa Lucia at Gustavus Adolphus College, "which increased my Scandinavian cred quite a bit." She and her non-Scandinavian husband, who plays the fast ice game of bandy, took their son on a trip to Västerås, a town northwest of Stockholm where bandy has old traditions. "I was just blown away at how people looked just like my relatives in Minnesota—these are my people!" she said.

In addition to those who pursued elected office, many Scandinavian women became active in radical politics in Minnesota. Signe Aurell, born in 1889 in Glimåkra-Osby in southern Sweden, came to Minneapolis in 1913. Working as a laundress and seamstress, she joined the Industrial Workers of the World (IWW), fought for fair wages and safe working conditions, and urged Scandinavian maids in the Twin Cities to organize. In 1900, 61 percent of the Swedish immigrant women in Minnesota worked as servants or waitresses. Aurell published frequently in the Swedish American press and wrote poetry and was published in *Allarm, Bokstugan,* and *Brand.* She translated into Swedish the last will of Joe Hill, a prominent Wobbly (IWW member) and a Swede. In 1920, she left Minnesota, possibly because of economic difficulties, and returned to Sweden, where she died in 1975.

Olive Malmberg Johnson was another Minnesota radical. Born in the university town of Lund in southern Sweden in 1872, she came to Minnesota as a teenager with her family, graduated from high school in Minneapolis, and then left for New York, where she joined the Socialist Labor Party and became the longtime editor of the party's weekly paper, *The People.* She wrote books about the revolution, women, and the socialist movement, which "furnishes all the opportunities for women. It is her only true and proper field of action." She also ran for political office, as the Socialist Labor Party's candidate for governor of New York in 1918, for mayor of New York City in 1929, and for the US Senate from New York in 1934, losing all three times. She died in California in 1954.

PARALLEL TO THE FIGHT for the right of women to vote, the other major political issue of the time, prohibition, played out with heavy Scandinavian involvement. When the Eighteenth Amendment to the US Constitution made liquor illegal in the United States in 1919, Ole O. Sageng—a lifelong temperance man as well as a longtime friend of the suffragists—achieved another political goal. Prior to that, in 1915, he and other temperance proponents in Minnesota's anti-saloon movement had succeeded in getting the Minnesota legislature to approve the so-called county option. It gave the voters in each county the power to decide whether liquor could be sold in the county or not. County option proponents were, at heart, prohibitionists. Before the end of the year, forty-five of Minnesota's eighty-six counties voted to go dry, and by the time the Eighteenth Amendment made prohibition the law of the land in January 1920, sixty-four of Minnesota's counties had voted to go dry.

It was Sageng's fellow Norwegian American, Andrew J. Volstead, also from western Minnesota, who launched the Prohibition Era by writing the National Prohibition Act, better known as the Volstead Act. He was the public face of Prohibition, to both opponents and proponents. He received praise as well as death threats. His name became tied to what would be considered a "failed social experiment," and former governor Theodore Christianson writes, "Certainly, the name of no Minnesota citizen has been spoken with more abuse and obloquy."

Born in Goodhue County, the son of immigrant parents from Norway, Volstead attended St. Olaf College and then studied law in Decorah, Iowa, before moving to Granite Falls, the county seat of Yellow Medicine County in western Minnesota. A Republican, he quickly became involved in the community and remained there all his life. Elected to the position of county attorney, Volstead became known as an earnest and vigorous upholder of the law, including the local option law that gave the municipalities the possibility to vote dry. A distinguished-looking man with a droopy mustache, Volstead continued to pursue local office and was elected president of the board of education, city attorney, and mayor of Granite Falls. Eventually, in 1902, he was elected to the US House of Representatives from the Seventh Congressional District, a position he held for twenty years.

In October 1919, the Volstead Act was approved in both chambers of the US Congress over President Wilson's veto. It allowed the federal government to enforce the War Prohibition Act of 1918, which prohibited the manufacturing and sale of liquor until the end of the war, and paved the way for the enactment of the Eighteenth Amendment. Beyond his advocacy of Prohibition, Volstead had a significant impact in Congress. He authored the Capper-Volstead Act, which established farm cooperatives and allowed them to operate without fear of antitrust prosecution. The Minnesota coops had a Norwegian friend in Washington. He was also supportive of federal legislation outlawing lynching, which was an unpopular stance at the time.

In 1922, "the Father of Prohibition" lost his bid for yet another term in the US House. Volstead returned to Minnesota, where he continued working on enforcing Prohibition. He was not a teetotaler and had never made a prohibition speech or, like Sageng, been a temperance activist. Still, he believed in Prohibition and he believed that the law should be followed. When Prohibition was repealed in 1933, Volstead moved back to Granite Falls and resumed his legal career, never talking much about the big social experiment that failed. He died in 1947. His old home is today a National Historic Landmark.

Halvor Steenerson, from Crookston in Polk County, was a contemporary of Volstead, and their political careers were quite similar. Both were born in America to Norwegian-born immigrant parents. Both became lawyers. And both were Republicans. Their careers also both ended in 1922 when they were each beaten by two Norwegians from the new Farmer-Labor Party, Ole J. Kvale and Knud Wefald. As progressive Republicans, not much separated Volstead and Steenerson. Both supported railroad regulation, income tax, woman suffrage, tariff reform, prohibition of child labor, eight-hour days for railway labor, and workmen's compensation. After serving as county attorney, Steenerson was elected to the Minnesota Senate, where he was instrumental in establishing the Railroad and Warehouse Commission that set freight rates on wheat and other grains, a hugely contested issue at the time and one that affected many of Steenerson's farmer constituents in the Red River Valley. Following extensive litigation, what was popularly known as the Steenerson grain rate case established the right of state control over railway charges. After his 1922 election loss, Steenerson returned to Crookston and resumed practicing law. He died in 1926.

Haldor Erickson Boen was another Norwegian-born politician from western Minnesota. Born in 1851, he came to America together with his two brothers when he was seventeen years old and eventually settled in Fergus Falls in Otter Tail County. Within a few years of arriving, he found work in the county auditor's office and was later elected county commissioner and registrar of deeds. In 1884 he helped form the Farmers' Alliance in the county and became its secretary. The Alliance became the populist People's Party, and when Boen was elected to the US House of Representatives in 1892, it was as a Populist, succeeding fellow Norwegian Kittel Halvorson. Boen won in spite of strong opposition from the Republicans in the county, led by the Norwegian-language paper the *Fergus Falls Ugeblad*. But he served only one term, losing his reelection bid in 1894. The Republican Party succeeded in putting a brake on the momentum of the Populists. Boen returned to Fergus Falls, where he bought and ran the *Fergus Falls Globe* and resumed farming.

Boen spoke softly and haltingly, and although his English was good, he was not a strong public speaker. But he had grit and ambition, and he was "a true leader of men." As the populist People's Party faded, so did Haldor

Boen's political career, and he never made a comeback after his defeat in 1894, in spite of trying. With time, he became more radical and politically more isolated. In Otter Tail County, the younger Ole O. Sageng, who had been a Populist himself, became a leading voice among the county's Norwegian Americans, as he moved them into his form of progressive Republicanism.

Jacob F. Jacobson, from Ryfylke in Rogaland, Norway, was a power broker in Minnesota politics. Called "Honest Jake" and the "Norwegian Giant from Lac qui Parle," Jacobson came to America in 1857, when he was eight years old. Eventually, he became one of the first European settlers in Lac qui Parle County in western Minnesota. He started a farm machinery business, which became quite successful. His political career started as county auditor before he was elected to the Minnesota house in 1889. Reelected repeatedly until 1902, Jacobson was also chairman of the Republican county committee and president of the county agricultural society, both for many years. He was an imposing man, and his voice could be heard by large audiences long before microphones and loudspeakers were invented.

Regarded as "the very personification of populism," according to the *St. Paul Dispatch,* Jacobson was always looked upon as a radical. To his supporters, Jacobson's strongest asset was his honesty, and his work was "above suspicion." Minnesota politics needs more people like Jacob Jacobson, the *Dispatch* wrote when he died. Others, however, thought Jacobson was a crude and bluff, unpolished man who loved to talk. Historian O. N. Nelson calls him "a coarse, grained, boisterous, uneducated, bankrupt individual" who was more feared than trusted. Still, former governor Theodore Christianson, who also came from Lac qui Parle, calls Jacobson one of the ablest men in the Republican Party in western Minnesota. "His force and energy were throughout aligned on the side of the people in combating the unrestrained aggrandizement and abuses of railroads, corporations and special interests." In particular, Jacobson never conceded anything to the liquor lobby. He backed a new state board of control and direct elections in primaries.

In 1908, Jacobson became the Republican candidate for governor, but he lost to the hugely popular and urbane Democrat John A. Johnson, who won a third term. He died in 1938, eighty-nine years old.

Roger Moe is a leading modern example of the central role of Norwegian immigrant politicians from western Minnesota, but unlike his predecessors, he was DFL. Moe was first elected to the Minnesota Senate in 1970. He became majority leader in 1981, a position he held until his retirement in 2003—longer than any senate majority leader in state history. Moe once described himself as a "left-of-center Democrat, raised in a family where my grandfather, a Norwegian Lutheran minister, was considered the 'leading liberal' in the area and my parents thought Franklin and Eleanor Roosevelt were second only to God."

Born in Crookston in Polk County, Moe has stayed true to his northwestern Minnesota roots and lives outside the little town of Erskine. "This was my world growing up, and this is home," Moe said of the 160-acre farm where the old homestead once stood, and which a cousin now farms.

Over 40 percent of the thirty thousand or so inhabitants in Polk County are of Norwegian ancestry. Moe says he is Norwegian American—"but I am American, of course, although I am very comfortable whenever I go to Norway." Moe has been there many times: "What attracts me about Norway? The importance of physical fitness, wellness, and health; the lifestyle is more simple. They don't waste space and they are very good models. They have a priority emphasis on the young and on the little kids. A focus! Look at maternity leave and the stairs with special rails for the baby carriages."

Both of Moe's grandfathers came from Norway. His mother's father, Lars J., or L. J., Njus, came from Leikanger in Sogn. Arriving in America in 1888 at the age of eighteen, he eventually settled in Polk County. Both he and his brother, Nils, became ordained Lutheran ministers, and they were among the original members of a fraternal insurance society for retiring Lutheran pastors, Luther Union, that became the well-known Lutheran Brotherhood Insurance Company. L. J. Njus was also a poet and essayist, and for several years in the 1920s an associate editor at *Decorah Posten*, a leading Norwegian-language newspaper in Decorah, Iowa. Upon returning to Polk County in 1929, he ran for county treasurer. "Any favors given my candidacy will be appreciated. Thank you," it said on his election flyer, along with this little verse:

> The ballot is the people's voice
> Which silently express their choice,
> I wonder what will be my fate
> When you select your candidate?

L. J. Njus lost. He never ran for political office again.

In 1970, only twenty-six years old, Roger Moe decided to run for office. By then, he had graduated from Mayville State University in North Dakota, completed graduate studies at Moorhead State and North Dakota State universities, and become a math teacher and wrestling coach at the high school in Ada, south of Crookston. As the campaign got started, Moe recalled, "I woke up one night and sat up in bed. I had the idea on how to advertise my campaign. I was going to use my grandfather's . . . name and the flyer came to say: 'My grandfather ran and now his grandson Roger Moe asks for your vote.' My grandfather was a leading liberal in the area at the time, and when I went door knocking, I could not get out of some of the homes. Everyone remembered my grandfather. He had baptized them, he had married them."

Moe's opponents were the longtime incumbent, Norman Larson from Ada, and the mayor of Crookston, Harold Thomforde, both conservative. The *Crookston Daily Times* supported Thomforde, and an editorial published just before the election said, "We cannot afford a relatively unknown senator to represent us." But Moe won, beating Thomforde (after Larson had surprisingly withdrawn) by 10,869 to 9,066 votes. That same year, Donald, Roger's brother, who lived in St. Paul, also ran for office for the first time and won a seat from District 45B in the Minnesota house. Ten years later, in 1980, Donald also became a state senator after winning the seat vacated with the death of majority leader Nick Coleman. The headline of the *Crookston Daily Times* boasted, "Two Sons in the Senate." The two brothers, both DFL, won in a year when Jimmy Carter lost the presidency to Ronald Reagan and two years after Al Quie, a Republican, had been elected governor of Minnesota.

After his first victory in 1970, Moe said his reelections were never really contested, but "it's a conservative district, and you need to be careful on the social issues." The senate district is as big as the states of Rhode Island, Connecticut, and parts of Massachusetts combined, and it includes two Indian reservations, White Earth to the south and Red Lake to the north. In 2003, the Red Lake Reservation, where Moe used to get 90 percent of the vote, adopted him and gave him a war bonnet and the name Ginew—Golden Eagle. "Some people criticized me for my work with the Indians," Moe says, "but my answer was always that I would stop advocating for them when their unemployment, their suicide rate, child deaths, alcoholism, and their education and ability to read and write all were equal to the state's average. Then, I will stop my advocacy, but until then, I am in public service and this is the right thing to do."

Roger Moe is not a talkative man. In a Minnesota Public Radio profile as Moe was ending his political career, he was described as "reserved, cautious, unflappable—not given to emotion or personal dynamism." Journalist Betty Wilson describes him as "not exactly the wide-eyed dreamer." With time, Moe developed a reputation as a master negotiator, and he earned the respect, even fondness, of his political opponents. Quie said he was "like a brother." And Steve Sviggum, the Republican speaker of the Minnesota house from 1998 to 2006 and one of Moe's political opponents, also expressed respect for Moe, his fellow Norwegian American. "We had our differences," he said, "and we yelled at each other, but we aimed for reasonable agreements. In 2000 or so, [during] budget negotiations, we had about $540 million left. Everything else was agreed on. But we had that money left. And we could not reach an agreement. So, finally, since we were not going to shut down the government, I think it was Roger Moe who suggested why don't we split it three ways, one-third for the senate, one-third for the house, and one-third for the governor: 'A tird, a tird, a tird.' . . . And you could hear that Scandinavian dialect coming through loud and clear when we went home and explained what we had done. Better with a tird, than shut down the government."

As majority leader, one of Moe's major accomplishments was overseeing the merger of the state's college and university system with its technical schools. In his hometown of Crookston, the University of Minnesota branch is called "Moe U." "I did not have only my hand in this," Moe said as we toured the pretty campus. "I had my whole arm."

Roger Moe twice ran for higher political office but lost both times. In 1998, he was the candidate for lieutenant governor and Hubert "Skip" Humphrey III's running mate. They came in third, after the winner, Jesse Ventura, and the Republican candidate, Norm Coleman. In 2002 Moe ran for governor, with Julia Sabo, the daughter of legendary Norwegian American politician Martin Olav Sabo, as the lieutenant governor candidate. They lost to the Republican, Tim Pawlenty. In both elections, as in many others in Minnesota's political history, third-party candidates muddled the political balance, with Ventura, Reform Party, winning in 1998 and Tim Penny, Independence Party, winning 16 percent of the vote in 2002.

A REMARKABLY LARGE NUMBER of Minnesota's Scandinavian politicians were journalists. Several governors were editors of small-town newspapers—country editors—such as John A. Johnson of the *St. Peter Herald*, Theodore Christianson of the *Dawson Sentinel*, and Hjalmar Petersen, owner and editor of the *Askov American*. As governor, Johnson surrounded himself with former journalists, including his private secretary and executive clerk, the secretary of state, and the state fire warden, librarian, and oil inspector. "He was the best example of how far a Minnesota country editor could go in progressive politics."

Many of the journalist-politicians came to America as teenagers, in their twenties, or even later. Many came from prominent families, were well educated, and were journalists before leaving for America. They became sort of a bridge between the old country and the new, for they often had contacts in the old country and were informed about events there. Their roles as journalists in the Scandinavian American community made them well known, and so, many times, the transition to political roles came naturally.

John W. Arctander, born in Stockholm, Sweden, in 1849, was one of these journalist-politicians. He was on his father's side a descendant of one of Norway's oldest families and of the Swedish Nobel family on his mother's side. After graduating from the university in Christiania (Oslo), he became a journalist. As a defender of the rights of the farmers and workers, however, his radicalism collided with the authorities, and he was forced into political exile at the age of twenty-one. After several years as a journalist with Norwegian papers in Chicago and New York, Arctander moved to Minnesota, studied law, and became a lawyer. *Svenska Amerikanska Posten* praised Arctander, a Democrat, as the best lawyer not only in Minneapolis but in all of Minnesota and said that all Democrats and Swedes should be honored when he was elected district judge in Hennepin County. Called the "workers' lawyer" and the "workers' judge," Arctander became a leading figure in the Scandinavian immigrant community.

Herman Stockenström also came from a prominent family, the noble von Stockenström family of Sweden. Born in Dalarna in 1853, he studied in Falun and Stockholm before leaving for America, also at the age of twenty-one, never to return. After a short stint at a Swedish-language paper in Moline, Illinois, he moved to Minnesota in 1878 and found a job, first at *Skaffaren/Minnesota Stats Tidning* in St. Paul and then at *Hemlandet,* two leading Swedish-language newspapers. Like many Scandinavian journalists at the time, Stockenström, a Republican, was deeply interested in politics and served many years as deputy secretary of state to both the Swede Hans Mattson and the Norwegian Fredrick Brown. He was also commissioner of statistics under Mattson. Stockenström died young, not yet fifty, while he was an editor at *Svenska Amerikanska Posten,* and was one of Swedish America's most respected journalists.

Luth Jaeger became a leading spokesman for the rapid Americanization of Norwegian immigrants. He left for America in 1871 when he was
twenty years old and eventually assumed the editorship of the liberal
Norwegian-language newspaper *Budstikken* in Minneapolis. In 1889, he and
his father-in-law, Hans Mattson, launched *The North*, an English-language
paper in Chicago devoted to Scandinavian interests. It folded five years later,
which ended the career of one of the most respected Scandinavian journalists in Minnesota. But Jaeger, a Democrat, remained politically active. At
one point, he ran for secretary of state against Mattson, but lost. With time,
he became less and less involved in the Norwegian immigrant community.
He had come to think that maintaining Norwegian nationalist interests was
a violation of Americanism. In a speech in 1909 at the Norwegian Society
of Minneapolis, he urged the use of English to break the isolation of the
Norwegians in America. The ultimate object of Norwegian immigration,
he said, was the assimilation of the Norwegians with the American people,
and that meant the renunciation of the Norwegian national identity: "We
cease to exist as Norwegians, consequently, also the Norwegian language
must become practically extinct." And one way of doing this, Jaeger said,
was to dispense with Norwegian newspapers in order to "be through and
through, wholly and fully, Americans." Jaeger died in his home in Minneapolis in 1925.

Søren Listoe was born in Copenhagen in 1846. His father was a journalist
in Silkeborg in Jutland before emigrating with his family to America in 1863,
when Søren was seventeen years old. In 1874, at the age of twenty-eight, Listoe became the first Dane elected to the Minnesota legislature. He went on
to have a prominent journalistic and political career, which included serving
as US consul to the Netherlands and Germany. Listoe's years as a journalist
included stints at *Nordisk Folkeblad*, a paper owned and edited by another
Danish immigrant, F. Sneedorff Christensen, who advocated "the greatest
possible participation by Nordics in the political life" of Minnesota. He remained close to Knute Nelson most of his life, especially during Listoe's years
in Europe. Like Nelson, Listoe remained faithful to the Republican Party.

Icelander Gunnar B. Bjornson, who owned and edited the respected
Minneota Mascot newspaper in western Minnesota, was also a leading figure in the Republican Party in the 1910s. He came to America as a boy in
1876 and later married Ingebjorg Augusta Jonsdottir Hurdal, who had immigrated to Manitoba in Canada in 1883. They settled in Minneota and spoke
Icelandic at home. The Bjornson family owned and ran the *Mascot* from

1900 to 1944. The local paper packed a punch in Minnesota politics that far exceeded its size, first under Gunnar B. Bjornson—who was also president of the Minnesota State Editorial Association—and then under his sons. Bjornson had a distinguished political career as a member of the Minnesota House of Representatives and, in 1914 and 1915, as chair of the Republican State Central Committee.

Valdimir, or Val, Bjornson, also a Republican, closely followed in his father's footsteps, in both journalism and politics. Val had his first byline when he was twelve years old as the school correspondent for the *Mascot*. After graduating from the University of Minnesota in 1930, Val went back to Minneota to work at the paper. In 1934 he paid his first visit to Iceland, where he also spent part of World War II as a naval intelligence officer. Val was there when Iceland declared independence from Denmark in 1944, paving the way for Iceland to join NATO after the war. In 1950, Val Bjornson was elected Minnesota state treasurer. Interrupted only by a failed run for the US Senate against Hubert H. Humphrey in 1954, he served as treasurer until 1975, when he resigned after a total of twenty-two years in the position. Bjornson was a "consistent Republican vote-getter," according to the Icelandic National League of North America.

Others in this group of distinguished Scandinavian journalists/ politicians include Henry Rines, whose original name was Hans Hansson. A Swedish immigrant from Orsa in the province of Dalarna, he was only one year old when his family settled in Mora, Minnesota. Hans's father died shortly after arrival and three years later his mother married John Fitzgerald Rines. Hans Hansson became Henry Rines. In 1904, he bought the *Kanabec County Times,* which he owned for over forty years. Rines, a Republican who had served as postmaster and county auditor, was elected to the Minnesota house in 1907. Reelected several times, he became speaker of the house from 1913 to 1915. From 1917 to 1926, he served two terms as Minnesota state treasurer and later also as state comptroller and chairman of the Commission of Administration and Finance.

Jens K. Grondahl was a journalist, editor and publisher of the *Daily Republican* in Red Wing for forty years. He was also a member of the Minnesota House of Representatives for three terms, starting in 1895. He had come from Norway to America with his parents when he was eleven and became a journalist after university studies in Minneapolis. He was also the author of poems and songs. His "America, My Country: The New National Anthem," with music by E. F. Maetzold, was first published in the *Daily Republican* in

1917. It has been called the greatest patriotic song/poem of World War I and was read into the *Congressional Record* the day the United States declared war on Germany. Here is the chorus:

> America, my country, I answer thy call,
> That freedom may live and that tyrants may fall;
> I owe thee my all and my all will I give—I do and die that America
>   may live.

Grondahl was a progressive Republican. In 1894, he was elected to the Minnesota house as its youngest member ever. An advocate of ethics in government and of limiting corporate financial influence, he was the only member of the legislature to refuse to accept free passes from the railroads, which eventually led to anti-pass legislation. He was also instrumental in abolishing the contract system at the Minnesota state prison to relieve free labor from the injurious competition from prison-made goods. He was the leader in the campaign for a better system of treating the chronically mentally disturbed, and he fought to preserve the beautiful landscape around Red Wing. Able to speak both English and Norwegian well, Grondahl often campaigned throughout Minnesota under the auspices of the Republican Party. In 1924, he declined to enter the Republican primary for governor.

Born in Paxton, Illinois, in 1871, Victor E. Lawson was the son of Swedish immigrants and one of fifteen children. He became a crusading newspaper publisher and a Minnesota state senator. As a young man in Kandiyohi County, he became involved in local affairs as deputy postmaster, justice of the peace, and village recorder. He eventually moved to Willmar, where he spent the rest of his life as editor/owner of the *Willmar Tribune* and as a local historian, and where he served three terms as mayor. In 1926, Lawson was elected to the Minnesota Senate and then reelected twice. He also once ran unsuccessfully for governor of Minnesota.

Originally a Republican, he broke with the party to support William Jennings Bryan, the candidate for the Democratic and Populist Party, in the 1896 presidential election and then continued to support progressive causes. He became chairman of the People's Party's state committee and twice ran state election campaigns. The Minnesota *Journal of the Senate* described him as "one of the builders of the liberal movement in Minnesota." Lawson's political power was "achieved without sacrifice of his principles and convictions. . . . Everyone knows where he stands and respects the vigor

of his opinions and convictions, but he probably has few if any personal enemies." Lawson, who died in Willmar in 1960, received the Order of Vasa
from the King of Sweden.

THE NORDIC IMMIGRANTS who established themselves in the politics of
their new home in Minnesota numbered in the thousands. They came from
many different backgrounds, from the well-educated to those with only a
few years of schooling, although nearly all were literate. Education for their
children and grandchildren was of primary importance for the Scandinavian immigrants and so, it turned out, were leading social and moral issues
of the times, such as women's right to vote, temperance, and prohibition.

Starting out locally, they soon broadened their sights, running for and
winning statewide political offices. The office of the secretary of state was
the first statewide political position won by a Scandinavian, and with time,
it became somewhat of a gateway into politics. Scandinavians held on to
this tradition for decades, all the way up until modern times in a remarkable
succession of elections.

The overwhelming majority of the early Scandinavian immigrant poli-
ticians were Republicans. But as new political winds blew over the state,
Scandinavian Americans turned to Populism and Progressivism, and the
Democratic Party made some inroads among them. Later, they turned in
large numbers to the agrarian protest movement under the umbrella of the
Nonpartisan League, and still later in the twentieth century, the hold of the
Republican Party eventually gave way with the emergence of the Farmer-
Labor Party.

From Protests to Repression

The difference is that a few would destroy democracy to win the war, and the rest of us would win the war to establish democracy.

Charles A. Lindbergh Sr., March 1918

For me, there are during this war but two parties, one composed of loyalists, the other of disloyalists.

Governor Joseph A. A. Burnquist, March 1918

SCANDINAVIAN IMMIGRANT POLITICIANS fully entered Minnesota politics at a momentous, even tumultuous time for the state. The decades around the turn of the twentieth century were years of political upheaval and discontent; agrarian protest movements rising up against the power of the corporations and income inequalities; increased radicalism; massive strikes among the miners on the Iron Range; the election of a socialist mayor in Minneapolis; and new political constellations. The deep Scandinavian loyalty to the Republican Party was coming to an end in the most contentious and scandalous gubernatorial election in Minnesota history. Abroad, the Russian Revolution and the rise of communism occurred as America entered the Great War in Europe.

It was also a time of violation of civil liberties and repression—a "reign of terror," many called it. These were dark years in Minnesota's history. The US Department of Justice called it "the most serious interference with civil liberties" in the whole country, and the National Civil Liberties Bureau pointed to the Nonpartisan League as the "principal victim" of political violence during World War I.

The various political forces had been building well before the turn of the century. The farmers were primarily and increasingly unhappy with the price of wheat and the high cost of transporting it on the railroads, and with restrictions on where they could sell and store the grain. The demands for reforms dramatically increased over the next few years, but it was not until the 1880s that Minnesota experienced the first effective protests among farmers and labor when the Farmers' Alliance and the Knights of Labor united to form the Alliance Labor Union Party in 1890. That year, the new party ran its own gubernatorial candidate, Sidney M. Owen. He finished third, supported by 24 percent of the vote, including tens of thousands of Norwegian American farmers who turned their backs on the Republican nominee. The election that year "marked the emergence of third-party protest on a large scale in the traditionally conservative state." Two years later, the People's, or Populist, Party ran its own gubernatorial candidate, Ignatius Donnelly.

The Populists went after the power of the railroad barons and liquor sales (many Scandinavian Lutherans saw the sale of alcohol as a moral/Christian issue) and worked for labor rights and woman suffrage. Later, the Progressive Party sought political reforms, including direct primaries, the ability to recall officeholders, and nonpartisan elections. By 1913, Minnesota adopted a nonpartisan state legislature with the purpose of decreasing the influence of political parties. It lasted until 1973. Although Populism lasted only a few years, it greatly influenced the progressive politics of the time and launched the Progressive Era with the 1898 election of a non-Republican governor, Swedish-born John Lind.

In these years of agrarian protests and discontent, the Scandinavian, primarily Norwegian American, farmers were not leaders of the protests—those were non-Scandinavians like Ignatius Donnelly and Arthur C. Townley—but they played a major role in both the Populist and the Progressive eras. As former close aide of Hubert Humphrey Arthur Naftalin later writes, the Populist Party "drew its strength chiefly from the Republican Party and principally from the Scandinavian nationalities," and since that time, the Scandinavians "have played a prominent role in Minnesota protest politics." Historian Carl H. Chrislock argues that the Scandinavian support of progressivism must be seen in the proper perspective and that "Midwestern progressivism was a regional, not a Norwegian or a Scandinavian phenomenon." At the same time, "the volatility of the Scandinavian vote" was a constant feature of these years. The Scandinavians responded to economic distress by supporting unorthodox remedies, but they also "seldom failed" to support candidates of Scandinavian descent.

By 1910, the Republican Party was in trouble, embroiled in a hard internal fight between the Old Guard and the Progressives. This internal split was vividly apparent when the progressive Republican Sydney Anderson—

lawyer, Spanish-American War veteran, half Swede, half Norwegian—
challenged incumbent veteran congressman James A. Tawney of the party's
Old Guard in the Republican primary for Minnesota's First Congressional
District in 1910. Anderson won in an upset called "the greatest progressive
triumph," according to Roger E. Wyman, and then went on to win in the
general election. He was only thirty years old; he was reelected six times.
For Wyman, the vote was one of Scandinavian solidarity. Nationality was
a prime determinant of voting behavior as the heaviest voting occurred in
counties with large Scandinavian populations. "When a Norsk, Swede or
Dane calls on the Scandinavians, it is politics and principle to the devil, as
shown by the vote," was one comment. But it was more than that. Sydney
Anderson represented a new style of politician that emerged in the Progressive Era, whose appeal was nonpartisan and based more on principles and
ideology, such as popular rule versus special interests, or democracy versus
bossism. Anderson appealed to the voters in the name of greater democracy.

The political decisions by voters swung back and forth, sometimes favoring ethnicity, sometimes the party. Thus, in 1908, the progressive Republican
Charles A. Lindbergh Sr., himself seeking reelection, came out in support of
his fellow progressive Republican candidate for governor, Norwegian-born
Jacob F. Jacobson, against his fellow Swede, the incumbent Democrat John A.
Johnson. Jacobson himself had urged, in a speech in 1906, faithfulness to the
party over ethnicity, according to the Swedish-language paper *Duluth Posten:*

> I myself was born in the old country, Norway. I'm not ashamed of
> my country. I came as a young boy to this country and received the
> benefits, rights and privileges that the most excellent government
> on earth can provide. I wish the old mother country well as all of
> you do who come from foreign countries, but when the question
> comes down to choosing between our motherland, which cannot
> support us, and the land in which we live and whose freedom,
> benefits and rights we enjoy, we ought to consider the meaning
> of the oath we swore as we received our citizenship. If you are a
> Republican and vote for a Democrat because he is Norwegian or
> Swedish, you are unworthy of your citizenship and break that oath,
> and if you are a Democrat and vote for a Republican because he is
> Norwegian or Swedish, you break also your oath.

The political solidarity among the Scandinavian Americans was challenged by the progressive movement, and in the 1912 presidential election,

the Republicans and Democrats were challenged by a third party, Teddy Roosevelt's Progressive, or Bull Moose, Party. Roosevelt lost nationally, but he won in Minnesota, mostly thanks to substantial support among the state's Scandinavian voters, many of whom also supported the Socialist Party candidate, Eugene V. Debs, in another protest vote. Debs came in fourth. Many of those who supported Roosevelt never returned to the Republican Party, according to Janet Nyberg, and instead transferred their loyalty to the Farmer-Labor Party.

Three years after the 1912 election the agrarian protests took a new, and more serious, turn when the Nonpartisan League was founded in North Dakota. Its aim was twofold: to restore the government to the people of the state, and to use its power for the benefit of its citizens while preventing exploitation and injury to the people.

A radical offshoot of the progressive movement, this "political prairie fire" soon blew over Minnesota. A "great fear" settled over the Minnesota State Legislature as the "cloud on the western horizon" was carefully watched. Again, Scandinavian farmers, mainly the Norwegians in North Dakota and in the Red River Valley along the border between Minnesota and North Dakota, played a major role. Recruiters worked hard among the farmers. Alfred Knutson, a Norwegian immigrant in North Dakota, spent a whole winter traveling on skis from farm to farm recruiting new members. In only a year, the new League became the "dominant force in North Dakota politics." It advocated a radical program that called for state ownership of a series of agricultural institutions: grain elevators, flour mills, insurance companies, banks. In North Dakota, the League purchased the Scandinavian American Bank and made it a League bank. By 1916, the Nonpartisan League candidate was elected governor of North Dakota with the greatest majority in history, and League members were in the majority in both houses of the North Dakota State Legislature. Meanwhile, the League was also spreading throughout the Midwest and into Canada, and in 1917, the League's headquarters moved from Fargo, North Dakota, to St. Paul, Minnesota, where fifty thousand people had signed up for membership. The Nonpartisan League was the leader of progressivism in Minnesota.

At its peak in early 1919, the Nonpartisan League had 250,000 paying members in thirteen states and two Canadian provinces, and it became "the starkest challenge to party politics in twentieth century America." As a voting bloc, it "had no peer." Its basis was an "anti-monopolist popular politics" that created new strategies for electoral success that "exemplified the push for democratic innovation during the Progressive Era." The League founded "path-breaking state-owned enterprises," urged women to get politically involved, and brought together farmers and laborers. Finally, it also proposed an alternate future for American capitalism. Many of its leaders and staff members were socialists, or former socialists, although the Socialist Party viewed the League as bourgeois and not radical enough, and there never were any organizational or ideological ties between the two groups.

The Nonpartisan League never intended to operate as a political party, preferring to participate within the Republican and Democratic parties by endorsing candidates with views and policies favorable to the League. They organized in each precinct and elected delegates to the district conventions that, in turn, chose candidates for the primary elections. Eschewing a third-party strategy, the League infiltrated the existing party structures through the primary elections and became a direct threat to the incumbent politicians, mainly the Republicans.

World War I broke out in Europe on July 28, 1914, and it came to America on April 6, 1917, when the United States declared war on Germany. The war split the people of Minnesota into basically three groups: interventionists, noninterventionists or neutralists, and the middle way of President Woodrow Wilson. The neutralists were strong. The German Americans and the Swedish Americans largely belonged to this group, as did the labor movement and rural Minnesota as a whole. The state's large German-language press argued hard for nonintervention. The progressive movement's strongly avowed neutrality continued to be an important part of progressivism until the United States entered the war.

In the US Congress, four of Minnesota's ten representatives in the House voted against the declaration of war—among them the Scandinavian Americans Harold Knutson, Ernest Lundeen, and Carl Van Dyke—while in the Senate, Knute Nelson supported the war declaration. Of the fifty members of the House of Representatives who voted against American participation in the war, thirty-five were from the Midwest. Further out on the left, Norwegian-born Frithjof Werenskjöld, an agitator for temperance and socialism, wrote in *Svenska Socialisten* shortly after war broke out:

> Cursed in history's letters of fire
> those, who have lit a fire in the states of Europe,
> Cursed those, who seek the halo of war,
> forever damn wily diplomats.

Just days after the United States entered the war, the administration of Governor Joseph A. A. Burnquist effectively declared war on what it called agitators and radicals and displayed a readiness to arrest all those who, in its view, preached treason. Burnquist sought to enforce "one hundred percent loyalty." On April 16, the state legislature approved the Minnesota Commission of Public Safety (MCPS)—the "Watchdog of Loyalty," as historian Carl H. Chrislock called it—granting very broad powers and a million dollars in funds.

Democracy in Minnesota was severely tested under this "virtual dictatorship" by the Commission that ruled in the name of loyalty to America, of super patriotism. "Its word was law in Minnesota, and its standards of 'loyalty' the norm." For Burnquist, the Commission had no other purpose than to be of patriotic service, but the years under the Commission constitute a dark interlude in Minnesota's long, progressive traditions. Under Burnquist's authority, a special Home Guard was established with more than three hundred officers and 7,300 men in twenty-three battalions, ostensibly

The Minnesota Commission of Public Safety, circa 1918: (left to right) *A. C. Weiss, Thomas E. Cashman, H. W. Libby, Governor Joseph A. A. Burnquist, Clifford L. Hilton, Ambrose Tighe, Charles Hoyt March, J. F. McGee*

to protect private property and public safety, but in reality used to enforce the orders of the Commission. Later, a Motor Corps was added, organized in a military fashion with 120 officers and more than 2,450 enlisted men in ten battalions.

In a state where fully 70 percent of the population was either first- or second-generation immigrants, mostly of German, Norwegian, and Swedish descent, "loyalty" became a "political weapon," and the "feeling of being a 'foreigner' became as dreaded as leprosy." Noncitizens were not allowed to teach school. Over two hundred thousand aliens were registered throughout Minnesota, and in his 1919 inaugural address, Burnquist asserted that illegal voting and holding of land were detected among immigrant communities.

Even members of the Commission acknowledged that parts of the bill that paved the way for its founding were unconstitutional. In a letter to former governor John Lind, Ambrose Tighe, the chief counsel of the Commission, writes that the Commission's "basic flaw" was "its departure from the principle of constitutional government." He adds, "The ruthlessness of the Commission's procedures shows if further evidence is required, how dangerous it is to vest even good men with arbitrary power."

The Commission had seven members, five of whom were appointed by Burnquist, while he, as chairman, and the state attorney general served ex officio. The dominant member came to be John F. McGee, a Minneapolis lawyer. His extremist rhetoric has been compared to that of Senator Joseph R. McCarthy in the 1950s, and McGee's high visibility created the perception that he, not the governor, was in charge.

McGee saw the Commission as an opportunity to suppress pro-Germans, trade unionists, the Nonpartisan League, socialists, pacifists, and everyone else who might doubt the wisdom of America going to war, writes Chrislock. Shortly after the Commission was established, McGee testified before a US Senate committee, where he called members of the Nonpartisan League "traitors" and said, "Where we made a mistake was in not establishing a firing squad in the first days of the war. We should now get busy and have that firing squad working overtime. Wait until the long casualty lists begin to come in and the Minnesota woods will not be dense enough to hide the traitors who will meet punishment for their crimes. These men who are fighting our soldiers and stabbing them in the back are going to die." And then McGee zeroed in on the "hyphenated" Americans, stating that "the disloyal element in Minnesota is largely among the German-Swedish people. The nation blundered at the start of the war in not dealing severely with these vipers."

Former governor John Lind had been an original member of the Commission, but he resigned following a confrontation with McGee, after McGee wanted to oust Thomas Van Lear, the socialist mayor of Minneapolis elected in 1916, because of his opposition to the war. Lind, convinced of Van Lear's loyalty and good faith, opposed McGee's plan. After a rancorous discussion, Lind walked out and told Burnquist that he could no longer serve with McGee. (Van Lear was able to finish out his term before being defeated in his reelection bid in 1918.)

In these times of loyalty versus disloyalty, McGee led his attacks seemingly without any interference from Governor Burnquist, although Chrislock writes that these attacks were helpful neither to Burnquist's reelection campaign nor to the Commission. Many protests followed, not the least from the German and Swedish Americans. While Burnquist said he disagreed with McGee on the disloyalty of those immigrant groups, he previously had said that there was no more patriotic citizen than McGee, and he showed no inclination to dismiss McGee from the Commission.

"The intolerance, openly and tacitly approved by the Commission, took forms of hatred toward Catholics, Jews, and Blacks," writes journalist Michael Fedo. On June 15, 1920, during Burnquist's last year as governor, a mob stormed the local Duluth jail and dragged out to the street three young African Americans from a touring circus who had been arrested on suspicion of having raped a young white woman. The mob beat them and lynched them by hanging them from a lamppost, one by one. No murder conviction was ever obtained. The tragedy took place at a time when the Ku Klux Klan (KKK) was flourishing in the Midwest, not the least in Minnesota, according to Elizabeth Dorsey Hale's book about the Klan.

ONLY ONE MEMBER OF THE Minnesota State Legislature initially voted against creating the Minnesota Commission of Public Safety (MCPS), a barber from the town of Two Harbors, up the coast from Duluth on Lake Superior's North Shore. His name was Ernest (in Sweden: Ernst) Gottfrid Strand, a Swedish socialist immigrant.

As the Minnesota house voted 116 to 1 in favor of the Commission, Strand's lone "no" vote was greeted with cries of, "Throw him out." The legislature's other socialist member, Norwegian immigrant Andrew O. (Andreas Olaf) Devold of Minneapolis, had abstained, an action for which he was heavily criticized by his fellow Minneapolis socialists. Two days later, Devold joined Strand in voting "no" to the final senate/house conference bill.

The two socialists were alone. No other legislator, Scandinavian American or otherwise, joined them in their opposition to the Commission.

Ernest G. Strand, who was born in 1883 in Långasjö parish in the province of Småland in Sweden, came to America in 1901. He was one of some twelve hundred people from Långasjö who emigrated to America between 1850 and 1930. In 1907 alone, 20 percent of the population in the parish left for America, and more than one-third of those immigrants came to Minnesota. In the Strand family, five of the eight siblings emigrated to America. Ernst followed his brother August, who had left Sweden in 1899 and settled in Two Harbors, where he became a blacksmith. Eventually, August was elected alderman from the Socialist Party.

The brothers came to belong to an active group of Swedish and Norwegian socialists in Two Harbors, a town of about five thousand inhabitants, of whom many were Scandinavians. Around 1910, one-third of all of Minnesota's iron ore was transported to Two Harbors by the Duluth and Iron Range Railroad (D&IR) and then shipped onward to Pittsburgh and other cities where the ore was converted to steel. Ernest Strand worked for three years for the railroad before moving to Minneapolis, where he became a barber. In 1907, he returned to Two Harbors, bought a barbershop, and joined the Socialist Party. His barbershop, a strict union shop, became an informal gathering place for the town's Scandinavian socialists. The Socialist Party earned a landslide victory in the local elections of 1911, capturing the majority of the aldermen positions on the city council, including Strand's, and the mayor's office. Strand was reelected in 1913, and a year later he was elected chair of the town council. In 1916 he was elected mayor. The *Two Harbors Socialist* expressed its confidence in the new mayor, writing that Strand "is known as one of the most progressive men in the community and well qualified." Later that year, Strand was elected to the state legislature, endorsed by the Nonpartisan League, and he resigned as mayor. He served three terms in the Minnesota house, from 1917 to 1923.

Strand's election to the Minnesota House of Representatives in 1916 was front-page news in the Chicago-based *Svenska Socialisten*, which proudly declared that "our comrade" had won, although the margin of victory was slim, only fifty-seven votes in Lake County and twenty-three votes in Cook County. In describing Strand, the paper says that he had not made much of a name for himself after he was first elected alderman in Two Harbors, and that he himself said that he was "too shy for politics," but he was always present and he cast his vote as an "intelligent and class conscious socialist."

Svenska Socialisten also describes him as a simple and modest man who is well liked by the fellow inhabitants, an "eager, energetic and self-sacrificing" party member. He had no bad habits, except his love for coffee, the paper writes. Strand's opponents, on the other hand, attacked him as unsuited for the task as alderman.

Strand was the second socialist elected to the state legislature from Two Harbors. The first was Nels S. Hillman, also a Swedish immigrant. A locomotive engineer, he served in the state legislature between 1911 and 1915. As the only socialist in the legislature, Hillman was called "one of the most intelligent and uncompromising of the progressives" by Lynn Haines, a muckraking journalist whose critical annual reports of the legislature were widely read. Hillman fought for all the progressive measures in the 1911 session, such as the county option regarding the sale of alcohol and all election questions.

The socialists in Two Harbors, who ran under the banner Public Ownership Party until 1912, had elected their first socialist mayor in 1907. They dominated the town's politics between 1911 and 1919. Wide-ranging reforms were instituted, and a number of construction projects, all owned by the city, were realized: a dock for coal shipment, a stone crusher, an icehouse, and an electric power station. Cooperatives were common. The Scandinavian socialists "were clearly reformist and moderately radical, working for practical reforms rather than the overthrow of capitalism."

In the 1912 presidential election, Socialist Party candidate Eugene V. Debs carried Lake County, where Two Harbors is located, with 38 percent of the vote. Leading Swedish socialist agitators visited Two Harbors in those years, among them August Palm and Ture Nerman. The leading IWW agitator Elizabeth Gurley Flynn twice spoke in Two Harbors, and the Socialist local and the IWW coexisted peacefully. Opposition to World War I also was widespread in Two Harbors. Some Swedish, Norwegian, and Finnish residents, wanting to avoid the draft, chose to return to their home countries. About thirty Finnish draft resisters received jail terms of one to six months, and in late 1918, seven Finnish draft resisters were deported back to Finland. Partly as a result of this antiwar stance at a time when questions of loyalty and Americanism were at the forefront, the influence of Scandinavian socialists receded. Beyond their antiwar positions, local issues dominated the political debate, and the socialists lost the "church and temperance vote." Opposition from the powerful Duluth and Iron Range Railroad, the largest employer in town, also played a role. After losing control of the Two Harbors City Council for a couple of years, the socialists made a strong comeback in 1919, when August Omtvedt, a railroad worker from Telemarken, Norway, was elected mayor, together with five socialist aldermen and a municipal judge.

During the 1910s, there were three socialist locals in Two Harbors—Scandinavian (Swedish/Norwegian), Finnish, and Anglo American. They worked well together. In 1913, the first issue of the newspaper *Two Harbors Socialist* was published with Juls J. Anderson, born in Trondheim in Norway, as editor. Anderson had come to America when he was four years old and had attended school in Wisconsin as well as in St. Paul, Minnesota, before coming to Two Harbors. He had been director of the monthly the *Minnesota Socialist* and was a member of the International Typographical Union. By the time he left the Two Harbors paper three years later it had doubled in size, to eight pages, with lots of ads. During those years, membership in the town's Scandinavian Socialist Federation Club #16 had increased steadily, from forty-two members in 1913, to ninety-eight in 1914, and 106 in 1918.

Two Harbors' Scandinavian local was still active in 1921, but by then, the "socialist bids for control of the public sphere seemed to have died down," according to Swedish scholar Jimmy Engren, and the election that year illustrated a shift from socialism and the role of radical Scandinavian immigrants in politics to trade-union politics. It was also a sign of more harmonious relations between the railroad company and workers, as there was no "company ticket" in that year's election as there had been in previous years, with candidates that the D&IR supported. A transformation to farmer-labor politics took place as the children of the Scandinavian immigrants entered the labor market and developed new perspectives after World War I. The vote tallies in the election for Minnesota governor in Lake County clearly show this transformation. While in 1918 the socialists received 277 votes and the Farmer-Labor Party 248, just four years later, in 1922, the socialists received no (zero) votes while 1,512 voted Farmer-Labor. In July 1918, the *Two Harbors Socialist* was published for the last time and was succeeded by the *Lake County Chronicle*. Clarence Hillman, a socialist and former railroad engineer, was its editor until the 1940s, during which time the paper was a leading supporter of the Nonpartisan League and Farmer-Labor candidates.

In 1914, Andrew O. Devold became the second elected socialist member (after Nels S. Hillman) in the Minnesota House of Representatives, and in 1918 he was elected to the Minnesota Senate. By the time of his death in 1939, he had served five terms in the state senate and played a prominent role in the formation of the Farmer-Labor Party, although he still identified himself as a socialist. Odd S. Lovoll calls Devold "one of Minnesota's most effective social activists, who argued the cause eloquently in Norwegian as well as in English throughout the state."

Devold, born in 1881 in Stockholm of Norwegian parents, was the step-son of Emil Lauritz Ludvigsen Mengshoel, editor of *Gaa Paa* (Forward), Minnesota's radical Norwegian-language paper. Settling in Minnesota with his mother in 1893, when he was twelve years old, Devold became an important ally of his stepfather and helped edit the newspaper. Emil Mengshoel had made Minneapolis his home soon after arriving in America. Born out of wedlock in 1866 in the town of Gjøvik, Mengshoel was raised by his grandparents, but at the age of eighteen he broke with them, and at twenty-two he went to sea, eventually jumping ship in Florida in 1891 to begin a new life in America, according to Norwegian scholar Odd-Stein Granhus. In 1896, Mengshoel arrived in Minnesota, where he went to work for various Scandinavian and English-language newspapers, including *Nye Normanden* (the New Norseman), a radical weekly in Moorhead. Eventually, he joined *Gaa Paa*, which he ran between 1903 and 1925. At its high point, the paper had about forty-five hundred subscribers, many outside of Minnesota.

Before he left Norway, Mengshoel had encountered socialism at the school he attended in Christiania (Oslo) for noncommissioned officers. The school was a hotbed of discussion about socialism and the struggle for a parliamentary democracy in Norway at a time when the country was still part of Sweden. In Minnesota he befriended another radical Norwegian, Olav Kringen, who wrote for *Nye Normanden* but returned to Norway in 1897 and became an important name in the emerging Norwegian labor movement. Mengshoel had by then married Helle Margrethe Crøger, whom he met in Minneapolis. Crøger was from a distinguished clergy family in Bergen, Norway, and was herself a political radical. In 1889 she had been one of the socialist leaders in a famous strike among women workers at a match factory in Christiania. The strike led to the first Norwegian labor union for women. Crøger left for America in 1893.

In 1901 the Socialist Party of America was founded and Mengshoel declared himself a socialist, and by the time he took over the ownership of *Gaa Paa*, there was no doubt that the paper stood for socialism, with its masthead proclaiming it the "Organ for Scandinavian Workers in America." The paper was a husband and wife effort, as editor and business manager, respectively.

Emil Mengshoel was a radical, at least for the times, but he was no revolutionary. As a parliamentary social democrat, he believed in the ballot and in elections. He was against anarchist bombs and industrial sabotage, and he deplored the fact that communists and syndicalists would not co-operate with the Socialist Party in elections. Mengshoel and Crøger were in constant touch with the leaders of the Norwegian Labour Party, many of whom Crøger knew before she left for America. The political bond with the old country was important and strong. Among these leaders were Olav Kringen, who continued to write for *Gaa Paa* after his return to Norway; Christian Holtermann Knudsen, editor of *Vort Arbeide* (Our Work); and Carl Jeppesen, one of the founders of the Norwegian Labour Party in 1887 and the first editor of its official organ, *Social-Demokraten*.

Mengshoel wrote of "our sister party," the Norwegian Social Democratic Party. His convictions owed much to the social democratic ideologies in Norway and in Scandinavia, which "included a pragmatic reform social-ism, confidence in the power of education, and a broad appeal to all anti-capitalist groups," the urban workers, farmers, and fishermen. And as long as he was editor of *Gaa Paa*, Mengshoel continued to support the Socialist Party and its belief in "cooperation with the promising coalition of Minne-sota farmers and labor unions in the Farmer-Labor Party."

Like many radicals and socialists in Minnesota at the time, Mengshoel opposed US entry into World War I. His *Gaa Paa* stood out as a "conspicu-ous exception" to the pro-war consensus of not only the American press at the time but also of most Norwegian and other Scandinavian American newspapers. His opposition to the war led to the end of *Gaa Paa* in Sep-tember 1918, when the paper lost its second-class mailing privileges for, it was said, having published material that violated US laws, among them the Espionage Act of 1917. In December 1918, the paper started appearing under a new name, *Folkets Røst* (the Voice of the People). Its slogan, "A newspaper for Norwegians in America," indicated a broader goal than just the "Scandi-navian workers" in America. Granhus concludes: "When the socialist alter-native failed, he [Mengshoel] readjusted his course somewhat and became a force behind the reform politics of the Farmer-Labor movement. During the war and the Red Scare, Mengshoel boldly confronted the powerful anti-radical and nationalistic movement and became one of the very few consis-tent Norwegian-American voices against the war."

After *Folkets Røst* closed in 1925, Mengshoel continued to write hundreds of articles for various Norwegian American newspapers, particularly during World War II, opposing fascism and the German occupation of Norway. He died in Minneapolis in May 1945, shortly after peace had come to Norway and Europe.

IN 1918, THE LAST YEAR of World War I, the political forces in Minnesota collided as the Republican establishment, led by Governor Burnquist and his Minnesota Commission of Public Safety, zeroed in on the Nonpartisan League as its main enemy. The establishment not only opposed the League's program of state socialism but accused it of being unpatriotic for condemning the war and US participation in it. Historian Carl Chrislock sees two main objectives of the "loyalty crusade"—to defeat the Nonpartisan League and trade unionism. The leading anti-labor group in Minnesota at the time was the Citizens Alliance of Minneapolis, a powerful business group formed in 1903 to keep Minneapolis a "non-union shop," meaning workplaces where union members were denied jobs. The conservative, staunchly Republican Citizens Alliance was a strong supporter of Burnquist and the Commission. In 1917, the Home Guard of the Commission of Public Safety was used to break the Twin City Rapid Transit Company workers strike. The power of the Citizens Alliance kept Minneapolis a non-union city for decades, and its control was not broken until the mid-1930s.

The Republican primary in the gubernatorial election that year pitted two Swedish Americans, Governor Joseph A. A. Burnquist and Charles A. Lindbergh Sr., against each other. They represented two opposite poles of opinion among Scandinavian Americans—one a leader of the Republican establishment who stressed loyalty and hundred-percent Americanism, employing, in the eyes of some, dictatorial powers to achieve it; the other a leader of the progressive Republicans, an insurgent, arguing for neutrality in the Great War and for fairness and equity for farmers and workers. The result was a bitter and vicious campaign, an epic battle for the soul of Minnesota's voters, not least that of the Scandinavian immigrant community.

Joseph Alfred Arner (J. A. A.) Burnquist was the son of two Swedish immigrants, Johan A. Björnkvist and Anna Louisa Johnson. He was born in 1879 in Dayton, Iowa, where his father became a successful merchant. The future governor received a fine education, first at Carleton College and then at the University of Minnesota Law School via Columbia University in New York. He was seen as a rising young lawyer and a gifted speaker, having won the first prize at the Minnesota State Oratorical Contest in 1901. In 1908, he was elected to the Minnesota house and reelected in 1910. Only thirty years old, Burnquist was regarded as a leading progressive voice among Minnesota's Republicans, as journalist Lynn Haines points out in his report about the 1911 legislative session, dedicated to "the progressives of Minnesota": "Strong insurgent leader. Progressive candidate for Speaker. An uncompromising progressive and he never failed to vote to give larger opportunities to the people. Took a prominent part in the fight for every fundamental fight for reform. Mr. Burnquist displayed unusual ability and courage in his legislative work and made some of the best speeches of the session."

In 1912, Burnquist was easily elected lieutenant governor, having received an endorsement from the National Progressive Republican League, the party of Robert La Follette. Elected governor that year was Swedish-born Adolph Olson Eberhart. In 1914, Burnquist was reelected as lieutenant governor, now with Winfield Hammond as governor, and when Hammond died in office in December 1915, Burnquist became governor and was subsequently reelected twice, serving from 1915 to 1921. "Once again a Swedish governor in Minnesota" was the proud headline in the Stockholm daily newspaper, *Svenska Dagbladet*.

As governor, Burnquist signed important progressive legislation, such as woman suffrage and child labor, and prior to that, as lieutenant governor, he had been a key figure in furthering the cause of temperance by supporting the county option. After declining to run again for governor in 1920, Burnquist went back to his law practice, only to reemerge on the political scene in 1939 when he was elected Minnesota's attorney general, a position to which he was reelected numerous times until his retirement in 1955. It was, in all, a long and splendid political career, although ultimately the Commission of Public Safety came to haunt him, and it's questionable whether his political reputation ever recovered from his years as a "war governor."

Three factors changed the focus of the Burnquist governorship from its progressive roots: the growing dissatisfaction of labor, the rise of the Nonpartisan League, and the United States' involvement in World War I. Burnquist went so far in his patriotic fever and insistence on loyalty to the nation that he advocated a ban on teaching foreign languages, particularly German but also Swedish, in Minnesota's schools. After a large antiwar rally in July 1917 in New Ulm, the unofficial center of the state's German population, the governor suspended the mayor and the city attorney for "malfeasance in office" after they spoke out against the war. A third official, the county auditor, was initially also removed but later reinstated for lack of evidence. In September, Burnquist prohibited the pacifist People's Council from holding its meeting in St. Paul because, he claimed, it would aid and abet the enemies of America. "This is a fight to the finish," Burnquist said at one point to the Scandinavian Odin Club in Minneapolis, "and I will use every power at my disposal to smash the Hun propaganda within our gates." Peace, he said on another occasion, "can never come until the great military monster which the German war lords have reared, has been defeated."

Burnquist's challenger in the 1918 Republican primary, Charles August Lindbergh Sr., also played an important role in Minnesota and American reform politics, spanning the progressive wing of the Republican Party, the Nonpartisan League, and the Farmer-Labor Party. To his biographer Bruce L. Larson, Lindbergh "is best remembered for his attack on the Money Trust, his support of the insurgent revolt in Congress, his opposition to American entry into World War I, and his deep commitment to the needs of the Midwestern farmer."

Charles August (Karl August) Lindbergh Sr., often called C. A., was named after Swedish King Charles (Karl) XV, a friend of his father. He came to Minnesota with his parents in 1859, not even one year old. His father, Ola Månsson, had been a member of the Swedish parliament (Riksdag) for over ten years, representing a district in the southern province of Skåne. He left for America not for reasons of economic hardship or famine, but because of political activities and business difficulties. He was a liberal, and he worked for political reforms, such as the abolition of the whipping post and to secure better laws for the common man. Often called radical and revolutionist, Månsson had many political enemies, who eventually brought charges of embezzlement against him. He was likely framed and guilty only in a technical sense, and when he left Sweden he was given a gold medal by his colleagues in parliament.

Leaving for America, Ola Månsson took the name August Lindbergh and the family settled on a homestead near the town of Melrose in central Minnesota. Pioneer life was harsh in their little home with the earth as a floor. There was not much money. At one point, August Lindbergh was forced to trade in the gold medal for a plow, and his wife Louisa's gold watch bought a cow. An accident while building a frame house caused August to lose an arm.

August and Louisa Lindbergh assimilated quickly and stressed the importance of using English as much as possible. In 1870, August became an American citizen. "It is a remarkable fact that the Lindberghs became completely American in a single generation," and that no one in the family married a Scandinavian, as was so common among the first immigrants. Their home became something of a community center, and August became active in the affairs of the community, serving as town clerk, village recorder, justice of the peace, and postmaster. In 1861, two years after their arrival, August organized the first school district around Melrose and later donated a granary on his farm to be used as a schoolhouse. It was the first school attended by his son Charles. August Lindbergh died in Little Falls in 1893, eighty-five years old, while Louisa Lindbergh lived until 1921. They had four children, two sons and two daughters. Charles's brother, Frank Albert, became a lawyer and settled in the town of Crosby on the Cuyuna Range in northern Minnesota, where he was elected the first mayor of the town and also served as postmaster.

C. A. Lindbergh also became a lawyer after graduating from the University of Michigan law school in 1883. He set up his practice in the town of Little Falls, north of Melrose, which became his home and his business and political base for his entire life. In 1906, to the surprise of nearly everyone near him, he decided to run for the US Congress. He had little political experience except for one term as county attorney. His daughter Eva once said, "Father had no idea of politics at the time." Lindbergh challenged an incumbent Republican, Clarence B. Buchman, who had served since 1903 and who had the support of Senator Knute Nelson. The Sixth District encompassed the central parts of the state, where over 21 percent of the population was foreign-born—mostly Germans and Swedes—and included the towns of St. Cloud, Brainerd, Alexandria, Sauk Centre, Little Falls, and Melrose. Lindbergh won the primary by 1,200 votes. A columnist in the *Minneapolis Journal* commented afterward that if Lindbergh had lost, it would have been very difficult to hold the Swedes in line.

Lindbergh had the support of the leading Swedish-language paper in St. Paul, *Minnesota Stats Tidning*, which urged its readers to support him not only because he was born in Sweden but because he had views similar to the progressive Teddy Roosevelt—Lindbergh, like Burnquist, supported Roosevelt for president in 1912. Swedish scholar Sten Carlsson does not view Lindbergh as a "typical ethnic politician," although he did receive strong support from the Swedes in his district and that support increased with the years, particularly because the Swedish American press endorsed him. His strongest backing, however, came in counties with a large German American population. The reason was, of course, his neutrality stand during World War I. According to Larson, "The origins of Lindbergh's reform thought lie in the liberal tradition of his father's Swedish career . . . [which] clearly indicates his deep concern for democratic change in the interests of humanity." Larson adds that although C. A. Lindbergh knew Swedish and would at times use it conversationally, he did not use it in his election campaigns and he did not speak it at home.

The easy victory in the general election in November 1906 was the start of a more than ten-year congressional career during which Lindbergh was easily reelected every two years. He earned a reputation as an independent man with strong convictions who was not prone to compromise. In the small so-called insurgent wing of the Republican members in the House of Representatives, he was consistent and the most radical. Russel B. Nye calls him a direct descendant of the Populists, "a lone wolf in politics, the most leftish of the group and a bitter hater of trusts and privilege." Lindbergh himself writes in a letter in 1917 to his daughter Eva, "I am a radical because I oppose the few and stand for the masses." He was willing to shed the party label because no party had a monopoly on progressivism.

After ten years in the US Congress, Lindbergh declined to run for re-election in 1916. He was looking for something else, as he thought he had accomplished his goals as a congressman. During his five terms, he had fought for labor and farm reforms, against big business and political bosses, for finance reform, for woman suffrage, for conservation and public ownership of water power, against violations of Indian rights, and for prohibition. He had published a magazine called *The Law of Rights, Realized and Unrealized* and books about banking and currency, in which he dealt with the increasing power of the money trusts. Shortly after he retired from Congress, his *Why Is Your Country at War* came out. Its purpose, he said, was to emphasize independence, by which, according to Larson, he meant a willingness to discuss the real causes of World War I—the promotion of the war by an inner circle of businesses for commercial purposes—and that the purpose of the war was "for profit." He attacked privileged Wall Street economic interests and the corrupt and unfair political system. His antiwar stand was closely connected to his wish for progressive economic reforms. Although the book sold very few copies, its content turned out to be "explosive," writes Barbara Stuhler, adding that it "could well have become the Bible for the disillusioned revisionists of the interwar period" and that its ideas "were almost identical to those which would nurture the Farmer-Labor Party." In a raid, federal agents ordered all copies and printing plates destroyed. The book was republished many years later, after Lindbergh's death.

Lindbergh was a constant and major opponent of the war. His reasons were economic. For him, the war was not about making the world safe for democracy, as President Woodrow Wilson had said, but rather was an undesired diversion from the problems that needed to be solved in America. He had resigned from Congress before the US declaration of war, which his successor, Norwegian-born Harold Knutson, together with forty-nine other House members, voted against. Had Lindbergh stayed in Congress, there is no doubt that he would have voted against the war declaration, writes Larson. Still, once the United States had entered the war, he supported the war effort, as he wrote to his daughter, "If we get in war, we will have to support it right or wrong."

The opportunity to seek other political challenges arose in 1918. Governor Burnquist was running for reelection, and the Nonpartisan League—the political prairie fire from North Dakota—was sweeping in over Minnesota, rapidly gaining support and new members. Although Lindbergh was not a member of the Nonpartisan League, he was sympathetic to it and had become actively involved in it. On March 19, 1918, the League endorsed Lindbergh as its candidate for governor in the Republican primary to be held a few months later. The die was cast: Burnquist vs. Lindbergh. The Republican Party faced an internal fight for the nomination of its gubernatorial candidate, a fight that became legendary in its acrimony and bitterness.

Lindbergh ran on the League's program to win the war for democracy, for state-owned pulp and paper mills, state insurance, free employment bureaus, old-age pensions, and an eight-hour workday. The push for domestic and economic reforms was combined with continued, deep skepticism about the war while still backing the American war effort. Lindbergh saw the League as the true representative of both farmers and workers, supporting legislation and progressive economic programs comparable to those in Australia and the Scandinavian countries. He also pointed to the importance of loyalty to one's country, and he dismissed Governor Burnquist's contention that the election was a fight between loyalists and disloyalists. Lindbergh said the difference between the two is "that a few would destroy democracy to win the war, and the rest of us would win the war to establish democracy."

The Republican establishment, the Minnesota Commission of Public Safety, and the state's business community led by the Citizens Alliance went "all-out" to defeat Lindbergh based on the themes of loyalty and the threat of the Nonpartisan League's socialist program. US Senator Knute Nelson stated that Lindbergh was "as disloyal as can be," and he strongly supported Burnquist, calling him a "Rock of Gibraltar in maintaining law and order."

While visiting the town of Two Harbors in northern Minnesota, Governor Burnquist spoke of the "German hordes," saying, "We have a state here in which we believe in law and order. . . . If any citizen is not loyal to this country, he should be deprived of the rights of citizenship and sent back to the country from which he came." Burnquist connected the Nonpartisan League with radical Wobblies, "red socialists," and "pacifists."

The state split, and even the Swedish voters in the state were divided,

Charles A. Lindbergh, Farmer-Labor candidate for governor of Minnesota, on the cover of the Nonpartisan Leader, *May 6, 1918*

although both of the leading Swedish-language papers, *Svenska Amerikanska Posten* and *Minnesota Stats Tidning*, supported Governor Burnquist. Their support showed the growing importance of the Swedish urban voters, who did not find Lindbergh's agrarian radicalism, or socialism, particularly attractive. On the other hand, farmers saw Lindbergh as a real Minnesota product, a man who knew from experience about the hardships of the pioneer farmer. Some said that you could judge him by his enemies: big business hates him, the "kept press" attacks him, but no man dares to say he has been false to the people—the farmers and workers of this state.

The crowds that came to listen to Lindbergh during the campaign were huge right from the start, and he was often greeted as a hero. But "violence followed Lindbergh everywhere." Once, when Lindbergh found his driver badly beaten after a meeting, he convinced the mob to let them leave, but it only happened in "a shower of bullets." Shots hit the campaign car, but Lindbergh sat up straight and instructed the driver: "Don't drive so fast, Gunny, they will think we are scared."

Nonpartisan League meetings were prohibited outright by many local authorities. In nineteen of the state's eighty-six counties, any public appearance by League members was outlawed. Larson writes that Lindbergh suffered personal abuse and physical danger, having been run out of towns, pelted with rotten eggs, hung in effigy, and even shot at, or just banned, as he was in Duluth and other towns, from speaking. But Lindbergh "displayed remarkable courage," according to Larson, who quoted Lindbergh writing to his daughter, Eva: "You must prepare to see me in prison or possibly shot, for I will not be a rubber stamp to deceive the people."

In this toxic and hysteric atmosphere, where hyphenated Americans—German-Americans, Swedish-Americans, Norwegian-Americans—had become something un-American, something ugly, Lindbergh refused to use patriotism as a political weapon. A quote from Mark Twain's book *The Mysterious Stranger* became a favorite of his during the campaign: "Before long you will see this curious thing: the speakers stoned from the platform and free speech strangled by the hordes of curious men who in their secret hearts are still at one with those stoned speakers—as earlier—but do not dare to say so. And now the whole nation—pulpit and all—will take up the war-cry, and shout itself hoarse and mob any honest man who ventures to open his mouth."

Prominent Swedish American politician Ernest Lundeen shot back with vigor when John F. McGee of the Minnesota Commission of Public Safety questioned the loyalty of the Swedish Americans, saying, "They [Swedish Americans] have fought in every war, the Revolutionary War, the War of 1812, the Mexican War, the Civil War, the Spanish-American War, and World War I. They have never been found wanting. The Swedish people first of all nations of the world recognized American independence. No punishment is too severe for this character assassin who so traduces and slanders our best citizens."

There were also voices of restraint within the Republican Scandinavian establishment and some openly critical of the Burnquist administration. Icelandic American editor and leading Republican Gunnar Bjornson was such a voice. He had supported Burnquist during the primary election campaign. But in October 1918, after several tragic campaign incidents—a German American farmer in Rock County was tarred and feathered and deported to South Dakota, and a Finnish immigrant was badly beaten and found dead hanging from a tree, probably lynched—Bjornson expressed his exasperation, even outrage, at what was going on in the campaign. After Burnquist had finally promised a reward for any information about what had happened to the murdered Finn, Bjornson responded in his *Minneota Mascot:*

> We hope that hereafter there will be no more stealing of banners, no more tearing off of the United States flag from cars that carry a Nonpartisan League banner, no more of the dirty, sneaking yellow paint brigades, no more of this tarring and feathering, no more of the disgraces that have taken place in Rock County, no more deporting of citizens, no more of the hundred and one different kinds of outrages that have gone unmolested and unnoticed, if not encouraged, by state and county officials.

In a record voter turnout, Lindbergh made a strong showing but lost the Republican primary to Burnquist, 199,000 votes to 150,000, or 41 percent to 54. It was an election pitting rural Minnesota against urban Minnesota. Lindbergh carried thirty counties, mostly in northwestern and western Minnesota, and captured three times more votes than the number of Nonpartisan League members in Minnesota. The Swedish population at the time represented 11.5 percent of Minnesota's total population, the second-largest nationality after the Germans. Lindbergh's support was strongest in the ten counties with the largest Swedish population, and he beat Burnquist in seven of them. He also did well in counties where Norwegians and Germans dominated. Thus, writes Swedish scholar Dag Blanck, "Lindbergh became the candidate of Minnesota's immigrants and their children, whereas Burnquist had a much greater appeal among native-born Minnesotans, whose foreign background was at least two generations away." To Blanck, the election should also be seen as an illustration of the divergent political views within the Scandinavian community, while the large support for Lindbergh also showed how strongly "protest politics" resonated among the Scandinavians. In the following decades, this would translate into support for the Farmer-Labor Party.

The loss was a big blow not only for Lindbergh but also for the Nonpartisan League. Neither one ever recovered. The League tried launching its own gubernatorial candidate, David Evans, in the November 1918 general election against Burnquist, this time under the name "Farmer-Labor"—the first time it was ever used. But Evans lost decisively to the incumbent governor. According to Chrislock, the 1918 election signaled the end of the Progressive Era in Minnesota. Charles A. Lindbergh Sr. ran again for political office, for the US House of Representatives, for the US Senate, and in 1924, once more for Minnesota governor. He never won. A brain tumor cut his efforts short, and he died on May 25, 1924.

Lindbergh's legacy was central to the development of the Farmer-Labor Party in the 1920s and 1930s. During the 1918 gubernatorial campaign, the impossible had happened—an alliance between farmers and laborers—and Lindbergh came to be known during the campaign as the farmer and labor candidate and soon simply the farmer-labor candidate. The seed was planted in Minnesota politics that would have long-lasting and fundamental implications for politics in the state and the nation.

In 1969, Walfrid Engdahl, a Swedish immigrant and radical activist and writer in Minneapolis, praised Lindbergh as "the incorruptible seeker after truth and justice, and when he thought he found them, he preached them freely and openly.... No one has shown greater courage, a more honest thoroughness in his searching, and no one has shown a greater empathy for the starving and suffering in society. For them, he sacrificed everything in his life."

Three years after his father's death, Charles A. Lindbergh Jr. flew alone across the Atlantic Ocean.

CHANGE WAS A KEY WORD in Minnesota politics in the decades around the turn of the twentieth century. The Republican Party's monopoly on power ended and new political constellations made their way onto the scene. For the state's Scandinavians this meant not merely the election of the first Scandinavian governors but also their complete political breakthrough on all levels of politics and society. It meant full engagement in the agrarian protest politics of the time, in both the populist and the progressive movements, and in voting for the first third-party gubernatorial candidate in 1890. It meant supporting the Nonpartisan League, and it meant having to choose during World War I between an anti-immigrant, repressive Swedish American governor and a progressive, antiwar Swedish American challenger from the same party.

Most of all, these years showed that the Scandinavian vote was far from monolithic.

Ethnicity was important in these years, judging from the Scandinavian-language press coverage of state politics and the frequent appeals to support Scandinavian candidates. At times it meant a choice between ethnicity and political party, and at times these same newspapers chose the latter over the former—party affiliation over ethnicity. It was never an easy choice, but rather a delicate balancing act.

At the end of this period, as the Farmer-Labor Party took the first steps that gave notice of a new era in Minnesota politics, the importance of ethnicity had waned. The war, and how the Scandinavians felt about it, underscored the political divisions among Minnesota's ethnic voting groups. The "patriotic fever" of the times was anti-immigrant and anti-ethnicity, and so it served to dampen ethnic expressions and celebrations.

By 1920, the first- and second-generation Scandinavian immigrants who had paved the way for the Scandinavian entrance into the state's politics were largely gone, replaced by Americanized Scandinavian political candidates for whom ethnicity was no longer as important. A new era was ahead for Minnesota's Scandinavian politicians.

5

Radicals in Exile

*I did not have "America fever." I would have preferred to stay in
Sweden. But there were no jobs.*

Walfrid Engdahl, 1978

"MY GRANDFATHER NEVER MELLOWED. He used to say to me, 'to be radical is to get to the bottom of things.'" Brad Engdahl, a successful lawyer in Minneapolis, remembers with fondness his grandfather Walfrid Engdahl, who was twenty years old when he arrived in Minnesota in 1910 after being blacklisted and forced to leave Sweden following the General Strike of 1909. Born in Ellenö in western Sweden's Dalsland province not far from the Norwegian border on March 5, 1890, Walfrid Engdahl was almost ninety when he died in Minneapolis on January 29, 1979.

Engdahl was among the Scandinavian immigrants who came to America in the second big migration wave after the turn of the twentieth century. They often came alone, looking for work and settling in America's cities. Many of them, like Engdahl, had been active in the battles for political and union rights in their home countries and were forced to emigrate for political reasons. They were, in a sense, radicals in exile in America, in a country that, it would turn out, had little appetite for their brand of politics. Like so many other immigrants, Engdahl made his way in the new country by doing odd jobs, working the railroads all over the West and Canada and eventually becoming a carpenter. He was for almost sixty years active in the labor movement, both as an organizer and a writer. He joined mainstream politics in Minnesota and held several positions in the state government before retiring in 1955. He became a leading voice in Swedish American organizations and a prominent pen in the Swedish American press. He left a mark.

These radicals in exile, these political firebrands, came from all over Scandinavia. Their newspapers tell their stories: Norwegian *Gaa Paa* (Forward) in Minneapolis; Finnish *Työmies* (the Worker), *Sosialisti*, and *Industrialisti* on Minnesota's Iron Range; and Swedish *Forskaren* (the Investigator) and

Allarm in Minneapolis. There were also radical papers in English: *New Times* came out in Minneapolis between 1910 and 1918 and was closely allied with the Minnesota Socialist Party and socialist mayor Thomas Van Lear, and *Truth,* started by Scandinavian socialists and published in Duluth between 1917 and 1923, was militantly socialist and a strong supporter of the Industrial Workers of the World (IWW). *Two Harbors Socialist,* published in the small North Shore town, was run for years by Swedish and Norwegian socialists.

The records of these radical Scandinavian immigrants are often limited. Some died unknown in the new country; some returned or were deported to Scandinavia, where they often continued their political and union activities. Some remained radical all their lives, while others joined the political mainstream and ran for political office as members of the Farmer-Labor Party or its successor, the Democratic-Farmer-Labor Party (DFL). Walfrid Engdahl's story is well documented and gives a good picture of the life of one of Minnesota's many radical Swedish immigrants through his unpublished and unfinished memoir, "My Life," and through lengthy interviews in English and Swedish for two oral history projects.

Walfrid Engdahl's father was a skilled carpenter and cabinetmaker and also cultivated a small piece of land. His mother, a midwife, was an avid reader of religious books but could not write. Walfrid had five siblings, including his twin sister, Ellen, who, he writes in his memoir, was the perfect playmate. She died just four months before he finally made it back to Sweden in 1966 for the first visit since leaving for America fifty-six years earlier. "That is something I regret, very, very much," he adds.

He left school at thirteen and landed a job as a bricklayer's assistant at a local hospital construction project. It paid "good money," six to eight Swedish crowns a day, about a dollar, most of which he gave to his parents so that his father could build a new home. The bricklayer Walfrid worked for was a man named Jonas Larsson, who had worked as a miner in Coeur d'Alene, Idaho, and been active in the radical Western Federation of Miners. Larsson fled to Sweden after the union members were rounded up following the murder of Governor Frank Steunenberg in 1905. Larsson, Engdahl writes, was one of the finest men he had ever met. He once gave him the book *Merrie England* by Robert Blatchford, a British socialist and journalist: "From then on I dedicated my life to socialism and to the workers. To me, no cause could be more worthy of one's dedication and efforts than to make the world a better place for all of us."

At fifteen, Engdahl moved to Stockholm, where he became a member of

Stockholms Norra, a social democratic youth club founded in 1892. By 1902, it had 130 members, many of whom would later find their way to America, where they continued their political and union activism. That same year, these young socialists participated vigorously in the big political strike for the right to vote, which Swedish men did not achieve until 1909 and Swedish women not until 1921.

Politics was often discussed at work. Henrik "Hinke" Bergegren and Hjalmar Branting were the two leading social democrats of the time. Branting's speeches were "genuine" road maps for how the "working class would win its socialist society," writes Engdahl. Meanwhile, Bergegren "wanted revolution in a bold, open way," arguing that politics could never establish a socialist society and that only a general strike could destroy the capitalist system. He favored a more revolutionary approach over the parliamentary strategy pursued by Branting, who later became Sweden's first Social Democratic prime minister. In 1908, Bergegren was expelled at the party congress.

The 1909 General Strike in Sweden was a turning point for Walfrid Engdahl and for thousands of other Swedish workers. The conflict was both a workers' strike and a massive lockout by employers. It lasted for more than three months and involved a total of three hundred thousand workers. The conflict led to 11.8 million lost days of work and losses of 25 million Swedish crowns. "It changed my whole career," writes Engdahl in "My Life." Anyone who took part in the General Strike of 1909 was assumed to have radical ideas and was blacklisted. As an activist in the syndicalist movement in Sweden, Engdahl was blacklisted, and he went home to work for his father until, "I shall never forget that day, when my father told me that I had to leave Sweden because of my activities in the strike of 1909 and my involvement in the radical labor movement in general," writes Engdahl. His father told him that the bank had refused him a loan for the construction of the community-owned poorhouse because Walfrid was on his payroll. He suggested that his son leave for America; he would lend him the money for the trip. "I did not have 'America fever,'" Engdahl later said in his 1978 interview with Lennart Setterdahl. "I would have preferred to stay in Sweden. But there were no jobs."

Engdahl left Sweden for America just as he turned twenty, arriving at Ellis Island in New York on April 1, 1910, one of thousands of blacklisted Swedish workers forced into exile during this period. According to official statistics, Swedish emigration jumped to almost 22,000 people in 1909 from 12,499 the previous year. The numbers were particularly high during the last months of 1909, after the General Strike. In December that year, the number of people leaving Sweden was three times as high as in December 1907. In 1910, the numbers climbed even higher, reaching almost 28,000.

During the General Strike, a total of eight hundred young socialists were criminally charged and five hundred were handed sentences ranging from fines to prison terms for giving speeches, insulting the monarchy, or trying to organize. Workers were persecuted at their jobs; many were fired and evicted from their homes. An estimated twenty thousand Swedish workers left for North America because the employers' blacklists made it impossible to find work. Once in America, many of these men continued to be active in politics and in the unions. They often joined organizations and clubs most similar to the ones they had left behind. The social democrats went to the Scandinavian Socialist Labor Federation, part of the Socialist Party, and to the identically named Scandinavian Socialist Labor Federation, a wing of the Socialist Labor Party. The young socialists and the syndicalists formed a Scandinavian section of the syndicalist/anarchist Industrial Workers of the World in the United States. The anarchists also gathered around a Chicago monthly called *Revolt*. Many joined temperance groups, such as Verdandi. Temperance was an important part of their identity, as it was for Engdahl—a lifelong temperance man.

The period following the 1909 General Strike was not the first time Swedish workers left for America after a labor conflict, although never before in such large numbers. In fact, these were years of extraordinary labor unrest, with some three thousand labor conflicts from 1879 to 1909. The Sundsvall strike of 1879 was the first big strike among industrial workers in Sweden. It was followed by the Norberg strike of 1891–92, and the Ljusne conflict in 1905–06. All of them ended in defeats for the workers, and all of them triggered a dramatic increase in emigration to the United States. In the Sundsvall strike around five thousand workers from twenty sawmills participated. The strike was broken up by the military, and work resumed under conditions set by the employers. Isidor Kjellberg, editor of the daily *Östgöten*, wrote after a visit to the Sundsvall area: "If any plan for the future can be called common there, it is that of leaving, the sooner the better, the present home for America, where many fellow workers—some say 2,000 counting wives and children—have already moved after the breaking of the strike. America is the thought for the day and the dream of the night." The Stockholm daily *Dagens Nyheter* wrote: "It is terribly sad for the stranger to come into contact with a whole population that has given up all hope and only wants to leave the country. All thoughts are concentrated on America and how they are to find the means to travel there."

Emigration numbers from the Sundsvall area during these years confirm that story. While six people emigrated in 1876 and only two in 1878, 264 people left for America in the strike year 1879, followed by 286, 330, 251, and 110 over the next four years. The events of 1879 "tended to destroy the hope of reaching a better position in the near future and induced them [workers] to carry out their plans to emigrate," and because of disappointment and frustration that better working and living conditions could not be attained, "the labor disputes in Sweden had a direct bearing on emigration to America." Swedish historian Fred Nilson writes that to emigrate became a choice between eating in America or starving in Sweden: "Emigration became for many in the working class an emergency solution to acute difficulties to survive that often resulted from the employers' blacklisting."

The Norberg strike of 1891–92 was actually three strikes in quick succession, with the last as the biggest, involving eight hundred to nine hundred iron mine workers. It lasted almost six months and hinged on demands from the workers for the right to participate in wage negotiations. The union was crushed and lay dormant for fifteen years, and none of the strike leaders could get a job afterward. In 1892, eighty people left for America and another forty-two in the first half of 1893. Several of the strike and union leaders were among those who left. In the Ljusne conflict of 1905–06, all political and union activities were prohibited and the right to organize was the core issue. Eventually, in 1906, out of a total labor force of twelve hundred, 105 people left for America, including forty-six members of the Young Social Democrats' Association, again pointing to "a clear connection between socialist political activity and emigration."

The General Strike of 1909 was the first nationwide labor conflict in modern Sweden, and the country came to a standstill. The conflict ended in a victory for the employers, as the strike funds for the workers dried up in spite of generous financial support from, among others, Scandinavian workers' organizations in America. The workers in Sweden had "experienced the tensions and the repressions of expanding industrial capitalism already before leaving for America," and so when they arrived in the new country, the "confrontation with industrial America was no shock to them." On the contrary, many of them "were well prepared to take part in the struggle of the American working class."

Engdahl, once in Minneapolis, wasted no time in rejoining the labor movement. He was equipped with the addresses of the American Federa-

tion of Labor Carpenters Union Local 7, founded in 1892 by a group of Swedish socialists, and the local branch of the IWW. He knew no English, but
the secretary of the union was a Swede, and with his help, Engdahl started
working immediately. His first job was to help build the first hospital unit
at the University of Minnesota. Work took him to the Dakotas, Montana,
Washington State, and British Columbia.

These first years did not seem to be particularly happy ones, judging from
Engdahl's three letters to Hinke Bergegren, the radical Swedish socialist. The
elegantly penned letters were written after Bergegren was expelled from the
Social Democratic Party. Engdahl laments the fact that Bergegren had resigned as editor of the young socialists' paper *Brand* (Fire)—"our beloved
newspaper": "I left Sweden almost a year ago and all my friends were almost
convinced that here we would forget our socialist, or, rather, anarchist, out-
look. You do not need to do that. If you start to stir in the American society it
is more and more likened with a dung heap, and a rotten one at that.... The
big and beautiful idea of syndicalism is much misunderstood here.... But,
the day will come when our revolution will appear and step forth just as thunderous and mighty as we have dreamed of." He thanks Bergegren for fighting
for his ideas, which "also are mine," and adds, "we will never forget you."

A new job at the Swedish-language paper *Forskaren* (the Investigator)
was the reason for Engdahl's return to Minnesota. It launched his career as a
journalist and writer. The paper was founded by two Swedes as "an organ of
socialism and free thought." *Forskaren,* called by the British scholar Michael
Brook "a Swedish radical voice in Minneapolis," was not the first radical
Swedish newspaper in Minnesota, starting already in 1876 with *Agatho-
kraten* (One Who Believes in the Rule of the Good), according to Brook,
and *Rothuggaren* (the Radical) in 1880. In 1891, *Gnistan* (the Spark), subtitled
"A Swedish Radical Weekly," was founded by the Reverend Axel Lundeberg, who had worked in Sweden with August Palm, the father of Swedish
socialism, before Lundeberg came to Minnesota. *Gnistan* closed in 1892.
Forskaren lasted much longer, first as a newspaper and then, for nineteen
years, as a periodical. It was closely associated with Frihetsförbundet (the
Scandinavian Liberty League), founded in Minneapolis by radical Swedes.
It held Sunday school for the children of the members of temperance groups
such as International Order of Good Templars and Verdandi together with
the First Scandinavian Unitarian Church in Minneapolis, started by David
Holmgren, an ordained minister who, facing imprisonment for financial ir-
regularities, fled to America in 1906.

Engdahl became a Wobbly—a member of the Industrial Workers of the

World—shortly after arriving in Minneapolis. IWW was a union founded in Chicago in 1905 by Eugene Debs, "Big Bill" Haywood, and a couple of hundred other delegates, among them some Swedish immigrants. The Wobblies urged direct action through strikes and other means, and they scorned the political process. Their rallying cry was "One Big Union." At the time, Minneapolis was said to have one of the biggest local IWW organizations in America.

In "My Life," Engdahl expresses great affinity and admiration for the IWW. There were "no secrets" there; the members were "resourceful and brave" and "enemies of private competitive capitalism in all its wasteful, brutal, and dishonest appearances. Some day they were going to take over the production and distribution of all commodities and urged its members to read and study the essential functions in a free society so that none would live in hunger, want, or slavery."

At the end of 1915, Engdahl started writing for *Allarm*, a Swedish-language monthly published by the Scandinavian Propaganda League of the IWW in Minneapolis. The paper had been founded in Seattle earlier in the year under the name *Solidaritet* (Solidarity), but had moved to Minneapolis. It had a circulation of about two thousand copies. "We tried to tell the truth the way we saw it," Engdahl said in the Minnesota Radicalism Project interview. "We have always criticized the profit motive, the competitive motive instead of the cooperative motive. We have told about the insane exploitation of the national resources. We have criticized the destruction of foods to hold up the prices."

One of Engdahl's first articles was about IWW activist and fellow Swede Joe Hill, whose songbook, *To Fan the Flames of Discontent*, the IWW published in 1916. Born Joel Emmanuel Hägglund in Gävle, Sweden, in 1879 and also known as Josef Hillström, Hill left for America in 1902 and became a migrant worker out west, eventually joining the IWW. He was sentenced to death and shot by a firing squad on November 19, 1915, in Salt Lake City, Utah, for a murder and robbery he most likely did not commit.

Engdahl writes in *Allarm*: "Today, I learned to my horror that comrade Hillström had been shot. Today, November 19, 1915. How can something like that happen today? Sleep well tonight, Mr. Governor! What crime has Josef Hillström committed? He was a discontented slave, and he was intelligent. God, that is enough to be criminal!" On the first anniversary of Joe Hill's death, Engdahl again wrote about his fellow IWW Swede, asking why he should be praised and answering, "because he was a man! In one of

Walfrid Engdahl, circa 1977. Photo courtesy of Brad Engdahl

his last letters, Hill wrote, 'Don't waste time over my memory—organize!' Those are manly words worthy of remembering for everyone."

Engdahl wrote for *Allarm* until its last issue in May 1918. He believed being a revolutionary was the "self-evident duty of the awakened worker," and it is "preferable to die as an honest revolutionary rather than to defend the mortal enemies on Wall Street. It is more honest to die for freedom than for the private capitalists. We are the defenders of freedom and nothing can suppress us." Is there anything "more rotten than politics," he asks in another article and calls the approaching World War I the "greatest curse." It was better to die in an "honest revolution than on the bloody and stinking battlefields." Engdahl believed that the IWW was the only group that dared to take action.

On September 5, 1917, agents of the US Department of Justice raided forty-eight IWW halls across the country and arrested 166 Wobblies on charges of violating the US Espionage Act. In the final six months of *Allarm*'s existence, much space was devoted to these arrests and the subsequent trial in Chicago. Among the arrested were three Swedes: the editor of *Allarm*, Carl Ahlteen; its business manager, Sigfrid Stenberg; and Chicago-based Ragnar Johanson, a painter, IWW activist, and frequent contributor to the paper. A fourth Swede, Edward Mattson, managed to avoid arrest by fleeing to Canada. Returning to Sweden, he became a leading figure in the syndicalist movement.

At the trial, Ahlteen was sentenced to twenty years in prison and fined $20,000, while Stenberg and Johanson each received ten-year prison sentences and fines of $30,000. They never served their full prison terms. In a deal with the US government, they were released in early 1923 and deported to Sweden. A photo in the Swedish syndicalist paper *Arbetaren* from January 24, 1923, shows three smiling young men in overcoats and elegant hats arriving by boat in Göteborg, welcomed by friends and colleagues.

Carl Ahlteen, spelled Althén in Swedish, came to America from Grimslöv in Småland in southern Sweden soon after the General Strike. According to Michael Brook, Ahlteen prided himself on his hardness and realism, always insisting that the workers must fight for themselves. Power and power alone must be the motto of the working class, Ahlteen writes in *Allarm* in June 1916, and when the worker wakes up, the time has come when "our comrades once again can breathe freely." Back in Sweden, Ahlteen's political and union activities faded, and it is possible that Ahlteen again left Sweden in the 1930s and that he died in Colombia soon after World War II.

Ragnar Johanson was a prominent syndicalist before leaving for America in 1912. Called "a silver tongued orator," he frequently wrote for *Allarm* and became a leading itinerant agitator for IWW among Swedish immigrants in America. Once back in Sweden he continued his syndicalist activities and was for many years a manager at the syndicalist publishing house Federativ. He died in 1959.

Sigfrid Stenberg, born in Stora Tuna in the province of Dalarna in 1892, worked in the lumber industry and as a painter before coming to America in 1912. He was *Allarm's* business manager until his arrest in 1917. The evidence on which Stenberg's conviction was based was a telegram he wrote that said in Swedish, "Sänd Allarm"—meaning "Send *Allarm*," the paper—which the prosecutor translated as "Send all weapons." Stenberg also continued his union activities in Sweden. He joined SAC, the Swedish syndicalist organization, and worked as a journalist at SAC's newspaper *Arbetaren* until his death in 1942, at the age of fifty.

The three, Engdahl writes in "My Life," "were intelligent, honest, and idealistic. They had the courage to follow their inner light regardless of consequences."

After *Allarm* ceased publishing, Engdahl started writing for other newspapers and periodicals, often about culture, literature, music, and poetry.

He wrote for Henry Bengston's *Svenska Socialisten* (the Swedish Socialist) in Chicago, the organ of the Scandinavian Socialist Federation, founded in 1910 in Chicago and which had at its height over thirty-seven hundred members, mostly Swedes. He wrote for *Bokstugan* (the Book Cabin), a literary magazine and official organ of the Verdandi Study League, also in Chicago, started in 1919 by Wallentin Wald, a young painter from Engdahl's Young Socialists Club in Stockholm who had left for America after serving a prison sentence for distributing pacifist leaflets in Stockholm. At *Bokstugan,* Wald surrounded himself with a group of enthusiastic literary contributors, among them Engdahl. They were not academically trained, but they were all "serious thinkers and well able to express themselves in both verse and prose." Bengston said *Bokstugan*, which published articles in both Swedish and English, "reached a, by far, higher literary standard than any of its Swedish contemporaries in the United States." September 1928 was its last issue. Wald died in 1946.

Later, between 1958 and 1969, Engdahl was a frequent contributor to *Kulturarvet* (Swedish Heritage), also edited by Bengston and published by the Swedish Cultural Society of America, which elected Engdahl its chairman in 1964. Engdahl also wrote a regular column for the *Minneapolis Labor Review* and showed great fondness for early progressive Swedish American politicians in Minnesota, such as Magnus Johnson and Charles A. Lindbergh Sr.

Parallel to writing, Engdahl worked as a carpenter, was active in the Twin Cities Carpenters' Union No. 7 in Minneapolis, and was secretary of the Twin City Carpenters' District Council. He also joined the American Federation of Labor (AFL). In a speech on the local radio station WCCO on May 8, 1931, published that day in the *Minneapolis Tribune*, Engdahl makes a strong case for the working man and for organized labor "to make this world a better place to live in." He said the "day is at hand when people will understand our motives. The day is at hand when through our effort there shall come an era of happiness such as the world has never seen before, when the morning sun shall shine upon the smiling faces of our children who, in turn, shall dedicate their lives to preserve the cause of liberty, justice and equality which the workers, through endless struggle and sacrifice have won for them."

In the early 1930s, Engdahl joined the Farmer-Labor Party and held several positions in Governor Floyd B. Olson's administrations. Until the mid-1950s, Engdahl was in charge of the construction and maintenance of the public welfare buildings in Minneapolis. Governor Olson also named him the first union representative of organized labor on the building commission for a new office building. When Engdahl was unable to prevent the commission from setting the pay scale 20 percent below union wages, he went to Olson ready to hand in his resignation. But the governor refused to accept it, and at a meeting to decide on the wages, Olson, according to Engdahl's account in "My Life," gave "one of the most factual and forceful speeches I have ever heard. When he was through, the chairman stated, 'Gentlemen, you have just heard one of the greatest speeches by the greatest governor in the USA supporting the proposition of establishing the union scale as the prevailing scale on our office building. It is up to you to decide what to do.'" The motion to pay union scale carried.

"We had a great governor," Engdahl writes. "We did not realize the magnitude of the man." In his interview with Lennart Setterdahl, Engdahl said that "Olson would have been a good president. There was no speaker like him. He was radical, but clever."

Walfrid Engdahl slowly made peace with the country that had pushed him away. When Augusta Engdahl went to Sweden in 1948 to visit her relatives, her husband chose not to go. For him, Sweden remained a "pariah," and it was not until the mid-1960s, when Walfrid and Augusta Engdahl spent almost a year in Sweden, that his picture of the old country changed. By then, Sweden was a nation transformed by democratic reforms and the rise to power of the labor movement to which he had helped give birth. To Setterdahl he said, "I got a very good impression of Sweden when I visited in 1967–68. There was a sense of security and happiness. I did not see one sad face during the whole year." And his grandson, Brad, recalled with a laugh that when his grandfather returned to America, "he said that Sweden was the greatest country, and he was so pleased and so impressed." Engdahl later wrote in *Kulturarvet* about Sweden's rich culture and the big changes that had taken place there: "Much of what we, in our youth, dreamed of has become reality. In a more fortunate way than in any other country, a bloodless revolution has transpired in Sweden, which has given the working people and the elderly free and joyous human dignity. The fear of destitution and old age is now only memory about hard and cruel times that are no more."

CARL SKOGLUND AND WALTER MALTE FRANK were contemporaries of Walfrid Engdahl in Minnesota. Both, also blacklisted, left Sweden for America as young men in their twenties in the immediate aftermath of the 1909

General Strike. And both left their mark on radical politics and labor relations in their new home country—Skoglund as a militant strike leader and a revolutionary communist until the end of his life, and Frank as a prominent union leader and a man of the political establishment in Minnesota who helped launch the Farmer-Labor Party of Minnesota and ran for political office—a "typical centrist," as Skoglund once called Frank.

For Skoglund and Frank, as for Engdahl, America did not seem to be "the thought for the day and the dream of the night," as Isidor Kjellberg had written after the Sundsvall strike in 1879. They were not struck by "America fever." Skoglund said in a 1960 interview for Minnesota's Radicalism Project, "I had not thought about leaving Sweden, or emigrating. I had intended to stay, but because of this situation I had very little choice." And Frank, who refused to serve in the Swedish army, later explained that his three choices were army, jail, or emigration, and he chose emigration.

Skoglund, born in 1884, hailed, like Engdahl, from the province of Dalsland in western Sweden, more precisely from Svärdlungskogen, near the town of Bengtsfors. Growing up in Sweden, Skoglund described a hard life of strife and great poverty, where "conditions were very primitive." His father was a "semi-feudal serf." "In reality, my generation became the break between the old semi-feudal life and the new industrial life," Skoglund said.

Skoglund barely had three full school years behind him when he went to work at a paper mill. At twenty-one, he was drafted into the Swedish army like all other young men at the time. After the army, he went back to school for six months and also went back to work at the paper mill, but as he became involved in organizing the workers, he quit, or was forced to quit, and found that there were no jobs anywhere for him. He left for America, arriving in Boston in 1911 and continuing directly by train to Minneapolis, where a series of different jobs followed—cement mixer, lumberjack, night fireman, and janitor. These were hard years. "At the time, I had carried in my mind to commit suicide and to sit on the Minnesota River to jump in and drown myself," he said.

Skoglund helped Engdahl edit *Allarm*, and by that time he had started working for the Pullman Company's railroad. He also started to write a column called "Kvarnstad Krönika" (Mill City Chronicle) for *Svenska Socialisten* in Chicago. At Pullman, he helped organize the Pullman workers into a new union, the Brotherhood of Railroad Car Men, affiliated with the American Federation of Labor (AFL). A nine-month-long strike in 1922 cost him his job, and Skoglund never worked for Pullman again.

Shortly after arriving in Minnesota, Skoglund became a member of the IWW, but he did not support its antipolitical syndicalist policies and moved on, joining, in 1914, the Scandinavian Socialist Federation of the Socialist Party. When the Socialist Party split after the Russian Revolution in 1917, Skoglund sided with the left wing, which went on to form the Communist Party of America. In 1928, he was expelled from the Communist Party for opposing Stalinism and supporting Trotsky, and in 1938 he helped form the Trotskyist Socialist Workers Party. By then, Trotsky lived in exile in Mexico, and Skoglund had planned to join other party leaders there for political discussions. He never went, fearing he would not be let back into America since he was not a US citizen. In a letter to Skoglund at a hotel in Laredo, Texas, on the border with Mexico, Trotsky writes, "I am profoundly chagrined that you are handicapped by some judicial obstacles to come here. . . . I would be very happy to meet a representative of the 'old guard' who many comrades consider their teacher. Natalia and I embrace you fraternally."

Following the outbreak of World War II, Skoglund and eighteen other Trotskyists were arrested under the Alien Registration Act of 1940, also known as the Smith Act. They were sentenced to jail and Skoglund spent 1944–45 in a federal prison. The Smith Act had made it a crime to advocate the overthrow of the US government and also stipulated that all non–US citizens had to register with the government.

Carl Skoglund, or "Skogie" as his friends and fellow workers called him, is best remembered for his central role in the 1934 Minneapolis Teamsters' Strike, a "landmark in the labor history not only of Minnesota but of the United States." The strike, which took place at the height of the Depression, when one-third of the workers in Minneapolis were unemployed, was led by Skoglund and Vincent Raymond Dunne. They had met in the Minneapolis coal yards and came to play "critical roles in the struggle for union recognition in Minneapolis." Dunne was of Irish and French-Canadian descent, born in Kansas City in 1889, but he grew up on a farm in central Minnesota. He became a lumberjack and a Wobbly and a socialist in his youth. In 1920 he joined the Communist Party and later became a Trotskyist, which he remained until his death in 1970.

"Skoglund was a socialist and a very able man," Dunne recalled in an interview for the Minnesota Radicalism Project. "He became a very well-known labor leader in this town. He was a thorough-going socialist, an international revolutionary socialist. Once he said to me, 'This is the place, Vincent Dunne, you have to learn what you didn't learn when you were a kid.' I took that seriously. I thought that was a great thing. He turned out to be a very, very good tutor. He was not only a skilled mechanic but he was also an intellectual of considerable stature. . . . He was my first real teacher in the party as a revolutionary socialist. Skoglund knew thousands, and thousands knew him, because he was one of their leaders in the strikes they held. He was one of the outstanding leaders because he was a man that was well educated and so forth, but still a working man." When Skoglund died in December 1960, his obituary in the *International Socialist Review* said, "the American working class lost one of its best, most experienced and loyal defenders."

Skoglund and Dunne had joined Local 574 of the Teamsters Union, and later Dunne's two brothers, Grant and Miles, also joined. Together, the four were "in competence, resourcefulness, and devotion to the labor movement without peers." In organizing Local 574, Skoglund and Dunne tried something new. Instead of organizing around occupational specialties, as was the tradition in the American labor movement at the time, they gathered all the workers together in a new industrial model, which, eventually, became the foundation of the CIO, the Congress of Industrial Organizations. Skoglund and Dunne "perfected a new motorized form of pickets as flying squads, roving the streets in their own trucks and cars, preventing strike breakers from making their deliveries." They demonstrated an effective mastery of 1930s communication technology, used their telephones effectively, and published a daily strike bulletin. Local mass rallies mobilized support for the strike.

Dunne and Skoglund were more than ideologues; they knew how to put their ideas into practice, and they were well liked among their fellow workers. Skoglund, described as stocky and well built, was a good mechanic and a man who loved astronomy, was a "generous and nice fellow and most of the fellas knew him and if he asked you to join a union, you pretty much had to." But Minneapolis's powerful pro-business, pro–open shop Citizens Alliance fought the union all the way and refused to negotiate with it directly. However, a short strike in February 1934 led to some modest wage increases, and union membership rose sharply, to nearly seven thousand by June. The battle now hardened. Encouraged by the New Deal's National Industrial Recovery Act of 1933, which gave labor the right to organize and bargain collectively, Local 574 leaders Dunne and Skoglund announced new demands for a closed shop, wage increases, and extra pay for overtime. But they acted on their own. The International Brotherhood of Teamsters, conservative and averse to strikes, refused to authorize a strike, and the AFL warned its affiliate, the Central Labor Council, not to cooperate with Local 574. The Teamsters charged that the "real objective of the Communists [in Local 574] is to enlist Minnesota in the revolution they hope to start in this country to overthrow the constitution and the laws of the land." The Citizens Alliance grew greatly alarmed over the development and decided to stand firm. Violence followed. Picketers were arrested. It was close to class warfare. The strike lasted thirty-six days, ending after intervention by Governor Floyd B. Olson, federal negotiators, and even, indirectly, President Franklin D. Roosevelt. The conflict cost Minneapolis $50 million and millions in lost wages for the workers and left four men dead and scores injured. But the union was recognized, Minneapolis ceased being an open-shop town, and "the dictatorship of the Citizens Alliance was smashed."

Carl Skoglund never returned to Sweden. Because he never became a US citizen, he lived under a constant threat of deportation for his political and union activities. At one point, the US immigration authorities had him on a Norwegian ship in New York harbor, preparing to deport him, but he was saved at the last moment by American socialist leader Norman Thomas. In a poem from 1949 called "The Saga of a Swede," Miles Dunne, chairman of the Minnesota Section of the Civil Rights Defense Committee, wrote:

> We'll never let him send him back
> Or start him on his way.
> Join the fight
> With all your might
> Away with darkness, welcome light.
> Carl Skoglund's here to stay.

Skoglund died in 1960 at the Marxist School in New Jersey. In Minneapolis in 1984, the hundredth anniversary of Skoglund's birth was celebrated with speeches and a Swedish smörgåsbord for the "profound contribution Carl made to maintaining the continuity of the revolutionary socialist movement."

Frank was, like Skoglund, involved with organized labor in Scandinavia before coming to America in 1913, with the Swedish sailors' union and in the machine and metal union in Oslo. Unlike Skoglund, he was raised in a fairly well-to-do family but disagreed with their philosophy of life and struck out on his own. Once in Minnesota, Frank studied engineering at the University of Minnesota. He joined the IWW and went to work out west in harvest

Violence erupts during the 1934 truck drivers' strike in Minneapolis

and lumber camps. During this time he met Joe Hill—"no doubt about that, he was framed," Frank said in an interview for the Minnesota Historical Society. Frank's later union activities involved the Lathers Union and the Building and Construction Trades Council. In a speech in Stillwater, Minnesota, on Labor Day in 1926, he urged his audience to join in the fight for a powerful, militant industrial union within the trade-union movement to build a true class-oriented Farmer-Labor Party. In 1932, he was appointed National Chairman of the AFL Trade Union Committee for Unemployment Insurance and Relief. He was active in the Farmer-Labor Party and ran for the state senate in 1930, but lost. In 1948, he ran for the US Congress as a candidate for the Democratic-Farmer-Labor (DFL) Party, but lost again.

Frank cooperated at various times with the more radical Popular Front and the Trotskyists, as well as with the Central Labor Union's moderates. He left the Popular Front after the Hitler-Stalin Pact in 1939, and in 1948 Frank was expelled from the Central Labor Union's political committee for supporting Henry Wallace's failed third-party efforts to the left of Harry Truman and the Democratic Party. Throughout the 1930s, Frank was often a main speaker at major political and union rallies in the Twin Cities, appearing together with prominent speakers such as Farmer-Labor governors Floyd B. Olson and Elmer Benson. Later in life he talked about the dangers of fascism in America and expressed strong views about the "mistake" of the Vietnam War. "I felt it necessary," he explained, "to participate in every endeavor to bring forth the real aspirations, principles and ideals, and the power of the working people, and all the connecting issues, and thus to participate also in the parliamentary . . . campaigns."

Like Skoglund, Walter Frank also encountered problems with the American immigration authorities, although he was a US citizen. In 1951, as he planned a trip to Europe that included a visit to his relatives in Sweden, he was denied a passport. The trip was deemed not to be "in the best interest of the United States," according to the US State Department. It took Frank more than four years to get his passport and only after interventions from, among others, Hubert Humphrey, then US senator from Minnesota, and after swearing that he had never been a member of the Communist Party. A letter from President Dwight D. Eisenhower on September 24, 1956, starting with the salutation "Dear Fellow Citizen," signaled the end of Frank's long fight to obtain a passport.

FROM THE LATE 1880s to the mid-1950s, a remarkable stretch of time, the Scandinavian Left provided leadership to the labor movement in Duluth. Richard Hudelson—labor historian, former philosophy professor at the University of Wisconsin–Superior, and a Duluth resident—points to the sheer number of Scandinavians in Duluth. By 1870 a third of the city's population was Swedish, along with 13 percent Norwegians and three percent Danes. The Finns came later. By 1920, 75,000 out of a population of 99,000 were foreign-born or children of foreign-born, and the Swedish population in Duluth was one of the largest concentrations of Swedish immigrants in the urban Midwest, proportionally larger than even Chicago and Minneapolis. And they became politically involved early. The members of the Duluth Scandinavian Socialist Local "brought a radicalism" with them from Sweden, and "there is strong evidence for the importance of the connection with Ljusne [labor conflict] in the history of the local" in Duluth.

In 1917, the radical Swedes in Duluth started a paper called *Truth*. It was an English-language paper, and not Swedish, clearly showing that the Swedes, who were the largest foreign-born group in the city, felt confident enough to reach out to other ethnic groups. Affiliated with the Scandinavian Socialist Federation in Chicago and the American Socialist Party (SP), Duluth's Scandinavian Socialist Local was one of the strongest in Minnesota. Its membership was almost entirely Swedish and largely blue collar. Socially, the members were close, spending free time together and holding Sunday picnics. Many members also belonged to the IWW, which had first established itself in Duluth in 1911.

As the official organ of the Socialist Party of Duluth, *Truth* saw its circulation quickly rise to twenty thousand copies. The Duluth Scandinavian Socialist Local's members, of which there were more than four hundred, provided the leadership behind their newspaper, "the rock upon which *Truth* was built." The paper eventually moved left and took its place on the side of revolution, which meant open support of the IWW as well as of the Russian Revolution.

Jacob O. (J. O.) Bentall was editor of *Truth* between 1918 and 1922. He had come from Sweden to Minnesota in 1871, only one year old, brought to America by his father, who began to farm in Meeker County. The son worked on the farm and then went to Carleton College in Northfield, Minnesota, graduating in 1896, followed by four years in graduate school at the University of Chicago. He had trained as a Baptist minister and had been a pastor of the First Baptist Church in St. Anne, Illinois, south of Chicago, as well as editor of the *Christian Socialist*, founded in 1904 by the Christian Socialist Fellowship. Bentall believed that the principles of Christianity were incompatible with capitalism and that socialism offered a way in which the Christian principles could be attained. He wrote that "to destroy Capitalism was our job." Bentall was imprisoned twice and ran for governor of Minnesota twice, first in 1916 as a socialist candidate, receiving 23,306 votes, or 6.7 percent of the total, then in 1928 as a candidate for the Communist Party with 5,760 people, or 0.6 percent, voting for him. He was a fierce opponent of World War I and was arrested in the summer of 1917 for violating the wartime Espionage Act. Appeal followed appeal until, in 1922, three years after the war was over and when Bentall was editor of *Truth*, he started serving a two-year sentence at the Leavenworth federal prison in Kansas. His comment on the verdict was, "Tell them I laugh at it, tell them I laugh at it. Ha, ha, ha."

President Warren Harding ordered Bentall's release in July 1923.

In 1929, Bentall was expelled from the Communist Party. By then, *Truth* had long ago ceased publication and the Duluth Scandinavian Socialist Local had faded away; in *Truth*'s last issue, its bitter comment was "due to lack of funds caused by the apathy of the workers."

When Bentall died in New York in 1933, he was called the "well-known communist leader" by the Swedish American newspaper *Vestkusten* (the West Coast). And Jack Carney, Bentall's predecessor as editor of *Truth,* wrote: "Comrade Bentall is no spotlight artist, he is one of the best and truest comrades that the movement has produced."

THE THOUSANDS OF RADICAL Scandinavians, mostly Swedes but also Norwegians and Danes, were often reluctant immigrants, forced into exile to find jobs, to survive. They left their home countries at a time of profound change, when a budding working class started its struggle for political and union rights. They lost that struggle, and they left for America.

Many of them, blacklisted for their political and union activities, continued to be activists in their new home country. Engdahl, Skoglund, and Frank belong to this group. The impact of these radical immigrants on Minnesota and state politics was never great. They often moved in narrow circles, among ideological and personal friends, socializing with one another and reading their own newspapers. The exception—and it is a big one—was the Minneapolis Teamsters' Strike of 1934, with Carl Skoglund as one of its leaders. The strike became a landmark in US labor history as the rights of the union were recognized and Minneapolis ceased to be an open-shop city.

Skoglund kept his communist faith all his life and remained a political outsider, while Engdahl and Frank mellowed politically with time, joining mainstream Minnesota politics as active members of the Farmer-Labor Party.

6

Finns on the Range

The story of Finland's immigrants is sometimes bitter,
sometimes sweet.

Michael G. Karni, Matti E. Kaups, Douglas J. Ollila Jr., 1975

IT WAS UP NORTH, on the Iron Range, that the Finnish immigrants made
their mark on Minnesota, and on America.

Politics were at the center. The Finns on the Range were far more political than the immigrants from the other Nordic countries. Theirs was a
radical brand of politics, and it was on the radical left that the Finns had the
greatest influence on Minnesota's politics and unions.

Few Finns reached state leadership positions. Only one Minnesota governor has had Finnish ancestry, C. Elmer Anderson, a Finland-Swede, born
in Brainerd, whose parents, Alfred A. and Anna L. Anderson, came from the
village of Esse in the heavily Swedish-speaking area along the Baltic coast in
western Finland. The Republican served as Minnesota's twenty-eighth governor, from 1951 to 1955, and before that was lieutenant governor for eleven
years. Only one Finn from Minnesota has been elected to a national office,
Oscar J. Väänänen Larson, an attorney from Duluth. He was also Republican and served two terms, 1921 to 1925, in the US House of Representatives.
The first Finn to be elected to a political office in Minnesota beyond the
local level was Charles Kauppi, also from Duluth, who came to America
in 1879 when he was fifteen years old. In 1896, he was elected to the first of
five four-year terms as a St. Louis County commissioner. And in 1904, John
Saari became the first Finnish American elected to the Minnesota State
Legislature. Born in Lapua in Finland in 1877, Saari arrived in Minnesota in
1892 and eventually became a co-owner of the Saari brothers grocery store
in Eveleth. During his first two years in the Minnesota house, Saari succeeded in getting a bill through the state legislature to improve safety in the
iron mines by establishing the office of mine inspector. Mining accidents
during his years in the state house had resulted in 177 deaths, and 77 of them

were Finns. After Saari, at least a dozen members with Finnish ancestry have served in the state house.

Life for the Finns on the Range was hard, as they faced both ethnic discrimination and cultural and economic oppression. They spoke a totally different language than their fellow Nordics. Ethnically, they were often erroneously, and with racist undertones, linked with Mongolians and American Indians. The Finns also were seen as problem drinkers. When John Svan, a miner, applied for US citizenship in 1907, he was turned down because, "being a Finn, he is Mongolian and not a 'white person'"; at the time, whiteness was a requirement of citizenship, as stipulated by US law. Shortly afterward, another fifteen Finns were denied citizenship. All were members of the Finnish Socialist Federation and had participated in the 1907 strike. The case was thrown out of court a few weeks later by a federal judge in Duluth, who declared the Finns to be white.

Early anti-Finn campaigns in local newspapers stereotyped them as "reds," "anarchists," and "drunks." Descriptions of Finnish immigrants tended to focus on "drinking, fighting, and radicalism," and one survey in the early 1920s found only 36 percent of the respondents willing to live next door to a Finn. Tavern signs could be found declaring "No Indians or Finns allowed." In 1918, Olli Kiukkonen, one of many Finns who had refused to register for the World War I military draft, was tarred and feathered and lynched by a vigilante group in Duluth. His gravestone in Park Hill Cemetery reads: "Victim of Warmongers." But other than some isolated acts of violence, Finns were never targeted as an ethnic group for systematic lynchings or attacks by vigilantes. Some, probably fewer than two hundred, were deported to Finland, mainly for violations of US immigration laws. Deportations for political activities were rare.

The young Finnish miners who had come and settled in northern Minnesota were single men, and they gathered either in the saloons or the cooperative boardinghouses on the Range. The first of these boardinghouses, or *poikatalot*, was founded in Duluth in 1881. Soon there were Finnish boardinghouses all over Minnesota. In 1926, there were still twenty-four such accommodations, and the largest of them was Toverila in Duluth, with 338 members. A major diversion for these men was, indeed, drinking. It was not made easier by the fact that, in 1912, there were three hundred fifty saloons, sixty of them owned by Finns, spread over fifteen Iron Range towns.

Work in the mines on the Iron Range was dangerous and poorly paid. More than three hundred Finns died in mining accidents from 1884 to 1930.

Pamela Brunfelt, Finnish American scholar and a native of the Iron Range, has called the conditions sweatshop-like. The miners had to pay for their own dynamite and candles and for tools they broke, and they only got paid when they mined the ore, not when repairs had to be done. Labor conflicts broke out almost as soon as mining started. Duluth labor historian Richard Hudelson estimates that about fifty strikes took place in northern Minnesota and Michigan during the first decade of the twentieth century. Three Finns were shot and killed by marshals during some early strikes. During the big Copper Country strike in 1913, tragedy struck at the Christmas ball in the Italian Hall in Calumet on Michigan's Upper Peninsula. A false cry of "fire" resulted in a stampede, killing seventy-three people, including forty-seven Finns. It came to be called the Italian Hall Massacre and was immortalized in a song by Woody Guthrie. An even greater calamity took place on Columbus Day in 1918, when 175 Finns, including women and children, lost their lives in the massive Cloquet–Moose Lake forest fire that swept through northeastern Minnesota. It was the deadliest tragedy for the Finnish community in America.

The Finnish immigrants were radicalized as a result of the "inhuman conditions" for workers in industrialized America. Three big labor conflicts of the early twentieth century—in 1907 and 1916 in the iron ore mines of Minnesota and in the 1913 Copper Country strike on the Upper Peninsula in neighboring Michigan—were led by Finns. The fight was about pay, mine safety, an eight-hour workday, and the right to organize. The 1907 strike involved twenty thousand miners and shut down all the mines on the Mesabi Range. All three strikes met with defeat for the striking workers. No unions were formed, and the mine owners fired and then blacklisted hundreds of strikers.

The mines in Minnesota remained "open shop" until the 1930s and in Michigan until the early 1940s, when the boom times for copper mining were long gone. "Condemn their illusions if you will," former communist agitator and functionary turned historian Carl Ross writes in a series of articles in *New York Uutiset* about the mine strikers, "but admire their courage. . . . It was no small feat for these men and women, largely of foreign birth, to stand as co-equals and even leaders of American working men and women, who had not yet won the right to trade unionism. They lost. That is all they can be criticized for. But they also pioneered."

Early Finnish radicals hoping to organize workers convened in Duluth in 1904 and established the Finnish American Labor League. At the convention, the members voted against joining the Socialist Party of America. Two

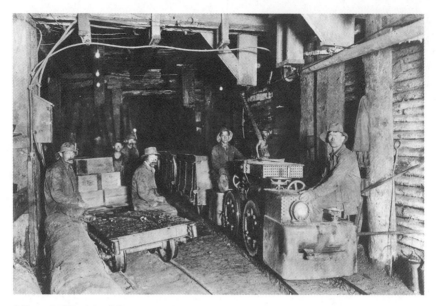

Miners in Virginia, Minnesota, circa 1910

years later, at a convention in Hibbing, the Finnish Socialist Federation was formed as part of the Socialist Party. By 1909, the federation had 5,183 members, and it grew rapidly to 15,525 members in 1914. It was the largest foreign-language group in the Socialist Party of America. The Finnish Federation also published four newspapers, ran a radical school in Duluth—Work People's College—organized clubs, and founded libraries and socialist halls that hosted lectures, dances, theater, and music. "Socialism became a way of life," writes Finnish American scholar Douglas Ollila. Between 20 and 25 percent of all Finnish immigrants were socialists. The Finnish American brand of socialism came to be called "hall socialism," where the Finn halls in the towns on the Range became centers for a wide range of daily activities as well as educational centers and centers for Marxist education. And when the American Communist Party, whose official name was the Communist Party of the United States of America (CPUSA), was founded in the early 1920s, over 40 percent of its members were Finns. In Minnesota in 1931, five hundred of the eight hundred communists were Finns. Overall, between 25 percent and 40 percent of all Finnish immigrants participated in various leftist political, cultural, and social activities.

How much of this political activism and organizing did the Finnish immigrants bring with them from their home country? There is little question that events in Finland at the turn of the twentieth century influenced both emigration and political radicalism. These were turbulent years in Finland, a time of almost constant crisis, from the Russification program of the 1890s to the General Strike of 1905, World War I, the Russian Revolution in 1917, and the civil war between Reds and Whites that followed Finland's independence from Russia in December 1917. While one single event in Sweden, the General Strike of 1909, resulted in thousands of radicals leaving for America, the Finnish radicals were forced into exile by a series of upheavals over many years.

The earliest immigrants exhibited forms of non-ideological discontent, but those who arrived in America after 1890 had been in varying degrees exposed to socialism: "Socialist ideas, quite simply, were in the air." And the General Strike in 1905 was a turning point. While before the strike the main influence would have been social democracy, after the strike, many Finns were more attuned to the idea that direct force could be used to solve social problems, writes K. Marianne Wargelin, immigration scholar and Finland's honorary consul in Minneapolis. Those who came to America after World War I were "radicalized and disenchanted from the experience of the bloody Finnish civil war and brought a new sense of urgency about the progress of socialism." To explain Finnish radicalism on the Range, Carl Ross has pointed out that it was the working class and the Social Democratic Party of Finland that led the national uprising toward independence and that the General Strike in 1905 was initiated by the social democrats, and so, he explains, when his father and the other immigrants came to America, they saw the socialist movement as the mainstream of Finnish politics, and they "expected to find a socialist movement here that could play a comparable role."

Before the 1890s, the overwhelming majority of the Finnish immigrants in America were farmers, most of them conservative. They had left to find work and to seek better opportunities, taking jobs in the mines or the lumber industry. They left in an act of defiance against the upper classes in Finland and in protest against the authoritarian Church of Finland. The departures were not viewed positively by the Finnish establishment, not the least by the conservative Lutheran clergy. The criticism sowed bitterness and alienation among those who left, and many never joined the Finnish church in America. With the traditional church increasingly irrelevant in the new world, many immigrants turned to anticlerical socialism, founded workers' societies, and built socialist halls. "If Finland prepared the immigrants for socialism, America ripened them." Oddly enough, this radicalization also drove many Finns to farming. Blacklisted miners on the Iron Range who could no longer find mining work were forced into the countryside to eke out a living on poor stump farms on cutover land where the soil barely lent itself to farming. By 1920, a quarter of all Finnish-born immigrants lived on self-owned farms, a higher ratio of ownership than most other immigrant groups—the landless from Finland had found farms in America.

The ascension of Czar Nicholas II in 1893 and the subsequent Russification program in Finland led by the Russian governor-general of Finland, Nikolai Bobrikov, introduced new reasons to leave Finland: political persecution and conscription into the Russian army. The czar's goal was to integrate Finland into his empire. Russian replaced Swedish as the official language. The Finnish army was abolished, and Finns now had to serve in the Russian military. "This political threat to Finland's traditional autonomy within the empire intensified the sense of discontent generally among Finns. . . . It no doubt strengthened the resolve of young men and others to emigrate." In 1903, Bobrikov, who had by then been given wide-ranging powers, was assassinated. The General Strike followed in 1905, after which the czar abolished the old Diet (parliament) and instituted a new one-chamber parliament. The right to vote was extended to all men and women. The new Social Democratic Party, formed in 1906, pressed for reforms. But these came too late, and Finns left for America in droves, many heading to northern Minnesota and Michigan. By 1905, the Finns were the largest foreign-born immigrant group on the Iron Range, comprising almost 40 percent of the fifteen thousand people living there, compared to 13 percent Swedes and six percent Norwegians.

In December 1917, the new Soviet state recognized Finland's independence, but the celebrations did not last long. A month later, civil war broke out, with forty thousand Russian troops still in Finland. In America, most Finnish papers backed the Reds—calling it class war and revolutionary war—while the "Church Finns" and temperance societies supported the Whites, or the official Finnish government. The brutal and bloody war, which lasted until May 1918 and left some thirty-one thousand dead, ended in a victory for the Whites. Thousands of radicals—socialists, communists, trade unionists, and strike leaders—fled the country to avoid imprisonment and even execution. About twelve thousand came to America in 1923 in the last big wave of Finnish immigration, while thousands of Reds headed east into exile and in Moscow formed the Finnish Communist Party, which was illegal in Finland.

This later wave of immigrants to America found an already politically organized community led by those who had earlier fled the Russification program. Because of the political crises at the turn of the century, "Finnish Americans obtained a very capable leadership that had a very great significance in the organization of the Finnish-American workingmen's movement in its early stages." Immigration scholar Peter Kivisto gives two primary reasons why radicalism took hold so quickly among Finnish immigrants: the timing of the immigration and the presence of intellectual leadership. Radical Finns, who were more urban and better educated than the rank and file of Finns in America, became in exile agitators for socialism. As "Apostles of Socialism," they traveled extensively in the Finnish communities all over America, setting their sights on playing a major role in changing American politics. Some stayed, some returned to Finland, both voluntarily and involuntarily, and some went back and forth between the old and the new worlds.

Alfred F. Tanner, one of the earliest of the radical leaders to leave Finland, was one of the Apostles. Others included Victor Kosonen, Martin Hendrickson, and Oskari Tokoi. They were active all over America, starting socialist organizations and newspapers in Massachusetts and New York and recruiting members on the Iron Range. Tokoi went back and forth between Finland and America and became a prominent politician, both speaker of parliament and prime minister, in the old country. The Apostles found a receptive audience among the Finns of the Iron Range, "whose antipathy to capitalism had progressively intensified" in America, and by 1903, they had gained "a solid foothold." In 1906, the radical paper *Työmies* moved from Massachusetts to Hancock, Michigan, and then, after the 1913 Copper Country strike, to Superior, Wisconsin, across the bay from Duluth, Minnesota.

Leo Laukki was a prominent radical leader who was an organizer and activist in the mining communities of northern Minnesota. His real name was Leonard Leopold Lindquist, a Finland-Swedish last name. Born to a proletarian family in Helsinki in 1880, he took a path common among working-class Finns and became an officer in the Russian army. He was also active in revolutionary activities, including in the General Strike of 1905. Laukki was eventually forced into exile because of his job as a journalist for a socialist newspaper. Once in Minnesota, he became an instructor when, in 1908, the Finnish Socialist Federation took over a school in Duluth originally opened by the Finnish Evangelical Lutheran Church. They renamed it Työväen

Opisto (Work People's College). Laukki, described as a charismatic and fiery radical, became the school's director and folded it into the IWW (Industrial Workers of the World). This hastened a split in the Socialist Federation in 1913 between the pro-IWW and anti-IWW factions. One wing kept control of the Finnish Socialist newspaper *Työmies*, headquartered in Superior, while the pro-IWW faction started a new paper in Duluth, *Sosialisti*, later renamed *Industrialisti*. Laukki became editor of the new paper, and with the help of IWW sympathizers within the Scandinavian Socialist Local in Duluth, IWW took control of the town's Socialist Party. Laukki, and the IWW, played a major role in the 1916 strike on the Mesabi Range. In the 1917 crackdown on the IWW that led to the arrest of 166 Wobblies and subsequent Chicago trial, Laukki and four other Finns were among those arrested. Laukki was sentenced to twenty years in prison. After a year in Leavenworth, he was released on bail, pending appeal, whereupon he and another jailed Finn also out on bail, Fred Jaakkola, fled to Russia. From that point on, the IWW was not a "significant force" within the ranks of Finnish American radicals. Leo Laukki was arrested and executed during the Stalin purges in 1938.

As director of the Work People's College in Duluth, Laukki recruited many gifted socialists as instructors, in particular Yrjö Sirola, who was one of Finland's foremost socialist theorists. Sirola is called by Finnish American scholars the "ideological father of Finnish-American communism" and "one of the important architects of the Bolshevik government under Lenin." Sirola's name was originally Sirén, also a Finland-Swedish name. After his studies, he became a teacher and later a journalist. In 1903, Sirola, like many other leading Finnish intellectuals, joined the Social Democratic Party. He was active in the General Strike and became deputy speaker in parliament. But as Russia tightened its grip on Finnish affairs, he, too, decided to leave, arriving in America in 1909.

Sirola didn't stay long in the United States, teaching for four years at the Work People's College before returning to Finland, where he became a communist and eventually the foreign minister in the Reds' provisional government during the civil war. When his side lost, Sirola fled to the Soviet Union, where he helped found the Communist Party of Finland. In 1925, Sirola secretly returned one more time to America under the name of Frank Miller to help persuade the Finnish American communists to reorganize the Finnish Federation of the Communist Party of America in accordance with Moscow's wishes. The reorganization was called Bolshevization, or Stalinization, and meant tighter control of all activities from Moscow. It would mean the assimilation of the Finns and the other foreign-born immigrant

This Is the School the Workers Built

IT WELCOMES YOU

The Following Courses Are Taught:

Marxian Economics   Organization Methods   Bookkeeping
Sociology   Labor Journalism   Mathematics
History of Labor   Public Speaking   Blue Print Reading
Movement   English   and Allied Subjects

THIS SCHOOL IS RUN BY WORKERS FOR WORKERS

IT IS OPEN FROM DECEMBER 1st TO MARCH 30th
It Costs You $39.00 per Month

SUMMER SCHOOL FOR JUNIORS:
June 22nd to July 17th for those aged 15 to 20
July 20th to August 14th for those from 12 to 15.

FOR FURTHER INFORMATION APPLY TO

WORK PEOPLE'S COLLEGE
Box 39, Morgan Park Sta.   Duluth, Minnesota

Advertisement for the Work People's College in Duluth, Minnesota, 1931

workers into one unit. In essence, that they would be Americanized. For the Finnish American communists, numbering about seventy-five hundred members, this would mean giving up their independence, their newspapers, cooperatives, boardinghouses, and socialist halls. "Hall socialism," a way of life for so many Finnish immigrants, was threatened, and they resisted. In the end, they had to give in, and the Finnish Federation of the Communist Party of America was dissolved. Moscow and its supporters in the American Communist Party paid a steep price. Party membership shrank by half as the Finnish American communists left the Party by the thousands.

Yrjö Sirola remained active in the Communist Party for the rest of his life and died in Moscow in 1936 at the age of sixty. John Wiita, also known as Henry Puro and one of the highest-ranking Finnish American members of the American Communist Party, met Sirola in Petrozavodsk in Soviet Karelia in 1932. "We talked all night," writes Wiita, "and I wondered whether Sirola was happy in the Soviet Union, but I did not ask, nor did he say anything."

Wiita had arrived in America in 1905, seventeen years old, and gone straight to Superior, Wisconsin, where he first worked as a longshoreman and a railroad car repairman. In 1907 he joined the Superior chapter of the Finnish Socialist Federation. It "lifted my morals, gave purpose to my life, raised my cultural level and aroused my eagerness to study and to understand social and political questions," Wiita writes. He became a journalist and worked on several radical Finnish American newspapers. He spent the World War I years in Canada under the name of Henry Puro to avoid the military draft. Later, he became dean of the Work People's College but then was forced out, a victim of the "destructive factional fight" when Laukki made the school into an IWW institute, "dragging it into the deep swamp of syndicalism." After resigning from the college, Wiita, together with other orthodox communists, was fired from the editorial staff of *Sosialisti*, again losing out to Laukki and the Wobblies. Throughout his career, Wiita always sided with the pro-Moscow faction of the Party, but by 1943, Wiita's ideological conviction had waned and he left the Party "quietly, without fanfare, as its aims, programs and action were no longer in accord with his views and especially because of what happened in Soviet Russia: Stalin's terror, the Stalin-Hitler Pact, and the treatment of those thousands of American Finns who re-emigrated, this time to Soviet Karelia to help build the new Soviet Russia." He moved to Connecticut and became a real estate agent. He died in 1981.

Ida Pasanen, born in 1872 in Asikkala, Finland, has been called a "founding mother of Finnish America" and a leading radical on the Range. She was the daughter of a Romani woman, and she never knew her father. She was self-educated and involved in the workers' movement before leaving for America in 1903, where she and her daughter Viena joined her husband in Cloquet, Minnesota. In 1907 she moved to Two Harbors on Lake Superior's North Shore, where she intensified her dedication to the socialist and union movements, woman suffrage, and feminism. By that time, she had participated as one of three women in the founding of the Finnish Socialist Federation in Hibbing. Although the federation was dominated by men— the Minnesota chapter had 2,308 men and 576 women—Finnish American women were significant players in the political and union movement on the Range. In 1911, they launched their own successful socialist newspaper, *Toveritar* (Woman Comrade). With a circulation peaking at ten thousand in 1921, it played an important role in increasing the egalitarianism of the Finnish socialist movement. Ida Pasanen was also heavily involved in education and in the Work People's College in Duluth. She was active in various cultural activities, such as theater productions, and she was a feminist, writes Wargelin, although a socialist first.

Her daughter Viena Rakel Pasanen—who was known, after her two marriages, as Viena P. Johnson and then as Viena Hendrickson—was a "tireless advocate of progressive forces." A popular public speaker, she was a leading member of the Farmer-Labor Party in the 1930s and '40s, serving as its campaign manager in Duluth in the 1936 elections. She was also president of the Duluth Farmer-Labor Women's Club and secretary-treasurer of the Minnesota Farmer-Labor Association. In 1934, she ran for the Minnesota Senate, but lost. Ten years later, she helped broker the merger of the Farmer-Labor Party and the Democratic Party to form the Democratic-Farmer-Labor Party (DFL). She and other activists in her generation on the Range viewed their work as a continuation of the struggle for justice of their immigrant parents: "Together, they saw themselves as engaged in a struggle between the forces of light and the forces of darkness. They shared a sense of historical importance of their time as a crossroads between an unjust past and a possibly better future. They poured their time, energy, and resources into this struggle."

PAMELA BRUNFELT OF Ely, Minnesota, is a third-generation Finn. She is a historian at Vermilion Community College in Ely. Her grandfather, who arrived in America in the 1890s, was very radical, something she is very proud of. He arrived radicalized after the Russification efforts in Finland. The new immigrants felt liberated when they arrived, Brunfelt told me, freed from oppressive Russian rule. There was a difference between the Swedish and Norwegian immigrants and the Finns, who "were not willing to play the political game." They never learned the English language well—it was more difficult for them than for the other Scandinavians—and they were less integrated into the community than the Swedes and Norwegians, who "chose to work within the system." But the IWW and the communists gave the Finns a voice, and they did not need to know English in their own federations. The Finns also brought a completely different kind of cooperative spirit, Brunfelt added, not based on production like the other Scandinavians with dairy and other products, but oriented to retail and other business—stores, halls, boardinghouses, funeral homes, insurance companies, credit unions. "When many of the Finns were blacklisted for their political activities, the cooperatives saved them," she said.

The Finnish immigrants pursued "collective action" as a way to adapt to the new country, finding solidarity in Finnish organizations and in cooperation in the new world. Informal community associations turned into formal organizations: first churches and temperance societies, then cooperatives, and then libraries, benefit associations, schools, choral groups, unions, political clubs, publishing houses, and newspapers—many, many newspapers. At the same time, they were divided between conservatives gathering around the Finnish Lutheran church and radicals in the socialist clubs and cooperatives. The Finns fought everyone, including each other: "Few ethnic groups of similar size have displayed such diversity—and turmoil—within their ranks."

The Finnish American communities in Minnesota gathered primarily around four institutions: churches, temperance societies, consumer cooperatives, and radical political groups. The Finnish immigrants felt freed, finding new energy leading to self-direction and independence. The immigrants were determined to build "the paradise they had crossed the ocean to find. . . . It was as though they had cast off the restraints of wardship and awakened to new aspirations . . . above all, they developed new, self-reliant leaders from their own untutored and inexperienced ranks, for the urgency of their concerns required immediate action."

One main group among the Finns was based on a conservative culture with traditions grounded in the Finnish Lutheran church and nationalism. It was out of this conservative culture that the True Finns Movement was founded in 1908, in a backlash to the 1907 strike on the Iron Range and the growth of radicalism. This movement was anti-socialist and devoted to preventing "nihilistic and anarchistic socialists" from coming to America. It ultimately failed, because the Finns were not strongly wedded to religion and to the church. The Finns were also divided along religious lines. When the Finnish state church was founded in Hancock, Michigan, in 1890 as the Suomi Synod to keep up the "absolute hegemony" of the Evangelical Lutheran Church of Finland, the religious melting pot that was America proved a potent adversary. Once in America, Finnish Lutheranism split into many competing factions, although the Suomi Synod, conservative and traditional, saw itself as the authentic offshoot of the Church of Finland and viewed the activities of the socialists as harmful.

While the role of the church in Finnish communities diminished in the United States, the cooperative movement stands out for its importance to Finnish Americans and Finnish immigration. Carl Ross argued that the cooperative movement "became the single largest business enterprise the Finns have undertaken in this country," and scholar Michael G. Karni called it the "most remarkable and most successful institution by Finns in America." While the Finns did not introduce cooperatives in America, "no national group has made a greater contribution toward the sound organization of the consumers' cooperative movement of this country, had a more idealistic concept of cooperation, or more consistently supported the idea of federation."

The movement offered a way of life for many Finnish immigrants. The first cooperatives were formed around 1878 on Michigan's Upper Peninsula, while Minnesota's first cooperative was established near Menahga in 1903, when thirteen Finnish farm families pooled their savings and contributed $170 to start a store. By 1917, there were sixty-five Finnish-sponsored cooperatives—often called "Finn stores" or "Red stores"—in Minnesota, Michigan, and Wisconsin. They dominated the retail landscape. The town of Cloquet, for example, was in the 1930s said to have the largest retail cooperative society in North America.

Finnish socialists found the idea behind the cooperatives compatible with their socialist ideology and argued that cooperatives liberated workers and farmers from capitalism. Coops became a political instrument in the class struggle. That was made clear already at the first convention of the Finnish Socialist Federation, where cooperatives were a major part of the federation's platform. During the three big Iron Range strikes, the cooperatives functioned as an outlet when miners were denied credit or services by private merchants and stores.

The last big political fight among the Finnish immigrants concerned the cooperative movement and its future direction. At issue was political neutrality and whether the coop movement should remain open to the whole working class and focus on economic change in America, or go hard left as part of the Communist Party. At the center of the conflict was the Co-operative Central Exchange (CCE), which had been formed in Superior, Wisconsin, in 1917, when fifteen cooperative societies came together to sell their products under the Red Star label, consisting of a red star with a hammer and sickle and reflecting its close ties with the communists. By 1928, the CCE supplied a hundred stores in three states and did $1.5 million in business that year alone. By 1929, the CCE was engulfed in a bitter internal struggle connected to the Bolshevization efforts in the Communist Party.

Michael G. Karni catches the atmosphere at the time: "Recalcitrant members of the CCE's board of directors were called to Moscow to explain their positions; the now-polarized Finnish radical press rose to unprecedented heights of polemic and vilification; families split over the issue; delegate votes were courted assiduously; operatives were sent to Superior from Moscow and New York; cablegrams crossed the Atlantic frequently; sporadic violence broke out; and clandestine strategy caucuses were held almost nightly."

Eventually, the battle developed into not only a serious crisis for the cooperative movement but also the most serious split among the Finnish American radicals. It had started almost innocuously when the CCE received a letter from the Communist Party of America requesting a loan of $5,000, a request that the CCE leaders turned down. Things then escalated. The CCE's annual meeting in April 1930 was dramatic. In the end, the takeover attempt failed, and the communists walked out singing the "International," although they had won the support from only 46 of the 233 delegates. The vote made clear that far from all of the twenty thousand Finnish coop members were communists or even sympathizers. With communism eliminated from the cooperative movement, the movement was free to devote itself to cooperation and making cooperative business work.

The cooperative struggle changed Finnish radicalism in America. It was the "beginning of the end" of Finnish American radicalism as an ethnic movement, and by 1940, the coop movement had little left of its earlier militant, proletarian character. The defeat of the communists "de-radicalized" many Finns and forced them "more into the mainstream of American values and culture, away from purely ethnic concerns." It marked an "important watershed" in the adjustment of Finns to American values.

In the end, sixteen cooperative societies with two thousand members followed the communists and left the CCE. They started their own Workers' and Farmers' Cooperative Unity Alliance (CUA), with nineteen stores in Minnesota, fifteen in Michigan, and five in Wisconsin. The venture lasted only ten years. Some of the stores rejoined the CCE, which had changed its name to the Central Co-operative Wholesale (CCW) and abandoned the Red Star label. Non-Finnish members also became more common, accounting for almost 30 percent of the CCW membership by the end of the 1930s. A Swede was even elected to the board of directors. By 1941 CCW claimed over fifty thousand members in 126 cooperative societies. By 1960 sales had increased to $37.7 million, but the Finnish domination had vanished. In 1963 CCW merged with Minneapolis-based Midland Cooperatives, Inc.

THE FINNISH COMMUNISTS remained active in the 1930s, rallying around their central cooperative organization, the CUA, throwing themselves into various political causes, and continuing to organize the unions and participate in the American Communist Party. For four decades, the Party was led by Gus Hall, who was born Arvo Kustaa Halberg in 1910 in Cherry, Minnesota, to Finnish immigrant parents. His father, Matti, and mother, Susanna, were blacklisted radicals on the Iron Range. Recruited by his father, Halberg joined the Communist Party at the age of seventeen and became an organizer for the Young Communist League in the Upper Midwest. He was in and out of jail for his political activities starting early in life, and he went to study at the Lenin Institute in Moscow. He returned to Minnesota and participated in the Minneapolis Teamsters' Strike of 1934, for which he was jailed for six months. After being blacklisted, he changed his name to Gus Hall and left the state. He served in the US navy during World War II. After the war, he was indicted for his political activities and sentenced to five years in prison under the Alien Registration Act. In 1951 the Supreme Court upheld the conviction and Hall fled to Mexico, but was quickly brought back to the United States to serve his sentence at Leavenworth. After his release, he resumed his political activities. In 1959 he was elected general secretary of the Communist Party of America, which he led for forty years. He ran for president of the United States four times between 1972 and 1984, at the most capturing 58,709 votes in 1976. Hall died in New York in 2000. He remained until the end a Stalinist hardliner and a Soviet loyalist.

While Gus Hall's political career took place mostly outside of Minnesota, another Finnish communist had more local impact. In 1932, Karl Emil Nygard became America's first communist mayor when he was elected to that post in Crosby, Minnesota. His victory was no accident but the "culmination of years of radical activity on the Iron Range," writes Pamela Brunfelt. It represented the "apex of radicalism in the United States before the New Deal."

Nygard was born in 1906 in Iron Bend, Wisconsin, to Finland-Swedish parents who moved to Crosby in 1911. His father had studied civil engineering at Uppsala University in Sweden but had run out of money, dropped out, and left for America, where he found work in the mines in Wisconsin and Michigan before coming to Crosby to work in the Cuyuna mines at the southern end of the Iron Range. The strike in 1916 made a big impression on ten-year-old Karl. He wrote in *New Pioneer*, the communist paper for children: "STRIKES IN THE MINES! . . . Streets Were filled with men, women and children. Deputies! Gun Thugs! Special Police! Banners were displayed. Striking miners and miners' wives marched in protest. . . . Through lines of deputies and gun thugs we marched and cheered for the solidarity of labor. What a grand day that was for me."

Nygard started working in the mines in 1923 before studying chemistry at the University of Minnesota. Lacking money, he dropped out and went back to working in the mines. He returned to Crosby in the Depression year of 1929 and became politically involved. "I couldn't understand," he said, "in this rich, wonderful country of ours . . . [why] we couldn't live a decent life, those that worked and labored and struggled to produce wealth in this country, were kicked out into the street. . . . What is wrong with this world? What is wrong with this country?"

He became an organizer and in 1930 joined the Communist Party and ran unsuccessfully for mayor of Crosby. He ran and lost again the next year, but in 1932, in his third attempt, he won, by 529 votes to 359. America had its first communist mayor.

During a visit to New York City after his election victory, Nygard said in a speech at Webster Hall in October 1933 that he had won because he had won the hearts of the workers and led them in militant demonstrations. He proclaimed that the communists would organize the workers not only in Minnesota but in the whole country. The Party "will continue to fight and grow and it will soon become the majority mass party of the American proletariat," he said. Shortly afterward, Nygard failed to get reelected, trounced by the voters, 735 to 277. His term ended quietly. In 1934, he again failed to recapture the mayoral office. Nygard never ran for political office again and soon left politics and the Communist Party, although he remained a Marxist until his death at the age of seventy-seven in 1984. "We're not Russians, we're not communists, I might say now we're Marxists, we're left-wingers as far as I'm concerned," he said.

Carl Ross also did not stay true to the Communist Party all his life. He was born Kalle Rasi in 1913 in Hancock, Michigan, of Finnish American parents, on the eve of the big Copper Country strike that year. The family soon moved to Superior, Wisconsin, where his father, John Edwin Rasi, a socialist activist who had arrived from Finland around 1900, worked as a typesetter for the communist paper *Työmies*. Father and son even lived for a while in a small apartment in the Työmies building. Growing up in Superior, young Carl's life revolved around the city's Finnish American institutions, and there was little contact with the non-Finnish community. He advanced from Midwest secretary of the Labor Sports Union, a communist youth organization in the early 1930s, to secretary of the Young Communist League of Minnesota and then to a national leadership position in New York. In 1946 he returned to Minnesota as the state secretary of the Communist Party and was active in the failed efforts by the Progressive Party to elect Henry Wallace president in 1948.

When the Communist Party decided to go underground in 1950, Ross disappeared and lived incognito on both coasts until he was arrested for harboring a fellow fugitive and served eighteen months in prison. He returned to Minnesota in 1955 but became more and more disillusioned with the Communist Party. He believed that it needed to adapt to American conditions in order to develop a theoretical basis for a domestic socialist movement rather than one guided from the Soviet Union. What was needed, he said, was "an American Marxism."

By 1956, following the Soviet Union's brutal suppression of the uprising in Hungary in October that year, Ross and his comrades could "recognize the degree and the depth of the disaster for the communist movement. It was difficult to function, it was impossible to function in Minnesota," according to Ross. Membership dropped to between three hundred and four hundred. In 1957 Ross quit the Party, realizing he was in a "no-win" situation that had gone "beyond the point of salvation." The shift he deemed necessary was never going to happen. After more than thirty years, he left the Party and politics, opened up a plating shop in Minneapolis, and started to study Finnish American history. As Ross explains, "the most important aspect was that life within the communist movement was a kind of a culturally, personally, politically integrated existence." One of its attractive features was the personal identity with a movement and its people, and undoubtedly at the bottom of it all, "a genuine sense of comradeship or fellowship." Ross had decided early in life that he wanted to be, "as Lenin used to say, a 'professional revolutionary,' a functionary in the communist movement, and I achieved that ambition. And I think that it makes for a full, interesting life. It's not one that I regret, or that I'm sorry about undertaking. . . . So in the terms of the past fifty years, at least I was not a bystander." Carl Ross died in 2004 in Minneapolis.

· · ·

> They took my friends' fathers and sometimes my friends' mothers; they took shopkeepers and musicians and actors and workers and teachers and men who swept the streets. And no one knew why. And they took my father. They took my father. They took my father.

In *They Took My Father: A Story of Idealism and Betrayal*, Mayme Sevander tells the story of her father, Oscar Corgan, who had sailed with his family from New York on April 4, 1934, to the Soviet Union to help build the new workers' paradise. Mayme was ten years old.

Oscar Corgan was born in 1887 in Nikkala, Sweden, near the Finnish border where the two nations meet at the northern tip of the Gulf of Bothnia. He left for America in 1907. His first stop was Hancock, Michigan, where he worked in the mines before settling in Superior, Wisconsin. He joined the newly formed Communist Party of America in 1919, becoming an activist and agitator while working at the newspaper *Työmies*. He was faithful to the Moscow faction of the Party through all the battles that culminated in the Party's defeat over control of the cooperative movement. Eventually, Corgan became one of two main recruiters in the effort to bring Finnish Americans to Soviet Karelia to help build the new workers' state in Soviet Russia.

Possibly as many as ten thousand Finns in North America responded to the calls to re-emigrate to Soviet Karelia. "America fever" turned to "Karelia fever." Corgan and his family were among the last to leave in this mass exodus, but it wasn't with great enthusiasm. His daughter writes that her father, a clear-eyed idealist, knew that life in Soviet Karelia would be hard. "But what else could he do? For better or worse, he had to follow his ideals. To do less would have been hypocritical, and my father was no hypocrite."

Three and a half years after arriving in Soviet Karelia, on November 4, 1937, Oscar Corgan was arrested by the Soviet secret police. He was never seen again, and it would take his daughter decades to find out what had happened to her father. He had been warned at least once, by none other than Yrjö Sirola, one of the top Finnish communists in Moscow, who had recommended that Corgan and his family return to America. Corgan ignored his advice. Sirola had expressed doubts about the future in a 1932 meeting in the Soviet Karelian capital Petrozavodsk with John Wiita, also a faithful, pro-Moscow communist, who never emigrated to Soviet Karelia. "Sirola had great reservations, as I did," Wiita writes. "He doubted whether Finnish Americans, who were used to a much higher living standard, could stand all the hardships that existed at the time in Soviet Karelia."

This was a time of great hardship also in the United States, and the disillusioned Finns left Depression-era America behind. But a return to Finland was out of the question. So they dreamed of the Soviet Union, and Soviet Karelia was next door to Finland with a language, Karelian, close to Finnish; many Reds had fled there after the Finnish civil war of 1918. The new Soviet state was the promised land for workers and a second chance for them to fulfill their dreams for a better and just world. For Karelia, the Finnish Americans brought technical skills and equipment as well as hard currency. But life in Karelia was much more difficult than they had ever imagined. Eventually, as many as half of the Finnish transplants left and returned to America and Canada, deeply disappointed. Some of them couldn't afford the trip home across the Atlantic, and they reached only Finland.

After years of searching, and two separate death certificates, Mayme Sevander finally learned the fate of her father. He had been executed on January 9, 1938, place of death unknown. By then, the other main recruiter of Finns to Soviet Karelia, Matti Tenhunen, had also become a victim of Stalin's terror. Stalin's propaganda now claimed that the Karelian exodus had been part of an anti-Soviet conspiracy whose aim was to destroy the socialist economy in Soviet Karelia and separate Karelia from the Soviet Union.

In total, several thousand Finns died in Stalin's Great Terror. Finnish immigrant Edith Koivisto of Hibbing, Minnesota, who had a passion for art, music, and acting and was active in the Finnish American radical movement, writes: "Sooner or later, they all disappeared in the bosom of Mother Russia—or were suffocated. I suppose they were looking for something, searching for a safe place to drop anchor. They were somewhat disappointed in America, they could not change the class society we have here, so they tried it elsewhere. We who stayed behind are resigned to our fate."

Mayme Sevander sums up her own fate: "I was only ten years old when my family moved to the Soviet Union. I was fourteen when my father was arrested, twenty-two when my mother died and just twenty-nine when the

Stalin era ended. A lifetime of heartbreak was packed in those nineteen years." But she was a survivor. She married and had children, became a Soviet citizen, and worked as a journalist and language teacher. Then, one day in 1986, an American delegation from Duluth arrived in Petrozavodsk and met a group of American Finns still living in the city. Sevander was one of them. Duluth and Petrozavodsk became sister cities, and eventually, after the collapse of the Soviet Union, Sevander moved to Minnesota to write and research and speak about her father and the thousands of other Finnish Americans who succumbed to "Karelia fever."

In the series of watershed moments for the radical Finns on the Iron Range in northern Minnesota, the tragedy of "Karelia fever" marked "the beginning of the decline of the Finnish-American communist movement." It lost thousands of active members of the Communist Party in this re-emigration. Carl Ross saw the Karelian emigration as "part of the recovery from the political collapse after the split in the cooperative movement." But it was, he said, "a fiasco, totally unrealistic, unnecessary, a running scandal" that separated families and uprooted people. Still, he did not see the Karelian exodus as the reason for the declining communist influence among the Finnish Americans. "The situation in the cooperatives in 1929–30 destroyed the base," he said, and so did the American Communist Party's support of the Soviets in the Finnish-Soviet War of 1939–40. That cost the communists "their intellectual or political credibility; they were literally wiped out."

Swedish immigration scholars Hans Norman and Harald Runblom view Finnish labor history in America as one of "intense frustration," seen among other things in the re-emigration to Soviet Karelia. Historians Karni, Kaups, and Ollila write about a time of "alienation, conflict and tragedy" but also about "triumphs and success, of fashioning a new culture shaped by the experiences in both Europe and America." In any case, the "total immersion," as Michael G. Karni calls it, of the Finns on the Range, "linking culture, class and labor philosophy as a way of life," is no more.

ALTHOUGH RADICAL, LEFTIST activity has long since faded from the politics of the Iron Range, the reminders of its ethnic and political past are still evident. Duluth, dubbed the Helsinki of America and the Finnish Capital of the United States, had only nine Finnish residents in 1880. But once the iron mines opened—in Vermilion in 1884, Mesabi in 1892, and Cuyuna in 1911—the Finns started arriving in great numbers. By 1920, Duluth had 3,120 Finnish residents, and they became the best organized politically among the immigrants. Duluth is still a labor town. Even today, eight of the nine members on the city council and five of the seven school board members have been endorsed by labor. *Labor World*, Minnesota's oldest labor newspaper, founded in 1896, is still published out of offices in the old Coca-Cola bottling plant, now called the Duluth Labor Temple and home to many union offices. The newspaper has a circulation of 16,700 and is edited by Larry Sillanpa (Finnish: Sillanpää).

Exploring the Twin Ports of Duluth in Minnesota and Superior across the bridge in Wisconsin, labor historian Richard Hudelson points to the many remnants of Duluth's radical past. One is Woodman Hall, a frequent spot for meetings and dances by Scandinavian socialists. Built in 1911, the hall was the scene of numerous rallies in support of striking workers. On September 14, 1916, the police prevented the Nonpartisan League's antiwar gubernatorial candidate Charles A. Lindbergh Sr. from speaking to an overflow crowd at Woodman Hall. The hall hosted speeches by Farmer-Labor governor Floyd B. Olson, as well as by leaders from the IWW and the socialist and communist parties. In the Smithville neighborhood of West Duluth, the once-thriving Work People's College doesn't look like much today, with kids' bikes strewn in front of the entrance. In 1915, the college had around 150 students, studying everything from English and bookkeeping to the works of Marx and Engels, and its teachers were the leaders of the Range's radical Finns. Across the bay in Superior, the desolate North End that borders the shipyards, docks, and railroad tracks has always been a working-class district. It was home to the radical Finnish newspaper *Työmies* as well as to the Central Co-operative Wholesale and the Tarmo boardinghouse, where as many as four hundred men stayed at one time. Finnish American life revolved around these three institutions, plus Finn Hall and the public sauna.

On an August evening, as a thick fog swept in over Duluth at the western end of Lake Superior, the city reminded me of San Francisco. The water without a horizon is not the Pacific Ocean but the world's largest inland lake, Lake Superior. The North Shore runs northeast, along Bob Dylan's Highway 61, past Two Harbors, Tofte, Lutsen, and Hovland, before it ends in Canada. The scenery is stunning. The area was settled by Norwegian immigrants, many of them fishermen, giving it the nickname the Norwegian Riviera. A few miles inland, in the middle of a landscape that could be northern Scandinavia, is the little town of Finland, settled by Finns in 1895. The town's cooperative general store has a mural covering an entire side of the building depicting life on the Range. The Finland Coop was founded in

1913 and is still member-owned, serving the town and surrounding communities. Already in the late 1920s, the store was making enough money to be sustainable, and a bigger building was constructed in 1931. As late as 1941, all board meeting minutes were written in Finnish. A sign at the entrance tells visitors that membership is still only ten dollars. To the north and west, through the deep woods, the towns of Ely, Embarrass, Palo, Virginia, and Hibbing all had sizable Finnish populations. They are located along a strip of land a hundred miles long and ten miles narrow, rich with iron ore. During the first half of the twentieth century, the Range provided 70 percent of the nation's iron ore.

"Without the iron ore of Minnesota, the later industrial revolution and massive urbanization would not have been possible," said historian Pamela Brunfelt. To her, the Range is like "an urban environment within a rural and isolated landscape," as diverse as New York City, with more than forty different ethnic groups. The towns, with synagogues and churches of all denominations, were even connected by trolley lines. The streetscapes had signs in many languages and food from many cultures. One synagogue is left, in the town of Virginia, which also has the last Jewish heritage site on the Range, the B'nai Abraham Museum and Cultural Center. The Socialist Opera House also still stands. Built in 1913, it was the headquarters for the local strike committee during the conflict of 1916. The building became a symbol for the struggle for equality and remained in the hands of workers' groups during the rest of its time as a public building. Over in Ely, the Ely Steam Bath is a reminder of the Finnish sauna heritage, and in Vaasa Township, the roads and gravestones bear Finnish names: Pulkinen, Teinila, Salo, Niemi, Kari, Koski, Mikkola, Paavola, and Heikkila. Some are World War II veterans, and most inscriptions on the gravestones are in English. Flowers and American flags decorate the graves. There are no blue-and-white Finnish flags. The Finns have become Americans.

East of Hibbing is Mesaba Co-op Park, a key institution in the history of the Finns on the Iron Range. In her book, Mayme Sevander recalls a summer as a child and "the big red flag with the gold hammer and sickle we flew, and the sky-blue skirt I wore and the red kerchief that meant I was a Young Pioneer. And I remember the camp songs we sang that said we were proud to be communists." Also called the People's Park, it was created as a result of a vibrant Finnish cooperative movement that reached its fullest expression on the Iron Range. The summers in the 1930s were "festivals of struggle," full of politics, sports, music, dances, and plays. The park was an integral part of the Finnish working-class struggle and culture on the Range, oriented toward kinship and ethnicity rather than individualism.

The main structure in the park, the pavilion, was erected on the shore of Lake North Star, and the opening dance was held here on June 29, 1930. Dances held twice a week soon drew crowds from across the Range. Regular Saturday night dances during the summer continued into the 1980s. Now in its eighty-sixth year, it's one of the few remaining coop parks in America. Finnish is no longer heard here, though one of the signs bids welcome in Finnish—"*Tervetuola!*" The campsites and cabins were quiet on a midweek summer day, and the sauna by the tranquil lake was cold. The dance pavilion, which looked exactly like an old-time *dansbana* decorated with birch branches, still found in many Scandinavian villages, was empty. On the weekend, Mesaba Co-op Park will come alive again.

7

Third Becomes First

I am not a liberal. I am what I want to be—a radical.

Floyd Bjornstjerne Olson, 1934

AS A NEW DECADE STARTED after the Great War, new political alignments were in the making, but there was no official third party yet. The war record of the Burnquist administration and the Minnesota Commission of Public Safety proved to be "important catalysts" for change, and through the Non-partisan League, important first steps in the Farmer-Labor movement had been taken. It would reach maturity in the two decades ahead.

Meanwhile, Minnesota's voters continued to choose Republican candidates as governors, as did the country at large when choosing presidents: Warren G. Harding, Calvin Coolidge, and Herbert Hoover. Minnesota voters also continued to put their trust in Scandinavian governors, in Jacob Aall Ottesen (J. A. O.) Preus, 1921–25, and Theodore Christianson, 1925–31, both Norwegian Americans.

"Good or bad, the Scandinavians monopolize Minnesota politics," said Sinclair Lewis, novelist, future Nobel Prize winner, and Minnesota native, in a 1923 speech. Scandinavians may be described as surly, socialistic, and unwilling to Americanize, he said, but the truth is that they Americanize only too quickly—much more quickly than the Americans. Lewis described former governor John A. Johnson as "a man of destiny; had he lived he would probably have been president, and possibly, a president of power and originality." And the two Farmer-Labor senators, Henrik Shipstead and Magnus Johnson, "vigorously represent everything that is pioneer, democratic, realistic, and American in our heritage."

By the end of the 1920s, the Scandinavian monopoly saw a shift in allegiances, as the long-standing bond between Scandinavian voters and the mainstream Republican Party was breaking up. The year 1928, when Christianson secured his third and final gubernatorial election victory, was in a sense the end of an era. It was the last time "the first generation Swedish and

Swedish-American editors were able to rally the entire Swedish American community to support Republican conservatism."

That shift had begun to take shape decades earlier, starting with the emergence of the Farmers' Alliance in 1890, and difficult economic conditions during the first decades of the twentieth century increasingly led voters to turn to third-party alternatives. In the aftermath of the loss by the Nonpartisan League, which supported Charles A. Lindbergh Sr. in the gubernatorial election of 1918, Scandinavian politicians such as Lindbergh, Knut Wefald, Ole J. Kvale, Henrik Shipstead, and Magnus Johnson began to gather around a new political force, the Farmer-Labor Party.

The Farmer-Labor movement was not primarily a Scandinavian ethnic movement—that would be a "distortion," writes historian Carl H. Chrislock. He points to three key parts of this political coalition: trade unionists in the Twin Cities and on the Iron Range, farmers in northwestern Minnesota, and Minnesota's German Americans, who resented the loyalty campaign during World War I. Although the first two groups were heavily Scandinavian, many Scandinavian Americans remained traditional Republicans.

The breakthrough for the new party came in 1922, when three of its four major candidates won their elections. Knud Wefald and Ole J. Kvale were elected to the US House of Representatives and Henrik Shipstead to the US Senate—all three were Norwegian Americans. Only Swedish-born Magnus Johnson failed to win, narrowly losing the gubernatorial election 295,479 votes to 309,560 for Republican J. A. O. Preus. In addition, Minnesota voters elected twenty-four Farmer-Labor candidates to the state senate and forty-six Farmer-Labor candidates to the state house. Both Wefald and Kvale beat incumbent Republicans and fellow Norwegians, Halvor Steenerson and Andrew Volstead. Their election victories were clear signs of what was to come in Minnesota politics.

Knud Wefald, born in Kragerø, Norway, in 1869, left for America when he was eighteen and eventually ended up in the town of Hawley, just east of Moorhead, in Clay County in western Minnesota. He became a manager of the Hawley Lumber Company and got involved in politics, serving as president of the Hawley village council and elected to the state house, where he served from 1913 to 1915. In 1922, he beat Steenerson to represent Minnesota's Ninth District in the US House of Representatives. After winning again in 1924, Wefald lost his reelection bid in 1926 to Republican Conrad Selvig, the son of Norwegian immigrants. Wefald then returned to Hawley, where he remained active in politics and served as an editor of *Normanden*, a Norwegian-language paper in Fargo, North Dakota. Like so many second- and third-generation Scandinavian immigrants, Wefald's son, Magnus Wefald, also became involved in Minnesota politics. A lawyer and a Republican, he was mayor of Hawley and a member of the state senate for twelve years.

Ole J. Kvale, born in Iowa in 1869, was one of six children of two Norwegian-born immigrants. He became an ordained Lutheran minister and served in the town of Benson, in Swift County in western Minnesota, where he launched his political career. After defeating Volstead in 1922, Kvale was reelected three more times to the US House of Representatives. He served until his death in 1929, when he was succeeded by his son, Paul J. Kvale, also Farmer-Labor, who served until 1939.

Henrik Shipstead became the first non-Republican US senator from Minnesota since 1863. Born in Minnesota to Norwegian immigrant parents, Shipstead was a dentist by training, and he set up his practice in Glenwood, Pope County, where he also launched his political career, first as president of the village council and then as mayor. In 1918, supported by the Nonpartisan League, he ran for US Congress but lost to Volstead, and in 1920, running for governor and again supported by the Nonpartisan League, he lost to the Republican Preus, another fellow Norwegian American. Following his 1922 election victory over incumbent Republican Frank Kellogg, Shipstead served in the Senate for almost twenty-five years. First elected as a member of the Farmer-Labor Party, he later ran as a Republican, having grown increasingly conservative and concerned about the expanding communist influence within the Farmer-Labor Party.

The fourth major Farmer-Labor candidate in 1922, Magnus Johnson, was born in Liljedal in the province of Värmland in Sweden in 1871 and came to America when he was nineteen years old. He had left school in Sweden at the age of twelve when his father died, and he went to work as a glassblower in the Liljedal Glass Works. As a young man, he discovered Hjalmar Branting and other social-democratic labor pioneers of the time, and they came to form the basis for his social and political philosophy. In America, he worked as a mill hand and lumberjack before he bought a forty-acre farm in Meeker County. Backed by the Nonpartisan League and later as a member of the Farmer-Labor Party, Johnson entered politics at the local and state levels—first as justice of the peace, township assessor, and clerk of the local school board and later serving in both chambers of the Minnesota legislature. Within months of his loss in the 1922 governor's race, Johnson was elected to fill Knute Nelson's seat after his death in 1923, making Johnson the first and only Swedish-born member of the US Senate.

Suddenly, both of Minnesota's US senators were from the Farmer-Labor Party. It did not last long. Johnson failed to get reelected in 1924 and then tried in vain in 1926 and 1936 to become Minnesota's governor. In 1932, he was elected to the US House of Representatives for one term.

Magnus Johnson championed the little people and the weak and worked for insuring bank deposits, social security, and equal pay for women. He was known for his tremendous voice that needed no microphone nor loud-speaker and for his heavily accented English. Here is how the "colorful" Swedish-born politician was described by Walfrid Engdahl, the radical ac-tivist and writer: "Bold, strong and unafraid, he stood upon the flag-draped platform, damning those who cause hardships to the farmers and the work-ers who held so fast a grip on his heart. He spoke of tariffs, of discriminatory laws, of broken pledges—his stentorian voice and his powerful fists raised against injustice and the men who plotted and schemed to beat the laboring man in an uneven contest for his very existence and life."

He challenged the US secretary of agriculture to milking contests, and once at a rally where there was no podium, he spoke from a manure spreader—that was the first time, he said, he had ever spoken from "a Re-publican platform." His opponents were not always kind, however. Johnson was called a "dirt farmer" and a "foreign socialist" as he proposed the sociali-zation of mines, railroads, power plants, and utilities. He was also for US recognition of the Soviet Union. He was often laughed at, and it was said that he was not house trained. But in the end, Magnus Johnson won praise even from those who fought against him. The *Minneapolis Journal*, Republi-can and conservative, writes that Johnson "always commanded respect and admiration even from political opponents." Former Republican governor Joseph A. A. Burnquist, a fellow Swedish American, called Johnson a "citi-zen of whom Minnesota has every reason to be proud. . . . His career is a splendid illustration of the opportunities offered in the new world to the young man of enterprise, determination and ability." When Magnus John-son died in 1936, his funeral was the largest ever in Meeker County, as many thousands paid their respects in the Litchfield Opera House.

JUST TWO YEARS AFTER Johnson came up less than fifteen thousand votes short in his bid to become the state's first Farmer-Labor governor, Floyd B. Olson, the hard-charging prosecutor from North Minneapolis, lost the 1924 election to Republican Theodore Christianson, 366,029 votes to 406,692. But the election solidified the Farmer-Labor Party's place as the main opposition party to the Republicans, as the Democratic Party's candidate came in a distant third with only 49,353 votes. The election laid the foundation for Olson's overwhelming victory six years later, thanks to a coalition of farmers, workers, socialists, isolationists, and progressives. His 1930 election victory was impressive: 473,154 votes to 289,528 for the Republican candidate, with the Democrat far behind at 29,109 votes. A Republican gubernatorial candidate had never before been beaten so badly in Minnesota politics. The 1930 victory ended twenty-five years of Republican dominance and made the Farmer-Labor Party the most successful third party in American history, so successful, in fact, that it was now Minnesota's largest political party. Olson "towered over the party and provided it with the dramatic leadership which it had lacked until his emergence." His election victory transformed Minnesota politics forever. The Floyd B. Olson era lasted until August 22, 1936. By then, after having been reelected governor twice, he was the Farmer-Labor candidate for the US Senate in the November elections. But that August day, Olson succumbed to stomach cancer and died, forty-four years old.

"His legacy is fundamental," said Minnesota historian Hyman Berman. "He established Minnesota as a progressive state, introduced reforms that are still with us today, such as the state income tax. He changed the political chess board."

Floyd Bjornstjerne Olson was born in North Minneapolis in 1891 to Paul A. Olson from Trondheim in Norway and Ida Maria Nelson from Värmland in Sweden. They had met in Minneapolis. It was not a happy home—"dysfunctional," as Berman described it. Floyd's father worked at the railroad but lacked ambition and liked his beer, while his mother, who had gone to eight years of school in Sweden, aspired to better things. Young Floyd (his mother wanted him to have an American first name while his middle name, Bjornstjerne, is supposed to have been a wish of his father, who admired the Norwegian poet and writer Bjørnstjerne Bjørnson) started to spend a lot of time around the poor, largely Jewish North Minneapolis neighborhood. He made friends and took part in the Jewish religious services as a "Shabbos Goy," a non-Jew who lit candles and performed various tasks that Jews were not permitted to do during the Sabbath. His best friend was Jewish: Abe Harris, who later became editor of the Farmer-Labor Party's newspaper and the governor's most trusted political aide. Harris was also an excellent boxer, and

Olson often served as his second during fights. Harris's family spoke Yiddish at home, and young Floyd became fluent in the language. "He was the only one who campaigned in Yiddish on the Jewish north side, and, of course, he got a hundred percent of the Jewish vote," said Berman with a laugh.

After graduating from North High School, Olson briefly entered the University of Minnesota before he took off west, to Alaska, Canada, and the Pacific Northwest, surviving on various odd jobs. In Seattle, he joined the radical Wobblies, the Industrial Workers of the World (IWW). But even then, writes his biographer George H. Mayer, Olson was more of a rebel than a radical. He admired rebellion for its own sake and was described as a "sincere crusader for the underdog." Mayer added: "Certainly, the effort to relieve human misery was the most consistent policy of his career." Eventually, Olson returned home and earned his law degree in St. Paul. In 1919, he became assistant attorney for Hennepin County, and a year later county attorney when the incumbent was forced to resign in the wake of a corruption scandal. Olson quickly made a name for himself as a tough prosecutor of racketeers and political corruption, like a modern Robin Hood dispensing justice. Olson also took on the Klan and "his successful handling of the Ku Klux Klan leaders in 1923 brought an end to the growing influence of that organization in Minneapolis." Still, Olson was something of a dark horse when he became Farmer-Labor's gubernatorial candidate in 1924, as he was almost unknown among the farmers in the reform movement. But when Charles A. Lindbergh Sr., then close to his death, withdrew his own candidature and endorsed Olson for governor, support increased substantially among the farmers. Still, Mayer writes, the nomination of Floyd B. Olson that year as the Farmer-Labor Party's gubernatorial candidate meant that the urban wing, the workers, had taken control of the party, and they remained in control until its decline in 1938.

"Many say that had Olson lived, he would have become president of the United States," said Berman. "He died just as he was about to be elected to the US Senate. He was close to Franklin D. Roosevelt when they were both governors. Had he lived he would have made a name for himself in the Senate, and in 1940, when Roosevelt chose Henry Wallace as his vice president, Olson would have been chosen. And had he been vice president when FDR died, he would have been president of the United States."

Mayer describes Olson as a man of "striking" physical appearance. He was well over six feet tall, with broad shoulders and blue eyes, "restless and half-defiant." His hair was dark, reddish brown. Admirers likened him to an "ancient Viking." Even his opponents could not resist his charm. He was a great speaker and a performer with the "effortless skill of a virtuoso." He liked people, and he loved to sing, dance, and play cards. Judge Joseph Poirier, who drove the governor around during election campaigns, once recounted that Olson, an inveterate tobacco chewer, would chew and "sing Swedish, Danish, Norwegian, and Yiddish songs by the hour," and many times he would practice yodeling.

Olson was a gifted orator, and when campaigning, he exuded self-confidence and was adept at handling even difficult moments. Bernhard LeVander tells the following story from a campaign event in northern Minnesota: A lady with a black shawl around her shoulders stepped up and asked Olson, who was accused of leading a fast life and enjoying his alcohol, "if it was in fact true that you lead a life that is less than exemplary and that these stories you hear are true about you." LeVander said that Olson "paused and waited for a moment, and then unhesitatingly said, 'Yes, lady, I'm afraid that many of the things you've heard about me are true. Would you go home tonight and pray for me?' And, of course, this electrified the audience and that ended that line of questioning."

Olson appealed for support among the Scandinavian voters in the 1930 election. An ad in the Norwegian paper *Minneapolis Tidende* said, "Floyd B. Olson—Norwegian father and Swedish mother—vote for him—Velg ham til vor Guvernør!" Politically, Olson ran as a moderate. At the Farmer-Labor Association's convention leading up to the election, which Olson had run "with such finesse that the delegates hardly knew that they had been bossed," all references to public ownership or socialist principles, including unemployment insurance, the forty-hour workweek, and state income tax, were absent from the party document. Clearly, a practical Olson felt that he and the party could only win with a moderate platform, declaring that it was the party's task "to restore the fundamentals of good government." Mayer even calls the party's platform "colorless." It "went far in removing the stigma of radicalism" from the party, and it was "bitter medicine" for many Farmer-Laborites.

As the Depression deepened—unemployment shot up to above 20 percent, prices for wheat, butter, milk, and other farm products fell drastically, and farm debt and farm foreclosures increased—the political situation for Minnesota's governor became ever more urgent. Olson supported FDR and the New Deal but felt it was not enough, and he set out, in the words of Mayer, "for a promised land halfway between Populism and Socialism."

In the election of 1932, the Farmer-Labor Party increased its control over the Minnesota governorship, as Olson captured over half a million votes compared to 334,000 for the Republican candidate. The Farmer-Labor Party now had an "unqualified mandate from the people," but impatience among Minnesota's voters, particularly among Farmer-Laborites, sharply increased. Demands for action, radical action, were heard ever more frequently, and Olson responded, becoming a "militant crusader" and the "public conscience of the state and the alter ego of the masses." That same year, Minnesota's voters gave for the first time ever their support to a Democratic candidate as president, when Franklin D. Roosevelt won the presidency.

In his inaugural address in 1933, Olson outlined a series of new actions, including unemployment insurance, protection against evictions caused by mortgage failures, a progressive state income tax, and public ownership although not pure state ownership of utilities. But the conservative forces in the state legislature were still strong, led by Anton Julius (A. J.) Rockne, a Republican lawyer and farmer, born in Minnesota to Norwegian immigrant parents. Rockne served between 1903 and 1947, both in the Minnesota house and senate. Called the Watchdog of the State Treasury, he fought Olson tooth and nail as a reflection of the "inborn distrust of rural Minnesota" toward Olson and his socialist ideas. The two collided head-on, forcing Olson at one point to threaten to declare martial law if his relief program was not approved by the legislature. Still, Olson emerged from the 1933 legislative session "with a stunning array of reforms," such as the state's first income tax, to be used for the state's public schools; reorganization of the banks; ratification of the federal amendment that prohibited child labor; a moratorium on farm foreclosures; an old-age pension system; thirteen new state forests; new incentives for business cooperatives; and shorter work hours for women in industrial jobs. Olson's final victory took place at the special legislative session at the end of the year, when five million relief dollars were appropriated. Olson's prestige and popularity stood at new heights. Using a state income tax rather than a sales tax to fund education was Olson's "notable contribution" to the state, and it "led Minnesota to develop strong public schools in spite of the Depression, something that became the hallmark of the culture in this state," Republican governor Elmer L. Andersen later wrote.

As he prepared for reelection in 1934, Olson went further than ever before at the Farmer-Labor Party convention that spring, declaring himself a radical with the ultimate goal of a "cooperative commonwealth," where the "government will stifle as much as possible the greed and avarice of the private profit system." He continued:

> Now, I am frank to say that I am not a liberal. I enjoy working on a common basis with liberals for their platforms, but I am not a liberal. I am what I want to be—I am a radical. I am a radical in the sense that I want a definite change in the system. I am not satisfied with tinkering. I am not satisfied with patching. . . . I want, however, an orderly, a sane and a constructive change. I don't want any visionary things any more than the hardest Tory or Conservative wants them. But I know the transition can take place and that, of course, it must be gradual. It can't come overnight, but I want to do all I can, to set it in motion and to keep it going steadily, not in jerks, or in jumps, or in spurts, but going steadily ahead.

Olson probably did not mean to say all this—he had deviated from his prepared text—but the audience's response was "deafening." It also caused the militants in the party to go all out in finalizing the party platform, as they interpreted the speech as a declaration of war on capitalism. The result was "the most extreme document ever drawn up by an American party actually holding political power," supporting higher taxes combined with sweeping public ownership of utilities, mines, transportation, banks, and factories. The party platform's preamble said: "We declare that capitalism has failed and that immediate steps must be taken by the people to abolish capitalism in a peaceful and lawful manner, and that a new, sane, and just society must be established, a system in which all the natural resources, machinery of production, transportation, and communication shall be owned by the government and operated democratically for the benefit of all the people, and not for the benefit of the few."

The term "cooperative commonwealth" had been used by radicals in Minnesota before, symbolizing a system based on individual freedom and the common good with an emphasis on grassroots economic organization through coops and public ownership. Its collectivism promised community participation rather than bureaucratic control.

Many in the Farmer-Labor Party were "petrified" following the adoption of this radical party platform, however. The term "political suicide" was even heard. Olson, who had left the convention early and gone to Washington,

DC, was forced to return for damage control. An amended platform was eventually hammered out without the clauses about public ownership. The leaders of the Farmer-Labor Party had in their amendment talks turned to the concept of "cooperation as a non-radical idea that fit with and yet moderated the platform's anti-capitalist rhetoric." The Scandinavian nations, they said, were model cooperative commonwealths, and the cooperative movement has made greater strides in Minnesota than anywhere else in America.

In Sweden at the time, the Social Democratic government of prime minister Per Albin Hansson had launched the idea of Folkhemmet, or the People's Home. As the Social Democrats began their long hold on power, between 1932 and 1976, it would come to mean a community that transcended the classes and aimed for a new order founded in democracy, justice, peace, and progress. Many viewed it as a third way between capitalism and socialism, where the Swedish society was built up like a family with everyone contributing and with free education and free universal health care. Swedish scholar Sten Carlsson writes that Floyd B. Olson resembled Swedish prime minister Hansson, who led the Social Democrats from 1928 to 1946. Both sought solidarity between the farmers and the workers, and Carlsson thought that Olson might have been directly influenced by Scandinavian politics. In any case, Carlsson believes that Olson, and also former Farmer-Labor senator Magnus Johnson, "went as far to the left as is possible in the United States without being shut out of the decision processes." Others have written that Olson was very much aware of the progress that Sweden had made in social and economic legislation, although, again, there was no evidence that Olson was directly influenced by Sweden. Floyd B. Olson and Per Albin Hansson never met, and the Minnesota governor never visited Sweden. Nevertheless, Olson at a minimum was aware of what was happening in Sweden. Speaking at Svenskarnas Dag (Sweden Day) in Minneapolis one year, Olson pointed toward Sweden and said, "The Swedish people understand how to use their government to promote the welfare of the people that it rules and serves."

In spite of the amended party platform, opposition to the Farmer-Labor Party persisted and continued right up until the election in the fall of 1934. Olson won again, albeit with the smallest margin of his career, 468,812 votes to the Republican's 396,359 and 176,928 for the Democratic candidate. His share of the vote had declined steadily, from 57 percent in 1930 to almost 50 percent in 1932 to 44 percent in 1934. He won thanks to the labor vote, while he lost in rural Minnesota except among the farmers in the Red River Valley. The election "foreshadowed the final disintegration of the unstable farmer-worker alliance."

Olson's last two years as governor were marked by continued political battles with the Republican-dominated Minnesota legislature, led by Rockne, under whose leadership the legislature exhibited "partisanship gone amuck." The big truckers' strike in the Twin Cities in 1934, led by Teamsters Local 574, tested the governor severely. There was no doubt where his sympathies lay, but the "employers could not forgive him for sympathy with the working-class aspirations, nor the leaders of Local 574 for refusing to join them behind the barricades." Although the governor had felt it necessary to declare martial law at one point, thanks to his political savvy he still emerged from the labor conflict with "enhanced prestige." The bitter strike ended with a clear victory for the union as its rights to negotiate were recognized. The victory came after decades of aggressive anti-labor policies, when the Republican Party and the Citizens Alliance had "ruthlessly," in William Millikan's words, used the patriotic fervor during World War I to virtually destroy the Nonpartisan League, the IWW, socialism, and the growing labor movement.

AS IT BECAME CLEAR THAT Olson would not run again for governor in 1936 but instead seek election to the US Senate, the jockeying for position among his potential successors began. Olson's health also suddenly became a factor when it was announced in December 1935 that he had undergone stomach surgery at the Mayo Clinic in Rochester and that a tumor had been found. His health deteriorated rapidly, and eight months later Floyd B. Olson was dead. His death resulted in widespread public grief, as thousands waited in line at the State Capitol to pay their respects to their "fearless and effective crusader for social justice."

Olson's governorship "remains the gold standard," and Abe Harris, Olson's boyhood friend, wrote under the headline "The Skipper Is Gone" in the *Minnesota Leader* shortly after Olson had passed: "It isn't true . . . only a dream—a more sincere man than Floyd B. Olson never engaged in public life in this or in any other state."

The power struggle that emerged within the Farmer-Labor Party after Olson's death was fierce. Although none turned out to be capable of following in his footsteps, those who felt called to succeed Olson were also Scandinavians: Hjalmar Petersen, Elmer Benson, and Magnus Johnson.

As Governor Olson's health deteriorated during the spring and summer of 1936, Hjalmar Petersen, his lieutenant governor, desperately wanted Olson to endorse him as successor before he died. In a much criticized letter to Olson, he suggested that Olson resign as governor and withdraw his Senate candidacy so that Benson could run for the Senate, and he himself for governor. Olson never replied. He died ten days later. Petersen, as lieutenant governor, finished out the remaining four months of Olson's term in office, but Benson won the party's nomination and would go on to be elected Minnesota's twenty-fourth governor in November 1936.

Hjalmar Petersen was another country editor/politician, and the last, at least so far, foreign-born governor of Minnesota. He is also, to date, Minnesota's only Danish American governor. Born in Eskildstrup, Denmark, in 1890, Petersen was the son of two shopkeepers, Lauritz and Anna K. H. Petersen. His family left for America shortly after young Hjalmar was born, settling in the Danish American town of Tyler in southwestern Minnesota. He started working at the local newspaper as a teenager. His formal

Eight Minnesota governors of Nordic descent, 1958: (left to right) *C. Elmer Andersen, Edward J. Thye, Elmer Benson, Elmer L. Andersen, Harold Stassen, Hjalmar Petersen, Luther Youngdahl, J. A. O. Preus*

education ended after seventh grade, and after a series of newspaper jobs, he moved to another Danish town, Askov, north of the Twin Cities, where he launched his own newspaper, the *Askov American*, in 1914.

During World War I Petersen sided with the Republican Party establishment in support of Governor Joseph A. A. Burnquist and his controversial Commission of Public Safety. But, writes his biographer Steven J. Keillor, Petersen started to move left after the war, closer to the Farmer-Labor Party, while still valuing his independence as a newspaper editor. He also got involved in the affairs of Askov, serving as both village clerk and mayor. By the time he ran for the Minnesota House of Representatives in 1930, he was a member of the Farmer-Labor Party. He served two terms before being elected lieutenant governor in 1934. While in the state legislature, he sponsored the state income tax law and urged that tax revenues be spent on public education. "It was undoubtedly Petersen's most important contribution to the state of Minnesota," writes Keillor.

Elmer A. Benson, the son of Norwegian immigrants, was born in 1895 in Appleton in Swift County in western Minnesota, where his father had moved after leaving Norway in 1866 to farm and to found a successful general store. His mother was the great-granddaughter of one of the signers of the 1814 Norwegian constitution, which declared independence from Denmark. As with most Scandinavians at the time, Benson's father was a traditional Republican until the ascent of Charles A. Lindbergh Sr., who became his hero. And like 90 percent of the citizens of Swift County, the father moved left to the Nonpartisan League and then to the new Farmer-Labor Party.

Governor Olson largely engineered Elmer Benson's political career, appointing him to several positions in securities and banking in his administration before asking him to complete the unexpired term of US Senator Thomas D. Schall, who had died suddenly in December 1935. Petersen strongly criticized the appointment of Benson, who had never held elective office. It was as senator that Benson won the Farmer-Labor Party's nomination as gubernatorial candidate to succeed Olson, the nomination Hjalmar Petersen had so much wanted and thought he was promised by Olson. But Benson was unanimously endorsed by the Farmer-Labor convention, and Petersen had to settle for the Railroad and Warehouse Commission, the forerunner to the Public Utilities Commission.

In the end, the 1936 election was a triumph for the Farmer-Labor Party. Elmer Benson became governor after beating his Republican opponent by almost 250,000 votes, and his fellow Scandinavian Farmer-Laborites captured almost all the rest of the state offices: Gottfrid Lindsten as lieutenant governor, C. A. Halverson as state treasurer, Harry H. Peterson as general counsel, and Hjalmar Petersen as railroad and warehouse commissioner. The only non-Farmer-Laborite to win a major statewide office was another Scandinavian, Republican Mike Holm, who was once again elected secretary of state.

Petersen's letter to Olson seeking his endorsement to succeed him as governor came at the worst possible moment, according to his biographer Keillor, and in a manner that was most damaging to his future standing within the Farmer-Labor Party. The bad blood it created between Benson and Petersen and their respective factions of the party came to mark the following two years as well as the 1938 election, when Benson sought re-election with Petersen once again challenging him. It became a bitter fight, maybe even more acrimonious than the 1918 Republican primary between Joseph A. A. Burnquist and Charles A. Lindbergh Sr.

Petersen took his case directly to the primary, realizing no doubt that Benson would likely be endorsed by the Farmer-Labor convention. Petersen, a "highly ambitious and unprincipled politician," according to historian Hyman Berman, zeroed in on two issues in his attempt to wrestle the nomination away from the incumbent governor: communism and anti-Semitism. In the anti–Olson/Benson propaganda, Jewishness was equated with communism and generally with radicalism, so that, in fact, the "anti-Semitic rhetoric of the 1930s was anti-Communist."

Local communist leaders had indeed been part of the Olson administrations, but neither the Farmer-Laborites nor the communists were interested in an alliance until the Communist International (Comintern) launched the idea of the Popular Front, which advocated alliances with local progressive parties to combat the growing fascism in Europe. In a secret meeting in October 1935, Olson and American communist leader Earl Browder agreed that individual communists could join the Farmer-Labor Party and hold office in return for communist support of the party. This alliance was strengthened in the Benson administration.

The anti-Semitic portion of Petersen's campaign focused on a small group of Jewish advisers in both the Olson and the Benson administrations, among them Olson's boyhood friend Abe Harris, who was editor of the Farmer-Labor Party newspaper the *Minnesota Leader*, and Roger Rutchik, Benson's executive secretary. Petersen did not directly attack these advisers but used the code name "Mexican Generals" to attack them and to make use of anti-Semitic innuendo, alleging that communist infiltrators had taken over the Farmer-Labor Party. At one point, Petersen explained what he meant with his "Mexican Generals" by mentioning three of them by name—Abe Harris, Roger Rutchik, and Art Jacobs—but mentioned none of Benson's non-Jewish advisers. Keillor writes that Petersen knew the facts surrounding these advisers and that there was no connection between them and the Communist Party. He argues that Petersen was not guilty of openly anti-Semitic attacks, but on the other hand, he "did little to stop and much to encourage" them. He "was simply careless about anti-Semitic appearances." But Petersen's own prejudices were revealed again and again, including in a letter quoted by Keillor: "To think of our state . . . populated by good Scandinavians, Germans, people of the British Isles, and others of that good sturdy type of citizenry, and then to behold the spectacle of such a commonwealth of two and a half millions of people being run by a little gang of individuals with whom most of our people would be ashamed to associate."

Floyd B. Olson was no communist, and he was never favorable to communist ideology and strategy. "I have not read Marx," he used to say. He did not think communism offered any hopes for changing politics in America. In a campaign speech in October 1934, he took on the accusation against himself and the Farmer-Labor Party, saying that their opponents used the Red Scare to try to frighten the good people of Minnesota: "The communists believe in the abolition of private property. We believe in its creation. The communists would confiscate whatever little private wealth the ordinary man now has. We would give him an opportunity to earn more. The communists believe the individual is created for the service and benefit of the state. We believe the state is created for the benefit and service of the individual."

In the end, Petersen lost the 1938 primary, although not by much, as only 16,030 votes separated him from Benson. He captured rural Minnesota while Benson won in the Twin Cities and on the Iron Range, winning 55 percent of the vote in Minneapolis and 79 percent in the Jewish neighborhoods in North Minneapolis. Petersen ran again for political office but lost every time. His political career was over, and "all he had left was his newspaper, his publishing company, and a house that was paid for." He did make somewhat of a political comeback in the 1950s when he was again elected to the Railroad and Warehouse Commission. He remained editor of his newspaper until his death in 1968. The *Askov American* is still published as a weekly.

Benson's political career also came to an end in 1938. Although he had once foolishly declared that he knew no communists, the issue of alleged communist affiliation, "more than any other," contributed to his defeat in the 1938 general election, which was full of "red-baiting." He received only 387,263 votes in 1938, compared to 680,342 in 1936. The Farmer-Labor Party's eight-year-long hold on power in Minnesota was over; the party never recovered. Benson was "deeply shocked and almost broken-hearted." He returned to farming near Appleton, but like his bitter enemy Hjalmar Petersen, he could not resist attempting a political comeback. In 1940, he ran for the US Senate but was crushed by Henrik Shipstead, who had by then returned to the Republican Party and collected 641,041 votes to Benson's 310,875. Benson tried again in 1942 but lost once more to another Republican, Joseph H. Ball. He never ran for office again.

By 1938, the Farmer-Labor Party entered what one scholar has called the decline, or the fourth and final stage in its history. In the first stage, from 1917 to 1924—emergence—farmers and workers joined forces to form the Nonpartisan League; the second stage, from 1924 to 1930—consolidation—led

Crown Prince Gustaf Adolf of Sweden, the future King Gustaf VI Adolf (center) with his wife, Louise Mountbatten, and Minnesota governor Elmer A. Benson (left), 1938

to Olson's election victory; and the third stage, from 1930 to 1938 was high tide, with Olson and then Benson as governors.

THE REPUBLICANS' RETURN to power in 1938 was led by a young lawyer named Harold Stassen. As head of the Young Republican League, he had set out to shift the Republican Party in a more liberal direction, calling it "enlightened capitalism." This desire for change came out of the defeats of the 1936 elections, as well as the rise of labor and class conflict during the decade. Stassen's internationalism was combined with the call for good government through civil service reforms and efforts to clean up corruption in state government. The Republican Party's long-standing policy of anti-unionism was discarded in favor of collective bargaining, including compulsory arbitration of labor disputes. Stassen called for a labor relations act modeled on laws in Norway and Sweden, and labor courts, such as the Swedish "Arbetsdomstolen," were cited as models. By 1938, at the Republican Party's Minnesota convention just a few months before the elections that won Stassen the governorship, the party platform supported a minimum wage, unemployment insurance, and social security on the state level. This was no rejection of Roosevelt's New Deal.

Stassen's election campaign stressed the charges against the Benson administration for "incompetence, corruption and blindness to communist infiltration." Stassen's efforts to cultivate a liberal image were "supplemented by an archconservative shadow campaign" of red-baiting and anti-Semitism. The Republicans picked up the anti-Semitic message of the Petersen primary campaign, and "what had largely been a whispering campaign and one of innuendo, became open, brazen, well-financed and successful." Stassen never repudiated this aspect of his campaign, although he was asked to do so by Jewish Republicans. He became governor in a landslide, 59 percent to Benson's 34 and only six percent for the Democratic Party's candidate. Historian Hyman Berman concludes, "So ended the most successful use of political anti-Semitism in the United States."

In 1948, during the first of his many failed attempts to be elected president of the United States, Stassen returned to the strong anti-communist message from his 1938 gubernatorial campaign. He tarred his opponent Thomas E. Dewey with the brush of communist sympathy and compared Dewey's hometown of New York with how Minnesota used to be, "one of the centers of communist activity." Stassen urged that the Communist Party be banned.

Stassen was of German-Czech-Norwegian descent. His father, William, was born in Minnesota, and his mother, Elsbeth Mueller, came to America from Germany when she was six years old. Stassen was reelected governor in 1940 and 1942 but resigned in April 1943 to join the war effort. He was followed as governor first by Norwegian American Edward J. Thye in 1944 and then by Swedish American Luther W. Youngdahl in 1946, 1948, and 1950. By then, the isolationism that so many Scandinavians in Minnesota had for so long advocated was dead. In fact, Stassen had said so already in a speech at the Gridiron Club dinner in Washington, DC, in December 1939: "I hope the senior leaders of my party realize it before it's too late for my party and country."

The Swedish Americans had tended to identify with Germany, much out of ethnic and cultural affinity. There is perhaps irony in the fact that so many of Minnesota's Scandinavians, many of them foreign-born and most of them with ties and relatives in their old home countries, were hostile to American involvement in the affairs of Europe. This desire to stay home and take care of the affairs of Minnesota and America transcended generations of Scandinavian immigrants. As World War II drew closer, Charles A. Lindbergh Jr., the son of the legendary congressman, followed in the isolationist footsteps of his father during World War I. Lindbergh Jr. involved himself deeply in the America First Committee, a leading antiwar organization that at its peak had over eight hundred thousand members but was dissolved three days after the Japanese attack on Pearl Harbor.

Nazi Germany's invasion of Denmark and Norway in April 1940 came as a shock for many of Minnesota's Scandinavians, and from that point on, isolationism did not have the same firm grip. At a big rally in Minneapolis on Syttende Mai—Norwegian National Day—barely a month after Hitler had occupied the two Scandinavian countries, US Senator Joseph H. Ball, a Republican and close political ally of Stassen's, attacked the America First Committee. He said that the whole point is whether we "sit back and try to stop Hitler at New York, Baltimore, and Charleston . . . or shall we help stop him at the cliffs of Dover?" The many thousands of Norwegian Americans at the rally gave Ball a standing ovation. In the fall of 1941, just a few months before Pearl Harbor, the young Lindbergh was joined by Senator Shipstead at an antiwar rally, which was met with strong criticism from internationalists in Minnesota such as Ball.

Henrik Shipstead became a leading isolationist spokesman in the US Senate, and he held on to his isolationism through and beyond World

War II. Historian Barbara Stuhler describes Shipstead's isolationism as "an intense fear of war, an aversion to the corrupt diplomacy and governments of Europe, a hatred of the powers of financiers, and a desire for America to stand perfected as an ideal for the world." His isolationism should be seen as a continuation of Charles A. Lindbergh Sr.'s opposition to American participation in World War I, and Shipstead held on through the years, opposing the League of Nations, the World Court, US entry into World War II, and the US signing the United Nations Charter. "I apologize to no one for thinking of my country first," Shipstead once said, but by the end of 1946, he would "discover that the ship had sailed." His long career in the Senate was over.

Charles A. Lindbergh Sr.'s successor as US representative from Minnesota's Sixth District, Norwegian American Harold Knutson, was also a strident isolationist. Born in Skien in Norway in 1880, Knutson was six years old when he arrived with his parents in America. Like many other Minnesota politicians, Knutson was also a journalist, editor of the *St. Cloud Daily Journal-Press*. A member of the Republican leadership, Knutson would be the only member of the US House of Representatives to serve from World War I to World War II. He voted against declaring war on Germany in 1917 together with three other Minnesota congressmen. Like Shipstead, Knutson briefly abandoned his isolationism in December 1941 to vote for the US war resolution the day after Pearl Harbor, only to return to it later, when Knutson voted against the Marshall Plan for postwar Europe and the Bretton Woods Agreements Act establishing the International Monetary Fund and the World Bank. Knutson ended his thirty-two-year career in Congress as a conservative and "unreconstructed isolationist," in contrast to Lindbergh, whose "radical isolationism embraced the progressive thinking on domestic reform issues." Still there was no question that Knutson, and Lindbergh before him, accurately reflected his constituents in the predominantly German Stearns County, where a survey of over fifty thousand voters had resulted in a ten-to-one vote against the United States entering World War II. The roll call votes in the House of Representatives between 1933 and 1950 put Minnesota as the sixth most isolationist state in the nation, and the Senate votes placed it between seventh and twelfth place. From 1939 through 1941, the nine members of Minnesota's delegation in the House of Representatives, eight Republicans and one Farmer-Laborite, rarely strayed from the isolationist doctrine.

The Republican Party's period of success during the 1940s were years of crisis for the Farmer-Labor Party, years of its "final disintegration." After 1940, the Farmer-Labor Party no longer had a US senator—Shipstead had switched to the Republican Party and Ernest Lundeen had died in a plane crash. Born of Swedish immigrant parents in South Dakota in 1878, Lundeen had served in the Minnesota state house and the US House of Representatives as a Republican during the 1910s, but switched to the Farmer-Labor Party, and in 1928 tried to break the Republicans' hold on Minnesota's governorship. He failed, defeated by Theodore Christianson. Eight years later, their roles were reversed as Lundeen handily beat Christianson to become the second Farmer-Labor US senator from Minnesota. He served only three and a half years, until his death in August 1940.

The crisis was even deeper for the Democratic Party, whose candidates for governor and senator consistently came in third, often a distant third, and no Democrats at all were represented in Minnesota's congressional delegations between 1940 and 1944. Scandinavians frustrated by the growing conservatism of the Republican Party never made the switch to the Democratic Party. Instead, they left for the Farmer-Labor Party and then largely followed it when it merged with the Democratic Party in 1944 to form the new Democratic-Farmer-Labor Party (DFL). "The merger leveraged the Scandinavian influence in Minnesota politics," said longtime DFLer David Lebedoff.

The merger talks had been encouraged by President Franklin D. Roosevelt, who sought reelection in 1944 and needed Minnesota on his side in order to win. The talks were led by Hubert Humphrey for the Democrats and Elmer Benson for Farmer-Labor, two Norwegian Americans. The April 15, 1944, merger was for Arthur Naftalin "simply the final requiem for a death" of the old Farmer-Labor Party that had occurred already in 1938. It did not end the bitter in-fighting between the new party's right-wing and left-wing factions, led by Humphrey and Benson, respectively. The DFL convention in 1946 ended in disaster for the Humphrey forces, and Humphrey himself was met by boos and shouts of "fascist" and "warmonger" in what one writer called "an outright coup." Another wrote that it was reason to believe that "for a brief period in 1947 and 1948, the Minnesota DFL became the only major American party ever to be controlled by communists."

The Humphrey faction barely managed to elect one of its own as party secretary, a young Scandinavian American named Orville Freeman. He would use his new position as a "beachhead" in the eventual comeback of the Humphrey faction at the DFL convention in 1948, when all communists and "fellow travelers" were ousted. For Hubert Humphrey, the mayor of Minneapolis since 1945, the 1948 elections were also a personal triumph as the voters of Minnesota overwhelmingly elected him the state's first US senator from the Democratic-Farmer-Labor Party.

The merger of the Farmer-Labor and Democratic parties and the subsequent ferocious battle over the future of the new DFL Party showed that Humphrey could play political hardball. Years later, in 1962, when the highly respected progressive Republican governor Elmer L. Andersen sought reelection, Humphrey paved the way late in the campaign for the DFL candidate, Karl Rolvaag, to defeat Andersen and become governor. The DFL charges against Andersen regarding a road construction project were a "smear campaign" led by Humphrey, Andersen writes bitterly in his memoir. Humphrey had never been a big favorite of Andersen's, calling him "exceedingly talented" and with "a good heart and a love for the people" but lacking "solidity of character. . . . He spent most of his political ammunition on personal advancement, not the betterment of his state."

Leading up to the 1948 presidential election, the Elmer Benson faction in the new DFL voted to support the candidacy of Roosevelt's former vice president, Henry A. Wallace. He had left the Democratic Party in December 1947 in protest against President Harry Truman's foreign policy and was running for president as head of the left-wing Progressive Party. But in the primary elections in September 1948, the nominees from the Humphrey faction won almost all important contests, and in November, Truman won an overwhelming reelection victory in Minnesota, capturing 692,966 votes to only 27,866 for Wallace.

For Benson, who had served as national cochairman of Wallace's presidential campaign, the election signaled the end of his political career. He returned, for good this time, to his farm near Appleton. In a 1980 article entitled "Politics in My Lifetime," Benson lamented the "disintegration of the progressive traditions" from the 1920s and '30s and that the current challenge was to have a "radical presence" in our politics. The Farmer-Labor Party was a "special coalition" in which the socialists always played a key role. And, yes, there were communists in the party, but "I have no apologies to make for my position . . . even though we were smeared for associating with the communist popular front point of view." About the merger and the creation of the DFL Party, Benson writes that he thought, at the time, it would renew progressive politics in Minnesota. "In retrospect . . . I think the merger was a mistake."

8

Two New Parties

"I have looked at Sweden, and I would say it is a very large part
of my overall philosophy."

Former Republican Governor Arne Helge Carlson, 2013

MINNESOTA POLITICS CHANGED dramatically during World War II and
the postwar years of the 1940s. There was no longer a third political force,
a third-party alternative. The two major parties left standing consolidated
and were, in a sense, new. Still, Minnesota's Scandinavians continued in
leadership positions as the two dominant political strains were formed: progressive Republicanism and DFL liberalism.

The Democratic-Farmer-Labor Party, whose merger was called a "mistake" by former governor Elmer Benson, became, and remains, a dominant
political force in modern Minnesota. By 1948, the fierce internal battle
within the new DFL Party was over, with the Hubert Humphrey–led faction victorious. An era closed, writes historian John Earl Haynes, and "a
decade of liberal civil war ended with the destruction of the Popular Front
alliance and the creation of an anti-communist consensus."

The Republican Party, too, was revitalized under the leadership of
Harold Stassen and evolved into a moderate and internationalist party—
as crucial as the formation of the DFL in heralding a new political era in
Minnesota. Stassen's gubernatorial election victory in 1938 was the start of
a sixteen-year reign of moderate/progressive Republicanism. Together with
Floyd B. Olson and Hubert Humphrey, Stassen "must be considered among
the founding fathers of Minnesota's modern political system," writes Albert
Eisele.

Out of this return to a more traditional, and more American, two-party
system in the postwar years, two giants in Minnesota politics stepped out
from under the DFL umbrella. Their names were Hubert Horatio Humphrey and Walter Frederick Mondale, both Norwegian Americans. Humphrey did not wear his Norwegian heritage on his sleeve, but he used it in

his political career from the start. "I used to say that when Humphrey was in trouble, he talked more about his Norwegian mother," Mondale said with a laugh.

Humphrey was born in Wallace, South Dakota, in 1911 to Christine Sannes (Kirsten Sandnes in Norway), the daughter of a sea captain. She was born at Tveit near Kristiansand in Norway in 1883 and came to America in 1887. His father, Hubert Humphrey Sr., was born in Oregon, and his family had been in America since before the Revolution. Both grandfathers were happy about the marriage, particularly the bride's father, because most Norwegian girls in the area married Swedes, whom he considered second-rate citizens.

"Dad was a Democrat among friends and neighbors who took their Republicanism—along with their religion—very seriously," Humphrey writes in his memoir. My mother "was a Republican, respectable, upstanding, and God-fearing." Humphrey's father idolized Woodrow Wilson, according to biographer Carl Solberg, who gives lovely insight into the politics of the family when Hubert was a boy in South Dakota. Once after a dinner, Solberg writes, when Hubert's mother had revealed that she had voted for the Republicans Warren Harding and Calvin Coolidge for president, his father gathered the children and said, "Now you treat your mother with respect. Don't argue with her and don't ever speak harshly to her because she's my sweetheart," adding, "But remember, sometimes she's politically unreliable."

Humphrey, a child of the Depression and a strong supporter of the New Deal, was a prairie progressive, a populist, but he was no isolationist, unlike so many from a similar background. He was an internationalist, and it was first Stassen and then Humphrey, together with the leading newspapers in the Twin Cities, who "swung the majority opinion in Minnesota over to the international side." Humphrey came to have frequent contacts with Scandinavia, both Norway and Sweden, during his political career, starting in the early 1950s. In an interview with Norwegian national radio in 1975, Humphrey talked about his relatives in Norway, about his visit in 1969 in connection with the funeral of the former United Nations secretary-general, Norwegian Trygve Lie, and about Norway's influence on his own politics. "I have a great loyalty to rural life. My family, including my mother, was mostly Republicans. My grandfather was a progressive Republican and supported Franklin Delano Roosevelt. He was a disciplinarian. Tough, hard as nails, physically. He lived until his 90s and when he was failing he said that if he could only get close to the ocean he would get well. There was a sense of hard work, frugal and self-reliant. I am very proud of my Norwegian ancestry, I truly am."

Humphrey's contacts with the ruling Swedish Social Democrats were frequent, with mutual visits starting in 1963, when he participated in a European socialist summit. Britain's Labour Party leader, Harold Wilson, and West Germany's Social Democrat, Willy Brandt, became his personal friends—"his kind of people." The summit took place at Harpsund, the summer residence of the Swedish Social Democratic prime minister Tage Erlander, just south of Stockholm. It was the beginning of a long friendship and many years of correspondence between Humphrey and Erlander. The letters start with "Dear Tage" and "Dear Hubert," even when Humphrey was US vice president between 1965 and 1969. In a letter to Erlander in December 1958, Humphrey writes to thank the Swedish leader for a luncheon in Stockholm, adding, "I will be deeply pleased if I can have the benefit of your continued judgment and counsel directly or through your embassy here. I have a high regard for you, as you know, and I will consider myself privileged to be able to hear from you further on matters of continuing interest to our two nations with all of their warm and friendly ties." And in a letter to Erlander after the election in 1964, Humphrey writes that he is looking forward to serving as vice president under Lyndon Johnson, and that "it will be my pleasure to do everything I can to help assure even more fruitful relationships between our two great and friendly nations." That year, he had wanted to attend the Harpsund summit again but, when asked, President Johnson said, "A socialist summit? My God, no!" In a 1966 New Year's greeting to Erlander, Humphrey writes, "My only regret is that I do not get to see you more often" but he looks forward to working together during the coming year. After a visit to Washington in 1965, Erlander expresses his gratitude for Humphrey's "great hospitality and generosity" with his time.

The relations between the United States and Sweden changed as the Vietnam War escalated and Erlander retired in 1969 after more than two decades as Sweden's leader. He was succeeded by Olof Palme, a major critic of the war. In November 1970, just after he was reelected to the US Senate, Humphrey jokingly asked a reporter from the Stockholm daily *Aftonbladet*, "Do you still receive Americans in Sweden? If that is the case, I will be there next year. How is Tage Erlander? Does he like being retired? Give him my best regards and say hello to Palme, too. I was going to meet with him this summer, but something came up. He is an intelligent boy."

After more than three decades in politics, beginning with his election as

Minneapolis mayor in 1945, Hubert H. Humphrey died of cancer in January 1978. Warren Spannaus, the former Minnesota attorney general, called him "an icon." Once, Spannaus recalled, Humphrey had told him never to leave a meeting until the last person had left. At a campaign stop in southwestern Minnesota during Spannaus's run for attorney general, the "whole place lit up and Humphrey spent his whole speech telling them to vote for me. Then there was a wedding in another room and we went in there and Humphrey danced with everyone. He electrified those crowds; the generosity with his time. You got to work hard. That's politics."

During Humphrey's term as mayor of Minneapolis—a city that, at the time, had a reputation for bigotry and anti-Semitism—civil rights became central to him as a political leader. His speech at the Democratic Convention in 1948, the year he ran for the US Senate for the first time, launched him as a leading liberal voice in America. The speech demanded the end of racial segregation. "The time has arrived," Humphrey said, "for the Democrats to get out of the shadow of state's rights and walk forthrightly in the bright sunshine of human rights." Humphrey won the support of a majority of convention delegates, but it led to a split in the Democratic Party and to the segregationists walking out and eventually forming the Dixiecrat Party, which nominated South Carolina senator Strom Thurmond as its presidential candidate.

Still, Harry Truman (Democrat) was reelected president, and Humphrey was overwhelmingly elected to the Senate. His subsequent sixteen years in Congress encompassed a wide range of accomplishments, from the Civil Rights and Voting Rights Acts to fair employment practices, Medicare, food stamps, Head Start, and nuclear disarmament. His solid liberal record led to the vice presidency during the Johnson administration, but his support for the Vietnam War cost him the presidential election in 1968.

Humphrey encountered both triumphs and defeats during his career, but no loss was more bitter than that to Richard Nixon in 1968. "Can you think of a politician other than Harold Stassen with more experience in losing," he said afterward. But he came back—the "happy warrior"—and was elected to the US Senate again. He just could not stay away from politics and the election campaign. But time had passed him by, an anti-communist and a Cold War warrior in the post-Vietnam era. He had inspired many, built a strong new political party in Minnesota, and gathered around him a remarkable group of public servants—from Orville Freeman to Walter Mondale.

Humphrey and Mondale had known each other since Humphrey's first Senate campaign in 1947–48, when Mondale was a young student campaign volunteer, recruited by Orville Freeman, the future governor. Many years later, when Mondale visited a dying Humphrey, the former vice president said to then–vice president Mondale: "Now it's your turn. You must carry on."

Walter Mondale, called "Fritz," was born in the little town of Ceylon in southern Minnesota in 1928. He first really took notice of his Norwegian heritage when his brother, Lester, took a trip to Norway in 1958. He was the first Mondale to visit the old country since the family arrived in America in 1857. "I started to feel a need to come closer to my Norwegian roots," Mondale told me. It was Mondale's great-grandfather who had first left for America from the village of Mundal in Sognefjord. He fought in the Union army during the Civil War. Mondale's father was a Methodist minister. He and his mother, who was of Scottish/English descent, loved Franklin Delano Roosevelt and Floyd B. Olson, Mondale writes in his memoir. They were compassionate people who believed in public service and who instilled in their son a sense of social obligation. "One thing," Mondale said, "was the belief in learning and education. There was no excuse for ignorance. You had to learn, you should learn, and you should respect learning." Journalist Finlay Lewis writes that Mondale's values were heavily influenced by the "moral vision and anger" of his father's "traumatic encounters with the vicissitudes of life" as a poor farmer and preacher who believed that the powerful would prey on the weak and "it was an article of religious faith that government had a duty to even the balance."

But, Mondale said, "they never put it to us as Norwegian values, but the idea for them was to be good Americans and learn the language, make their way in America as Americans, and while they were proud of their background, my dad never sat down and talked to me about my Scandinavian background as being uppermost as to how we should think about issues."

Mondale did not visit Scandinavia until the end of his term as vice president in the Carter administration. As he stepped off the plane in Stockholm, he is reported to have breathed deeply and said, "It smells like Minnesota!" Later he said, "I had an immediate sense of connection. You don't have to explain yourself. It's comfortable; they are very aware of the relations over here in America. They want to stay connected with those families. It was a wonderful experience." He met Olof Palme, a major critic of the Vietnam War—"We had a wonderful talk; he loved Humphrey." And in a speech in Stockholm, according to the memoir of Wilhelm Wachtmeister, Sweden's ambassador to the United States, Mondale said about Vietnam, "you were right and we were wrong." That was a brave thing for a US vice president to say, Wachtmeister writes.

In a 1975 interview with Norwegian national radio, Mondale was asked if his Norwegian ancestry influenced his political views; his answer was yes. He said he believed in education, good economic policies that create jobs, good health care, and protecting the environment, and some of this stems from those Norwegian roots. And in Minnesota, "while it is not necessary to be of a Scandinavian background, I think Minnesotans feel very comfortable with leaders of Scandinavian background." Mondale also admired the fact that the Norwegians have taken the income from their oil and placed it in a foundation for future needs and that Norway puts education and youth first. And, he added, look at Finland and its education system and the Scandinavian countries' health insurance—"I hope we will have that, too."

While expressing his admiration for Scandinavian politics and policies, Mondale thought it would be hard to draw a line from Minnesota's Scandinavian political legacy and say that the Scandinavians did this and others did that. Citing the large waves of Norwegian and Swedish immigrants coming to Minnesota and entering politics in the early twentieth century, Mondale said that this "huge presence of Scandinavian Minnesotans has had a big effect and continues to have a big effect on the fundamental direction of our state." That legacy is not a thing of the past, but it has merged with our values in Minnesota, he said, as reflected in our laws, the standards that are expected by public officers, the honesty and integrity, the basic sense of justice and decency to be found all throughout the state. Again and again Mondale brought up the issue of education and cited an example from World War II, when Minnesota had the lowest number of rejected draftees in the nation because "our kids were better trained and better educated." He gave credit to several Republican governors for supporting this tradition of putting kids first to improve the chances of the next generation. "Is what you are doing helping the next generation? That's the test. Education is the reason for our success," Mondale said. "The values we have talked about have helped nudge the state in a very positive direction."

Walter Mondale has been called "lucky" in his political career, but more than that, perhaps, he had political allies, and good friends, in the right places at the right time. Many of these were fellow Scandinavians. In 1960, Governor Orville Freeman appointed Mondale, then only thirty-two years old, Minnesota's attorney general to fill a midterm vacancy. Mondale was reelected to the office in 1962. Two years after that, Governor Karl Rolvaag appointed Mondale to fill the US Senate seat vacated by Hubert Humphrey upon his election as US vice president. Mondale was elected senator two years later and reelected in 1972. In 1976, he was elected vice president as Jimmy Carter's running mate, but they lost their reelection bid in 1980 to Ronald Reagan. In 1984, Mondale secured the presidential nomination for the Democratic Party, but he lost again to Reagan, in a landslide; Minnesota was the only state Mondale won. He ran for political office one last time in 2002, when, less than two weeks before the elections, he was asked to be the DFL's senatorial candidate following the death of incumbent Senator Paul Wellstone in a plane crash. Mondale lost to Norm Coleman, but not by much, fewer than fifty thousand out of a total of 2.245 million votes. Coleman "stood for everything I opposed," Mondale writes in his memoir. "That race was the only election I ever lost in Minnesota, and it's hard to get over that."

Like Humphrey, Walter Mondale nearly reached the pinnacle of public office in the United States, the presidency, but unlike Humphrey, he never became a leading liberal voice and was never a New Deal crusader, although his

US Secretary of Agriculture and former governor Orville Freeman, Senator Walter Mondale, Governor Karl Rolvaag, and Vice President Hubert Humphrey, 1967

political record was solidly liberal. As Minnesota attorney general, he prominently supported the right of defendants to have a lawyer, a right ultimately guaranteed by the Supreme Court in 1964. At the Democratic Convention that year, he also fought hard, but unsuccessfully, to get the Mississippi Freedom Democratic Party, a pro–civil rights party, seated at the convention. Later, as US senator, Mondale was a leader in the fight for fair housing and for fair warning regarding defective automobiles, and he fought President Nixon's antibusing school legislation. He staunchly supported President Johnson, both domestically and regarding the Vietnam War, but in the early 1970s, his position on the war changed, and he voted to end American military actions in Cambodia and to set a timetable for the withdrawal of troops from Vietnam. He also cosponsored the War Powers Resolution and was an active member of the so-called Church Committee investigating covert activities by the CIA and FBI. In the mid-1970s he led the successful effort to reform the Senate by making it easier to end a filibuster.

As the Democratic nominee for president in 1984, Mondale selected Geraldine Ferraro as his running mate—the first woman ever nominated on a national presidential ticket by a major political party. And under President Jimmy Carter he staked out a stronger partnership role as vice president, which has subsequently become the norm for the modern vice presidency.

AS HUBERT HUMPHREY MOVED onto the national political scene, not only Walter Mondale but a whole generation of successful Scandinavian candidates from the DFL Party followed him into politics. None of them were from old families or old money. Rather, they came out of very modest backgrounds, dedicated, intelligent, and able. "They made their own way," Dan Ostrom, professor emeritus at Gustavus Adolphus College, said. One of them was Orville Freeman, of both Norwegian and Swedish descent, who had become friends with Humphrey when they were students at the University of Minnesota. He used to go to Humphrey's house on Saturday nights for a pancake supper, which would often be his only hot meal of the week. Freeman not only became friends with Humphrey, he also became his closest aide and vitally important in organizing the Farmer-Labor/Democratic Party merger in 1944. Freeman earned his law degree from Minnesota, and after running unsuccessfully for governor in 1952, he was elected to the office in 1954 and then reelected for two more terms, serving from 1955 to 1961. After his terms as governor, he served eight years as US secretary of agriculture in the Kennedy and Johnson administrations.

"My father spoke Norwegian as a kid and he understood it," said his son Mike Freeman, the Hennepin County attorney general and a DFL veteran, and he shared a story that is part of the family lore from the time the first immigrants in the Freeman family arrived in Minnesota: "One of them ended up [working] in a lumberyard and went to get his pay. He said, 'I am Olof Johnson and I am here to get my pay.' 'I have already paid several Olof Johnsons,' was the reply. 'Well, I am Olof Johnson, I worked hard, so pay me!' 'I will pay you next week,' the man said, 'but you have to come back with a new name.' Next week, Olof Johnson came and said the same thing, whereupon the paymaster said, 'Aren't you the one I told to come back with a new name?' 'Yes, but I like my name.' 'Well, if you want to get paid, you get a new name.' 'Okay,' he said, 'I am Olof Freeman. I came here to be a free man. I am a free man, so pay me!' And he did."

Mike Freeman said his father "was a progressive, a very liberal man. He appointed the first black judge in Minnesota, and he got awards from Jewish organizations. Now, where did this come from? I don't know. We never talked about the old country or going back. We were Americans, and that was it." His parents took one trip to Scandinavia when Orville Freeman was governor—"not like Roger Moe who has probably been a dozen times, or Wendy Anderson." His father was never like that. "We didn't talk about it. We sometimes joked that we were mongrels, part Swedish and part Norwegian, plus a bunch of other nationalities."

Mike Freeman said that his father's Scandinavian legacy was "working hard, trying very hard to do the right thing, believing in education, believing in family, and believing in trying to leave the world a little better place—that is him, and that is me." He concluded that the Scandinavian political legacy in Minnesota is "the legacy of good government, of working hard, of caring for other people, of a strong education and providing opportunities."

Karl Rolvaag was one of Orville Freeman's close friends, and he was lieutenant governor during Freeman's governorship. In 1962, Rolvaag became the first Minnesota governor to be elected to a four-year term. He was also perhaps the most Scandinavian of all of Minnesota's postwar governors. According to his daughter, Kris Garey, Rolvaag considered himself Norwegian by nationality. "Norway was very important to my father," she said.

Rolvaag, who died in 1990, was the son of Ole E. Rølvaag, the Norwegian immigrant author of *Giants in the Earth*, the epic series about Norwegian immigration to the Dakotas and Minnesota. Rølvaag, together with Sweden's Vilhelm Moberg, was the greatest fictional chronicler of Scandinavian immigrants to America. When his father died, Karl, sixteen years old, ran away from home and worked as a logger and a miner and on the railroad out west for six years, joining the radical IWW, the Industrial Workers of the World. Upon returning home to Northfield, Minnesota, he enrolled at St. Olaf College, where his father had taught. He was drafted into the army in 1941 and was seriously wounded as a tank commander during World War II. After the war he took his whole family to Norway for a year on a Fulbright scholarship. "He thought he wanted to become an academic," said Garey. But when the family returned to America, Rolvaag entered politics.

When Rolvaag was first eligible to vote in a presidential election, in 1932, he cast his vote for the socialist candidate, Norman Thomas. His experience out west and in the army "pointed my whole direction into the DFL Party," he once said. He eventually became head of the DFL Party and achieved his first elected office in 1954 when he became Freeman's lieutenant governor.

In his lone four-year term as governor, Rolvaag did not see major accomplishments, mainly due to the fact that the state legislature was controlled by Republicans. However, he brought about reform to institutions serving the mentally ill, and he reorganized Minnesota's junior colleges into a coordinated statewide system. When he sought reelection in 1966, Rolvaag suffered the humiliation of his own party endorsing his lieutenant governor, A. M. (Sandy) Keith. But Rolvaag persisted and easily defeated Keith in the Democratic primary. He lost, however, to Republican Harold LeVander in the general election that year. He later served as US ambassador to Iceland but stayed out of politics, fighting his toughest battle: alcoholism.

Rolvaag's loss preceded what could be called the DFL's decade—the 1970s. It was the decade of the Minnesota Miracle, when the DFL controlled the governorship and had majorities in both the state senate and house. Swedish American scholar Bruce L. Larson calls the 1970 election, when thirty-seven-year-old Wendell "Wendy" Anderson became the youngest governor in the nation, a "pivotal shift in political party history to virtual one-party control of state government." He compared it to a similar Republican period, from Harold Stassen in 1939 to C. Elmer Anderson in 1955. The DFL decade was also a time when "the modern governorship and the modern legislature" took shape, according to Norwegian American politician Martin Olav Sabo. Carleton College professor Steven Schier agreed, saying that the "modern Minnesota government got its origin with the Minnesota Miracle."

Wendell Anderson won the 1970 election rather easily, claiming over 54 percent of the vote—much thanks to the support from Minnesota's Scandinavian Americans, according to Bruce Larson. Anderson "will go far," Hubert Humphrey once said to a Swedish reporter. "You have exported a lot of good people from Sweden."

Born in St. Paul in 1933, Anderson had Swedish heritage on both his father's and mother's sides. Three of his grandparents were born in Sweden, in the provinces of Västergötland and Hälsingland. He recalled that growing up, "my grandmother still read the bible in Swedish." He played ice hockey for the University of Minnesota and was a member of the silver medal–winning US team at the 1956 Winter Olympics. He remembers playing against the Swedish stars Lasse Björn, Rolle Stoltz, and Sven Tumba Johansson. Anderson says he must have been to Sweden forty times and to Norway twenty times in his life.

He loved Sweden. "I am a Swede who happens now to live in America," he wrote when he was named "Swedish American of the Year" in 1975. "I believe my Swedish heritage and the experiences and attitudes of my parents and grandparents had a significant impact on my political philosophy." He pointed to his years as governor, from 1971 to 1977, when he drastically increased state aid for education, displayed commitment to a tax system that would help redistribute wealth and care for the truly needy, and worked to protect the environment, reflecting his love for the outdoors. To him, he also wrote, "it was only natural" that a grandson of farmers and of a streetcar motorman who had lost his job because of his labor activities would join the party of Roosevelt, Truman, Kennedy, and Humphrey.

When Anderson died in 2016, the classic Swedish hymn "Tryggare kan ingen vara" (translated to English as "Children of the Heavenly Father") was sung in both languages at the memorial services at Mount Olivet Lutheran Church in Minneapolis. A Swedish flag and the blue and yellow colors greeted the hundreds of attendees at the reception after the ceremony, at which Governor Mark Dayton had called Anderson one of the state's "greatest governors"—someone straight out of central casting, tall and handsome, and with a last name ending in "son," the "quintessential" Minnesota governor. Former Minnesota Senate majority leader Roger Moe called Anderson's years as governor the "most productive" in Minnesota history. "What a legacy he leaves," Moe said.

Anderson first landed in the national spotlight in 1971, at the start of his four-year term as governor, when he followed up on his campaign promise to raise taxes so that the state would be responsible for a larger share of school financing. He won passage of an omnibus tax bill in the Minnesota legislature that raised $588 million in new taxes for increased state funding for public education from kindergarten through twelfth grade. The bill was a "fundamental reform of school finance" in the state, as described thirty-five years later by Sabo, the DFL's minority leader in the Minnesota house at the time. It raised "just about every state tax in sight" and increased the state's support for education from 43 percent of operating costs to 65 percent while reducing property taxes by more than 18 percent. It was a drastic change. Previously most of the resources for education came from local property taxes, which had been rapidly increasing and causing massive and angry protests. In the end, 72 percent of the DFL caucus and 43 percent of the Republicans in the house supported the tax bill, while the support in the senate was 88 percent and 35 percent, respectively. It was a truly bipartisan compromise.

"They came together," DFL Party chairman Ken Martin said, "and they said that if Minnesota is going to be something else but a cold Omaha, then we need to improve education and make it the cornerstone of our state. And for decades they have, together, made significant investments in education. They understood that was going to make our state prosperous."

The bill was part of what came to be called the Minnesota Miracle—the high tide of liberalism in Minnesota—not only because it raised taxes to such a degree but also, and maybe even more so, because it was done when both the state senate and house were controlled by Republicans. On August 13, 1973, Governor Anderson landed on the cover of *Time* magazine with the headline "The Good Life in Minnesota." The article described Minnesota as "the state that works," led by a governor with "athletic dash and youthful charm," reminiscent of John F. Kennedy.

The Republicans controlled the state legislature, but the Scandinavian Republicans were split on the big tax bill. In the house, majority leader Ernest A. Lindstrom was strongly opposed, while in the senate, majority leader Stanley W. Holmquist became an ally of the governor. Holmquist, a former teacher, principal, and superintendent of Grove City schools "was philosophically with us and made a great difference," former governor Anderson said in a Minnesota Miracle roundtable discussion many years later, to which Sabo added, "I don't think there's any way you would achieve the bipartisan support without Stan Holmquist's involvement." Holmquist was former Republican governor Elmer L. Andersen's brother-in-law, and Andersen later wrote in his memoir that Holmquist was no "penny pincher" when it came to education and he "deserves a great deal of credit for convincing the senate to go along" with Governor Wendell Anderson. Holmquist's father, Victor, had emigrated at a young age from Sweden with his parents and settled in Hallock in Kittson County in the northwestern corner of Minnesota, close to the Canadian border. The father had also been a member of the legislature, first supported by the Nonpartisan League and later as a conservative, but then becoming a Democrat.

The 1972 elections resulted in a big DFL victory. The party won majorities in both the state senate and the house. Norwegian American Martin Olav Sabo became speaker of the house and Irish American Nick Coleman the party's first senate majority leader. The legislators who had supported Anderson and the tax bill met with success in their reelection efforts, as 89.8 percent of those house members who ran again earned victory. The fact that so many of those who voted for the tax hike were reelected, from both parties, tells you, Wendell Anderson said, "that Minnesota voters are willing to accept some pain if they understand why it's necessary."

Anderson's hold on the electorate continued in 1974, when he won over 62 percent of the vote and came out ahead in all of Minnesota's eighty-seven counties. Other leading DFL officeholders were also reelected, and the DFL increased its majorities in both the state senate and house. The election success produced a series of bills that were approved during the following legislative sessions, many of which passed with support from Republicans, including the future governor, Swedish American Arne Carlson, who was then an assistant minority leader in the state house. The bills included an expanded Environmental Policy Act (MEPA), expanded health care, the state's first handgun control bill, a statewide minimum wage, one of the nation's most comprehensive ethics and election reform bills, and a new data privacy law, drafted by Swedish American legislator John Lindstrom from Willmar with the help of the young Swedish American lawyer Brad Engdahl, based on a Swedish privacy model. "It was Brad who found the Swedish law," Lindstrom recalled. "It was so clear and comprehensible.... There was nothing like that in Minnesota at the time."

The DFL success did not last forever. The decline began when Wendell Anderson resigned as governor in late 1976 to assume the US Senate seat Walter Mondale had vacated upon his election as vice president. It was a politically unpopular move, and Anderson lost his election bid for a full Senate term in 1978. His successor as governor, lieutenant governor Rudy Perpich, of Croatian descent and Minnesota's first Catholic governor, also lost in his bid for a full term. So did the DFL's other Senate candidate, Bob Short. The

Republican sweep ended Anderson's political career and the DFL's reign in the Minnesota legislature. Writes former DFL legislator Tom Berg, "The 1978 election marked the end of a historic era, an era in which the sovereign state government began to respond to the legitimate concerns of the majority of the people of the state and not just the concerns of a handful of powerful special-interest groups."

THE DECADE THAT HAD STARTED with the Minnesota Miracle ended with the Minnesota Massacre. It was a "massacre" for the DFL Party but a triumph for the Republican Party.

Among the Republican winners in the 1978 election were a new governor, Norwegian American Albert (Al) Quie, and two new US senators, Dave Durenberger and Rudy Boschwitz, both German Americans. The victories of Durenberger, a Catholic, and Boschwitz, Jewish and born in Germany, constituted a "notable ethnic leap for the Republican Party, which had traditionally run Scandinavian Lutherans for statewide office."

Quie, and later Arne Carlson in the 1990s, belongs to the long string of Scandinavian Republican governors in Minnesota since World War II, along with Luther W. Youngdahl (1946–51), Elmer L. Andersen (1961–63), and Harold LeVander (1967–71). Quie's three Republican predecessors represented a progressive Republicanism of a type not seen in today's Minnesota, nor in today's America, for that matter. Historian John E. Haynes attempts to describe their leadership, writing, "One is tempted to see progressive Republicanism as a sort of secularized Scandinavian Lutheranism: earnest, moralistic, well-meaning, and moderate."

They "fit a distinctively progressive mold of Republicanism that has shaped Minnesota and helped produce a state that for many decades has been described as one of the most successful and prosperous in the nation," Russell Fridley and Dane Smith, two experienced observers of Minnesota history and politics, wrote in 2008. And as an illustration of how impossible this kind of politics would be today, they offered the following: "Picture a Republican governor . . . proudly calling himself a 'liberal,' pushing for tax increases and higher-education improvements, advancing civil liberties and human rights, setting aside thousands of acres of wilderness protections and embracing the very concept of government as the way we do things together. This actually happened."

The three, Youngdahl, Andersen, and LeVander, had much in common. They were all born in America, children of Scandinavian immigrants.

Youngdahl's father came to America from Malmö in Sweden in 1886, twenty-six years old. Andersen's father, Arne Kjelsberg, changed his last name to Andersen after he came to America from Solør in Norway; Andersen's mother was the daughter of a Swedish-born seaman and a Norwegian woman from Christiania who had met in Muskegon, Michigan. LeVander's father was born out of wedlock in Småland in Sweden, the son of a deaf-mute maid and a local pastor, N. P. Löfvander. At the age of nineteen, he left for America and took the name LeVander and also became a pastor. Harold LeVander's mother was born in Michigan, the daughter of two Swedish-born immigrants. According to Harold's brother Bernhard, their father was not politically active but might have been sympathetic toward the Nonpartisan League and was an admirer of Floyd B. Olson. The sons, however, became Republicans. Harold worked in Harold Stassen's law firm, and Bernhard got involved in Stassen's first campaign for governor in 1938 and became a leading member of the so-called Stassen Group. In 1946, Bernard became chairman of the Minnesota Republican Party. That year, in this capacity and as an emissary of Stassen, he asked Luther Youngdahl if he would be interested in running for governor.

Youngdahl played football in college and loved the outdoors. He was not really a politician. His first love was the law. He was a municipal judge and an associate justice of the Minnesota Supreme Court before being elected governor in 1946. After resigning from the governorship in 1951, he returned to the law as a federal judge in Washington, DC. Bernhard's reasons for asking Youngdahl to run for governor were, according to Youngdahl's biography, his public service record on the bench and in the community, his reputation as a public speaker, his familiar Scandinavian name, his remarkable record for winning large majorities in judicial elections in areas of the state where the Republicans were weak, his reputation for integrity, and his liberal political views. Youngdahl's biographer, Robert Esbjornson, adds:

> It was not just his [Youngdahl's] name that was political capital,
> but his personality as well. A man who "always takes a good pic-
> ture," he is an excellent example of the Nordic type of personality
> that has been idealized in Minnesota cultural traditions. He is a
> physical specimen reminiscent of the legendary "big Swede" of
> pioneer days whose feats are glorified in the mythical Paul Bunyan
> stories. Standing over six feet tall and weighing over 200 pounds,
> he possesses what seems to be an inexhaustible supply of energy.

Silver-haired, with a ruddy complexion and blue eyes, and a hearty disposition, his physical attributes distinguish him as the kind of man no one could mistake for anything but a Swede.

As governor, this "big Swede" became a crusader, launching a series of measures as part of a program that came to be called Honesty and Humanity in Government. He took on the strong gambling industry in Minnesota, and slot machines were outlawed. He served as a labor mediator and headed off several strikes during his first term as governor. He launched a new school aid program, and the University of Minnesota received the most money in its history during his first term. He threw his energy into improving Minnesota's mental health program, and Bernhard LeVander described him as "the father of a new day for mental health in Minnesota." His campaign for the mentally ill, called the "Crusade for Forgotten Souls" by the press, was waged on the radio and in speeches around the state. At Anoka State Hospital, he personally set fire to a pile of straightjackets, straps, and manacles as a symbol of his efforts to reform the mental health system. The bonfire produced big headlines, and by the spring of 1949, during his second term in office, a sweeping new mental health bill was approved with bipartisan support in the state legislature. Youngdahl also ended segregation in the Minnesota National Guard by executive order in September 1949, and under his leadership, Minnesota became the first state to help displaced persons in Europe after World War II—by October 1949, the state had received twenty-five hundred. And he just kept on winning at the polls. Youngdahl's third and final election victory, in November 1950, came with the largest plurality of his career, as he drew more than 60 percent of the votes.

Luther Youngdahl and Harold LeVander—"oh, they were really Swedes," said former Minnesota Supreme Court justice and LeVander's former law partner Paul H. Anderson. LeVander was "so proud" of his Swedish heritage: "He wore a ring from his father with words inscribed that drove his governorship: "To succeed—serve!" He served, adhering to his father's message that you don't go into government to destroy it, you go to serve, to make it work for the people. Did LeVander's Swedish heritage influence him as a governor? "Oh, yes, absolutely," Anderson said.

When Governor LeVander visited Sweden in July 1968, on the first annual *Minnesotadagen*—Minnesota Day—the Stockholm daily *Aftonbladet* reported about the minister's son from Småland who conversed freely in Swedish. Twenty years earlier, *Aftonbladet* had also amply covered Governor

Youngdahl's trip to Sweden and Norway. The 1948 visit included a gala dinner and dance, hosted by Prince Carl Bernadotte and with the diplomatic corps in full attendance. There was also a large reception, hosted by the Minnesota governor in Stockholm's city hall, for relatives of Swedes in Minnesota. And Elmer Andersen writes in his memoir about his own trip to Norway, Sweden, and Finland after he narrowly lost his reelection bid in 1962. The trip included visits with relatives in Norway and Sweden and a lunch with Finland's president Urho Kekkonen in Helsinki, where the former governor was awarded the Commander Cross of the Order of the Lion of Finland.

These were well-educated men. Two of them, Youngdahl and LeVander, were lawyers. All three were steeped in the Lutheran church. Youngdahl was raised by strict Lutheran parents, LeVander was the son of a Lutheran minister, and Andersen met his future wife when they were students and attended Grace University Lutheran Church, where they also both taught Sunday school. They were Republicans, but not party men. They were independent. A progressive pragmatism guided them in politics. They were not easy to pinpoint, and Paul H. Anderson described LeVander as a conservative but also as a prairie progressive. All three had "this sense of obligation to a larger community." Their goal was good and clean government; their goal was to do good. Andersen says that he learned to be "honest, decent, kind, generous, civil" at his church.

Elmer L. Andersen was often called "Minnesota's leading citizen." In his memoir, *A Man's Reach*, published in 2000 when he was eighty-nine, four years before he died, Andersen describes himself as a liberal Republican who admired Franklin Roosevelt but never voted for him and who became more independent "as the Republican Party has moved steadily toward the right." He continues, "It grieves me that my Republican Party ... is so far off track." It is unfortunate, he adds, that a "militant anti-abortion minority has held sway for two decades or more in the state Republican Party." He was "never in favor of cutting taxes" and could not support the party's "anti-Federalism philosophy." He goes on: "I see government as the people's partner, a useful tool in getting the people's work done. I hate the impression that some politicians convey today that government dominates people and that they have to minimize government. Government is the way people have of getting together and cooperating to get things done." As a consequence, Andersen explains, in his later years he has supported Democratic candidates.

Historian Hyman Berman said that he did not believe that Elmer Andersen was a Republican at the end of his life: "I saw him about a month or so before he passed away just before the Kerry-Bush election [in 2004], and he asked me to come by his house. I did not know his address, but I knew approximately where he lived, and he said, 'don't worry, you'll find my house.' It turned out to be the only one that had a Kerry sign on the lawn in front of the house. All the others had Bush signs."

Andersen followed in the tradition of Youngdahl and emphasized humanitarian issues, human values, and welfare. He served for nine years in the Minnesota Senate, where he championed a groundbreaking Fair Employment Practices Act, similar to what Youngdahl had advocated that failed to win legislative approval. Andersen was also instrumental, together with fellow Scandinavians like Al Quie and Stanley Holmquist, of pushing through programs for special education for children. As governor, Andersen opposed a sales tax, unlike many Republicans, because, he argued, it was unfair to low-income and senior Minnesotans; he championed a new fair housing bill, which he saw as an "important companion" to the Fair Employment Practices Act; he ensured fair taxation for the taconite industry; and he led the way for the establishment of Voyageurs National Park, although he gives much credit for its ultimate success to Charles A. Lindbergh Jr.

Andersen's reelection loss in 1962 to the DFL's Karl Rolvaag was a heartbreaker for Andersen and the Republicans. Bernhard LeVander said "it should never have happened." But, he added, Andersen always played his cards close to the vest, tended to compromise too quickly, and never developed a network. "If Elmer would have listened, taken advice and sought advice, developed some loyalty, and charged ahead on some issues," he would not have lost.

Bernhard LeVander was a close advisor to his older brother Harold, who defeated Rolvaag for governor at the next election, in 1966. The elder LeVander brother had been a top athlete as a young man and set several state collegiate track records. He was often seen as a non-politician and was less politically active than his brother Bernhard. Harold pretty much stuck to being a lawyer, but he was also active in his Lutheran church and in the Lutheran Brotherhood. He had never held elective office before he surprisingly decided to run for governor, and he returned to his law practice after his equally surprising decision not to seek reelection in 1970—paving the way for the governorship of Wendell Anderson.

During his one term as Minnesota's governor, from 1967 to 1971, LeVander followed in Youngdahl's and Andersen's footsteps as progressive Republicans, although he introduced a sales tax that Andersen had vigorously opposed. LeVander established the Metropolitan Council to spearhead regional planning in the Twin Cities and created the state's Pollution Control Agency and its Human Rights Department. Education was a priority, as it had been for Youngdahl and Andersen, and the state's education budget increased dramatically.

Following the DFL decade of the 1970s, the next two Scandinavian governors, Al Quie and Arne Carlson, both ran initially as Independent-Republicans, as the state party sought to distance itself from the national party tainted by the Watergate scandal.

All four of Al Quie's grandparents were Norwegian Americans, while Arne Helge Carlson, born in New York City, was the son of Swedish immigrants—his father from Göteborg and his mother from Visby on the island of Gotland in the Baltic Sea. Quie, born in 1923, is an imposing man with the powerful hands of a farmer and a horseman. His Norwegian heritage is important to him. "My parents spoke Norwegian and my mother made sure we learned both English and Norwegian. Yes, Norway and the culture and the language were a big part of my childhood and upbringing, but in politics, I had gotten beyond that," he said. Asked whether he ever tried to implement something that he learned about Scandinavia in Minnesota, after some reflection he answered "no." To Quie, a deeply religious man, being a politician allowed him to "serve in politics and to serve the Lord at the same time." He said he admires a legislator who is open-minded and seeks the facts, studies the issues, knows the history, and lays out where we should go. He said Elmer L. Andersen was a perfect example of a person who operated this way. But, he asked, "is that the Scandinavian legacy in Minnesota? I can't give you an answer."

As the social issues of abortion and gay rights came to the forefront in the political debate all over America during the 2010s, Quie took a hardline conservative stand, opposing abortion, and he left the Evangelical Lutheran Church in America (ELCA) when it decided to ordain practicing homosexuals. "That's contrary to the Bible," Quie said, "but we go to an ELCA church because of my wife's illness, where we know everyone, and I think that's more important."

During his one term as governor from 1979 to 1983, Quie had been an independent who openly declared that he was going to do the right thing even if it meant going against his own party. Decades later, in December 2010, in what was reported in the media as a "dramatic display of the new Republican order," Quie, Arne Carlson, and sixteen other prominent party members in Minnesota were banished from the state Republican Party as a punishment for supporting a third-party candidate for governor, the Republican-turned-Independent Tom Horner. "I am still a member of the national Republican Party though," Quie explained with a laugh.

Quie did not seek reelection in 1982. He had served under difficult economic times for the state and faced a serious budget deficit, and although opposed to raising taxes, he finally approved a tax increase to balance the budget. Quie was also instrumental in taking politics out of the selection of state judges by creating a "merit system" that is now the law. When he left the governorship, he was sixty years old. During his long political career, Quie had earned respect across party lines. Before serving as governor, he had been a state senator (1955–58) and for more than twenty years (1958–79) a member of the US House of Representatives. He had been mentioned as a possible vice president when Gerald Ford became president after Richard Nixon's resignation in 1974. He has stayed involved in public life in Minnesota and has for years been active in the Prison Fellowship program both in Minnesota and nationally. "A truly remarkable man," as Roger Moe once wrote.

"Arne Carlson—I thought he had a wonderful name for a Minnesota politician—a short Scandinavian name that is distinctive and easy to remember," writes Elmer L. Andersen about Arne Helge Carlson, Minnesota's thirty-seventh governor and the last of the century's moderate-progressive Scandinavian Republican governors. Born in New York City during the Depression, Carlson did not have an easy childhood. His parents were poor and for a while the family lived in a tarpaper shack in the poorest section of the Bronx. In 1947 the whole family moved back to Sweden to look for new opportunities, and the future governor went to school in Visby and Göteborg. But the family soon returned to America. Arne Carlson was a good student and received a scholarship that allowed him to attend the Choate School, a prestigious private boarding school in Connecticut. From there, again on a scholarship, he attended the equally prestigious Williams College in western Massachusetts before he came west to graduate school at the University of Minnesota. He stayed in Minnesota, where his brother, Lars, and his parents eventually joined him. Carlson's first elected office was as a Minneapolis city councilman from 1965 to 1967, and he served in the Minnesota house before he was elected state auditor, a position he held from 1979 until his inauguration as governor in January 1991.

Carlson started out as a Democrat, campaigning for Hubert Humphrey, but he became a Republican largely because of governor Elmer L. Andersen: "I was very fond of him, a wonderful person, very principled, very focused," Carlson said. Arne Carlson likes to talk, and he likes people who speak truthfully, and he laments, as he sees it, that people have become so guarded. He thinks people respond well to candor even if they don't agree: "I tried to be truthful, and it allowed us to have a high trust level with people."

As governor, Carlson took office at a time when the state faced serious financial problems. Eventually, he turned the deficit into a budget surplus, restored the state's AAA bond rating, and oversaw welfare and workers' compensation reform as well as health care reform through the newly created MinnesotaCare, which gave many low-income Minnesotans access to health care. As with previous Scandinavian governors, education was a priority for Carlson. He was a proponent of school choice and paved the way in 1991 for the first charter schools, not only in Minnesota but in the whole country, and for new school choice legislation in 1996. "Arne was a moderate Republican and the candidate I most identified with, an excellent governor," said Paul H. Anderson. "He was the epitome of the old, progressive Republican Party."

In the 1994 gubernatorial election, Carlson became the first sitting Republican governor in Minnesota history to be denied his party's endorsement. "I don't know how many times in American history a sitting governor was denied endorsement. But the rudeness was rather stunning," Carlson said in an interview. The party chose Allen Quist, a conservative anti-abortionist with a Scandinavian last name, who opposed Carlson's pro-choice position and regarded him as too liberal. But Carlson won the Republican primary and went on to crush his DFL opponent, John Marty, by over half a million votes, 63 percent to 34.

Carlson's bonds with and affinity for Sweden are strong: "I would say it [Sweden] is a very large part of my overall philosophy. I think there is a level of care and a level of decency that I would like to see in the United States." He said he never bought into labeling Sweden "socialist": "We have to take off our blinders which say that under no circumstances are we going to emulate those socialist countries. That's nonsense. No, I think the parameters that the Swedes have set up are very valid and they should play a role here. We are not doing enough for the disadvantaged. Homelessness is not getting better; it is getting worse. Head Start is cut.... Now, tell me if that is a sign of a civilized society." He continued, as if referencing his own poor childhood, "I think that the US is a very difficult country [in which] to be poor. Poverty here is real poverty, young people living in tents and trying to go to school—that's a serious problem. I believe that Sweden has nothing that even remotely resembles that kind of poverty. On the other hand, they don't have the extreme wealth, so what they have appeared to have done is to build a broader middle, and I think the US has to begin to evaluate how we rebuild the middle class."

Arne Carlson, Minnesota's governor from 1991 to 1999, thinks most people see him as "the last of the old-time governors." Like Elmer L. Andersen, Carlson has supported local non-Republican candidates after he left office, and he supported Barack Obama for president in 2008. Asked if he is still a Republican, he answered, "I think it is fair to say, and to be truthful to myself, I am very independent, always have been, a bit of a contrarian. No, I have no identity with the new group of people in the Republican Party who have taken over and have the audacity to say that god is on their side.... We have lost that sense of progressivism which was such a large part of our history." In 2016, he endorsed Hillary Clinton.

Carlson has kept politically active in retirement. He likes the phrase "the common good" and often comes back to it, arguing that in today's Minnesota "we are not pulling together for the common good." He has publicly opposed conservative former Republican congresswoman Michele Bachmann, and he once wrote, "I truly hope this new Republican Party gets out of the Ayn Rand syndrome and begins to recognize the role of balance and the strength of community." He pleaded for action by politicians and the community to save the Minnesota Orchestra, which went silent during a year-long labor conflict. He and Wendell Anderson cochaired the campaign for the Legacy Amendment in 2008, when Minnesotans by a margin of 56 to 39 voted to raise the state's sales tax by three-eighths of a cent to create four funds to "preserve Minnesota's history and cultural heritage." Since then, over one billion dollars for the arts, the outdoors, and clean water have been authorized.

In 2012 Carlson was involved in contentious political battles when he went against his own party and opposed two Republican-supported constitutional amendments—one banning same-sex marriage, the other favoring new voter photo IDs. Minnesota's voters said no to both amendments. The same-sex marriage amendment was a "dreadful proposal clearly aimed at helping this new Republican Party to get out the vote," Carlson said. And the new voter IDs—"what an insidious thing that was," he added. The former Republican governor teamed up with former Democratic vice president Walter Mondale to fight it: "It started out with about 80 percent support for

Portrait of Governor Arne Carlson, painted by Stephen A. Gjertson

photo IDs, but, ultimately, once Minnesotans understood, it went down to defeat. I think you have to take the rascals on."

In the state legislature, there are still many members, in both parties, with Scandinavian names. Both DFL leaders in the senate and the house are Scandinavians, Tom Bakk and Paul Thissen. Bakk's ancestors are Finland-Swedes and Finnish/Norwegian, while Thissen's came from Norway many generations ago. The two don't know much about who came before them, and neither one of them has visited Scandinavia. "I don't think of myself as a Scandinavian politician," Thissen told me, "although in some sense I guess I do because it allows me to connect with people in a particular way. It's still an asset in Minnesota to be of Norwegian or Scandinavian descent." And Bakk, who comes from the Iron Range, sees his district as still largely Scandinavian, where "government is part of the solution to the problems in our community." Bakk's father's only Swedish expression, which his mother used to tell him in Swedish, was "an education is not very heavy to carry around."

ALTHOUGH THE NUMBER OF Minnesota state legislators with Scandinavian names is not what it was a century ago, Scandinavian ancestry is still important to many. Laurie Halverson, with a family steeped in politics, is part of the new generation of Scandinavian Americans in state politics: "I feel so connected to Sweden, but I have never been there. I dream to go. My son is adopted from Korea and I named him Kai."

In November 2014, as the DFL's "Get Out the Vote Statewide Bus Tour" left the State Capitol in St. Paul and headed out across Minnesota, state representative Halverson was waiting in suburban Eagan a few miles to the south to join them and plead her case to the voters for their continued support after her first term in the state house. Eagan is in House District 51B, a typical swing district. None of the officeholders in the four elections prior to 2014 had been reelected. "And if history is a judge," a staffer said a few days before that year's election, "Laurie will lose." But even as her party lost control of the Minnesota house, Halverson went against the tide and won reelection, actually squeezed through. She beat her Republican challenger by 391 votes. That was a lot fewer than the 912 votes by which she won her first election in 2012. That was a banner year for Democrats, with President Barack Obama winning big not only in Minnesota but in the country as a whole and with Democrats winning majorities in both houses of the Minnesota legislature.

Laurie Halverson's maiden name is Nelson. She was born in Lindström (officially spelled with the umlaut) in Chisago County, the epicenter of early Swedish immigration to Minnesota. She studied Swedish in high school and worked in a nursing home with lot of old Swedes—one woman always called her "Swedish girl." She is a sixth-generation Minnesotan with both a Danish and a Swedish branch among her ancestors. Her maiden name comes from the Danish side of her family after her Danish-born great-great-grandfather, Jens Nielsen, who changed his last name to Nelson. Her great-grandfather's uncle, George A. Nelson, was born in 1873 in Milltown, in an area called West Denmark, in Polk County, Wisconsin, across the St. Croix River from Chisago County. He was a dirt farmer and active in the cooperative movement. After hearing the socialist Eugene Debs speak in town, he joined the Social Democratic Party of America and, in 1899, was elected to the Wisconsin State Assembly, where he served as speaker in 1926. In 1934 he was the Socialist Party's gubernatorial candidate in Wisconsin and received 45,000 votes, or 4.7 percent of the total. The Progressive Party's Philip La Follette won with 373,000 votes. Two years later, in the 1936 presidential election, George A. Nelson was the vice presidential running mate of the Socialist

Party's Norman Thomas. They captured 187,910 votes, just 0.4 percent of the total popular vote. Nelson continued to be active in politics, running for lieutenant governor in 1938 and for governor in 1944. He also published agricultural pamphlets, including "The Farce of Farm Relief" and "Farmers: Where Are We Going?" He died in 1962, almost ninety years old.

Halverson said that George A. Nelson was the political hero of her grandfather, Howard Nelson. "I chuckle, because my father, George A. Nelson, who is named after him, is a hardcore Republican, and I tease him and say you are named after a socialist. He is still a Republican and the fact that I am DFL is hard on him. But he has been very supportive of me."

On the Swedish side of her family, the first immigrants were Johan Petter Johanson and his wife, Charlotte, who came from Åsby in the province of Östergötland in 1856. He eventually changed his name to Palmquist. When the Civil War broke out, he joined the Union army at Fort Snelling and was present at Appomattox when General Lee surrendered to General Grant. He died in Chisago in 1909.

Growing up in Lindström, Halverson feels more Swedish than Danish. "You learned really bad Swedish," she said and laughed. She particularly felt Swedish around Christmas, with lutfisk and all the food: "My grandfather had a meat market where he made Swedish sausages, which he once served to the king and queen of Sweden when they visited. We had so many visitors from Sweden, we were constantly connected. A Swedish exchange student once said to me, 'You Minnesotans are so funny, you are just like us but a hundred years ago.'" Halverson said that her Scandinavian heritage played into, both consciously and unconsciously, why she became involved in politics. She remembered when she was little and participated in her grandfather's election parades and campaigns, dressed in Swedish clothes, in blue and yellow, and with all his campaign signs also in blue and yellow. "We were raised with a value of public service," she said. "My Republican grandfather, Howard Nelson, served in both the Minnesota state house and the state senate and then as mayor of Lindström; his son, Peter, also a Republican, was state legislator and mayor of Lindström; my dad was mayor of Chisago City. So, getting involved and serving our community is really part of our family value, passed down through my Scandinavian ancestors." Her own civic activities are numerous and have included the Eagan Parks Commission, Citizens League, Dakota Regional Chamber of Commerce, Eagan Rotary, League of Women Voters, Eagan Foundation, and volunteering for her Lutheran church.

"The notion that you can effect change in your life and in other people's lives was very much a part of this. It surprised me that other people did not understand that the political system was a way to effect change. A lot of people see a lot of barriers in the political system; there is a lot of cynicism about politicians and that they are bad and corrupt. But to me, I grew up with the value that politicians go and serve, and if you are called to serve, you do it."

When Halverson decided to join the DFL Party, she sat down with her Republican father to tell him. "He said, 'Well, I wish you were on my side, but I know you will do great.' And he drives the truck in my parade, and there is my poor Republican dad with my t-shirt full of DFL stickers—what a trooper!" She is the first woman and the first DFLer in the family elected to a political office. Why DFL? "You can't be a woman in the Republican Party and be pro-choice. You can't support equal rights for gay and lesbian couples. You just can't. You can't be independent, and that sounds harsh. You can't represent your district in the Republican Party. It was very calculated how that party got rid of any independent voices and incredibly upsetting that they punished women who went against the party."

Halverson said that her grandfather lived by the slogan "moderation in all things" and she calls herself a moderate. She is sad that the Republican Party of today is a very different party from the one with which she grew up, with its progressive history. "I tried to hang in there because of my family history, and I did not take it lightly to cast off my Republican heritage. But I realized I cannot effect change in the Republican Party. The old Republican Party of Minnesota is gone. The DFL has taken over the old progressive role of the Republican Party in Minnesota, which historically had been quite progressive with leaders such as Elmer L. Andersen and Arne Carlson. But there is no way the current GOP would claim these former leaders today."

Her father, George A. Nelson, the former mayor of Chisago City and now retired, acknowledged that his daughter came and talked to him after she decided to switch to the Democrats, which she did largely for social issues. But Laurie is not a zealot, he said. She works for the common good on the premise of what we can do together. "The fact is, I agree with Laurie probably on 98 percent of the issues she is going to vote on. I would vote the same way if I was in there."

Her grandfather, Howard Nelson, was a conservative Republican. "Well, he was very much for local control," her father, George Nelson, explained. "Things got accomplished best at the local level, and the only things the federal government should do were things we could not do at the local level, military protection and a strong defense. The rest—leave it to us!" He described his father as being very active in the community and belonging to many local organizations. "For us kids, it was normal to be involved, sitting around the kitchen table, stuffing envelopes and licking stamps and knocking on doors for him. He was always giving, always trying to make the community a better place. He was a very measured person as how to get things done. He never considered people who didn't agree with him as an enemy. He did not speak ill of people, not at all. He was a man of terrific moral conviction." Nelson also said his parents did not join the Republican Party until later in life: "The party was not important to them, but their beliefs were. He hated party politics, and he was always against issues becoming partisan, and I think he was exactly right."

"I am a Republican and believe very much like my father did that we can get things done at the local level and you only do as much on the federal level as you have to. We need to think about what we can get done for the good of the community, for the good of the state, because a lot of this should just be common sense. Instead of throwing mud at each other, which is the downside of partisan politics, instead of bad-mouthing people, it should be: what can we agree on? That is how you get things done."

His daughter, Laurie Halverson, fills in. "I come from a place where we have always valued the collective, always valued the 'we.' We understand that we do better when we do things together. My grandfather Howard understood that. He built the fire department in Lindström, he built the boy scouts, the Masonic lodge—he built the community in Lindström. And that community and those organizations did a lot of good for everybody."

When Halverson was first elected in 2012, she declared she was going to "bring the spirit of cooperation and compromise to St. Paul," and she followed that up before the 2014 election by stating, "During my service, I have consistently put community ahead of partisan politics. I am committed to bringing Minnesota values back into policy-making by exchanging the tiresome gridlock of the past for action on issues that matter to Minnesotans." For her, those issues mean excellence in education, all-day kindergarten for every Minnesota child, property tax relief, regulation of e-cigarettes, a homeless youth act, mental health, chemical dependency treatment support, middle-class jobs, and business tax cuts.

She ran for a third term in 2016. Her opponent, Pat Hammond, a political unknown, filed his candidature on the last eligible day, May 31. But, taking no chances, Halverson started knocking on doors early, and this time, many people knew her name and her reputation. She said that it was a bit of a surprise and very different from her previous campaigns, adding, "I am feeling a great deal of support. People feel pretty negative about Washington, but they seem happier at the local level."

She was right. Laurie Halverson was easily reelected despite the fact that her party lost its majority in the Minnesota Senate and failed to recapture the majority in the house. Her narrow election victories in 2012 and 2014, with 51.9 and 51.1 percent of the vote, respectively, turned into a decisive victory in 2016 as she received 13,311 votes, or 56.5 percent of the total.

Next year, she hopes to finally visit Sweden with her father.

IN THE DECADES AFTER World War II, the two dominant strains in Minnesota politics became progressive Republicanism and DFL liberalism. In the process, Minnesota went national and became more like the rest of America—a two-party state—while the Scandinavians continued in leadership positions in both local parties.

In the DFL, two political giants, Hubert Humphrey and Walter Mondale, led the way, while the leading Republicans were Luther Youngdahl, Elmer L. Andersen, Al Quie, and Arne Carlson. Still, there were exceptions to the two-party system. One was the state's Republican Party declaring its independence from the national party in the aftermath of the Watergate scandal in the 1970s, and another was when the Reform Party's Jesse Ventura was elected governor in 1998 in a three-candidate election that upset the status quo just like the Farmer-Labor Party had done in the 1930s.

The following eight years, with conservative Republican Tim Pawlenty as governor, can be seen as the end of traditional progressive Republicanism in Minnesota. The nationalization of the state's Republican Party meant a more conservative profile, and its chief spokesman, Governor Pawlenty, politically did not fit in the progressive traditions of Youngdahl, Andersen, or Carlson. Longtime DFL leader Martin Olav Sabo underlined this change when he noted, "the Republicans today are not like the ones I served with in the 1970s. They were not anti-government folks, they were not hostile to the existence of government like they are today, totally different—night and day."

On the other hand, the DFL remained firmly progressive in the hands of Humphrey and Mondale and later Orville Freeman, Wendell Anderson, Rudy Perpich, and Mark Dayton. In that sense, it stayed true to its Scandinavian roots, while the Republican Party became ever less Scandinavian.

At the same time as this was happening, Minnesota was changing, becoming demographically much different with an influx of new immigrants from very different countries and cultures: Hmong and Somali.

9

From Snoose Boulevard to Little Mogadishu

"If you don't have political clout, no one will take you seriously."
Abdi Warsame, Minneapolis City Council, 2013

ON NOVEMBER 5, 2013, SOMALI IMMIGRANT Abdi Warsame impressively beat the incumbent council vice president, Robert Lilligren, in the race for the Sixth Ward seat on the Minneapolis City Council.

Capturing almost 64 percent of the votes, Warsame became not only the first Somali American to win such an election in Minnesota but the first to reach such a high elective office anywhere in the United States. In so doing, he defeated a strong opponent who had served the ward's thirty thousand residents for almost ten years. Lilligren, a member of the White Earth Band of Ojibwe, was the first American Indian on the city council and one of two openly gay council members. But, as the great-great-grandson of a Swedish immigrant (whose last name was Liljengren) and one-quarter Norwegian, he was by no means the city council's first Scandinavian.

The 2013 election was the first time the Somalis in Ward Six came out in force to vote. To achieve political power, the Somalis took a page out of the Scandinavian handbook, written a century earlier in the same ward. In what was once a historic Scandinavian neighborhood on the eastern fringe of downtown Minneapolis, the torch now passed—to paraphrase President John F. Kennedy's famous line from his inaugural address in January 1961— to a new generation of Minnesotans, this time from East Africa, refugees from a war-torn country named Somalia.

"This is a very old American story, and it's a good one," commented Larry Jacobs, professor at the University of Minnesota's Humphrey School of Public Affairs. David Lebedoff, a veteran DFL Party insider and author of the book *Ward Number Six,* was more emotional: "In recent years, a couple of things have moved me greatly, almost brought tears to my eyes," he said. "One was the election of Barack Obama and the other was the Somali take-over of the Sixth Ward, my old ward. . . . In Minnesota, the first were the

· 195 ·

WASPs, and then the Scandinavians, and now the Somalis. . . . It was the continuation of what had happened to the Swedes a hundred years earlier. A group moves in and instead of remaining outside the system and having no part of it, they take over the system. Yes, it's only one city council seat, but it gives them hope and it gives them leverage."

At the raucous victory celebration at the Mixed Blood Theatre in Minneapolis's Cedar-Riverside neighborhood, Warsame, who is a member of the DFL Party, told the hundreds of joyful Somali Americans from the nearby Riverside Plaza apartment complex, home to around six thousand members of the growing Somali community in Minneapolis, "I'm an American who happens to be Somali, and this is my base and I am proud of it."

"We crushed them," a jubilant young Somali American volunteer shouted.

Warsame, a thirty-five-year-old Somali immigrant, began his journey in early childhood, first moving to London and then, in 2006, to Minnesota after completing his university studies in England. In Minneapolis, he worked as executive director of the Riverside Plaza Tenants Association and was board chair of the Cedar-Riverside Neighborhood Revitalization Program. His campaign headquarters were located in the Riverside Mall, the Somali shopping center in the shadow of the Riverside Plaza high-rises. On the day before the election, his office was packed with young campaign workers, all Somalis. Warsame was constantly on the phone giving instructions.

"Swedish! I have been to Sweden," he said to me immediately on hearing about my Swedish roots. "I have a brother in Göteborg who is married to a Swedish woman, and they have five children, all born in Sweden." Sweden is another center of the large Somali diaspora, and the Somali connection between Minnesota and Sweden is strong. Many in Minneapolis's Somali American community have relatives in Sweden; some had even lived there before coming to Minnesota and spoke good, even fluent, Swedish.

For Warsame a lot has happened in the eight years since he came to Minnesota. "This is why America is such a great country," he said. "You have a lot of opportunities here. I am excited, a once-in-a-lifetime experience to galvanize a whole community." But he also felt the weight of his young community, so near to gaining real political clout for the first time and moving in from the margins. "If we lose, it will maybe take another ten years or so to again be at the cusp of winning an election," he said. "So that for me is a lot of pressure. This means a lot to a lot of people."

Minneapolis city council member Abdi Warsame at a discussion at the Humphrey School of Public Affairs, 2014. Photo by the author

He knows the path ahead as well, calling the Sixth Ward's Cedar-Riverside the Ellis Island of Minnesota—the place where you first settle before moving up and maybe out to the suburbs. "So the experience of the Africans right now is similar to what the Scandinavians experienced earlier. We are following in the footsteps of the Swedes and the Scandinavians when they came to this country and got politically involved."

Robert Lilligren, who has lived in this part of Minneapolis for over twenty years and who identifies more as Ojibwe and gay than as Scandinavian American, welcomes the Somali activism. By his fourth election campaign, the boundaries of the Sixth Ward had changed to include the heavily Somali Cedar-Riverside neighborhood. "The Somali involvement is a good sign," said Lilligren. "This community has been a gateway forever, a rough and tumble part of the city. It's a good sign, a sign of engagement."

Scandinavian immigrants started to trickle into Minneapolis in 1851, but it was not until after the Civil War that they began to make the city their home in bigger numbers. By 1870, Minneapolis had 2,676 Swedish-born residents, 2,263 Norwegians, and 153 Danes. Some twenty-five years later, when Minneapolis's population topped 192,000, 32 percent were foreign-born—including more than 35,000 from the Nordic countries. Most of the Scandinavians settled where Cedar and Riverside Avenues intersect, just south of Seven Corners at Cedar and Washington Avenues. The area became known as Snoose Boulevard—a play on the Swedes' love of their snus, a kind of snuff.

Around the turn of the twentieth century, as free land for the farmers became harder to find, more and more Scandinavian immigrants settled in the cities, particularly the Swedes. By 1905, over 60 percent of the residents in the Cedar-Riverside section of Minneapolis were Scandinavians. By 1920, the Swedes were the largest ethnic group in eleven of the city's thirteen wards.

"The extent of ethnic concentration was remarkable . . . and knowledge of English was unnecessary," writes Byron Nordstrom, professor emeritus at Gustavus Adolphus College. Swedish immigrant journalist Alfred Söderström and his Norwegian immigrant colleague Carl G. O. Hansen describe, in their respective books about Minneapolis, the Scandinavian dominance in the Cedar-Riverside area. Hansen writes about Scandinavian "high life" in the Twin Cities in the 1880s, when the cities' prominent Scandinavian residents gathered for elegant social evenings with the Scandinavian ambassadors from Washington, DC. Practically every business along Cedar and Riverside Avenues was run by Swedes or Norwegians. These included grocery stores, furniture dealers, shoe and drug stores, bakeries, photography studios, cigar factories, tailor shops, feed stores, mortuaries, barber shops, and saloons. The police station was located in the basement of Skandia Bank, established in 1883 at the corner of Cedar Avenue and Fourth Street South. The police captain, a Norwegian named Louis Ness, was in charge of mostly Scandinavian policemen. Söderström traces the history of Scandinavian-run bookstores, pharmacies, jewelry shops, stores, real estate companies, and saloons all the way back to 1877. The Scandinavians covered the gamut of professions, including painters, butchers, carpenters, blacksmiths, lawyers, and shoemakers. All fifty-six members of the Tailors Union, except one Irishman, were Scandinavians. They started newspapers and singing clubs. They founded churches (forty-seven out of Minneapolis's total 185 churches were Scandinavian) and temperance societies. They worked in many of the city's twenty mills. When the Washburn A Mill exploded in May 1878 in one of the city's worst industrial accidents ever, two Swedes and one Norwegian were among the eighteen dead.

Nils Vaag, the Norwegian immigrant and main character in Ole E. Rølvaag's novel *The Boat of Longing,* settled in the Sixth Ward and worked as a janitor cleaning saloons and local businesses for nine dollars a week. Nils lives in "Babel," one of the area's many boardinghouses at Fourth Street and Thirteenth Avenue South, which was for Nils an "oasis in the great, strange city." Rølvaag writes, "The saloons were the worst, for they required two cleanings daily. Nils couldn't understand how people could make such beasts of themselves; they scarcely resembled human beings any longer— no, not even animals. And they were Norwegians, too, many of them."

With time, Scandinavian involvement in the many facets of life in Minneapolis expanded into politics. Hansen writes that the early Scandinavians in the city were quite interested in politics and most of their newspapers were partisan organs. But, he adds, the Norwegians at that time were far from a politically homogeneous group. Their differences could be seen in the two leading Norwegian newspapers at the time: *Folkebladet,* the organ of the Norwegian-Danish Lutheran Conference, and *Budstikken,* the organ of the opposition and critical of the clergy and church leaders. This feud between the papers was one of the "bitterest in the history of the Norwegian-American press," according to Hansen.

Still, Söderström writes, Minneapolis's American-born population started to fear that the Scandinavians were about to take over power in the city as more and more of them won elections and jobs in the city administration. Of the city's three hundred firemen, for example, thirty were Scandinavians—fourteen Swedes, thirteen Norwegians, and three Danes. Of the 213 policemen, seventeen were Swedes, nineteen were Norwegians, and four were Danes. They started political clubs like the Swedish American Republican Club and the Swedish American Union. As Söderström points out, the Norwegians took the lead in politics and had for years a clear advantage over the Swedes because the Norwegians had a stronger national sentiment and would always support their own, regardless of political affiliation. By 1899, Söderström writes, the Swedes were waking up, "even if they still are rubbing the sleep out of their eyes," and doing away with the "shameful epitaph" of Swedes as "voting cattle."

The first significant Scandinavian political victory in Minneapolis took place in 1870, when a Norwegian immigrant, George H. Johnson, was elected sheriff of Hennepin County. Born near Rosendal in Norway in 1843, Johnson came to America with his family when he was six. He moved to Minneapolis in 1865, after fighting for the Union as a member of Battery M of the First Illinois Light Artillery. A Republican like most Scandinavians in those years, Johnson was sheriff for six years, and he was followed in the position by several Norwegians and Swedes, including P. P. Swenson, John E. Holmberg, and Philip Megaarden.

In 1874 the Minneapolis City Council got its first Scandinavian member when A. H. (Aron Henrik) Edsten, a Norwegian and a Republican, was elected alderman from the Tenth Ward, which later became Ward Six, kicking off the council's Scandinavian era. Edsten was born at Edsten in the province of Bohuslän in Sweden in 1837, but he moved to Sarpsborg in Norway in 1855. He married a Norwegian woman, and in 1864 they and their two children left for America. Once in Minneapolis, Edsten became one of its first furniture dealers with a store at Third Avenue South and Washington Avenue. He was also active as a lay reader in the Swedish Augustana Evangelical Lutheran Church and one of the founders of the Norwegian Trinity Lutheran Church. He was an early trustee of the Augsburg Seminary, founded by Norwegian Lutherans, which later became Augsburg College.

In 1877 Norwegian immigrant physician Karl Bendeke, a Democrat, was elected to the city council from Ward Six. He was born in Christiania (Oslo) in 1841 and then moved to Trondheim. After finishing his medical education in Norway, he served for a while as the surgeon on an emigrant ship that went between Christiania and Quebec in Canada. It was during a visit to Chicago on one of those trips that he decided to stay in America. He moved to Minnesota in 1870. Bendeke served only one term on the city council, declining to run again because of his busy practice as a prominent eye specialist. Bendeke was an impressive member of the Norwegian immigrant community and "a gentleman of the old school," writes Söderström.

Republican Andrew C. (A. C.) Haugan, one of the most popular members of the city's Norwegian community, writes Hansen, served on the city council from Ward Six for ten years. Haugan had come to Minneapolis in the late 1860s from Strinda near Trondheim and for many years ran a big grocery store downtown. After serving as president of Washington Bank, which had a large Scandinavian clientele, he was elected city treasurer four times before his career ended in a scandal in 1897, when he was forced to resign after having been indicted and convicted on two counts of misappropri-ating city funds. "The fact that he misappropriated public money is beyond question," wrote the *Minneapolis Tribune*. "That he was to some extent the victim of circumstances and was caught in the maelstrom of false notions of official duty, so widely prevalent during the boom times, may be admitted. But as his was the responsibility, his must also be his punishment."

Other Scandinavians followed as aldermen from Ward Six for many years without interruption: Swedish Democrat Clarence Johnson, Nor-wegian Republican Chris Ellingsen, Swedish Republican John A. Swen-son, Norwegian Democrat Lars M. Rand, and Swedish Democrat Andrew Anderson. Other wards in the city also elected Scandinavians, including George Peterson, a Danish Democrat from Ward Twelve; Fred A. Schwartz, a Norwegian Democrat from Ward Ten; John A. Nordeen, a Swedish Re-publican from Ward Seven, and A. L. Skoog, a Swedish Republican, Peter Nelson, a Swedish Democrat, and Claus O. Peterson, a Swedish Republican, from Ward Eleven.

Scandinavians were also elected coroner, board president of the public library, county superintendent of schools, chief engineer of city waterworks, inspector of streetlights, vice president of the board of police commis-sioners, postmaster, and county attorney. In short, they were involved in every aspect of the affairs of the city in a wide variety of roles, except one—mayor of Minneapolis. Not until 1931 did the voters in Minneapolis elect a Scandinavian mayor: William A. Anderson from the Farmer-Labor Party, with a father from Norway and an American-born mother. He served only one term. In 1945 another Scandinavian American was elected mayor: Hubert H. Humphrey. That victory kicked off a national political career that reached far beyond Minnesota. He was succeeded by Swedish-born Eric Gustav Hoyer, from the town of Lidköping, when Humphrey was elected to the US Senate in 1948. Hoyer was reelected four times and served as mayor until 1957. He had come to Minneapolis in 1919 at the age of twenty-one to settle the estate of his dead brother. He stayed, working in construction and interior design. In the 1930s, he worked in Floyd B. Olson's gubernatorial campaign and was then elected to the city council, rising to its chair before becoming mayor.

Minnesota has long prided itself on its good and clean government. This has, among other things, meant the absence of political bosses among the Scandinavians. One exception to this was Lars M. Rand, nicknamed "Little Lars" or "the Little Norwegian." Called an "old-fashioned ward boss and skilled parliamentarian," Rand represented Ward Six on the Minneapolis City Council for two decades, from 1890 to 1910, and came as close to being a true political boss as anyone in Minnesota's history. He retired, undefeated, and died in September 1913, only fifty-six years old. As Rand lay in state in his home, thousands came for a last look at "Little Lars," reported the *Minneapolis Tribune*. Most of those who came to pay their respects to the "dead chieftain" were from Ward Six, where "the millionaires are scarce, indeed." They were sewer diggers, saloon keepers, preachers, and clerks. The mayor of Minneapolis and the members of the city council came—so many politicians attended that "it was like a political event of years long past, a page out of forgotten history." "The barefoot boy is dead" was the sad message passed by word of mouth through the Cedar-Riverside neighborhood. "The barefoot boy" was coined in a speech by Rand himself many years earlier when he told about how "on the rocky coast of Norway, there was born of poor but honest parents a barefoot boy. Who was that boy? That was me, Lars M. Rand."

The Rand organization was for twenty years an important entity in Cedar-Riverside. It provided the predominantly immigrant community with jobs, entertainment, and a social center while also helping it to integrate in the American political system: "The spectacle of an immigrant politician holding his own against the massed opposition of the Minneapolis power structure must have been encouraging."

Born in 1857 on the Rand farm in Nordfjord, Norway, Lars M. Rand came to America as a teenager with his family. They settled in Chippewa Falls, Wisconsin. Young Lars eventually moved to Minnesota, first to Northfield and then to Winona, where he started working as a janitor in a bank. He continued to study at the Winona State Normal School and then studied law. He gained admission to the Minnesota bar in 1884, only nine years after arriving in America. That same year he was elected a municipal judge. In 1885, Rand and his American-born wife moved to Minneapolis, which was experiencing a rapid population growth at the time, its thriving economy based on the flour and timber industries. The Rands settled in the heart of Ward Six, at 1920 Fourth Street South, and Rand "plunged into Democratic politics," according to historian Carl H. Chrislock. He became not only a delegate at the Minnesota Democratic convention in 1886 but also chair of the platform committee, apparently encouraged and supported by Michael Doran, the leader of Minnesota's Democrats, who actively sought to recruit Scandinavians, who were at the time overwhelmingly Republican.

In 1890, after a short stint as assistant city attorney, Rand ran for a seat on the Minneapolis City Council from Ward Six on a platform of "personal liberty," a code expression indicating opposition to antiliquor laws and support for the eight-hour working day for public employees. He crushed his Republican opponent, 2,252 votes to 516, starting a run of two decades as a city alderman. The Rand era had begun.

At that time, city aldermen were elected to four-year terms, and each of the city's thirteen wards had two seats on the council, which was the real center of power, controlling both the purse and the patronage. Rand successfully fought off a resolution that would have given preference in city government to full-fledged citizens over so-called first-paper citizens, i.e., foreign-born immigrants. Rand also cultivated the reputation of incorruptibility by refusing to accept a free streetcar pass and paying for each ride himself. He built coalitions and teamed up with his fellow Democrat from the Third Ward, a German ex-butcher named Joseph L. Kiichli, to defend the party's platform on personal liberty, which was largely about keeping the saloons open on Sundays.

Rand opposed the temperance movement, the strength of which was found among the Scandinavian immigrants, and he was attacked as a friend of the saloons. Norwegian American pastor M. Falk Gjertsen once took Rand and a Norwegian American Republican alderman, C. H. Blichfeldt, to task, saying their stand "brings a deep blush to my cheek," adding, "God have mercy on a man who will shame his friends and dishonor his home, his word, his church and his pastor."

But Rand was just getting started. In 1892 he maneuvered to elect fellow Democrat Andrew Anderson, a Swedish American, as the Sixth Ward's second representative. And in March 1893 Rand cemented his power not only in Ward Six but on the council as a whole by orchestrating the election of Kiichli to replace the previous duly elected Republican city council president. The council session lasted until three in the morning, with constant parliamentary maneuvers from both sides. Rand introduced 144 motions before achieving final victory. In addition to getting Kiichli as council president, Rand also secured for himself the position of chair of the public grounds and building committee, which gave him virtual control of the labor in city hall, and he became a member of the committee on gas, fire department, and railroads. Afterward, Rand's opponents went to court to overturn his maneuvering, but the Minnesota Supreme Court upheld Kiichli's and Rand's victory.

Rand never made a secret of his Norwegian background. In fact, he was proud of it and was a member of Norwegian clubs such as Sons of Norway. His English had a distinct Norwegian accent, but he preferred not to give speeches in Norwegian. The leading Swedish-language newspaper in Minneapolis, *Svenska Amerikanska Posten,* was a strong backer throughout Rand's political career. When Rand ran for reelection the first time, the paper wrote glowingly about him under the headline "En *folkets man*"—a man of the people—and "En *arbetarnes sanne vän*"—a true friend of the worker—as one of the best aldermen the city has ever had. It described how Rand was a faithful political friend of the Swedish Americans in Ward Six. Soon after he became alderman, Rand successfully defended Swedish American Andrew Bergström, chief engineer at the city's waterworks, against a Republican attack. Thanks to Rand, the paper also reported, Ward Six has a new police station, the best gas and sewage system in the city, and the streets have sidewalks of stone. And he had always been a true friend of the working people, advocating for the eight-hour day, defending the rights of the unions, and fighting for cheaper streetcar fares and municipal ownership of public utilities, such as gas and electricity. And he remained the only alderman who paid his own way on the streetcars.

The paper also cited a political battle in April 1893, when Rand fought and defeated a resolution, clearly directed against newly arrived Scandinavians, stipulating that only citizens and residents of the city for five years could get jobs in the public sector. In 1894 he supported state auditor Adolph Biermann, a Norwegian immigrant, for renomination in spite of opposition from the Democratic Party leadership. And in 1896 he backed John Lind, the Swedish-born candidate for governor on the Fusion Ticket, consisting of Democrats, Populists, and Silver Republicans. Lind did not win the governorship that year, but Rand made sure he carried Ward Six.

Rand was not only an ally to Scandinavian politicians, however. He was a proponent of immigrant solidarity and made sure that his organization was not exclusively Norwegian or Scandinavian. His closest aides included men with names such as Flaherty, Sweeney, and Walsh. Rand believed that all immigrants "shared an interest in maintaining a common front against the power of the city's 'Puritan-Yankee elite.'"

Rand—"the workingman's friend"—never seemed interested in running for mayor of Minneapolis. He was satisfied with representing Ward Six. With time, he encountered growing opposition from urban reform movements such as the Good Citizenship League, particularly in 1898, when

Rand was seeking a new four-year term. But the contest was not even close. Rand beat his Republican opponent by 1,172 votes to 681, and John Lind, for whom Rand eloquently spoke at a campaign rally at Norrmanna Hall in Ward Six, was elected governor of Minnesota.

But Rand faced new challenges. In 1900, the Minnesota State Legislature enacted a law requiring that all officials in Hennepin County who were running for office were to be nominated by a direct vote rather than by a caucus/convention system. This diminished the ability of the ward bosses to pick their preferred candidates.

The challenges against his political power and his organization in Ward Six continued. Being called "patriarch," "dean," or "nestor" of the city council, suggested, according to Chrislock, that Rand had attained a sort of elder statesman's status, although he was not even fifty years old. In 1902 he beat back a new Republican challenger, the Norwegian-born attorney John F. Dahl. The next year, another reform organization, the Minneapolis Voters' League, was formed with members from the city's elite, notably among them also Norwegians Sven Oftedal of the Augsburg Seminary and Andreas Ueland, an attorney. In 1906, the Voters' League launched a broad attack on Rand, who was described as "an oily . . . unscrupulous ward boss" who had been "a dangerous influence on city affairs during all his sixteen years" on the council. The League, which railed against Rand as an agent of the railroads and public service corporations, launched its own reform candidate, a Norwegian by the name of Peter Gunderson. Rand crushed Gunderson in the Democratic primary and then went on to beat the Republican John Peterson, a progressive Teddy Roosevelt Republican, in the general election. Still, Rand's margin of victory was the narrowest yet, at 1,026 votes to 805, with another 116 votes going to the socialist Public Ownership Party.

Rand proved adept at parrying accusations of cronyism or corruption and that he was amassing wealth. Charges that he was interested in politics in the Sixth Ward "only as a means of making a fat living for himself," as the Voters' League claimed, were "manifestly unfair." When Rand died, he left an estate worth a little over $32,000, "not a pauper's legacy but hardly evidence of 'fat living.'" In 1910 Rand chose to retire, explaining his decision: "I go out of the council at peace with all my colleagues and city officials and with only friendliness for everyone, excepting always the Voters' League," the *Minneapolis Journal* reported. One of his last initiatives was a bill to finance a public bath on Riverside Avenue in the Sixth Ward, a longtime dream of Rand's, according to the *Minneapolis Tribune*. The facility, the city's first year-round public bath, cost $20,000. "Little Lars" now also became known as the "Father of the Sixth Ward bath."

WHILE THE BOUNDARIES OF the Sixth Ward changed over the years, it almost always included Seven Corners and nearby Cedar-Riverside. Even though the Scandinavians dominated, the area was at the same time one of the most diverse in the city. When David Markle moved to the Cedar-Riverside neighborhood in 1962, remnants of the historic Scandinavian community were still evident. The University of Minnesota had not yet spread to the West Bank, and the freeways through the city had not yet split and isolated Minneapolis neighborhoods. The liquor patrol limits from 1884 were still in effect, trying to keep alcohol out of most residential areas, and the Salvation Army band still played on Sundays at the Cedar Avenue mission. At Ellison's on Cedar Avenue, raw lingon, anchovies, and pickled herring were sold, and Swedish was spoken. Brodahl's Restaurant served lutfisk every day, and Ray's Lunch offered yellow pea soup once a week. The Samuelson sisters sold *Svenska Dagbladet* and other Scandinavian newspapers. And in the Four Corners Saloon, across the street from Dania Hall, the jukebox still played "Nikolina" and "Johan på Snippen." The saloon was one of more than twenty liquor establishments on the nine blocks of Cedar Avenue north of East Franklin Avenue. The neighborhood, which had a bad reputation, was actually one of the safest in the city. It was also one of its liveliest and remained a real neighborhood, where there was "a rare degree of tolerance that seemed to be an old tradition: 'Nobody was any better than anybody else.'"

The area known as the Danish Flats, later called the Bohemian Flats, was a poor community on the banks of the Mississippi River full of immigrants' shacks and was part of Ward Six. Today, the tranquil park along the river is a popular weekend destination, and part of the old neighborhood above the flats is dominated by a steadily expanding University of Minnesota campus on the west bank of the Mississippi River. The names of many university buildings on its West Bank campus are reminders of the Scandinavian leaders of the city and the state: the Carlson School of Management, after prominent businessman Curtis Carlson; the Hubert Humphrey School of Public Affairs, after the former senator and vice president; the Walter F. Mondale School of Law, after another former senator and vice president; and the Elmer L. Andersen Library, after the former Republican governor. Norwegian Trinity Lutheran Church at Twenty-Second and Riverside Ave-

Charles Samuelson in front of Samuelson's Confectionery, a Scandinavian-owned business at Seven Corners in Minneapolis's Cedar-Riverside neighborhood, 1890

nues has been around for more than 140 years: "We've gotten very good at change. Norwegian is out. English is in. So are Amharic and Tigrinya, the native languages of our Ethiopian and Eritrean members. The old church building is gone, and we're now at home in Augsburg College's Foss Center. Less maintenance, more outreach. We embrace our traditions, but also strive to practice radical hospitality and outreach."

The venerable Dania Hall, at 427 Cedar Avenue South, was designed for the Dania Society by Norwegian-born architect Carl F. Struck and was completed in 1886. It quickly became a focal point for the Scandinavians in the city. Lars Rand spoke at its opening, saying that "within whose walls the spirit of intelligence, unity, friendship and brotherly love will be taught, not only among Danish citizens of Minneapolis, but the Norwegians and the Swedes as well." The magnificent five-story Dania Hall, where the curtain across the stage read, in Danish, *"Ej blot til lyst"* (Not for fun only)—just like the curtain at the Royal Danish Theatre in Copenhagen—was the premier center for Scandinavian social activities in Minneapolis for decades. It hosted concerts, plays by August Strindberg and Bjørnstjerne Bjørnson, and lectures by luminaries including Norwegian novelist Knut Hamsun. Dania

Hall was also the birthplace of Scandinavian vaudeville, with acts like Olle i Skratthult, whose real name was Hjalmar Peterson and who recorded the immensely popular "Nikolina" in 1915, which is still sung at Swedish American festivities. Every big gathering originated at Dania Hall, including one in 1897 when thousands gathered for a march to Loring Park to join tens of thousands in the unveiling of Jacob Fjelde's statue of the Norwegian violinist Ole Bull.

The glory days of Dania Hall ended with the Great Depression, and it fell into disuse despite being placed on the National Register of Historic Places in 1974. The Snoose Boulevard Festival celebrating the Scandinavian musical heritage in Cedar-Riverside was a shot in the arm for the neighborhood for a few years, but restoration and renovation ideas for Dania Hall fell to naught, and then, on February 28, 2000, the Scandinavian landmark burned down. At a memorial a couple of days later at Cedar Cultural Center, participants lamented the loss of Dania Hall. A 1975 recording of the classic Swedish immigrant song "Hälsa dem där hemma" (Greet Those at Home) by Olle i Skratthult's first wife, Olga Lindgren-Nilsen, was played. The lot where Dania Hall once stood is still empty as of 2017. Other important neighborhood venues, including Mozart Hall, Norrmanna Hall, and Peterson Hall, are also gone.

Today, Snoose Boulevard is known as Little Mogadishu, the epicenter of Minnesota's Somali community. The neighborhood has four mosques, and many of the six thousand residents in the thirteen hundred apartments in the Riverside Plaza towers are Somali immigrants or of Somali descent. Nearby is a Somali shopping mall. The neighborhood bears little resemblance to what scholars once called the Scandinavian "cultural community."

As a sign of the times, and as part of the efforts to build closer ties to its new neighbors, the American Swedish Institute, located in Ward Six, has had a Somali board member, and in its Story Swap program, older members of the Swedish American community share their immigrant stories with the newer generation of immigrants. Next door on Park Avenue, the Lutheran Social Service Center for Changing Lives is a cooperative venture between the Lutheran Social Service (LSS) of Minnesota and the Messiah Lutheran Church, a former Swedish church. The center is half Lutheran and half Muslim and a symbol of the important role the Lutherans and their churches have played for many years in aiding thousands of refugees and new arrivals to build new lives in Minnesota. A large majority of the residents in the neighborhood have incomes below the poverty line, and the center helps with housing for homeless and poor families. There is free lunch once a week. A Muslim prayer room was donated by Oliver and Ida Bergeland. The daycare center is run by a Somali, and a young Somali woman teaching a small group of Somali children the alphabet greets me with, "Oh, Sweden—I have relatives there!"

Lutheran Social Service of Minnesota was founded in 1865 by Swedish immigrant pastor Eric Norelius. That year, in the village of Vasa in Goodhue County south of the Twin Cities, Norelius heard of four orphan children in St. Paul, so he hitched up his blind horse, fetched the children, and brought them back to Vasa. The basement of his one-room church became Minnesota's first orphanage and the foundation of the Lutheran Social Service. Vasa had been founded a few years earlier by a group of Swedish immigrants led by Hans Mattson, future Civil War colonel and Minnesota secretary of state. Initially, the village was called Mattson's Settlement. Norelius changed the name to Vasa in honor of Swedish King Gustav Vasa, and he founded the Vasa Lutheran Church with eighty-seven members. Among the congregation's members was Swan Turnblad, the future owner and publisher of *Svenska Amerikanska Posten* and the builder of the Turnblad Mansion that is now the American Swedish Institute. As it grew, the orphanage changed location several times, including once as a result of a tornado in 1879 and then following a fire in 1899. The fourth and current location is in a private home in a bend on Old Childrens Home Road, just north from the red brick church and the first orphanage, which is now a museum.

Pastor Norelius died in 1916 and is buried in Vasa. His legacy, the Lutheran Social Service of Minnesota, is now one of the largest nonprofit social service agencies in the state, with over twenty-two hundred employees and $121 million in total revenues and charitable support. Its main services include housing for people with disabilities, in-home service to the elderly, homeless youth services, senior nutrition, and mental health counseling. Jodi Harpstead, CEO of Lutheran Social Service, said the biggest supporters and donors are disproportionately members of the Swedish Augustana Lutheran Church (Augustana Synod) that Norelius founded. "You would think that, today, that would have disappeared, but it has not," she said. The Scandinavian heritage is "still very much alive" in Minnesota, "a strong social conscience, always a strong sense of community, and when people ask me why, when I go to other states, I always chalk that up to our Scandinavian heritage." Harpstead, who calls herself "one hundred percent Danish" and who is married to a Norwegian American, said her organization is committed to helping the next generation of immigrants. She pointed to the Faith in the City program, which involves five Lutheran institutions working in the Cedar-Riverside neighborhood, mentoring the heads of Somali nonprofits and helping them get their organizations off the ground: "We are passing along our experience. We asked them and they wanted help with their leadership questions. This is, I think, a fundamentally Scandinavian impulse."

The refugee settlement in which LSS has played a vital role has now gone on for seventy years. Minnesota is a welcoming state, Harpstead said. "We have a track record, which is why all these organizations have been built up." She has heard that in the refugee camps in Kenya they had learned two words: "Minnesota" and "Lutheran." Still, she acknowledges some strains due to the ethnic and religious differences between the older residents and the new arrivals, although, she added, the fact that their work only concerns legal refugees and that the US State Department decides where the refugees settle make their role less controversial.

For Norwegian American Joanne Negstad, who volunteers every week at the Lutheran center next to the American Swedish Institute, Minnesota's Lutherans have "a consistent story" of caring for their own and their old people, which is also a reason that many refugees chose the state. "Minnesota has been a state that really cares for its people," she said, and if it "was not seen as this caring state, I don't think the refugees would have come here."

Although Minnesota is still an overwhelmingly white state populated primarily by people of European heritage—with only about seven percent of its population foreign-born, compared to a national average of 13.5 percent—the state is changing. An estimated forty thousand Somalis live in Minnesota, more than half of them born in Somalia. Of the nearly fifty thousand Hmong from Southeast Asia who live in Minnesota, about half are foreign-born. Mexicans constitute the largest group of foreign-born Minnesotans, at seventy thousand. The top ethnic groups also include Indians, Thai, and Chinese. The three most common non-English languages spoken are Spanish, Hmong, and Somali. Since 1979, Minnesota social service agencies have helped resettle about one hundred thousand refugees—mainly Hmong, Somalis, and Vietnamese, although more than three-quarters of the refugees during the first decade of this century have come from Africa. Swedish-born Minnesotans rank forty-ninth among foreign-born residents, and there are even fewer from the other four Nordic countries. Of the state's four hundred thousand foreign-born residents, 75 percent live in the Twin Cities metro area. The Hmong and the Somalis are heavily concentrated in this urban area, while other immigrant groups, such as the Mexicans, are more spread out over the state.

A prime "pull factor" for the recent waves of immigrants and refugees has been Minnesota's powerful humanitarian nonprofit sector, led by Lutheran Social Service and Catholic Charities, which has played a "huge role in the resettlement of refugees." The state started welcoming refugees after World War II, mainly from the Baltic States, and then from Southeast Asia after the Vietnam War. The majority of these new Minnesotans were Hmong, as Minnesota, along with California, became one of the main destinations for new settlers through the 1975 Indochina Migration and Refugee Assistance Act, which both Minnesota senators at the time, Hubert Humphrey and Walter Mondale, strongly supported. The Hmong mainly settled in St. Paul and today constitute the largest Hmong community in America. They wrestle with similar problems as the Somalis, with almost 30 percent living below the poverty line, eight percent not speaking English, 42 percent without high school education, and 21 percent unemployed, triple the state average.

The political activities among the new immigrants vary. Most have flocked to the DFL Party. DFL chairman Ken Martin said he is very excited to see all the new faces and how passionate they are about participating in American democracy. "That is a good thing for our party," he said. He expressed hope that this was going to be a long-term political engagement and a deeper involvement in the political process, reflecting a Scandinavian heritage, which, in Minnesota, means civic mindedness, high voter turnout, participation in government. "I am very hopeful," Martin said, "the new immigrants will take on this legacy and this tradition.... I hope they will understand the importance of government in their lives."

In 1992, the first Hmong American rose to public office in Minnesota when Choua Lee was elected to the St. Paul school board. The 2002 election of Mee Moua to the Minnesota state senate as the first Asian woman to serve in the state legislature was seen as the beginning of a big push among the Hmong for a bigger role in Minnesota politics. Born in Laos in 1969, she moved to the United States in 1978 and later became a lawyer and political activist. After two terms in the Minnesota Senate she chose not to run again in 2010 and is now president and executive director of Asian Americans Advancing Justice, an advocacy group and service provider based in Washington, DC. But the big push by the Hmong community into politics never happened. After Moua, the next Hmong elected official in Minnesota was Foung Hawj, a small-business owner who was elected to the state senate in 2012. Like Moua, he represents St. Paul and like all Hmong and Somalis elected to political offices in Minnesota, he is a member of the DFL Party.

In 2014 two Hmong Americans were elected to the Minneapolis and St. Paul City Councils. Dai Thao in St. Paul and Blong Yang in Minneapolis both came to America as children from refugee camps in Thailand and both represent heavily African American districts. Said Thao, an information technology manager, to the local media: "I may not have the same experience as African Americans, but I have similar experiences of being marginalized, of discrimination." Being the first elected Hmong, he also said, "is no different from the first Irish, German, Swede, African American, Polish, and so on. You not only carry the extraordinary expectations but also the hopes and dreams of your own community." As Minnesota's Hmong celebrated the fortieth anniversary of their arrival in the state, Lee Pao Xiong at St. Paul's Concordia University described their long journey: "We were Hmong, then Hmong Americans and American Hmong. Now, we are Hmong Minnesotans."

The Somalis started arriving in America in the 1980s, fleeing protracted conflict and civil war. They first settled in San Diego, California, but then found their way to Minnesota in the early 1990s, where more jobs were available. As Ahmed Ismail Yusuf writes in *Somalis in Minnesota*, it all began with a May 20, 1992, jobs ad in the *Argus Leader*, the local paper in Sioux Falls, South Dakota. The Heartland Food Company's poultry plant in Marshall in western Minnesota, close to the Dakota border, was hiring at a starting wage of $6.95 per hour, with benefits. The day after the ad appeared, four Somalis from Sioux Falls showed up at the plant and were hired on the spot, and they were told to tell their friends and families that there were more jobs. Word quickly spread to San Diego, where four young men jumped in a car and drove all the way to Marshall. Even though the plant had hired twenty more Somalis by the time they arrived, they also found immediate employment. "Now, anybody who was seeking work or ways to support one's family was heading to Marshall or thinking of how to get there."

What they found was a state with much lower unemployment than the national average, coupled with a lower cost of living and a higher minimum wage. From the 121 Somalis who relocated to Minnesota in 1993 directly from refugee camps, the numbers jumped quickly, reaching more than eleven thousand in the official 2000 census. The largest number of Somali immigrants to Minnesota came as a secondary wave, when people heard that there were jobs in Minnesota that did not require particular skills or language fluency. And they stayed once they found that Minnesota's hospitality turned out to be "durable." Resettlement assistance from social service agencies helped them out and made them feel welcome, and economic assistance helped the newcomers begin their new lives. By now, the Somalis have established "their own Minnesota identity." They feel they have come to a welcoming place with an "inclusive political environment that has fostered a tolerant climate."

Former Minneapolis mayor R. T. Rybak, who is of Czech descent, said that in Minnesota politics greater emphasis is placed on "common purpose, inclusion and social justice" than in the rest of the American heartland. He said that while some of this sentiment can be traced from the people who came here from the East Coast, "much more important were the Scandinavians who settled here, especially from Sweden." This mixing of American individualism with the Scandinavian sense of the common good "became the bedrock of Minnesota politics, a sort of a magic mixture in Minnesota." And because of this, Minnesota is disproportionally involved in global relief efforts that have influenced the state in a dramatic way. Humanitarian groups such as the Center for Victims of Torture, American Refugee Committee, Doctors Without Borders, the Lutheran Social Service, have gone all around the world and "spread the gospel of Minnesota."

Rybak, who was first elected in 2001 and served as mayor for three terms, said that the Scandinavian value of inclusiveness has been instrumental in attracting other immigrants to Minnesota. This, in turn, has led to dramatic changes in the complexion of this community and improved its ability to compete in a global environment. "I absolutely adhere this to the Scandinavian heritage," Rybak said.

Rybak has a history of supporting political candidates from the city's Somali community. At his final press conference in 2013, Mayor Rybak named a new pedestrian and bicycle bridge linking Cedar-Riverside with downtown Minneapolis "Samatar Crossing." It honors one of Minnesota's most prominent Somali Americans, Hussein Samatar, who died of leukemia in August 2013 at the age of forty-five. Samatar paved the way for other Somali Americans to enter Minnesota politics. "Samatar was the brightest light, and when he died that was a huge loss," Rybak said. Elected to the Minneapolis school board in 2010, Samatar founded the African Development Center in 2002 to help Somali businesses. Located at the corner of Cedar and Riverside Avenues, the center lends money and mobilizes other funds through banks and other businesses. Calling himself a proud Minnesotan, Samatar made several trips to Sweden and Denmark, comparing the fate of Somali immigrants on both sides of the Atlantic. His goal, he wrote on the center's website, was to realize his vision of "an integrated and successful Somali community in Minnesota and all Scandinavian countries."

While often viewed from the outside as a homogenous country, Sweden has become a country of immigrants, even more so than modern Minnesota, and another center for the Somali diaspora in the world. Driven by war and internal conflict, a total of 129,000 Somalis have made their way to the Nordic countries: 58,000 in Sweden, 36,600 in Norway, 18,600 in Denmark, and 15,750 in Finland. That's almost on par with the number of Somalis in the United States. Of Sweden's total population of 9.7 million, about 16 percent are foreign-born, up from 11 percent in 1998. Of Norway's 5.1 million people, 14.9 percent have a foreign background, compared with 12 percent in Denmark and 5.5 percent in Finland.

The Somalis in Sweden have not had the same success as those in Minnesota, sparking debate and academic studies. Professor Benny Carlson, an economic historian at Lund University in southern Sweden, has concluded that the differences are stark. The Somalis in Sweden live largely as "outsiders" and are the refugee and immigrant group with the greatest difficulties in the labor market. While 73 percent of the total Swedish population between ages sixteen and sixty-four are employed, only 21 percent of the Swedish Somalis work. That gap of 52 percent compares with a 13 percent gap in the United States, where 67 percent of the total population and 54 percent of the Somalis are employed. In Sweden, only 0.5 percent of the Somalis own a small business, compared with 5.1 percent in the United States.

In fact, Somalis in the United States are better entrepreneurs than the population as a whole. In the middle of the last decade, there were eight hundred Somali-owned small businesses in Minnesota, compared to thirty-eight in Sweden. By 2012, that number had risen to 223 in Sweden. According to Carlson, one important explanation for the difference is that the Somali Swedes are less educated than those who went to the United States. About 70 percent of the Somalis in Sweden have low or an unknown amount of education, and 60 percent of them are recent arrivals—after 2006. The higher educational levels among the Somalis in America and the fact that they have been in the country longer are important explanations for why the American Somalis have fared better. The fact that the United States is an English-speaking country is also an advantage, since many Somalis already speak some English on arrival, while practically none knew any Swedish. Finding a job is also more important in the United States because it has a less generous safety net. It is also much easier to start a business. As one Minnesota Somali said, comparing Sweden and Minnesota, "Here you don't need a PhD to get a driver's license."

Professor Carlson also points out that Minnesota, in contrast to the Scandinavian countries, is an "old" immigrant country that has built up an "accepting environment" for foreigners and other cultures, while the Nordic experience with immigration only goes back to just after World War II. Minnesota has strong public/private networks, including the Lutheran Social Service of Minnesota, to support new arrivals. The Somalis have also fought dispersal by US authorities to different parts of the country and have been able to form an "ethnic enclave" in Minneapolis of "critical mass," allowing them to organize, work to help each other, and further their interests.

So did the early Swedes and Norwegians in Ward Six, according to Professor Byron Nordstrom, where they lived and worked and where "virtually all the needs of an ethnic population could be met." The Somali enclave in Cedar-Riverside, he argues, is no different in its residents' search for economic and social support, education, culture, religious institutions, and, with time, political roles and leadership positions. Such enclaves are seen as a natural complement, or alternative, to the public sector, but, writes Carlson, such enclaves are seen in Sweden as a threat to the public sector and to the Swedish model. While the "ethnic enclaves" can retard integration into the mainstream and learning the language, in the case of Minneapolis they have had largely positive effects. Carlson thinks it is time to rethink and re-evaluate the Swedish model. The authorities can't do everything and don't have the necessary knowledge about the backgrounds and ambitions of the immigrants, and he argues that more responsibilities and resources instead should be "devolved to those most affected."

Rahma Dirie, who moved from Somalia to Sweden with her family when she was eight, visited Minnesota in 2010 as part of an exchange program between Sweden and Minnesota to discuss the Somali immigrant experience. The visit was an eye-opener for her. She writes, with fascination, about how Somalis in Minnesota had settled where the Swedes had once lived, and how the two cultures could exist side by side. "My cultural worlds were joined," she writes, as she learned about the history of the Swedish Americans and how they stuck together and sought each other out. Dirie compares yesterday's old Swedish immigrant neighborhoods of Snoose Boulevard in

Minneapolis and Swede Hollow in St. Paul with today's Stockholm suburbs, teeming with immigrants and refugees. It wasn't easy for those early Swedes either, yet their immigrant experience differed: "They were allowed to develop on their own and at their own pace and be integrated into the majority society." Dirie left Minnesota impressed with how the state's Somalis had mobilized collectively, their ambition, their faith in the future, and how much they had become part of the American society.

Professor Nordstrom underscores that the negative aspects of the Scandinavians living in Minneapolis's Sixth Ward should not be forgotten or glorified: "The people of the Ward were hard-working, largely unskilled, poorly paid outsiders in the city. They were separated from the established, English-speaking culture of the city. Their options for employment were severely restricted by their foreign status, as well as by their own economic and linguistic limitations."

He could have been writing about the Somalis in today's Ward Six. It's still not a wealthy part of the city. The population density in Cedar-Riverside is almost twice that of Minneapolis as a whole, and the $22,000 median income is less than half. Some 44 percent of the ward's population are foreign-born compared to 15 percent for the whole city; 60 percent live below the poverty line versus 24 percent in all of Minneapolis; 40 percent don't have a high school diploma; 24 percent of the population speak poor or no English; and only 54 percent of the adults are working.

There is a dark cloud hanging over the Somali community in Minneapolis, and that is the recruitment of young Somali Minnesotans to terrorist groups, including al-Shabaab in Somalia and the Islamic State (ISIS) in Syria. In 2013 two women were sentenced to stiff prison terms for conspiring to send money to al-Shabaab, and in 2014 and 2015 nine young Somali Americans in Minneapolis were arrested and charged with terrorist involvement. Six pleaded guilty of plotting to travel to Syria and join ISIS. Three refused a plea deal. They were found guilty by a jury after a trial in the spring of 2016 and received prison sentences from time served to ten years. The Twin Cities are now part of a new federal pilot program, Countering Violent Extremism, to try other approaches to fighting radicalization that do not necessarily include prison sentences. Parents and other members of the community can take their concerns to "intervention teams," where matters can be discussed without involving law enforcement. In the end, police will be contacted if a person is deemed serious in wanting to join a terrorist group. In Europe, such "softer" approaches have been tried, and the US attorney in Minnesota,

Andrew Luger, traveled to Denmark to learn about that country's approach to combating radicalization among Muslim youth there.

For Abdi Warsame, the Minneapolis City Council member, the number one issue for Somali Minnesotans is unemployment or underemployment. He believes the city needs to do a better job in making sure people have the skills to get jobs, giving people the means to actually enrich their lives. Half of the city's business startups are in the immigrant community, but the Africans don't have the tools or the educational background, Warsame said. He would like to act as "a bridge" between the many different communities in Ward Six. Besides jobs, other top issues are housing, violence, crime, and traffic. "All of these things are local politics," Warsame said. The message to Somali voters is that "if you do not have political clout, no one will take you seriously. If you actually have political power, then some of these issues will be addressed and you will be taken seriously." Warsame said he joined the race to make sure that the largest Somali community in the United States grows and participates in political life, and, in the process, becomes more confident, more integrated, and, in the end, more tolerant.

Warsame has followers in Minneapolis's Somali American community. In 2014 Mohamud Noor, a young computer scientist, executive director of the Confederation of Somali Community, and a member of the Minneapolis school board, challenged liberal Democrat Phyllis Kahn, who was first elected to the Minnesota House of Representatives in 1972, for her seat in the state legislature from District 60B. The DFL nomination caucus ended in a draw, as neither candidate captured the necessary 60 percent of the delegate votes to win the party's endorsement. In the primary that followed, Noor came up short as Kahn won 54 percent of the vote. In his concession speech to his supporters, who had gathered in Currie Park, in the shadow of the Riverside Plaza towers, he said, "It's been an incredible night and we have done our best and we congratulate Phyllis Kahn." Switching between English and Somali, Noor said that "the bitterness in this campaign ends tonight. We are united, not divided. It's now about supporting the DFL Party. Democracy is alive and well. We live in the best state in this nation. This is not the end but the beginning."

As another election approached in November 2016, the seventy-nine-year-old Kahn found herself challenged again, this time by two Somali Americans. In addition to another attempt by Noor, a thirty-three-year-old Somali American woman, Ilhan Omar, also DFL, declared her candidacy. Omar had supported Noor in his first attempt to defeat Kahn.

"I am running," Omar told me, "because we don't feel we are represented by the person currently holding this seat." The district is one of the most diverse in Minnesota, with racial disparities and a huge student population from the University of Minnesota, but, she continued, Representative Kahn has been "complacent" in serving the different populations in the district. "I am running because I believe there is an urgency in tackling these disparities.... I don't run because I think Somalis need a representative but because there is an urgency and they need a voice."

Omar had fled Somalia with her parents when she was eight. After four years in a refugee camp in Kenya, the family arrived in Minneapolis's Cedar-Riverside neighborhood in 1997. College educated and married with three children, Omar is the director of policy and initiatives at the Women Organizing Women Network. She also previously served as the senior policy aide for a Minneapolis City Council member and as DFL vice chair in her district. Omar has called herself an "unapologetic progressive," and in a *MinnPost* interview she said, "I was raised by people who've always dreamed of being part of a free political process. For me, this is exhilarating. This is the American Dream."

At the DFL nomination caucus in April 2016, Omar won 55 percent of the votes, eleven votes shy of the total needed for the endorsement; Kahn received 33 percent of the votes to Noor's 12 percent. Noor's supporters voted not to endorse anyone, although Noor had dropped out after the second ballot, having failed to secure the necessary 20 percent. All three candidates—Kahn, Omar, and Noor—competed in the DFL primary in August to decide the party's candidate for the general election in November.

With two Somali candidates potentially splitting the Somali vote, Kahn seemed to stand a good chance of being reelected once more. City council member Abdi Warsame threw his support behind Noor with the purpose, some sources say, of splitting the Somali vote and paving the way for Kahn's reelection. Warsame had supported Kahn in 2014. There was also speculation that the Somali men were sticking together against a young woman, but Omar said, "This is really about power." Still, she found it "really disappointing" that they needed to have a potentially divisive primary when a clear victory could have been had. Noor, she said, "had the opportunity to be a hero, but he chose not to."

In the end, Ilhan Omar won a resounding upset primary victory, claiming 41 percent of the 5,868 total votes, followed by Noor's 29.6 and Kahn's

29.4 percent. "Tonight, we made history," she said in an emotional speech at a local restaurant full of jubilant, dancing, flag-waving supporters, young and old, black and white. "It's time to move forward together." Omar had held her own in the Somali precincts in Cedar-Riverside and Seward, and she made serious inroads in the district's non-Somali precincts, particularly among University of Minnesota students. She won because she reached out beyond her ethnic community and put together a coalition of new immigrants and white, mainly young, Minnesotans. Her victory "reaffirms what an amazing, truly welcoming state Minnesota is," Abdi Warsame wrote in the *Star Tribune* after the primary.

Her victory in the general election on November 8, 2016, was never in question. House district 60B is a DFL stronghold. In addition, her Republican opponent, also a Somali American, had suspended his campaign well before the election. Omar won 79.8 percent of the vote. Minnesota, and America, had its first Somali American state legislator. It was truly historic.

Somali immigrants' entrance into Minnesota politics has not been without controversy. Robert Lilligren, for example, filed a protest against Warsame for alleged intimidation and excessive voter pressure. Lilligren said that Warsame's campaign implied that people should not vote for him because Lilligren is gay. The DFL Party leaders did not see it that way. The hard-fought 2014 campaign between Kahn and Noor also produced negative headlines, as police had to shut down the nomination caucus after violent confrontations between supporters in which Omar was injured. A second caucus went off without incident.

The Somali Americans seem to be in Minnesota politics to stay, seeking to build political clout just like the Scandinavian immigrants had done before them. As David Lebedoff put it: "The enduring contribution—and I hope this will never end—of the Scandinavian presence in Minnesota is the civic participation to build a stronger society. And that was the reason I was so stirred by the Somali take-over. It was the continuation of what had happened to the Swedes a hundred years earlier: a group moves in, and instead of remaining outside the system and having no part of it, they take over the system. Yes, it's only one city council seat, but it gives them hope and it gives them leverage."

Will the new immigrants change Minnesota's political culture? Margaret Anderson Kelliher, a former speaker of the Minnesota state house and DFL gubernatorial candidate, said the culture is going to be different. But the new immigrant groups will be influenced by the experiences of previous immigrants. "It is pretty deep in our DNA, some of these communal values," she said.

And in the words of a longtime veteran of Minnesota politics, former US vice president Walter Mondale: "It always takes a while with a new generation coming up. It's the old American process at its best, and it's going pretty well. And when they get hold of part of the power structure they help stabilize the community, and they become a model of what happens, a positive model." For Mondale, it's all part of a "process of healthy assimilation." He added, "I don't think that the Somalis feel that they are being cordoned off, separated. They can see where they can become part of America. They see a more open and tolerant society, even better than from which they came."

10

On the Scandinavian Road

"What a glorious new Scandinavia might not Minnesota become!"

Fredrika Bremer, 1853

"If only everyone could be like the Scandinavians, this would all be easy."

President Barack Obama, 2016

ONE OF THE FIRST SCANDINAVIAN visitors to notice the similarities between Minnesota and Scandinavia was Swedish writer Fredrika Bremer, born in the town of Åbo in 1801, when Finland still belonged to Sweden. In 1850, she traveled alone through the United States and arrived in St. Paul, writing, at first sight: "This Minnesota is a glorious country, and just the country for northern emigrants; just the country for a new Scandinavia. . . . What a glorious new Scandinavia might not Minnesota become!"

By 1890, Bremer's vision had become a reality, with Scandinavians making up nearly half of Minnesota's population. Today, 32 percent of the state's 5.4 million inhabitants identify themselves as Scandinavian or Nordic—16.8 percent Norwegian, 9.5 percent Swedish, and 4.7 percent Danish, Finnish, or Icelandic.

The similarities between the two lands are not lost on the descendants of Scandinavians. Former governor Wendell Anderson once wrote about Minnesota, "Any Swede visiting today would feel at home here. He would see in the countryside, in the faces of people, and even in our institutions, reminders of home." That was something Swedish prime minister Tage Erlander seemed to confirm in his diary entry from a visit to Minnesota in 1952: "Nowhere during my trip have I felt so at home as here." And former Minneapolis mayor R. T. Rybak drew applause and laughter when he said in a speech at the American Swedish Institute, "On St. Patrick's Day, it is always said that everybody is Irish; in Minneapolis, every day, everyone is Swedish." Yes, "Minnesota sees itself as a Scandinavian state and Minnesotans are conscious of their heritage, but it is no longer a driving force in their lives," journalist Albert Eisele said. "I don't think there is any doubt that Minnesota has a Scandinavian American culture," Macalester College professor emeritus David Lanegran said.

Kjell Bergh came to Minnesota from Norway in 1967 to go to college and now runs the state's largest dealerships of Swedish Volvos. "It's comfortable here as a Scandinavian," he said. "We are both respected and appreciated for what the Scandinavians have accomplished." Bergh talks about the key elements for a successful life—good education and good health care. "This is without a doubt reflected in the politics of Minnesota." The early Scandinavian immigrants brought a focus on helping each other, as well. Bergh's fellow Norwegian immigrant, Eivind Heiberg, who also came to America to go to college and who heads Sons of Norway and serves as Norway's honorary consul in Minnesota, said that as a native Norwegian in the Twin Cities, you almost get "a red carpet treatment. People are so proud of their roots. . . . It's an incredible feeling: they welcome you and embrace you." Sons of Norway, founded as a self-help society in 1895 by eighteen Norwegian immigrants, today has over $360 million in assets with four hundred local chapters and lodges. For Lena Norrman, who teaches Swedish at the University of Minnesota, life in the state can be described with three simple words, "values, quality, nature"—without doubt important ingredients of life in her native Sweden.

"It's amazing how the Scandinavian legacy is kept alive in Minnesota," said Lutheran pastor David W. Preus, a Norwegian American. "There's a consciousness, and it is hard for me to see that it has diminished at all." His father still spoke Norwegian in church and to the congregation, but he, himself, does not speak Norwegian. The language is just about gone in his family. "We were six children, all about four years apart, and only the three oldest spoke Norwegian. For the last three, our parents made sure we didn't speak Norwegian, because by then, we were doomed to be Americans and they would only hurt us by trying to hang on. . . . It's most unfortunate—it would have been nice if it had been another way. Not only did they not want us to be caught in another language, they did not want us to have the accent, because the Norwegians and the Swedes were the butt of jokes. It had to happen, I guess."

Bruce Karstadt, president of the American Swedish Institute (ASI), describes its mission as a "dynamic interplay between the two values of preserving and celebrating heritage while connecting to contemporary Nordic cultures." But for many, the older picture of Scandinavia lingers, as the modernity and progressiveness that has come to characterize the five Nordic countries after World War II have largely passed them by.

IN MINNESOTA, THE ABUNDANCE of Scandinavian surnames is instantly noticed. There are thousands of people named Anderson and Carlson and Johnson and Peterson. There is Soderberg's Flowers, Carlson Printing, Mortenson Construction, Lundborg Funeral Home, Marie Sandvik Center, Settergren Hardware store, Sven Clothing. Minnesota's media seem to carry more stories about Scandinavia than newspapers in other parts of the United States. And they are more knowledgeable, even making the unusual effort of spelling the Scandinavian names correctly, with all the umlauts and diacritical marks in the three extra letters in the Scandinavian alphabets—the Swedish Å, Ä, and Ö, and the Norwegian and Danish Å, Æ, and Ø.

The decision to stop using the Swedish "ö" sparked a controversy in the spring of 2015 when the Minnesota Department of Transportation dropped the umlaut on signs leading into the town of Lindström, founded in the mid-1850s by Swedish immigrant Daniel Lindström. "Välkommen till Lindström . . . Where the Kaffe's Always On!" is the slogan on the big coffee pot water tower that greets visitors on Main Street. The "ö" did not conform to the rules in the Standard Alphabets for Traffic Control Devices so it would have to be a simple "o." "Why," asked one Minnesotan in a letter to the editor at the *Star Tribune*, "are the Swedish cities of our state denied the proper spelling of their names on highway signs? Allow us to retain our cultural history. Give us our umlauts." It sounded serious, and it was. The "umlaut crisis" spread nationally, reaching the *New York Times* and Swedish media. Quick action was necessary, and Governor Mark Dayton did not wait long to issue an executive order reinstating the umlauts on the city signs. "If I have to drive to Lindström and paint the umlauts on the city limit signs myself, I will do it," the governor stated. The next day, crews from the Department of Transportation put the umlauts back.

Scandinavian royalty who visit the United States almost always make a stop in Minnesota—even if Minnesotans may need a primer on which country the dignitaries are coming from. "In the interest of fjord-like clarity," Kim Ode wrote in the *Star Tribune* prior to a 2013 visit by Sweden's King Carl Gustaf and Queen Silvia, she explained that the visitors were from

Sweden, "the birthplace of Ikea, Volvo, Nobel prizes, Abba, and smörgås-bords. Sweden, where the girls can have dragon tattoos or walk around be-fore Christmas with lighted candles on their heads."

Culinary connections are also evident. Swedish immigrant baker Arvid Peterson introduced the RyKrisp, a kind of *knäckebröd*, or crisp bread, to Minnesota and America in 1904 from the bakery on Lyndale Avenue. Al-though that bakery is no more, the city now has both the Scandinavian-inspired Bachelor Farmer and Fika, a popular lunch spot in the American Swedish Institute. And where else in America are you given the chance to attend a traditional Swedish August crayfish party—*kräftskiva*—where you can enjoy crayfish cooked in lots of dill, Västerbotten cheesecake, salad, beer, and, of course, aquavit, the potent spirit distilled from grain or pota-toes, flavored with caraway, fennel, anise, and other spices, served ice-cold in shot glasses and drunk with a song called a *snapsvisa*, and a *"skål"*—cheers!

Central Minneapolis is dotted with signs of its Scandinavian past.

The American Swedish Institute's classic Turnblad Mansion—Minne-apolis's only "castle"—was donated by Swedish newspaper publisher Swan Turnblad in 1929 and now has a modern exhibition wing. Only blocks away are Den Norske Lutherske Mindekirken (The Norwegian Lutheran Memo-rial Church), where services are still held in both English and Norwegian every Sunday, and the new Norway House. Danebo, the Danish American Center, lies a little further east, on the western banks of the Mississippi River. And in between, the Finns gather at the simple but stunningly beau-tiful Christ Church Lutheran, a national historic landmark first designed in 1949 by Eliel and Eero Saarinen, the Finnish father and son architects who made America their home.

Ingebretsen's Scandinavian food and gift store has done business on East Lake Street for more than ninety years. It has survived through the neigh-borhood's ups and downs on a stretch of the street once dominated by Scan-dinavians. When the old streetcars from downtown reached Lake Street, the area blossomed with businesses like Marie Narum's shoe store and Axel's lunchroom, both now closed. The old Swedish record store, Suneson Music Center, once next door to Ingebretsen's, closed in 2000. Across the street, on what is now an empty lot, the Gustavus II Adolphus Society had its Minneapolis headquarters. Founded in 1886, the society served the growing number of Swedish immigrant men. Its three-story building opened in 1924 "to demonstrate that Swedes were substantial citizens" and became a com-munity hub. Membership grew until the 1960s. As the Swedish immigrant community aged, and other groups entered the neighborhood, the building was sold, and it then burned down in January 2004, according to the sidewalk plaque, which is written in English and Spanish, but not in Swedish or Norwegian. Today, on the same block as Ingebretsen's are the Mexican eateries La Poblanita, El Diamantito, and Panaderia San Miguel, revealing the neighborhood's current demographics. Across the street, Durdur Bakery and Grocery sells halal meats, including beef, goat, and camel, catering to the growing Muslim population, and on the next block is the first Somali museum in the United States, the Somali Museum of Minnesota, opened in October 2013. "Somalis are playing the role European immigrants played in the 19th and 20th centuries," said museum outreach director Sarah Larsson to *MinnPost*.

In St. Paul, Payne Avenue was once the main street for the city's Swedish population, but it too has seen major changes. Anderson Shoes still exists, but the other Scandinavian names have been replaced by La Chica Fashion, Muong Pha Asia Grocery, La Pela Tortelleria, La Palma Supermercado, and Morelli's Alimentari. The Phalen Creek ravine, better known as Swede Hollow, is now a park with pleasant walks, picnic tables, and a creek running through. In the late 1800s, it was home to thousands of Swedish immigrants, who lived in real poverty in ramshackle houses, without heat or running water. The Swedes eventually left the hollow—moved up in the world in the classic immigrant pattern—and were replaced by other immigrant groups. In 1956, the last fourteen families (Mexican by this time) were evicted and their homes were burned after the spring that had supplied the water for Swede Hollow for a century was declared unsafe. Next to the park is Swede Hollow Cafe, a friendly lunch place. But if you are looking for Swedish treats, you will look in vain.

There is, seemingly, a Lutheran church on every corner in the Twin Cities. Minnesota's Scandinavians were, and still are, a church-going people. They talk about "my" church or "our" church and still go to the traditional lutfisk dinner and to listen to choral songs at Christmas. In today's Scandinavia, few people, only three percent of the population, attend church, and it stopped long ago being a community hub.

On a short stretch of Seventh Street South in Minneapolis, next to the new house of Sunday worship—the Minnesota Vikings' football stadium— three churches are monuments of a bygone era, when downtown was dominated by the Scandinavian immigrants from nearby Seven Corners and Cedar-Riverside. Their Swedish names—Augustana Lutheran from 1866,

Svenska Missionstabernaklet from 1886, and Svenska Missions Templet from 1895—are still visible on their red brick facades, but there is little else Swedish about them today. Services in Swedish haven't been held since 1957.

Svenska Missionstabernaklet, now the First Covenant Church, calls itself a "diverse, multi-generational, urban Christian community" and is still bilingual—but now it's English and Spanish. There is a gospel choir, a Latino evening, an Ethiopian gathering, and sister churches in Malawi in Africa. Its huge sanctuary is rarely even half full, but there is a mixture of young families and elderly couples. There are also signs of the old days, including the Swedish Room outside the sanctuary that honors the old immigrants with furniture and antiques, including an old grandfather clock, a classic *Moraklocka*.

Augustana Lutheran launched one of the earliest social ministry programs in Minneapolis to help women, orphans, the elderly, and the infirm. Augustana Care now includes three health centers, three senior living buildings, and an adult daycare center. The Swedish Hospital was founded next door and is now part of the Hennepin County Medical Center. The church now has only about a hundred members, and after it was recently sold and gave way to Hope Community Church, the old congregation moved to the nearby former First Swedish Methodist Church, from 1873.

Mindekirken, the Norwegian Lutheran Memorial Church, at the corner of East Twenty-First Street and East Franklin Avenue, is the epicenter of Norwegian Minneapolis, although no Scandinavians live in the neighborhood anymore. The Norwegians have for a long time watched the success of the nearby American Swedish Institute, perhaps with a tinge of envy. Finally, in 2015, a new center for Norwegian American culture and business, called Norway House, opened in the old bank building next to the church. Calling itself a "convener, connector, and facilitator of Norwegian American business, educational, social, and cultural organizations," Norway House "serves as a bridge between Americans and contemporary Norway" and confirms the strong ties between Minnesota and Scandinavia.

On May 17, 2014, Syttende Mai, Minneapolis celebrated the two hundredth anniversary of Norway's constitution. The festivities kicked off with a gala dinner attended by leading Norwegian Minnesotans, including Minnesota's chief justice Lorie Skjerven Gildea, St. Olaf College president David Anderson, and former state senate majority leader Roger Moe. The next day, a beautiful Sunday morning, Mindekirken was packed. The church was draped in Norwegian and American flags, the Norwegian Glee Club sang,

Pastor Kristin Sundt leads the parade from the Norwegian Mindekirken in Minne-
apolis on Syttende Mai (May 17), Norway's national day. Photo by the author

and the church bells rang. Children played games; there was a picnic, fiddle
music, and folk dancing. The traditional *folketog* (people's parade) through
the neighborhood—past the corner with the Somali Village Market and
Gulet Deli and Grocery—left some current residents wondering what was
going on, including one who said, "I think it's a Swedish parade."

228 · *Scandinavians in the State House*

EACH OF MINNESOTA'S TWIN CITIES is home to remarkable sculptures that reflect the cities' ties to Scandinavia and have become iconic symbols of the region. In the St. Paul City Hall and Ramsey County Courthouse, Carl Milles's *Vision of Peace* towers in the building's glorious Memorial Hall lobby. Unveiled in 1936, the statue draws on a Native American ceremony that the Swedish-born Milles had witnessed in Oklahoma. Milles spent most of his adult life in the United States before he returned to Sweden, where he died in 1955. He has left behind hundreds of sculptures at Millesgården in Stockholm and at the Cranbrook Academy of Art outside of Detroit, Michigan. Milles originally called the St. Paul sculpture *Indian God of Peace*, but it was renamed *Vision of Peace* at a ceremony in 1994 involving the state's major Native American tribes. It's made of white Mexican onyx, and it is gigantic—thirty-six feet tall and weighing sixty tons. It fills the hall and is truly magnificent.

In Minneapolis, *Spoonbridge and Cherry* by the Swedish-born Claes Oldenburg and his Dutch-born wife, Coosje van Bruggen, lights up the Sculpture Garden at the Walker Art Center. Oldenburg came to America as a young boy and grew up in Chicago, where his father was consul general. In the 1980s, he and his wife created their iconic sculpture, which is as remarkable in winter as in summer.

But those two statues are not the only ones in the Twin Cities by Scandinavian artists or with Nordic themes. Descendants of immigrants formed many fundraising committees and placed statues in parks all over the Twin Cities to commemorate their heritage. In Minnehaha Park, for example, there's the statue of Gunnar Wennerberg (1817–1901), a now largely forgotten Swedish poet and composer. A call to action in *Svenska Amerikanska Posten* urged the erection of a statue in honor of Wennerberg to "proudly remind the world that this man was a Swede." On Svenskarnas Dag in 1915, twenty-five thousand people gathered at the park to witness the unveiling of the big bronze statue by Swedish artist Carl Johan Eldh. Another literary-inspired sculpture was erected in 1955, when a replica of Arvid Backlund's statue of Selma Lagerlöf, the 1909 Nobel Prize–winning author, was installed in the garden of the American Swedish Institute. Backlund's original work stands in Rottneros Park in Värmland, Sweden.

In other city parks, Norwegians erected memorials of famous countrymen, many created by immigrant artist Jacob Fjelde. A bust in Como Park of Henrik Ibsen, the Norwegian playwright, was a gift from the Sons of Norway in 1912, and a statue of Norwegian violinist Ole Bull stands in

Loring Park near downtown Minneapolis. Fjelde's son, Paul, was also a sculptor, and his bust of President Abraham Lincoln, a gift to Norway from the people of North Dakota, stands in Oslo's Frogner Park. It is said to have served as a symbol of resistance during the Nazi occupation of Norway.

A bit less visible, on Kellogg Boulevard in downtown St. Paul, are plaques honoring two Swedish engineers at the entrance of the Hans O. Nyman Energy Center, the largest hot water district heating system in North America. Nyman and his successor, Anders Rydaker, were lured to St. Paul by mayor George Latimer to replace the old steam system. In the process, it has helped make Minnesota's capitol an energy-efficient, environmentally friendly city. "It's been absolutely wonderful for St. Paul," said Latimer.

JUNE IS MIDSOMMAR, and, in the Swedish tradition, flower-decked maypoles are raised across Minnesota. The small town of Nisswa, located about two hours northwest of Minneapolis, is the site of the annual Nisswa-stämman Scandinavian Folk Music Festival. *Stämma* in Swedish here means a group of people coming together to play music. And that's what they do in Nisswa. For two whole days and late into the nights, musicians from the Nordic countries joined with local Minnesota bands like Olle Olsson's Oldtime Orkestra, Skålmusik, the American Swedish Institute's Spelmanslag, Twin Cities Nyckelharpalag, and the Finn Hall Band.

Fiddlers Paul Dahlin and his son Daniel, third- and fourth-generation Swedes, together with uncle Bruce Johnson, are from Minneapolis. They call themselves Ivares Pojkarna after Paul's maternal grandfather, Ivares Edvin Jonsson, who came to Minnesota in 1924 from Röjeråsen in the province of Dalarna. He was nineteen years old, and his mother did not let him bring his fiddle. She told him he was going to America to work. But Jonsson came to spend the rest of his life in Minnesota playing his beloved music from Dalarna and passing on his fiddle music to his children, and to his grandson Paul, who was in 1996 awarded an NEA National Heritage Fellowship. In Nisswa, Paul, Daniel, and Bruce played the roof off in the cramped barn.

Eight towns in Chisago County—Chisago City, Lindström, Center City, Scandia, Taylors Falls, Shafer, Almelund, and North Branch—have sister cities in Sweden. This is the heart of Moberg Country, where the first Swedish immigrants arrived in 1850 and whose stories were immortalized by Vilhelm Moberg in the Emigrants series, his four-part epic about Karl Oskar Nilsson and his Kristina. A replica of the Karl Oskar and Kristina statue from the harbor in Karlshamn, the town on Sweden's southern coast

Midsommar festival at Minneapolis's American Swedish Institute. Photo courtesy of the American Swedish Institute

from which they left for America, stands in front of the Chisago County Press building in central Lindström, "America's Little Sweden." The Karl Oskar House, Nya Duvemåla in Lindström, was the inspiration for Karl Oskar and Kristina's home from Moberg's story. It is now a museum located near the Glader Cemetery from 1855, the first burial ground in the new country for Swedish immigrants. In Chisago City's Moberg Park, there is a statue of Vilhelm Moberg with his bike, which he used to get around and interview area residents while researching his epic in 1948.

In Scandia, director Lynne Blomstrand Moratzka has helped put together a remarkable heritage museum. Called Gammelgården, it is located next to the Elim Lutheran Church and its cemetery, where headstone names like Carlson, Mattson, Olson, Anderson, Lindgren, and Peterson leave no doubt about their origin. The museum dates from 1972, when the congregation at the Elim Church stepped in to save some historic log buildings. "We talk about immigration with a Swedish flavor," she said. "You are asked every day what to keep and what to let go of your ethnic heritage. So we say, we are here to tell a story of long ago but more importantly we are here to encourage you to keep whatever ethnic traditions you have, because they are important and they make you. Take some pride in your ethnicity. Don't deny it."

In a sign of this fading sense of ethnic heritage, Svenskarnas Dag, Swedish Heritage Day, is no more. In 2015, after more than eighty years, the Swedes joined forces with the Norwegians for the first "Scandinavian Summer Fest." Ted Noble, chair of Svenskarnas Dag, had been looking for a younger generation to take over and keep the legacy alive, but they are not easy to find, he said. Once, in 1938, Swedish crown prince Gustaf Adolf was welcomed by a hundred thousand people. "I had to pinch myself in the arm to be sure I was not dreaming," he supposedly said as he addressed the huge crowd in Swedish. For many years Svenskarnas Dag was a "must-stop" for Minnesota politicians running for office. On its eightieth anniversary, in 2013, maybe a thousand had gathered in Minneapolis's Minnehaha Park. It turned out to be the next to last Svenskarnas Dag—a sign of the times.

If June is important to Scandinavian traditions, so is December with its short days and long nights: Christmas songs, candles, julbord (Christmas buffet), and Santa Lucia, the blond girl with candles in her hair who makes her entry on December 13, one of the darkest days of the year, in the magnificent big room in the American Swedish Institute's Turnblad Mansion.

At Gustavus Adolphus College, founded by Swedes in 1862 and located in St. Peter, south of the Twin Cities, the traditional Christmas in Christ Chapel combines food, music, and song. The Christmas buffet includes herring, smoked salmon, oysters in hot mustard, Swedish meatballs and sausages, flatbread and rye bread, Norwegian lefse with lingonberries, Santa Lucia rolls (*lussekatter*), gingersnap cookies, and, finally, lutefisk—in Swedish spelled without an "e" in the middle, but somehow the Norwegian spelling is preferred even here at Gustavus Adolphus.

Lutfisk is not a big part of the Christmas table in Sweden anymore, but it dominates the Christmas season in Minnesota. At Mount Olivet Lutheran Church in South Minneapolis, founded by Swedes and one of the biggest Lutheran churches in America, twelve hundred pounds of lutfisk were prepared for as many as eighteen hundred guests at the traditional Christmas Lutefisk Dinner. But this traditional Nordic dish is not to everyone's liking. Bill Holm, the Icelandic American writer from Minneota in western Minnesota, asked in one of his books: "Is lutefisk food at all?" Good question.

WHEN MINNESOTA POLITICIANS head overseas, the five Nordic countries are a natural destination. In 2013 Governor Mark Dayton visited Norway and Sweden, as well as Germany, to increase Minnesota's exports and attract foreign investments to the state. Sweden's economic impact on Minnesota is not negligible. The state's total export of goods to Sweden is valued at $113 million per year. Swedish companies support a total of more than 6,600 jobs in Minnesota.

Keith Ellison, an African American and a Muslim who succeeded Norwegian American political veteran Martin Olav Sabo in the US House of Representatives, went to Norway on his first foreign visit to learn about peace and justice issues. The US attorney for Minnesota, Andrew Luger, went to Denmark in 2014 to learn about how the Danes battle extremism and what lessons Minnesota could learn as it tries to combat radicalism among its East African population. Jodi Harpstead, head of Lutheran Social Service of Minnesota, has been to her ancestral Denmark to see how the Danes work with people with disabilities. When University of Minnesota president Eric Kaler made his one official foreign trip in 2014, he headed to Norway, where the University of Oslo has long been a partner, particularly on climate change issues. Kaler told the *Minnesota Daily* that this relationship is important "given Minnesota's Scandinavian heritage." However, that heritage was not deep enough to save the university's Department of Scandinavian Studies, officially established in March 1883 by the Minnesota State Legislature. Swedish-born Nils Hasselmo, the university president from 1988 to 1997, once described the department as Scandinavian ethnic self-assertion in education. After a merger, however, the department no longer exists and is now called the Department of German, Scandinavian and Dutch. There are no permanent professors in the Nordic languages; Danish is not offered at all, and modern Icelandic only as a special six-week course.

Despite the loss of a Scandinavian department at the university, Minnesotans young and old can still learn Norwegian, Swedish, Finnish, and Danish—along with eleven other languages—at the Concordia Language Villages. Located in dense forest at Turtle Lake just north of Bemidji, the language villages were a brainchild of Gerhard Haukebo, professor at Concordia College in Moorhead, Minnesota, to initiate a program using immersion techniques to teach languages. Today there are fifteen villages on eight hundred acres with ten thousand participants every year, including the Norwegian Skogfjorden, Swedish Sjölunden, Finnish Salolampi, and Danish Skovsøen. Students come back year after year, and many return as teachers. Families come, with parents and grandparents. It becomes a community for learning. "We open up the world for the children via a foreign language," said Tove Dahl, dean of the Norwegian language village, "a sort of door opener to other cultures to help young people grow as responsible world citizens."

SOUTHEAST OF THE TWIN CITIES, toward the rolling hills where Minnesota meets Wisconsin and Iowa, the American and Norwegian flags greet visitors with a "Velkommen" at the entrance to the town of Spring Grove, the state's first Norwegian settlement. Eventually it became one of the densest Norwegian settlements in all of the United States.

Starting in 1852 with three Norwegians from Hallingdal, Spring Grove by 1870 had 1,135 Norwegian inhabitants, with only a handful of other nationalities. Spring Grove is still very Norwegian. Of the sixteen churches in the area, nine are Lutheran. A Syttende Mai Hus sits in the Viking Memorial Park in the middle of town, where two bronze figures commemorate *Han Ola og han Per*, a memorable comic strip by native son Norwegian American Peter Rosendahl. In the old Norwegian Ridge Cemetery behind Trinity Lutheran Church, every name on every gravestone is Norwegian.

On Main Street, the Giants of the Earth Heritage Center opened in the old Ballard House in 2009. The center is next to Norski's Saloon, where all five Nordic flags hang from the rafters. The murals in the Heritage Center were painted by Sigmund Årseth, a Norwegian artist who often visited Spring Grove and who taught rosemaling and landscape classes at Vesterheim Norwegian American museum in nearby Decorah, Iowa. A memorial statue of Årseth, who died in 2012, stands in the little garden behind the center.

As the first Norwegian settlement in Minnesota, Spring Grove is intent on keeping its heritage alive. It's a means of survival as many small towns fight for their existence on the plains. But even here, the memories and traditions of the pioneers are fading as the generations succeed each other. In 2014 Spring Grove's Syttende Mai celebration was shortened from three days to one due to lack of volunteers and declining attendance, according to Corey Anderson, president of the Syttende Mai committee.

After 1870, when there was no more available farmland around Spring Grove, the Norwegians headed west, to the Red River Valley on the border to North Dakota. The Hjemkomst Center (Homecoming Center) in Moorhead is a tribute to those Norwegian forebears, with its full-scale replicas of a Viking ship and of the Hopperstad Stave Church built by two local Norwegian Americans.

THE YEAR 2014 WAS an important one for Minnesota's Finnish population, marking 150 years since the first immigrants arrived from Finland.

That summer, the annual FinnFest was held in Minneapolis, a remarkable gathering of hundreds of Finnish Americans from all over America to celebrate their heritage and hold serious discussions about language and history. At the University of Minnesota, a two-day forum with educators from Finland discussed similarities and differences and the importance of education as "an element in the culture, as part of our societies," the Finnish minister of education said. There is no better model for Minnesota than the Finnish educational model, according to a speaker from Minnesota, who underscored the trust, respect, and cooperative nature of the highly regarded Finnish system as something to be emulated.

Earlier that year, blue-and-white Finnish flags were waved jubilantly in the crowd at Minneapolis's Orchestra Hall as an ovation greeted Finnish conductor Osmo Vänskä and the Minnesota Orchestra for their first concert in a year, following a lengthy labor conflict.

Cokato, about an hour west of Minneapolis, is Minnesota's oldest continuously Finnish community. The Finns first arrived in 1864, and by the end of 1869 there were twelve families and a few single men in Cokato. Five years later another fifty families arrived, and in 1876 twenty-five new families came from Finland. Now, 150 years later, on the Finnish Pioneer Memorial Highway around Cokato you can view the old and new Apostolic Lutheran Church, the old homesteads, the Finnish pioneer cemetery, and Finnish Pioneer Park with its Temperance Hall, schoolhouse, and Savu Sauna.

Farther west, Willmar was long dominated by Scandinavians and today is the hometown of veteran Scandinavian lawmakers Dean Johnson, Alec G. Olson, and John Lindstrom. Johnson, a Norwegian, is a Lutheran pastor who was the Republican minority leader and then, after switching parties in 2000, the DFL majority leader in the Minnesota Senate. He also serves as chair of the Board of Regents at the University of Minnesota. Lindstrom, Swedish, was a DFL member of the Minnesota house and then a district judge for many years. Olson, who still speaks Swedish pretty well, is a farmer and a former US congressman, state senator, and lieutenant governor. He talks of civic duty and responsibility and how this was taken seriously by the Scandinavian immigrants. Johnson and Olson once ran against each other for the state senate seat. Johnson tells the story of when he was knocking on doors during the campaign and came to a German farm. After he introduced himself, the farmer asked who his opponent was. "I told him, Alec Olson, whereupon he said, 'Well, I don't think I will be voting this year.'"

Today, Willmar is a microcosm of modern Minnesota, with many new immigrants, including between three thousand and four thousand Somalis. About 15 percent of the town's population are people of color. They have come for the jobs, mainly at the Jennie-O turkey plant, named after Jennifer Olson, the daughter of Earl B. Olson, whose parents, Olof and Anna (Anderson) Olson, were immigrants from Sweden. Olson—called the "turkey king of the world"—started his turkey business in Willmar in 1940. Between seven hundred and eight hundred Somalis now work there.

On Litchfield Avenue, the main street in downtown Willmar, life and business seem to be dominated by the Somali immigrants, whereas in 1905, at least seventy-nine of the listed 153 businesses were owned or operated by Scandinavians. There is an African Development Center, the Somali Star restaurant, the Somali grocery store Bihi's Shop, and the Somali Connection, another grocery store.

Beyond Willmar, still farther west, the Icelandic and Danish immigrants settled in the little towns of Minneota and Tyler. In Minneota, not much is left of the old Icelandic community other than their churches and cemeteries. Here, their most famous sons are buried, among them the Bjornson family—Gunnar B. (1872–1957) and his son, Valdimir "Val" (1906–87), both prominent journalists and politicians—as well as the writer and poet Bill Holm (1943–2009).

"Gone but not forgotten" reads the inscription on the Holm family gravestone in Westerheim Icelandic Cemetery, at the windblown corner of County Road 10 and County Road 61 outside Minneota. Here is where Bill Holm's Icelandic grandparents once settled, and where the cemeteries are full of Arnasons, Björnsons, and Gislasons. A plaque at the cemetery tells us that they brought little, because they had little: "Perhaps their most precious possessions were their sincere interest in public affairs and their traditional love of learning." They established schools, churches, libraries, reading societies, and the only Icelandic language newspaper in the United States, the *Vinland*, and they started businesses and farms.

Val Bjornson and Bill Holm were of different generations, but they knew each other as members of the small Icelandic immigrant community. In 1954, an eleven-year-old Holm met Bjornson for the first time when Bjornson was running for the US Senate against Hubert Humphrey. They met at the Swede Prairie Town Hall, and young Bill got Bjornson's autograph, which he kept all his life, he writes in his 1996 memoir. Bjornson lost to Humphrey, but "after an election so calm, dignified, literate, full of content, and completely without personal attacks on the part of either man—my memory of its honor and eloquence is one foundation of the energy I've spent as a writer praising failure in America." Holm described Val Bjornson as a great man, despite being a Republican, a man famous for his oratory and wit, "a writer, a talker, a word man"—just like young Bill Holm wanted to be.

The little town of Tyler is in the "Danish heartland," a few miles southwest of Minneota. The Danes, just like the Icelanders and the other Scandinavians, came here to farm, and they brought with them their traditions and their emphasis on education. Beginning in 1885, they founded the Danebod Folk School, a church, and a gym hall, now part of the Danebod Historic Complex on the south side of Tyler. At Christmas, there is still the traditional dancing around the Christmas tree, and in July, all of Tyler celebrates Aebleskiver Days, named after a special Danish pancake.

The businesses in town are a reminder of Tyler's Danish past: Jorgensen's financial services, the Kronborg Inn, Petersen's law office, Knudsen's insurance, and the little Nissemaend, the Danish elf who comes out so mysteriously at Christmas. But otherwise, there is not much Danish anymore in Tyler, Minnesota.

Alexandria, the hometown of legendary Norwegian American governor and US senator Knute Nelson, lies about two hours northwest of the Twin Cities. It calls itself the "birthplace of America" by virtue of the famous Kensington Runestone, housed in its own museum. The town is also home to "Big Ole"—maybe the biggest and most hideous Viking statue ever erected. A runestone in Minnesota is of course an odd occurrence, and debate has raged about its authenticity, among experts and amateurs alike. It was supposedly "placed here by Vikings in the year 1362," says the inscription on the runestone, having been found and dug up in 1898 by Swedish immigrant Olof Öhman on his farm in nearby Kensington. In 1949, the Swedish runologist Sven B. F. Jansson at Uppsala University concluded that it was a hoax. Runes are an old Scandinavian alphabet from the Viking Age that ended in 1050 or so, but the text on the Kensington stone was written in the late 1800s, not the 1300s. That did not prevent it from becoming one of the most famous and most discussed runestones in the world, exhibited at the Smithsonian Institution in Washington, DC, at the World's Fair in New York, and even in Scandinavia.

The stone has become a "cultural icon," and "its disputed authenticity only serves to make it more interesting and more symbolic," writes Uppsala Professor Henrik Williams. For the town of Alexandria, this debate does not seem to matter. Hoax or not, the Kensington Runestone and its museum, created in 1958, have become important tourist destinations.

WINTER IS ALSO SOMETHING that Minnesota has in common with northern Europe, and with that the winter sports. In the State of Hockey, just like in Sweden and Finland, ice hockey is big. Minnesota's National Hockey League team, the Minnesota Wild, has a distinct Scandinavian flavor. "Finns to the Left, Finns to the Right" was the headline in the *Star Tribune* just before the playoffs in April 2014, when the team featured three Finnish forwards: Mikko Koivu, Mikael Granlund, and Erik Haula, from Turku, Oulu, and Pori, respectively. That winter another Finn, Sean Bergenheim, was added to the mix alongside Swedish defenders Jonas Brodin and Christian Folin and Finnish goalie Niklas Bäckström.

What most people don't know is that Minnesota is also the State of Bandy—although most people probably don't even know what bandy is. This classic winter sport, which existed long before hockey, is played almost exclusively in the Nordic countries, in Russia, and, it turns out, in Minnesota, at the Guidant John Rose Minnesota Oval in Roseville, just north of St. Paul. The local team, the Minnesota Bandolier, are US champions. Like hockey, bandy is a fast game, played on ice, but on a soccer-size field and with shorter sticks, with a hard red ball instead of a black puck, and with eleven players on each side, including a stick-less goalie defending a soccer-sized goal.

And let's not forget skiing. Minneapolis's City of Lakes Loppet (Swedish for "the race") is an annual urban cross-country ski festival. On a perfect winter day, with clear blue skies, a warming sun, and deep snow, over ten thousand cross-country skiers of all ages race through the city on groomed trails, from park to park, from lake to lake, to the finish line at Lake Calhoun. All funds from the racing fees go to support the nonprofit Loppet Foundation's youth activities. The weekend after Loppet, the town of Mora, in heavily Swedish Isanti County north of the Twin Cities, hosts Vasaloppet as a yearly winter tradition. It takes its name from the massive ninety-kilometer cross-country ski race held each year from Sälen to Mora in the province of Dalarna in Sweden. The race traces the route taken when the first Swedish king, Gustav Vasa, fled on skis in the early 1500s to rally the Swedes against the Danish occupiers. Entering Mora, Minnesota, you are welcomed by a statue of "Mora-Nisse," one of the most famous Swedish cross-country skiers of all time. His real name was Nils Karlsson, from Mora, Sweden. He won dozens of Swedish championships and an Olympic gold medal in 1948, but, most importantly, he won Sweden's Vasaloppet a record nine times. In

1981 he also completed the Minnesota version. And the exchange has continued. In 2014 about twenty skiers from Mora, Sweden, took part in Vasaloppet in Mora, Minnesota.

AND SO THE SIGNS OF SCANDINAVIA and of those hundreds of thousands of Scandinavians who made Minnesota their home are still everywhere to be found, in all corners of today's Minnesota. Minnesota did become that "new, glorious Scandinavia" that Fredrika Bremer described. The question is, does that also still pertain to Minnesota's politics? Does its politics still have that Scandinavian flavor, and what does the future of its politics hold?

"I sort of think that Minnesota is to the United States what Scandinavia is to the world," said Ryan Winkler, a DFLer and budding star in the state legislature until he decided to leave politics in 2015 when his Swedish-born lawyer wife, Jenny Lindström Winkler from Karlstad in Värmland, took a new job in Brussels. He became a stay-at-home dad for their three children—just like many Scandinavians.

Don Ostrom, professor emeritus at Gustavus Adolphus College and a former DFL state representative, said, "If Canada is halfway culturally between the US and Europe, then Minnesota is halfway between the US and Canada. . . . I think the Swedish and Norwegian political culture is reflected in the general culture": dignity of ordinary people, the idea of helping your neighbor, cooperative activities, and the notion that we are all in this together.

"Historically, we have been a state with higher taxes and better services than most—and we have had clean politics, and, historically, people in Minnesota have felt that they were part of the government and not separate and removed from it," former Minnesota house speaker and US congressman Martin Olav Sabo said.

Minnesota is a state where education has long been a priority and the less well-off are taken care of, where the progressive traditions of Scandinavian public policy and the social conscience of the Lutheran church combine with uniquely American demographic and character traits. The Scandinavian immigrants and their descendants were at the forefront of every phase of the state's political history. They fought for the Union and helped shape the Republican Party; their switch to the Democratic/Populist Party sparked a shift in the statewide party power balance; they were leading participants in the agrarian protest movements such as the Farmers' Alliance and the Nonpartisan League; they were among the leaders in Minnesota's radical politics with the rise of socialism and communism in the early twentieth century; they were the strike leaders in the mines on the Iron Range; they were isolationists who also led the anti-immigration and loyalty efforts during World War I; they were leaders in the Farmer-Labor movement and led the efforts to merge the Farmer-Labor Party with the Democratic Party to form the Democratic-Farmer-Labor Party (DFL); they produced a series of progressive and respected Republican governors in the post–World War II era; they stood at the forefront of the Minnesota Miracle in the 1970s; and two of them became vice president of the United States.

For David Lebedoff, political veteran and campaign manager for former governor Wendell Anderson, the Scandinavian political legacy in Minnesota "has been extraordinarily important—in fact, the most important for Minnesota." The role of the Scandinavians is "probably the single largest reason for Minnesota's prosperity and clean politics." Their "enduring contribution—and I hope this will never end—is the civic participation to build a stronger society."

But Minnesota politics has also "shown signs of schizophrenia," with radical protest movements occurring at the same time as traditional conservatism. Its progressivist traditions have not developed in a straight, unbroken line. Its record is not unblemished, as witnessed by the Commission of Public Safety during World War I, the Duluth lynchings and Ku Klux Klan activity in the 1920s, the decades-long anti-labor and anti-union policies of the Citizens Alliance; anti-Semitism in Minneapolis in the 1930s and '40s, when the city was called the "capital of anti-Semitism in the United States" and where "an iron curtain" separated Jews from non-Jews.

"To be honest, the picture has not always been pretty," said Sabo, who also said that when he was challenged by a man named Johnson in his second election in 1962, "I decided I had better start using my middle name, Olav, and since then, I always had some 'Olav' votes. . . . The Scandinavian legacy will live on; its foundation is strong enough."

And what is the Scandinavian political legacy? Ostrom sees it as the "absence of corruption, honesty in government, making people less opposed to high taxes than in other states because they don't think that it is all going to waste, and the value placed on education. . . . There is not that great fear of government in Minnesota that there is in so many states."

"It's a question of equity more than anything else," said Ken Martin, chair of the DFL Party, and "that is a Scandinavian issue, opportunity and equality for all."

Issues concerned with quality of life are central to the political debate in Minnesota today, issues that could easily be high on the political agenda in Scandinavia. They reflect the notion, as Macalester professor David Lanegran put it, that government is supposed to work for and serve the people. That is what Lanegran would call the "Scandinavian ethos," a government based on a "puritanical political structure." For example, the Minnesota legislature recently refused, once again, to allow liquor sales on Sundays—a "no-no" in most Scandinavian countries, where state liquor stores at times have even been closed on Saturdays. The opposition to the new senate office building in St. Paul and suggestions that the money should be given to those in need sound very Scandinavian. So does the new anti-bullying law. Abortion rights and same-sex marriage are, of course, old hat in Scandinavia, so is all-day kindergarten, and the ongoing debate in Minnesota about allowing the unionization of kindergarten teachers rings Scandinavian, where unions are still strong.

Former Republican speaker Steve Sviggum said he had been particularly influenced by the tough drunk-driving laws in Scandinavia. Our laws, he said, are still not as tough, although we have tried to enhance them. And for Ryan Winkler, "family support"—child care, or *dagis*, to use the popular Swedish term for daycare—stands out. "What I think Scandinavia is really doing well is creating a little 'cocoon of stability' around children, and that's what these early childhood scholarships are all about," Winkler said. That, plus paid sick leave and family leave are some of the things Minnesota takes from Scandinavia. This might be a little too much social welfare for Minnesota, "but because it is built around children I think people would find it more acceptable."

There are also exceptions to the similarities in the political debate in Minnesota and Scandinavia. Gun rights are the most obvious.

Minnesotans are proud of their state, and rightly so. Few people move away. Minnesota often comes out on top, or close to the top, in rankings for quality of life and state pride, and Minnesota's politicians and media love to cite these numbers and rankings that show the progress and general well-being of the population in the North Star State. In particular, Minnesotans love to compare their state to neighbor and rival Wisconsin, where the latest job growth numbers, under conservative Republican governor Scott Walker, put Wisconsin forty-fourth among the fifty states. Walker has cut education spending and taxes on the wealthy, fought the unions, banned gay marriage, refused to participate in the Affordable Care Act health exchange and expand Medicaid, and imposed photo IDs for voters. Minnesota governor Mark Dayton has done the opposite. He raised taxes on the top two percent, which brought in over two billion dollars, three-quarters of which went to education; raised the minimum wage; instituted free all-day kindergarten; and defeated two constitutional amendments, supported by the Republicans, banning same-sex marriage and introducing new photo ID requirements for the state's voters.

Minnesota's recent success is unquestionable. A progressive in the style of previous Scandinavian American governors, Dayton is also stunningly unglamorous and totally devoid of charisma or eloquence, in typical Scandinavian fashion. In 2014, he was the only Democratic governor to win among nine midwestern states, underscoring Minnesota's exceptionalism. The budget deficit inherited from his predecessor Tim Pawlenty has been turned into a healthy one-billion dollar surplus. Since January 2011, when Dayton took office, more than 170,000 new jobs have been created, and in April 2016, the state added a record 15,500 private-sector jobs. Unemployment stood at 3.8 percent, compared to five percent nationally. Median household income was $60,828, with 11.5 percent of the population below the poverty line, compared to 15 percent nationally. More than 90 percent of Minnesotans have a high school diploma or higher. In 2014, Dayton signed a bill to extend unpaid leave for pregnant women from six to twelve weeks. He also proposed six weeks paid leave for new parents employed by the state, describing paid leave as a key to building a more productive and successful workforce.

Minnesota allows early voting, no-excuse absentee voting, online voter registration, and same-day registration. As a result, the state leads the nation in voter participation, which some say is an indication of the interest in civics inherited from northern Europe—Sweden, for example, had an 85.8 percent voter turnout in the 2014 parliamentary election. In nine consecutive elections, Minnesota's voters turned out in greater numbers than any other state in the country, with 78 percent in 2004 and 2008 and 76 percent in 2012. Then, in 2014—a non-presidential-election year—only half of all eligible voters turned out. Minnesota fell to sixth place. Alarm bells rang. We must be number one again, proclaimed the new secretary of state, Steve Simon. He almost succeeded in 2016, when voter turnout increased to 74.7 percent, second best to California's 75.3 percent. Sweden has also experienced lower voter turnout. But, "since World War II this is a trend in all democracies," said Sören Holmberg, election expert and political science professor at the University of Göteborg, Sweden. "It seems that democratic decision-making no longer is as important for people as it used to be in our globalized world."

Minnesota, according to Gallup, Politico, CNBC, AARP, and other sources, has been ranked number one in job creation, best for business, best place to retire, number one in workplace satisfaction, second best for working mothers, and second in home ownership. Politico named it the second strongest state, taking into account fifteen separate criteria, including income, poverty levels, infant deaths, life expectancy, violent crime, well-being, math and reading scores, and so on. Minnesota ranks tenth highest in per capita income and eighth lowest in number of people living below the poverty line. It has more cooperatives per capita than any other state, and more Fortune 500 companies per capita than any other state. Minnesota was home to the nation's first shelter for battered women and the first public charter school law; it has the second highest high school graduation rate and ranks eleventh among all states in people with college degrees or higher. Minnesota also has the second lowest imprisonment rate in the nation and is the tenth safest from violent crime. The state ranks sixth in overall health among its citizens, with the lowest number of deaths from heart disease in the nation and the second highest life expectancy at birth; its citizens are the ninth slimmest. Only 5.9 percent of Minnesotans lack health insurance—the fifth lowest rate in the nation—and the state is the third happiest, after Colorado and Hawaii.

The Twin Cities of Minneapolis and St. Paul—home to more than 3.5 million people in its metro area—also regularly rank high in various quality of life measures among American cities. The Twin Cities are the healthiest and fittest cities in America; Minneapolis is the most bike-friendly city in the nation; and the two are the best cities for public parks in the nation. In 2015 Minneapolis was named the nation's most literate city, while St. Paul came in fourth place. The Twin Cities have also been named the third friendliest metro area.

Minnesota also stands out for its volunteerism and its contributions to nonprofits. It is "still unique in the United States as to corporate philanthropy," according to Swedish American Marilyn Carlson Nelson, former president, CEO, and board chair of Carlson, the global hotel and hospitality company founded by her father, Curtis. The spirit of corporate philanthropy was spurred, she said, when President Lyndon Johnson, during a Minnesota visit, encouraged her father and others to give more than the one percent that was common at the time. So, she said, "they created a culture of giving five percent." Today, while corporate giving is between one and two percent nationally, is between two and five percent in Minnesota. Nelson, a member of the Committee Encouraging Corporate Philanthropy (CECP), says that this culture of giving "has been consciously built by CEOs here in Minnesota, particularly those early founders of their corporations. They had a vested interest for the long term in this community, a lot of commitment to the quality of life here in Minnesota."

New CEOs in town get visits from someone in CECP and are encouraged to become members and to participate. "It's part of the fabric of our social life," she said, and "one of the unique characteristics of our corporate culture here in Minnesota is that we all feel responsibility to give back to the community." Her list of civic engagements through the years is long and includes, among others, the Minnesota Orchestra, the Mayo Clinic, United Nations Global Compact, the National Endowment for Democracy, and the University of Minnesota Foundation. In a speech in 2014, she spoke warmly of Hubert Humphrey, "my father's friend," and his fight for civil rights, which fueled "my own advocacy" to fight the 2012 Republican proposal for a constitutional amendment to ban same-sex marriage in Minnesota. "I, along with my husband, Glen, my daughter Wendy and many hundreds of other advocates felt strongly that rejecting the codification of discrimination in our state's constitution was 'the right thing to do.'"

The Clean Water, Land and Legacy Amendment to the Minnesota constitution, passed in 2008, also makes the state special—and echoes the Nordic countries' strong emphasis on the environment. That year, the voters gave their overwhelming support, 56 percent to 39, to raise the sales tax by three-eighths of one percent and to spend the new money on the arts, the outdoors, and clean water. The program goes until 2034. The tax revenues are distributed into four Legacy Funds: clean water, outdoor heritage, arts and culture, and parks and trails. The Legacy Amendment followed an earlier constitutional amendment in 1988, when the state's voters approved the Environment and Natural Resources Trust Fund, which, by 2016, has distributed about $500 million, generated by the Minnesota Lottery, to a thousand projects around the state.

Minnesota is also an exception in the Upper Midwest when it comes to abortion rights. Jan Malcolm, former Minnesota Health Commissioner and a leading health expert who, although "a hundred percent Danish," was born in the Swedish Hospital in Minneapolis, talked about a state that is still grounded culturally in the Scandinavian heritages of community obligation and concern, and about the "communitarian approach to policy making, which has been the real hallmark of health care in Minnesota." She said a "very comprehensive coverage was the norm in Minnesota, and we have been filling in the gaps in the coverage system for a long, long time." Minnesota was the first to start a high-risk insurance pool, it has been generous with Medicaid coverage and instituted a children's health insurance plan in the 1980s and MinnesotaCare in the 1990s, offering universal coverage and a one fee schedule to low-income Minnesotans, which was signed by Governor Arne Carlson. That was "pretty radical," and "so when Obamacare was passed, we here in Minnesota already had 91 to 92 percent health coverage."

MINNESOTA IS CHANGING. Old ethnic identities have faded, and new ones have arrived with the influx of immigrants from beyond Europe. The new immigrants have not yet changed Minnesota's general population, "but I feel it is close to happening," said Susan Brower, the Minnesota state demographer. "Some communities, whose major source of population growth is from international immigration, have definitely been transformed, but the Twin Cities and Minnesota as a whole are still largely white Scandinavian, especially people of power." Still, in 1960 only one percent of Minnesotans were people of color, whereas census numbers from 2015 estimate that about 19 percent of the state's 5.5 million residents today are people of color. In 2014 Minnesota, a top destination, received 2,232 refugees from twenty-four countries. Almost half were from Somalia, followed by Myanmar and Iraq. That's more per capita than any other state, just like Sweden, which received 160,000 refugees in 2015—more per capita than any other European nation.

US senator Amy Klobuchar said that Minnesotans tend to be a bit more open to immigrants and talked about a "sense of internationalism." A recent story about the Islamic Center in the town of Winona that burned to the ground in 2013 bears witness to this, as the Central Lutheran Church and other area churches reached out and offered their space to the members of the Islamic Center to meet and worship. The broad response allowed Muslims to meet in a new church every week. But there is also opposition to immigration. In 2013, for example, the Tea Party in St. Cloud, a town that already had thirteen thousand Somalis, demanded a moratorium on new refugees settling in the area. In February 2016, a full-page ad in the *Star Tribune* urged Minnesotans not to be un-Minnesotan and to reject bigotry toward Muslims—"our fellow Minnesotans." The ad was the brainchild of

DFL congressman Keith Ellison, a Muslim American, and Republican businessman John Taft, the great-grandson of Republican president William Howard Taft. "We must come together as a diverse and vibrant community. If you're a Minnesotan, you know this to be true. . . . We can't be tricked into betraying our values. It'd be so very un-Minnesotan of us." Many Democrats signed the ad, including Governor Dayton and both US senators from Minnesota. So did a series of leading CEOs, education leaders, and former Republican senator David Durenberger, but no current Republican officeholders.

Blue, red, or purple—Minnesota has even been called polka-dotted—the state is today seen as liberal, with "soft socialist policies," as *MinnPost's* Eric Black put it. Even if it is not a totally blue state, it still is an anomaly in the Upper Midwest. In presidential elections between 1828 and 2012, Minnesota and North Dakota have voted for the same presidential nominee only 42 percent and Minnesota and South Dakota 48 percent of the time. The number for Wisconsin, the neighbor to the east, is 79.5 percent. Between 1860 and 1928, Minnesota's voters always supported the Republican nominee for president, except in 1912, when Teddy Roosevelt split from the Republican Party and ran as a candidate for the Progressive Party. Since 1932, the state's voters have been more faithful to the Democrats than any other state, wavering on only three occasions, voting for Eisenhower in 1952 and 1956 and for Nixon in 1972. The Democratic presidential candidate has won every Minnesota election since 1976. Minnesota continues to be part of that northern tier voting bloc, just like a hundred years earlier, stretching from New England and New York to Michigan, Wisconsin, and Minnesota, only this bloc now supports the Democratic Party. Despite this long DFL dominance, the 2014 elections marked only the third time in its history that the DFL Party won all the statewide races. At the same time, the party lost its majority in the Minnesota house, ending the "single-party DFL rule." A divided government followed, with a DFL governor and a DFL-controlled senate but with Republicans in charge in the house. It was the fourth time in ten years that the majority in the house had switched, and, just like in Washington, the ability to govern was severely weakened.

Proof of that was the "do-nothing" session of 2016 in the Minnesota legislature, which had seen increased partisanship over the previous two years. Republicans voted with other Republicans 92 percent of the time, and Democrats with other Democrats 86 percent of the time, according to a *Pioneer Press* study. The sixteen most partisan lawmakers were all Republicans.

Laurie Halverson, the DFL representative in Eagan and a self-professed moderate in a swing district, voted with the Democrats 75.6 percent and the Republicans 49.9 percent of the time.

Although the two political parties in Minnesota have often thought of themselves as independent and insulated from the national trends in American politics, both parties are now "national" parties. Since the merger in 1944, the DFL has adhered closely to the national Democratic Party. Members of the Minnesota Republican Party, which even called itself the Independent-Republican Party to distance itself from the national party following the Watergate scandal of the 1970s, today tends to take the same hard right positions as their fellow Republicans in the rest of the country. The fact that Marco Rubio beat Ted Cruz and Donald Trump in the 2016 Minnesota Republican primary could, perhaps, be seen as a sign that they are not completely dominated by the national party's hard right conservatism, but it is still largely a party that rallies around purity. Those who don't follow the party line don't seem to have much of a future, as witnessed by the resignation of state senator Branden Petersen, whose support of same-sex marriage was not well received by his Republican colleagues and constituents.

Steve Sviggum, a veteran Republican lawmaker, was a member of the Minnesota house from 1979 to 2007, both as minority leader and as speaker, and he now teaches at the University of Minnesota. He calls himself a "hundred percent Norwegian," and when he entered politics, he said, "I leaned on my old Norwegian values, family, loyalty, trust, hard work, individual responsibility, faith—my faith is very important to me." He served in a divided government, with maverick governor Jesse Ventura followed by Republican governor Tim Pawlenty, while the senate stayed in Democratic hands under the leadership of Roger Moe, his fellow Norwegian American. He tried to bring people together, "which did not mean that we did not have our differences—Roger and Ventura yelled at me and I yelled at them— but I tried very, very hard to bring people together in the best interest of Minnesota." He mentioned issues such as DUI laws, property tax reduction, investment in nursing homes, and the new baseball stadium, Target Field. "Now, if you are philosophically pure, which I am not, you would say that there is no way that taxpayers should contribute to sport, like now with the new Vikings stadium. But Minnesota without the Vikings, if they were to move from Minnesota, would be a disaster, and I would hate to be speaker then. Or, in 2006, I would have hated to have the Twins sold and moved if there had not been Target Field."

Sviggum underscored that he "feels very, very strongly" about his conservative values, but that does not mean all is black and white. "You got to have government. You got to do those things together that we cannot individually do by ourselves, the simple things such as roads, schools, public safety, and they have to be done together. . . . I am one who believes that you have to be able to govern." And to do that, "You have to cooperate to govern. Respect now seems to be gone at times. Both parties have become so extreme and so radical that it is harder for them to get together and govern in the best interest of Minnesota." Asked if this worried him, he answered, "Yes, I am worried, not that we drift to the right, but that we lose our sense of cooperation, our sense of respect and compromise." He said he does not need to get everything he wants immediately. He is okay with incremental progress. "That makes me a little less extreme, a little less radical and more pragmatic." That seems pretty Scandinavian, I said. "Yes, I would think so," he replied.

To Paul H. Anderson, former Minnesota Supreme Court justice, that is the mindset that runs through the terms of Stassen, LeVander, and Youngdahl—that "sense of obligation to a larger community of which you are a part." The question we need to be prepared to answer is, "What did you do to make things better?" and, Anderson added, "I think that was on the minds of these Scandinavian immigrants. They came here to find a better life, and for the most part they did. So, if things are better for us, don't we have an obligation to make things better for the next generation?"

Fourth-generation Norwegian American David W. Preus, legendary Lutheran pastor and former president of the American Lutheran Church, said that the biggest Scandinavian legacy in Minnesota is the religious legacy and, "stemming from that, the political participation, which has been terrific." He said he grew up in a Republican home, which was progressive and for the Nonpartisan League, but also for Farmer-Labor, and the spirit of all that still exists, as does the awareness of Scandinavian socialism. "Of course, we all steer away from the word socialism, like mad. . . . We tend to admire the way the Scandinavians have kept a positive political and business system while they have managed to clamp down on excessive wealth going to a handful and a bunch of impoverished people at the bottom. And I would guess, and it's only a guess, that the Scandinavians of Minnesota would overwhelmingly go for health care following the Scandinavian models."

Preus, who became a Democrat at age twenty-five and a leading voice in civil rights and later in the anti-apartheid movement in South Africa, said that there is a Scandinavian ethos of which he is very conscious. "I became aware of it in the army during World War II when, suddenly, I was the only one from the Upper Midwest of Scandinavian descent. Everyone was something else, and I discovered that the trust level was so amazingly different. I came out of a setting where you assumed that other people were trustworthy—until they proved otherwise. And now it was just the opposite. It is still so, and this is where you feel the Scandinavian influence."

If there was anything that the Scandinavian immigrants brought to Minnesota, as Nils Hasselmo, the Swedish-born former president of the University of Minnesota, sees it, "it was the sense of responsibility for your own community." But Hasselmo also pointed out that the political culture of the early Swedish immigrants was quite compatible with American political culture. Just like the Americans, they talked about freedom and independence. There was an "amalgam of Swedish traditions of freedom and independence very much in harmony with American ideology." He said, "True Swedes, and true Norwegians, but they were also true Americans."

How was it, then, to be surrounded by all these Scandinavians?

"Well, they are all very clannish, you know, and Wendy [Anderson] was the worst of the bunch," Warren Spannaus said with a laugh. "Wendy always talked about Swedish this and Swedish that, and I said, well, I am an American, and then he said, well, you don't want to talk about your ancestors. . . . Once, on the campaign, there was a question from the audience about how many Andersons had been governor in Minnesota, and Wendy answered, 'not enough.'" Spannaus, former state attorney general and of German descent, sees a combination of factors behind why so many Scandinavians became political leaders in Minnesota. "For one thing," he said, "they looked like Minnesotans, and they had the names—Johnson, Anderson, Swenson, Carlson—that reminded people probably of someone they knew, old Scandinavians. But, also, they were nice people, they were working people. The Scandinavian morality was progressive, and they believed in helping people that needed help, and I think that has carried through pretty much. . . . The Scandinavians did a hell of a job for Minnesota, and the precedents they set are still here, although, unfortunately, not as strong as they used to be."

There has been no Scandinavian governor of Minnesota, from either party, since Arne Carlson in the 1990s. It's possible that the 1998 elections can be seen as a sort of last Scandinavian hurrah, when the sons of three legendary Scandinavian American politicians—Hubert Humphrey, Walter Mondale, and Orville Freeman—all ran for governor. They all lost. Humphrey's son, "Skip," beat Mike Freeman and Ted Mondale in the DFL primary, and then in the general election, Humphrey lost to Jesse Ventura, the third-party (Reform Party) candidate. Ventura, the former professional wrestler and mayor of suburban Brooklyn Park, won with 37 percent of the vote, followed by Republican candidate Norm Coleman's 34 percent, and Humphrey's 28 percent.

Are we, in fact, seeing the end of the line of Scandinavian governors in Minnesota? "Yes, I think so," Arne Carlson answered.

> There is no new Scandinavian generation. This will have an enormous effect on Minnesota. What the Scandinavians brought was a word I dearly love—prudence. They brought a lot of prudence into developing their communities. They would be considered progressive on social issues but they were also very prudent as to how they spent their money. They would spend money on education. I would say that they were willing to spend money on what they would call "the common good." And I think their track record is extraordinary. But they were not prone to anything that would even remotely smack of waste, very intolerant of waste. It was fine to pay a tax dollar if it were to be spent in a prudent fashion. And, frankly, that has served them remarkably well, and I think we have lost a lot of that.

Former vice president Walter Mondale does not believe that the position Minnesota has created for itself will be threatened. "What threatens us is this train-wreck brand of politics where the only word you have to know is 'no.' You see that in Washington, and it is sickening. It was here for a while but I think it has gone away, thank God, and I hope it will never come back." He described Minnesota's Tea Party movement with Michele Bachmann as "an emotional fever that was incurable—unrelenting, negative, the politics of paralysis. And we almost got a critical mass of that here in Minnesota." But Nils Hasselmo does not exclude the idea that the state might be "affected by this national disease of radical and rightist politics and digging ideological trenches rather than solving problems." Former Governor Al Quie is also worried. "I think Minnesota politics is in trouble. The extremes in both parties have too much influence," he said.

Arne Carlson also shares these concerns. "Minnesota is a wonderful state," he said, "but I think we need to be smart enough to realize that we need to make some very intelligent and gutsy decisions to stay competitive. If you don't make steady progress you will lose ground, and Minnesota can no longer afford that because we excelled in the sixties and seventies. Minnesota then wanted to be discovered, and the result was a tremendous sense of community. Both political parties agreed on the goals although they disagreed on how to achieve those goals. But they always came together, and there was a lot of respect, as it ought to be. They competed in the world of ideas, and they knew how to govern. And they did well." But today, "I would contend that we are not pulling together for the common good."

Political scientist Daniel J. Elazar writes about three political cultures in the American political system: traditionalistic, individualistic, and moralistic. Minnesota belongs to the moralistic tradition, shaped by the Yankees from New England and the Scandinavians from northern Europe. Both shared a communitarian ethic. No other US state, writes Elazar, "provides as pure and undiluted an example of the moralistic political culture as Minnesota." There was the notion of the commonwealth, the common good, and they combined this moralistic tradition with a strong entrepreneurial spirit. The Scandinavian immigrants often went directly to Minnesota after arriving in America, which meant that their Americanization was shaped entirely by their experience in Minnesota, according to Elazar. That also meant that the immigrants influenced Minnesota's political system and reinforced the original contribution of the Yankees, who had arrived earlier. Minnesotans see politics as a public activity based on a notion of the public good and advancing the public interest. He writes, "the tone set by the state's political culture permeates Minnesota's civil society, its politics and government, giving Minnesota a 'clean' image." The result is a state with a healthy and growing economy, a high quality of life, a clean and active government, a moralistic culture, and a state that is, in many areas, a national policy leader and innovator.

Elazar's analysis, writes Carleton College professor Steven Schier, "helps us understand why Minnesota's politics is issue-oriented, intolerant of corruption, and focused more on the common good than in individualistic and traditionalistic states." Schier, who recently spent a semester as a Fulbright fellow at Uppsala University in Sweden, told me "the Swedish welfare state has an echo here in our institutions" and so do the broad moral concerns found in Scandinavia. He sees the Yankee/Scandinavian tradition in Minnesota politics as two complementary streams, with a similar cultural orientation: "very rational, very frugal." These two streams, both interested in broader moral principles, have created Minnesota with the support of a vibrant and active Lutheran church, which has helped "maintain the Scandinavian cultural tradition.... These things change very slowly." That tradition of Scandinavian leadership is so "entrenched" and has such "staying power" in Minnesota, that Schier believes the new immigrants, the Somalis and the Hmong, will accept the Yankee/Scandinavian political culture and function within it. "The culture replicates itself, and it will persist. There are no major movements of rival elites coming in, nothing to replace it. It is here to stay."

Larry Jacobs, professor at the University of Minnesota, talked of a "strong, lingering, entrenched northern European culture that tends to view Minnesota with a communitarian spirit." He thinks this will persist even in today's Minnesota with new immigrants from very different cultures and even as the number of Swedes and Norwegians decline in the state. "There is an embedded, historical, and institutional presence that continues to be very much present." Jacobs pointed to the eight years under very conservative Republican governor Tim Pawlenty (2003–11), which included government shutdowns, and said that "what is really striking is how much of the northern European welfare state of Minnesota was left after he was gone." Groups to the right, the Tea Party and others, were critical of this, of how much big government he left in place. "But the reality was that Pawlenty could not go much further without being thrown out of office. He was at the edge."

Jacobs noted that the Minnesota connection with its Nordic heritage runs deep. "The air that all Minnesotans breathe is air that has been filtered through a northern European, Swedish, Norwegian heritage.... It's rooted in the earth of Minnesota ... it's part of the soil." He mentioned a national conference he participated in on health reform, where he talked about what was happening in Minnesota, and one speaker commented, "Minnesota doesn't count. You are already doing a kind of European welfare state, sort of 'Minnesota exceptionalism.'" Jacobs once hosted the annual state legislature retreat with members from both parties and the theme, "One Minnesota—our state, our future." "That to me," he said, "captures the northern European way of thinking of things ... the communal model of governance where you look for ways to bargain, to negotiate between labor and management, between different groups. You are not in a silo. We are not going to run you over." He added that he did not want to romanticize this but there is a "culture of deliberation," which is very striking compared to the polarization in America as a whole: "You hear it everywhere in Minnesota—this is repugnant, this is not the Minnesota way, this is not the way we do things in Minnesota."

So, I asked him, are you saying that Minnesota is a special state and will continue to be a special place with special political traditions? "Yes, exactly," Jacobs answered. "It's like a fork in the road, and you can go this way or that way, and Minnesota has taken the Scandinavian way, and even though the Scandinavians are not running the state, we are on the road that the Scandinavians have put us on."

Acknowledgments

THIS BOOK HAS BEEN a wonderful and challenging project during which I have made many new discoveries and many new friends. So there are many without whom this book would not have been possible and many to thank.

First of all, I would like to express my deep gratitude to all those who agreed to be interviewed for this book. They all taught me so much about Minnesota's history, politics, and culture.

I owe deep gratitude to many journalist colleagues for their support and constant encouragement, such as my fellow Washingtonians, Tom Hamburger, Finlay Lewis, and Doyle McManus, as well as my son, Jonas, at Bloomberg News in Oslo, Norway. My thanks also go to Minnesota journalists Gregg Aamot, Steve Berg, Eric Black, Roger Buoen, Nick Coleman, Michael Fedo, Dave Hage, Dane Smith, Doug Stone, and Lori Sturdevent. I could not have completed this project without the invaluable support from immigration scholars on both sides of the Atlantic: Philip J. Anderson, William Beyer, Dag Blanck, Pamela A. Brunfelt, Jørn Brøndal, Benny Carlson, Richard Hudelson, Michael J. Lansing, Bruce L. Larson, Odd S. Lovoll, Byron Nordstrom, and Marianne Wargelin.

In Minnesota, I had two homes away from home. One was the American Swedish Institute with its president and CEO Bruce Karstadt and his welcoming staff, and the other was the Gale Library at the Minnesota Historical Society, where Patrick Coleman, Deborah Miller, and their colleagues extended invaluable help during many research hours. Other Minnesotans who made me feel welcome include Patrick Coleman and Sally Johnson, Eric and Katy Dregni, Brad Engdahl, Cliff Greene, John Lindstrom, Roger and Paulette Moe, Don and Colleen Moe, Kris Mortensen, Lois Quam, Ewa and Anders Rydåker, and Anelise Sawkins—thank you all.

This book would not have been possible without the librarians in various institutions, and I am most grateful to so many: Daniel Necas at the University of Minnesota's Immigration History Research Center; Gordon Anderson and Timothy Johnson at the University of Minnesota Libraries; and Anna-Kajsa Anderson at North Park University's Brandel Library and

Katy Darr at the Newberry Library, both in Chicago. Thank you also to the Swenson Swedish Immigration Research Center at Augustana College, Rock Island, Illinois; the Norwegian-American Historical Association at St. Olaf College, Northfield, Minnesota; Kungliga Biblioteket, Riksdagsbib-lioteket, and Arbetarrörelsens Arkiv och Bibliotek in Stockholm, Sweden; Nasjonalbiblioteket in Oslo, Norway; the Library of Congress in Washing-ton, DC; and to Kerstin Ellert, Jämtlands Lokalhistoriker, and Eva Olander, Orsa Hembygdsgård, in Sweden.

A generous stipend from the Axel and Margaret Ax:son Johnson Foun-dation in Stockholm, Sweden, made the many trips to Minnesota for re-search and interviews possible, and for that I am particularly grateful.

Finally, I want to thank Josh Leventhal, Shannon Pennefeather, Ann Regan, and their colleagues at the Minnesota Historical Society Press for believing in this project and for seeing it through.

Notes

Chapter 1: "The Beginnings"

page 3   "Outside of the Nordic countries . . .": Sten Carlsson, *Skandinaviska politiker i Minnesota*, 243.

page 7   Hjelm-Hansen's speech: *Swedish Historical Society Quarterly* (October 2005).

page 7   Biographical information on Hjelm-Hansen: Carlton C. Qualey, NAHA.

page 8   "It is true that . . .": Mattson, *Minnen*, 138.

page 8   Mattson's Civil War speech reprinted in *Minneapolis Morning Tribune*, January 1918.

page 9   O. Fritiof Ander, "Public Officials," in *Swedes in America*, eds. Benson and Hedin, 322.

page 9   On role of F. Sneedorff Christensen: Lovoll, *The Promise of America*, 121.

page 9   "greatly responsible for . . .": Ander, *T.N. Hasselquist*, 152.

page 10   "To be branded a Democrat . . .": Luth Jaeger's speech on January 25, 1909, from NAHA archives.

page 10   "represented Protestantism . . .": Lovoll, *The Promise Fulfilled*, 26.

page 10   "No slavery for either black or white": Lovoll, *The Promise of America*, 71.

page 11   "My grandfather read . . .": interview with Al Quie, June 13, 2013.

page 11   "marked a decisive phase . . .": Lovoll, *The Promise of America*, 75.

page 12   "were the peasant foot soldiers . . .": interview with William Beyer, August 22, 2013.

page 12   "They were starving": interview with Steve Sviggum, March 24, 2014.

page 12   Immigration numbers from Holmquist, *They Chose Minnesota*.

page 13   John Rice on Swedes in *They Chose Minnesota*, ed. Holmquist, 248–76.

page 14   Top year numbers from Runblom and Norman, eds., *Transatlantic Connections*, 288–93.

page 15   Top year numbers from Runblom and Norman, eds., *Transatlantic Connections*, 288–93.

page 15   "They preferred this . . .": Semmingsen, *Norway to America*, 40.

page 15   Muskego Manifesto: Lovoll, *The Promise of America*, 51.

page 15   "leap-frogged": Semmingsen, *Norway to America*, 69.

pages 15–16   Carlton C. Qualey and Jon A. Gjerde on Norwegians in *They Chose Minnesota*, ed. Holmquist, 220–47.

page 16   "perhaps, because immigrants . . .": Keillor, *Shaping Minnesota's Identity*, 100.

page 16   Top year numbers from Runblom and Norman, eds., *Transatlantic Connections*, 288–93.

page 17   Ann Regan on Danes in *They Chose Minnesota*, ed. Holmquist, 277–89.

page 17   Top year numbers from Runblom and Norman, eds., *Transatlantic Connections*, 288–93.

page17   "the glory of mercantile Minneota . . .": Holm, *The Heart Can Be Filled Anywhere on Earth*, 87.

pages 17–18   Ann Regan on Icelanders in *They Chose Minnesota*, ed. Holmquist, 290–95.

page 18   Timo Riipa on Finns in *They Chose Minnesota*, ed. Holmquist, 296–322.

page 18   Top year numbers from Runblom and Norman, eds., *Transatlantic Connections*, 288–93.

page 18   "It was unique . . .": interview with Marianne Wargelin, August 17, 2013.

page 19   Many were political refugees . . . : Carl Ross in *New York Uutiset*, June 1975–August 1976.

page 19   "The church was the first . . .": Hansen, *Third Generation Immigrant*, 15.

pages 19–20   "It is by no means . . .": Stephenson, *Religious Aspects of Swedish Immigration*, 133–34.

page 20   "plagued by disharmony . . .": Lovoll, *The Promise Fulfilled*, 20.

page 21   "it must bear a portion . . .": Stephenson, *Religious Aspect of Swedish Immigration*, 17–18.

page 21   "no issue concerned . . .": Lovoll, *The Promise of America*, 104.

page 22   "advancing their skills . . .": Paul George Hummasti, "Fighting for Temperance Ideas," in *Finns in the United States*, ed. Kostiainen, 99.

page 22   "took the Finns beyond . . .": Kolehmainen, *Finnish Temperance Societies in Minnesota*, 391.

page 22   "They gained experience . . .": interview with Odd S. Lovoll, June 10, 2013.

page 23   "underrepresentation": Carlsson, "Scandinavian Politicians in the United States," 153.

page 24   "The German story . . .": interview with Margaret Anderson Kelliher, February 6, 2014.

page 24   "The Germans were mainly . . .": interview with Hyman Berman, March 14, 2013.

page 25   "was seen as useless . . .": Keillor, *Shaping Minnesota's Identity*, 94.

page 25   "to protect Swedish religious ways": Keillor, *Shaping Minnesota's Identity*, 99.

page 25   "unlike Minnesota's Scandinavians . . .": Conzen, *Germans in Minnesota*, 62–63.

page 25   "sidelined the Germans . . .": Conzen, *Germans in Minnesota*, 81–82.

page 26   Success in the new place: Atkins, *Creating Minnesota*, 94.

page 26   "built farms . . .": Blegen, *Minnesota*, 175.

page 26   "as staunchly antiliquor . . .": Blegen, *Minnesota*, 217.

pages 26–27 "if it took a lot of money . . .": interview with Don Ostrom, March 31, 2014.

page 27 "the Scandinavians fit . . .": interview with Lori Sturdevant, March 24, 2013.

page 27 "Yes, you can't discard . . .": interview with Paul H. Anderson, July 28, 2014.

Chapter 2: *"Four Pioneers"*

page 28 "'Swede' Governor": Eberhart, "The American Way of Life," 131.

page 30 "dubious advantage": Stephenson, *John Lind of Minnesota*, 35–37.

page 31 "he read, he worked . . .": Gieske and Keillor, *Norwegian Yankee*, 23.

page 31 "salty, gruff . . .": Blegen, *Minnesota*, 387.

page 31 "I feel that . . .": Gieske and Keillor, *Norwegian Yankee*, 98.

page 32 "I am a Norwegian . . .": Gieske and Keillor, *Norwegian Yankee*, 217.

page 32 "unchallenged Republican . . .": Blegen, *Minnesota*, 388.

page 32 "a practically unbeatable . . .": Nye, *Midwestern Progressive Politics*, 81.

page 32 "I will fix him": Gieske and Keillor, *Norwegian Yankee*, 166.

page 32 "Stryparen Knute": *Svenska Amerikanska Posten*, November 1, 1892.

page 33 "Let's see in two years": *Svenska Amerikanska Posten*, November 29, 1892.

page 33 "rising sun": Gieske and Keillor, *Norwegian Yankee*, 170.

page 33 "ultimate success story": Lovoll, *Norwegians on the Prairie*, 211.

page 34 "nearly all Norwegian Americans . . .": Chrislock, *Ethnicity Challenged*, 36.

page 34 Background on John Lind: Stephenson, *John Lind of Minnesota*.

page 34 "Bravo, John Lind": Stephenson, *John Lind of Minnesota*, 187–88.

page 35 "we cannot afford . . ." and "jealous" . . . "suspicious": Stephenson, *John Lind of Minnesota*, 91–92.

page 35 "was the shrewd . . .": Stephenson, *John Lind of Minnesota*, 91–92.

page 35 "blackest eye . . .": Stephenson, *John Lind of Minnesota*, 113.

page 36 "Without him": Strand, *Swedish-Americans in Minnesota*, 78.

page 37 "an oracle of . . .": Stephenson, "The John Lind Papers," 159–60.

page 37 Background on John A. Johnson: Day and Knappen, *Life of John Albert Johnson*.

page 38 "greatest personal . . .": Folwell, *A History of Minnesota*, 2:275, 279.

page 38 "more like an Irishman . . .": Helmes, *John A. Johnson*, 29.

page 38 "the most widely known . . .": Helmes, *John A. Johnson*, 66.

page 38 "only recognized . . .": Helmes, *John A. Johnson*, 158.

page 38 "there will be no easy . . .": Helmes, *John A. Johnson*, 190.

page 38 "like a Western breeze . . .": *Washington Post* quoted by Day and Knappen, *Life of John Albert Johnson*, 170.

page 39 "hardly been equaled . . .": Folwell quoted Cyrus Northrop in the *Pioneer Press*, September 22, 1909.

page 39 "Lincoln of the Northwest": Strand, *Swedish-Americans in Minnesota*, 89.

page 39 "Swedish-America's . . .": obituary by Victor Nilsson, *Valkyrian*, November 1909.

page 39   "great friendship": Eberhart, "The American Way of Life," 81.

page 39   "I had only one political . . .": Eberhart, "The American Way of Life," 95.

page 39   "was partly luck": Strand, *Swedish-Americans in Minnesota*, 97.

page 40   "There is in the truest . . .": Eberhart, "The American Way of Life," 5.

page 40   "simply irresistible": Day and Knappen, *Life of John Albert Johnson*, 147.

page 40   "pioneers in the settlement . . .": speech cited by Day and Knappen, *Life of John Albert Johnson*, 304–5.

pages 40–41   "Scandinavians could boss state politics": *Minneapolis Tribune*, April 14, 1909.

page 41   "Governor Nelson seems . . ." and "unforgivable": Gieske and Keillor, *Norwegian Yankee*, 189.

page 41   "our friends in peace . . .": Stephenson, *John Lind of Minnesota*, 337.

page 42   "I was in every sense . . .": Eberhart, *The American Way of Life*, 131.

page 42   "to be good": Gieske and Keillor, *Norwegian Yankee*, 233–42.

page 43   "bind up their wounds . . .": speech cited by Day and Knappen, *Life of John Albert Johnson*, 307.

page 44   "was to draw a line. . .": Gieske and Keillor, *Norwegian Yankee*, 269.

page 44   "illogical and unfair": Eberhart, "The American Way of Life," 85.

page 44   "risky office . . .": Gieske and Keillor, *Norwegian Yankee*, 174–80.

page 45   "survived the risks . . .": Gieske and Keillor, *Norwegian Yankee*, 198.

page 45   "blueprint for reform": Chrislock, *The Progressive Era in Minnesota*, 9.

page 45   "added impetus and respectability": Chrislock, *The Progressive Era in Minnesota*, 14.

page 45   "accomplished none . . .": Lass, *Minnesota*, 208.

page 45   "outstanding progressive . . .": Chrislock, *The Progressive Era in Minnesota*, 19.

page 46   John A. Johnson's visit to the Iron Range: Helmes, *John A. Johnson*, 218–25.

page 46   Reforestation (Sweden and Norway): Lass, *Minnesota*, 243–45.

page 47   "artful coup": Chrislock, *The Progressive Era in Minnesota*, 48.

page 47   "completely revolutionized": *Minneapolis Journal*, June 18, 1912, quoted in Lass, *Minnesota*, 213.

page 47   "experienced and skilled": Blegen, *Minnesota*, 467.

page 48   "relic of the past": Bessler, *Legacy of Violence*, 152.

page 48   "the interests of justice": Bessler, *Legacy of Violence*, 168.

page 48   "I have always been opposed . . .": Bessler, *Legacy of Violence*, 171.

page 49   "No people . . .": *Compendium of History and Biography*.

Chapter 3: "Soon There Were Thousands"

page 50   Nelson, *History of the Scandinavians*.

page 50   "What has always struck me . . .": interview with David Lanegran, February 6, 2014.

page 50   "surprising": Sten Carlsson, "Skandinaviska politiker i Minnesota," in *Utvandring*, ed. Kälvemark, 240.

page 51   "spontaneous, almost irresistible impulse": Hansen, *Third Generation Immigrant*, 12, 16.

page 51   "voluntary pluralism": Blanck, *Becoming Swedish American*, 14, 221.

page 52   1847–1905 statistics: Ulvestad, *Norwegians in America*, vol. 1.

page 52   1860–1900 statistics: Nelson, *History of the Scandinavians*.

page 52   "impressive political bloc": Wefald, *A Voice of Protest*, 28.

pages 52–53   Democratic experience in Scandinavia: Brøndal, *Ethnic Leadership and Midwestern Politics*, 121–22.

page 53   "fostered an exclusiveness . . .": Ander, "Public Officials," in *Swedes in America*, eds. Benson and Hedin, 324–28.

page 53   "handicap of nationality": Norlie, *History of the Norwegian People*, 497.

page 53   "no novices": Lovoll, *Norwegians on the Prairie*, 74.

page 53   "banner county . . .": Soike, *Norwegian Americans and the Politics of Dissent*, 61.

pages 53–54   "extreme localism . . .": Lovoll, *Norwegians on the Prairie*, 8, 28, 74.

page 54   The Norwegian immigrants . . . county offices: Soike, *Norwegian Americans and the Politics of Dissent*, 24–26.

page 54   "unrelentingly progressive . . .": Wefald, *A Voice of Protest*, 3.

page 54   "common goal . . .": Wefald, *A Voice of Protest*, 4.

page 54   "hostile to competitive capitalism": Wefald refers to *A Study of Cultural Change* by Peter A. Munch, Oslo, 1956.

page 54   "more complex": Runblom and Norman, eds., *From Sweden to America*, 227.

page 54   "not wholly convincing": Qualey, "Norwegians in the Upper Midwest," 18.

page 55   "left-of-center tilt": Chrislock, "The Norwegian-American Impact on Minnesota Politics," 115.

page 55   "played a part . . .": Lovoll, *The Promise of America*, 131.

page 55   "these rebellions . . .": Youngdale, *Third Party Footprints*, 23.

page 55   "diversity rather than cohesion . . .": Grepperud, "A Study of Three Norwegian Newspapers."

page 55   "with weak party attachments": Soike, *Norwegian-Americans and the Politics of Dissent*, 188.

page 56   "The truth is": Chrislock, *Ethnicity Challenged*, 116.

page 56   "sizeable": Soike, *Norwegian-Americans and the Politics of Dissent*, 56.

page 57   "needed a patriotic American . . .": Shutter, *History of Minneapolis*, 2:712–15.

page 58   "there should be no distinction . . .": *Minneapolis Tribune*, August 13, 1869.

page 58   "cunning" and "crafty": *Svenska Amerikanska Posten*, November 1, 1892.

pages 58–59   "For the first time in our country . . .": *Minnesota Stats Tidning*, November 2, 1898.

page 59   "self-made man": *Svenska Amerikanska Posten*, September 29, 1920.

page 59   "community—you are responsible . . .": interview with Joan Anderson Growe, June 11, 2013.

page 60   "largely responsible...": Stuhler, *No Regrets*, 4.

page 60   "although we did not win...": Joan Anderson Growe quoted in Stuhler, *No Regrets*, 90.

page 61   "progressive folk hero": Chrislock, *The Progressive Era in Minnesota*, 62.

page 61   "most enduring friend": Stuhler, *Gentle Warriors*, 127.

page 61   "than any other man in Minnesota": Johnson, *Minnesota's Ole Sageng*, 387.

page 62   "remarkable political comeback...": Johnson, *Minnesota's Ole Sageng*, 6.

page 62   "was symbolic...": Brenda Ueland quoted in Johnson, *Minnesota's Ole Sageng*, 5.

page 62   "the suffragists adored Sageng": Stuhler, *Gentle Warriors*, 128.

page 62   "consented to espouse our cause...": Minnesota Woman Suffrage Association report quoted by Stuhler, *Gentle Warriors*, 127.

page 63   "His mother. His mother": daughter quoted in Johnson, *Minnesota's Ole Sageng*, 385.

page 63   "suffrage follower...": Johnson, *Minnesota's Ole Sageng*, 387.

page 63   "members of the SWSA...": Peterson, "Minnesota's Scandinavian Women Suffrage Association."

page 63   "My parents were...": Brenda Ueland quoted in Stuhler, *Gentle Warriors*, 35.

page 64   "rather formidable": Brenda Ueland quoted in Bauer, ed., *The Privilege for Which We Struggled*, 83.

page 64   "Ethnicity was a means...": Peterson, "Minnesota's Scandinavian Women Suffrage Association."

page 65   "even those who did not defend...": Bauer, ed., *The Privilege for Which We Struggled*, 137.

page 66   "so long a friend": Clara Ueland on Knute Nelson in Stuhler, *Gentle Warriors*, 147.

page 66   "more Scandinavian-American men...": Peterson, "Minnesota's Scandinavian Women Suffrage Association."

page 67   "my father put his head down...": interview with Margaret Anderson Kelliher, February 6, 2014.

page 67   "Yes, there is a Scandinavian trait...": interview with Margaret Anderson Kelliher, February 6, 2014.

page 68   "furnishes all the opportunities...": Malmberg Johnson, *Woman and the Socialist Movement*.

page 69   "failed social experiment": Eighmey, "Andrew Volstead."

page 69   "Certainly, the name of...": Christianson, *Land of Sky-Tinted Waters*, 9.

page 70   "a true leader of men...": Soike, *Norwegian-Americans and the Politics of Dissent*, 90.

page 71   "His force and energy...": Christianson, *Land of Sky-Tinted Waters*, 8.

page 72   "This was my world growing up": interviews with Roger Moe, July 31 and August 1, 2014.

page 73   "My grandfather ran...": interviews with Roger Moe, July 31 and August 1, 2014.

page 73   "We cannot afford...": *Crookston Daily Times*, October 29, 1970.
page 73   "Two Sons in the Senate": *Crookston Daily Times*, November 5, 1970.
page 73   "Then, I will stop my advocacy": interviews with Roger Moe, July 31 and August 1, 2014.
pages 73–74   "reserved, cautious, unflappable...": Michael Khoo, "Profile: Roger Moe," Minnesota Public Radio, September 16, 2002.
page 74   "not exactly the wide-eyed dreamer": Wilson, *Rudy!*, 163.
page 74   "like a brother": interview with Al Quie, June 3, 2013.
page 74   "In 2000 or so...": interview with Steve Sviggum, March 24, 2014.
page 75   "He was the best example...": Keillor, *Hjalmar Petersen of Minnesota*, 22.
page 76   "We cease to exist...": Luth Jaeger speech on "Norwegian-American Journalism," at the Norwegian Society of Minneapolis, January 25, 1909.
page 76   "the greatest possible participation...": Lovoll, *The Promise of America*, 121.
page 78   "one of the builders...": Minnesota *Journal of the Senate*, March 29, 1961, 1092.
pages 78–79   "achieved without sacrifice...": Christianson, *Land of Sky-Tinted Waters*, 614.

Chapter 4: "From Protests to Repression"

page 80   "The difference is that...": from Lindbergh's acceptance speech as gubernatorial candidate for the Nonpartisan League, quoted in Larson, *Lindbergh of Minnesota*, 222.
page 80   "For me, there are...": Burnquist letter to Arthur LaSueur, March 11, 1918, J. A. A. Burnquist Papers, Minnesota Historical Society.
page 81   "marked the emergence...": Blegen, *Minnesota*, 388.
page 81   "drew its strength chiefly...": Naftalin, "The Tradition of Protest and the Roots of the Farmer-Labor Party."
page 81   "Midwestern progressivism...": Chrislock, "The Norwegian-American Impact on Minnesota Politics," 112.
page 81   "the volatility of...": Barone, "Social Basis of Urban Politics."
page 82   "the greatest progressive triumph": Wyman, "Insurgency in Minnesota."
page 83   Transferred their loyalty: Nyberg, "Swedish Immigrant Press."
page 83   "political prairie fire": Robert L. Morlan's book with that title.
pages 83–84   "the starkest challenge to party politics...": Lansing, *Insurgent Democracy*, ix.
page 84   "Cursed in history's letters of fire...": *Svenska Socialisten*, December 17, 1914.
page 85   "virtual dictatorship": Chrislock, *Watchdog of Loyalty*, 60.
page 85   "Its word was law...": Morlan, *Political Prairie Fire*, 129.
page 86   "loyalty": Jensen, "Loyalty as a Political Weapon."
page 86   "basic flaw": Chrislock, *Watchdog of Loyalty*, 203.

page 86 "Where we made a mistake . . .": McGee testimony in US Senate, Chrislock, *Watchdog of Loyalty*, 299.

page 87 "The intolerance, openly and tacitly . . .": Fedo, *The Lynchings in Duluth*, 29.

page 87 "Throw him out": Chrislock, *Watchdog of Loyalty*, 57.

page 88 "is known as one . . .": *Two Harbors Socialist*, September 16, 1916.

page 88 "our comrade": *Svenska Socialisten*, December 7, 1916.

page 89 "were clearly reformist . . .": Engren, "Railroading and Labor Migration."

page 90 "socialist bids for control . . .": Engren, "Railroading and Labor Migration."

page 91 "one of Minnesota's most effective . . .": Lovoll, "Going With the Leftward Tide."

page 91 On Emil Lauritz Mengshoel: Granhus, "Socialist Dissent among Norwegian Americans," 27.

page 92 "our sister party": Lovoll, "*Gaa Paa*."

page 92 "cooperation with the promising . . .": Granhus, "Socialist Dissent among Norwegian Americans," 27.

page 92 "conspicuous exception": Chrislock, *Ethnically Challenged*, 66.

page 92 "When the socialist alternative failed": Granhus, "Socialist Dissent among Norwegian Americans," 27.

page 93 Two main objectives: Chrislock, *Watchdog of Loyalty*, xi.

pages 93–94 "Strong insurgent leader . . .": Haines, *The Minnesota Legislature of 1911*.

page 94 "Once again a Swedish . . .": *Svenska Dagbladet*, January 28, 1916.

page 95 "to smash the Hun" and "Peace can never come": *Minneapolis Morning Tribune*, April 7, 1918, and February 16, 1918.

page 95 "is best remembered for . . .": Larson, *Lindbergh of Minnesota*, 3.

page 95 "It is a remarkable fact . . .": Haines and Haines, *The Lindberghs*, 10.

page 96 "Father had no idea of politics at the time": daughter quoted in Larson, *Lindbergh of Minnesota*, 25.

page 96 "typical ethnic politician": Carlsson, *Scandinavian Politicians in the United States*, 153.

page 96 "The origins of Lindbergh's . . .": Larson, *Lindbergh of Minnesota*, 12.

page 97 "a lone wolf in politics": Nye, *Midwestern Progressive Politics*, 247.

page 97 "I am a radical . . .": quoted in Larson, *Lindbergh of Minnesota*, 217.

page 97 "explosive . . .": Stuhler, *Ten Men of Minnesota*, 43.

page 98 "If we get in war . . .": Larson, *Lindbergh of Minnesota*, 204.

page 98 "as disloyal as can be . . ." and "a Rock of Gibraltar in maintaining law and order": Chrislock, *Watchdog of Loyalty*, 295, 302.

page 98 "German hordes . . .": Burnquist quoted in *Journal News* after visiting Two Harbors, April 19, 1918.

page 100 "violence followed Lindbergh everywhere": Jensen, "Loyalty as a Political Weapon."

page 100   "Don't drive so fast . . .": Larson, *Lindbergh of Minnesota*, 237.

page 100   "You must prepare to see me . . .": Larson, *Lindbergh of Minnesota*, 241.

page 101   "We hope that hereafter . . .": Bjornson quoted in Chrislock, *Watchdog of Loyalty*, 291.

page 101   "Lindbergh became the candidate . . .": Dag Blanck, "Swedish Americans and the 1918 Gubernatorial Campaign in Minnesota," in *Swedes in the Twin Cities*, ed. Anderson and Blanck, 317, 327–28.

page 102   The impossible had happened: Morlan, *Political Prairie Fire*, 191.

page 102   "the incorruptible seeker . . .": Engdahl, "Charles Augustus Lindbergh Den Äldre."

Chapter 5: "Radicals in Exile"

page 104   "I did not have 'America fever'": Engdahl to Swedish oral historian Lennart Setterdahl, 1978, author's collection.

page 104   "My grandfather never mellowed . . .": interview with Brad Engdahl, April 24, 2014.

page 107   "If any plan for the future . . . ": Isador Kjellberg quoted by Hildeman, "Swedish Strikes and Emigration."

pages 107–8   "It is terribly sad for the stranger . . .": quote from Dagens Nyheter in Bjorn Rondahl, "Ljusne 1906: en politiskt motiverad utvandring," in *Utvandring*, ed. Kälvemark.

page 108   "tended to destroy the hope . . .": Hildeman, "Swedish Strikes and Emigration."

page 108   "Emigration became . . .": Nilsson, *Emigrationen från Stockholm till Nordamerika*, 250.

page 108   "a clear connection . . .": Tedebrand, "Strikes and Political Radicalism in Sweden."

page 108   "experienced the tensions . . .": Tedebrand, "Strikes and Political Radicalism in Sweden," 194.

page 109   "I left Sweden almost a year ago . . .": from Walfrid Engdahl's letters to Hinke Bergegren, Arbetarrörelsens Arkiv, Stockholm, Sweden.

page 109   "a Swedish radical voice in Minneapolis": Brook, "Radical Literature in Swedish America."

page 110   "We tried to tell the truth . . .": Walfrid Engdahl interview for the 20th Century Radicalism in Minnesota Oral History Project, 1972.

pages 110–11   On Joe Hill: Engdahl in *Allarm*, November 19, 1915, and November 19, 1916.

page 112   On Ahlteen: Bengston, *On the Left in America*, 198.

page 112   "a silver tongued orator": Hokanson, "Swedes and the I.W.W."

page 113   "serious thinkers": Bengston, "Chicago's Swedish 'Book Cabin.'"

page 114   "Olson would have been a good president": Engdahl to Setterdahl, 1978.

page 115   "America fever": Carl Skoglund interview for the 20th Century Radicalism in Minnesota Oral History Project, 1960.

page 116   "I am profoundly chagrined ...": letter to Carl Skoglund from Leon
Trotsky in Mexico, March 21, 1938, quoted in special anniversary issue,
Svenska socialisten, November 1915, Augustana College, Rock Island, IL.

page 116   "landmark in the labor history ...": Blantz, "Father Haas and the Minneapolis Truckers' Strike."

page 116   "critical roles in the struggle ...": Korth, *Minneapolis Teamsters' Strike
of 1934*, 8.

pages 116–17   "Skoglund was a socialist and a very able man": Vincent Dunne
interview for 20th Century Radicalism in Minnesota Oral History Project,
April 27, 1969.

page 117   "the American working class lost ...": obituary, *International Socialist
Review*. 22, no. 1 (1961): 2.

page 117   "in competence, resourcefulness, and devotion ...": Mayer, *The Political Career of Floyd B. Olson*, 188.

page 117   "perfected a new motorized form of pickets ...": Nathanson, *Minneapolis in the Twentieth Century*, 79.

page 117   "generous and nice fellow ..." coal worker quoted by Iric Nathanson,
Minneapolis in the Twentieth Century, 74.

page 118   "real objective ...": *Minnesota Journal* cited in Mayer, *The Political
Career of Floyd B. Olson*, 204.

page 118   "the dictatorship ...": Solberg, *Hubert Humphrey*, 64.

page 118   "We'll never let him send him back ...": Miles B. Dunne, October 8,
1949; *Svenska Socialisten*, November 1915.

page 118   "profound contribution ...": Riehle, "A Life We Can Learn From."

page 120   "I felt it necessary ...": Walter Frank interview with Minnesota Historical Society, August 11, 1969.

page 120   "brought a radicalism ...": Hudelson, "The Scandinavian Local of the
Duluth Socialist Party."

page 120   Swedes ... felt confident: Hudelson and Ross, *By the Ore Docks*, xxi.

page 121   "the rock upon which Truth was built": Richard Hudelson, "*Truth* in
Duluth," Voices of Dissent Conference, May 8, 1989.

page 121   "to destroy Capitalism was our job": J. O. Bentall in *Truth*, October 15,
1920.

page 121   "Tell them I laugh at it ...": *Minneapolis Morning Tribune*, April 13, 1920.

page 121   "due to lack of funds caused by the apathy of the workers": *Truth*, April
13, 1923.

page 122   "Comrade Bentall is no spotlight artist ...": Jack Carney on J. O. Bentall in *Truth*, April 12, 1918.

Chapter 6: "Finns on the Range"

page 123   "The story of Finland's immigrants ...": Karni, Kaups, and Ollila, eds.,
The Finnish Experience, 1.

page 124   "being a Finn, he is Mongolian ...": Peter Kivisto and Johanna Leinonen, "Ambiguous Identity: Finnish Americans and the Race Question," in *Finns in the United States*, ed. Kostiainen, 76.

page 124 On Kiukkonen: Alanen, *Finns in Minnesota*, 57.

page 125 "inhuman conditions": Ollila, "From Socialism to Industrial Union-ism (IWW): Social Factors in the Emergence of Left-Labor Radicalism Among Finnish Workers on the Mesabi, 1911–19," in *The Finnish Experience*, eds. Karni, Kaups, and Ollila, 170.

page 125 "Condemn their illusions if you will . . .": from articles by Carl Ross, *New York Uutiset*, June 1975–August 1976.

page 126 "Socialism became a way of life," Ollila, "From Socialism," in *The Finnish Experience*, 156.

page 127 "Socialist ideas, quite simply, were in the air": Al Gedicks quoted in Peter Kivisto, *Immigrant Socialists in the United States*, 70.

page 127 "radicalized and disenchanted . . .": Marianne Wargelin, "Finnish Americans," 2.

page 127 "expected to find . . .": Carl Ross interview for the 20th Century Radi-calism in Minnesota Oral History Project, 1986–88.

page 127 "If Finland prepared . . .": Hoglund, *Finnish Immigrants in America*, 57.

page 128 "This political threat . . .": A. William Hoglund, "No Land for Finns: Critics and Reformers View the Rural Exodus from Finland to America Between the 1880s and World War I," in *The Finnish Experience*, eds. Karni, Kaups, and Ollila, 45.

page 129 "Finnish Americans obtained . . .": Reino Kero quoted in Kivisto, *Immigrant Socialists in the United States*, 93.

page 129 "Apostles of Socialism": Kivisto, *Immigrant Socialists in the United States*, 93.

page 129 "whose antipathy to capitalism . . .": Kivisto, *Immigrant Socialists in the United States*, 95.

page 130 "significant force": Kivisto, *Immigrant Socialists in the United States*, 157.

page 130 "ideological father . . .": Carl Ross, *The Finn Factor*, 109.

page 130 "one of the important architects . . .": Ollila, "From Socialism," in *The Finnish Experience*, 161.

page 132 "I did not ask, nor did he say anything": John Wiita Papers, Immigra-tion History Research Center, University of Minnesota, Minneapolis, MN [hereafter, IHRC].

page 132 "destructive factional fight": Wiita Papers, IHRC.

page 132 "quietly, without fanfare . . .": Wiita Papers, IHRC.

page 133 A socialist first: Ross and Wargelin, *Women Who Dared*, 141.

page 133 "tireless advocate of progressive forces": Alanen, *Finns in Minnesota*, 61.

page 133 "Together, they saw themselves . . .": Hudelson and Ross, *By the Ore Docks*, 214.

page 133 "were not willing to play the political game": interview with Pamela Brunfelt, August 29, 2013.

page 134 "Few ethnic groups . . .": Alanen, *Finns in Minnesota*, 6.

page 134   "the paradise they had crossed the ocean to find . . .": Hoglund quoted in Karni, "For the Common Good."

page 135   "became the single largest business enterprise . . .": Ross, *The Finn Factor*, 94.

page 135   "most remarkable and . . .": Karni, "For the Common Good."

page 135   "no national group has made . . .": Parker, *The First 125 Years*, 311–12.

page 136   "Recalcitrant members . . .": Karni, "Struggle on the Cooperative Front: The Separation of Central Cooperative Wholesale from Communism, 1929–1930," in *The Finnish Experience*, eds. Karni, Kaups, and Ollila, 187.

page 136   "beginning of the end . . .": Karni, "Struggle on the Cooperative Front," in *The Finnish Experience*, 199.

page 138   "culmination of years of radical activity . . .": Brunfelt, "Karl Emil Nygard."

page 138   "STRIKES IN THE MINES . . .": Brunfelt, "Karl Emil Nygard."

page 138   "I couldn't understand . . .": Karl Emil Nygaard interview with Northwest Minnesota Historical Center, September 1973.

page 138   Nygard speech: "The First Red Mayor in America in Action," Workers Library Publishers.

pages 138–39   "We're not Russians . . .": Nygard interview.

page 139   "recognize the degree . . .": Ross interview for the 20th Century Radicalism in Minnesota Oral History Project.

page 140   "They took my friends' fathers . . .": Sevander, *They Took My Father*, 78.

page 141   "Sirola had great reservations, as I did . . .": John Wiita Papers, IHRC.

page 141   "Sooner or later, they all disappeared . . .": Edith Koivisto Papers, June 1975, IHRC.

page 142   "the beginning of the decline . . .": Reino Kero, "Emigration of Finns from North America to Soviet Karelia in the Early 1930s," in *The Finnish Experience*, ed. Karni, Kaups, and Ollila, 212.

page 142   "part of the recovery . . .": Carl Ross in 20th Century Radicalism in Minnesota Oral History Project.

page 142   "intense frustration": Runblom and Norman, eds., *Transatlantic Connections*, 235.

page 142   "alienation, conflict and tragedy": Karni, Kaups, and Ollila, *The Finnish Experience*, 1.

page 142   "total immersion": Karni, "For the Common Good."

page 144   "Without the iron ore of Minnesota . . .": interview with Pamela Brunfelt, August 29, 2013.

page 144   "the big red flag with . . .": Sevander, *They Took My Father*, 15.

page 144   "festivals of struggle": Alanen, *Finns in Minnesota*, 61.

Chapter 7: "Third Becomes First"

page 146   "I am not a liberal . . .": Floyd B. Olson, speech at Farmer-Labor Convention, March 27, 1934, in *Third Party Footprints*, ed. James M. Youngdale, 239.

page 146   "important catalysts": Larson, *Lindbergh of Minnesota*, 249.

page 146　"Good or bad, the Scandinavians monopolize . . .": Sinclair Lewis, "Minnesota—The Norse State," speech, These United States Symposium, New York, *The Nation*, May 30, 1923, 626.

pages 146–47　"the first generation Swedish and Swedish-American editors . . .": Capps, *From Isolationism to Involvement*, 105.

page 147　"distortion": Chrislock, "The Norwegian-American Impact on Minnesota Politics," 113.

page 149　"Bold, strong and unafraid . . .": Engdahl, "Magnus Johnson."

page 149　"a Republican platform": Engdahl, "Magnus Johnson," 123.

page 149　"always commanded respect . . .": *Minneapolis Journal*, September 14, 1936, quoted by Engdahl, "Magnus Johnson," 135.

page 149　"citizen of whom Minnesota has . . .": Burnquist, *Minnesota and Its People*, 637.

page 150　"towered over the party . . .": Naftalin, "History of the Farmer-Labor Party of Minnesota," 163.

page 150　"His legacy is fundamental . . .": interview with Hyman Berman, March 14, 2013.

page 151　"Certainly, the effort to relieve . . .": Mayer, *The Political Career of Floyd B. Olson*, 256.

page 151　"his successful handling of the Ku Klux Klan leaders . . .": Fridley, "What Would Floyd B. Do?"

page 152　"sing Swedish, Danish . . .": McGrath and Delmont, *Floyd Björnsterne Olson*.

page 152　"if it was in fact true . . .": LeVander, *Call Me Pete*, 25.

page 152　"Floyd B. Olson—Norwegian father . . .": *Minneapolis Tidende*, October 30, 1930.

page 152　"with such finesse . . .": Mayer, *The Political Career of Floyd B. Olson*, 44.

page 152　"went far in removing the stigma . . .": Mayer, *The Political Career of Floyd B. Olson*, 45.

page 152　"for a promised land . . .": Mayer, *The Political Career of Floyd B. Olson*, 109.

page 153　"unqualified mandate from the people": Naftalin, "History of the Farmer-Labor Party of Minnesota," 218.

page 153　"militant crusader" and the "public conscience of the state . . .": Mayer, *The Political Career of Floyd B. Olson*, 120.

page 153　"with a stunning array of reforms": Fridley, "What Would Floyd B. Do?"

page 153　"notable contribution . . .": Andersen, *A Man's Reach*, 44.

pages 153–54　Olson speech in Youngdale, *Third Party Footprints*.

page 154　"deafening": Mayer, *The Political Career of Floyd B. Olson*, 171.

page 154　"the most extreme document . . .": Mayer, *The Political Career of Floyd B. Olson*, 171.

page 154　"petrified" and "political suicide": Mayer, *The Political Career of Floyd B. Olson*, 171–72.

page 155　"cooperation as a non-radical idea . . .": Keillor, *Cooperative Commonwealth*, 317.

page 155   "went as far to the left . . .": Carlsson, "Skandinaviska politiker i Minnesota," in *Utvandring*, ed. Kälvemark, 242.

page 155   "The Swedish people understand . . .": Roy W. Swanson, *American Swedish Monthly*, February 1935.

page 156   "foreshadowed the final disintegration . . .": Mayer, *The Political Career of Floyd B. Olson*, 251.

page 156   "partisanship gone amuck": Mayer, *The Political Career of Floyd B. Olson*, 266.

page 156   "employers could not forgive him . . .": Mayer, *The Political Career of Floyd B. Olson*, 215.

page 156   "enhanced prestige": Mayer, *The Political Career of Floyd B. Olson*, 221.

page 156   "ruthlessly": Millikan, "Defenders of Business."

page 156   "fearless and effective crusader . . .": Mayer, *The Political Career of Floyd B. Olson*, 301.

page 156   "remains the gold standard": Fridley, "What Would Floyd B. Do?"

page 156   "The Skipper Is Gone": Abe Harris, *Minnesota Leader*, August 29, 1936.

page 158   "It was undoubtedly Petersen's . . .": Keillor, *Hjalmar Petersen of Minnesota*, 95.

page 159   "highly ambitious and unprincipled politician": Berman, "Political Antisemitism."

page 160   "did little to stop and much to encourage . . .": Keillor, *Hjalmar Petersen of Minnesota*, 157.

page 160   "To think of our state . . .": Keillor, *Hjalmar Petersen of Minnesota*, 157.

page 160   "The communists believe . . .": Mayer, *The Political Career of Floyd B. Olson*, 239.

page 160   "all he had left was . . .": Keillor, *Hjalmar Petersen of Minnesota*, 217.

page 161   "more than any other . . .": Shields, *Mr. Progressive*, 163.

page 161   "deeply shocked and almost broken-hearted . . .": Shields, *Mr. Progressive*, 218.

page 161   The decline: O'Connor, "Toward the Cooperative Commonwealth."

page 162   "incompetence, corruption . . .": Mitau, "The Democratic-Farmer-Labor Party Schism."

page 162   "what had largely been . . .": Berman, "Political Antisemitism."

page 162   "So ended the most successful use . . .": Berman, "Political Antisemitism."

page 163   "I hope the senior leaders of my party . . .": Werle, *Stassen Again*, 89.

page 163   "sit back and try to stop Hitler . . .": speech by Senator Ball cited in Stuhler, *Ten Men of Minnesota*, 127.

page 164   "an intense fear of war . . .": Stuhler, *Ten Men of Minnesota*, 97.

page 164   "discover that the ship had sailed": Werle, *Stassen Again*, 147.

page 164   "unreconstructed isolationist": Stuhler, *Ten Men of Minnesota*, 74.

page 164   "radical isolationism embraced . . .": Stuhler, *Ten Men of Minnesota*, 75.

page 165   "final disintegration": Naftalin, "History of the Farmer-Labor Party of Minnesota."

page 165   "The merger leveraged . . .": interview with David Lebedoff, June 5, 2013.

page 165   "simply the final requiem for a death . . .": Naftalin, "History of the Farmer-Labor Party of Minnesota."
page 165   "an outright coup": Solberg, *Hubert Humphrey*, 113.
page 165   "for a brief period in 1947 and 1948 . . .": Eisele, *Almost to the Presidency*, 62.
page 166   "exceedingly talented . . .": Andersen, *A Man's Reach*, 243.
page 166   "In retrospect . . .": Benson, "Politics in My Lifetime."

Chapter 8: "Two New Parties"

page 167   "I have looked at Sweden . . .": interview with Arne Carlson, June 12, 2013.
page 167   "a decade of liberal civil war ended . . .": Haynes, *Dubious Alliance*, 217.
page 167   "must be considered": Eisele, *Almost to the Presidency*, 47.
page 168   "I used to say . . .": interview with Walter Mondale, August 23, 2013.
page 168   Second-rate citizens: Eisele, *Almost to the Presidency*, 13.
page 168   "Dad was a Democrat . . .": Humphrey, *The Education of a Public Man*, 27, 29.
page 168   "Now you treat your mother with respect . . .": Solberg, *Hubert Humphrey*, 43.
page 168   "swung the majority opinion in Minnesota . . .": Solberg, *Hubert Humphrey*, 83.
pages 168–69   "I have a great loyalty to rural life": Humphrey interview on Norwegian National Radio (NRK), September 16, 1975.
page 169   "his kind of people": Solberg, *Hubert Humphrey*, 304.
page 169   "A socialist summit? My God, no!": Solberg, *Hubert Humphrey*, 221.
page 169   The letters start with "Dear Tage" and "Dear Hubert," and can be found in Arbetarrörelsens arkiv (Labor movement archives), Stockholm, Sweden.
page 169   "Do you still receive Americans . . .": *Aftonbladet*, November 4, 1970.
page 170   "an icon": interview with Warren Spannaus, April 10, 2014.
page 170   "Can you think of a politician . . .": Solberg, *Hubert Humphrey*, 415.
page 171   "Now it's your turn. You must carry on": Lewis, *Mondale*, 4.
page 171   "I started to feel a need . . .": interview with Walter Mondale, August 23, 2013.
page 171   "moral vision and anger": Lewis, *Mondale*, 280.
page 171   "they never put it to us . . .": interview with Walter Mondale, August 23, 2013.
page 171   "It smells like Minnesota!": Wachtmeister, *Som jag såg det*, 231.
page 171   "I had an immediate sense of . . .": interview with Walter Mondale, August 23, 2013.
page 172   "you were right and we were wrong": Walter Mondale quoted by Wachtmeister, *Som jag såg det*, 197, 231.
page 172   "while it is not necessary to be . . .": Walter Mondale interview on Norwegian National Radio (NRK), June 16, 1975.

page 172 "That's the test . . .": interview with Walter Mondale, August 23, 2013.

page 173 "stood for everything I opposed": Mondale, *The Good Fight*, 332–33.

page 174 "They made their own way": interview with Don Ostrom, March 31, 2014.

page 175 "My father spoke Norwegian as a kid . . .": interview with Mike Freeman, April 16, 2014.

page 175 "working hard . . .": interview with Mike Freeman, April 16, 2014.

page 175 "Norway was very important to my father": interview with Kris Garey, August 29, 2013.

page 176 "pointed my whole direction . . .": Karl Rolvaag oral history interview, Minnesota Historical Society, August 31, 1989.

page 176 "pivotal shift . . .": Bruce L. Larson, "Gubernatorial Politics and Swedish Americans in Minnesota: The 1970 Election and Beyond," in *Swedes in the Twin Cities*, ed. Anderson and Blanck, 331.

page 176 "the modern governorship . . .": interview with Martin Olav Sabo, March 13, 2013.

page 176 "modern Minnesota government . . .": interview with Steven Schier, June 10, 2013.

page 177 "You have exported a lot of good people from Sweden": Hubert Humphrey, *Aftonbladet*, November 4, 1970.

page 177 "I am a Swede who happens now to live in America": Wendell Anderson in *The Swedish Americans of the Year*, Karlstad, Sweden, 174–81.

page 178 "fundamental reform of school finance": Martin Olav Sabo quoted in Dornfeld, "The Minnesota Miracle."

page 178 "just about every state tax in sight": Dornfeld, "The Minnesota Miracle."

page 178 "They came together": interview with Ken Martin, April 25, 2014.

page 178 "I don't think there's any way . . .": Sabo, in Dornfeld, "The Minnesota Miracle."

pages 178–79 no "penny pincher": Andersen, *A Man's Reach*, 303.

page 179 "that Minnesota voters are willing to accept . . .": Wendell Anderson in Dornfeld, "The Minnesota Miracle."

page 179 "It was Brad . . .": interview with John Lindstrom, August 23, 2013.

page 180 "The 1978 election marked the end . . .": Berg, *Minnesota's Miracle*, 213.

page 180 "notable ethnic leap for the Republican Party . . .": Wilson, *Rudy!*, 105–6.

page 180 "One is tempted to see progressive Republicanism . . .": John E. Haynes, "Reformers, Radicals, and Conservatives," in *Minnesota in a Century of Change*, ed. Clark, 381.

page 180 "fit a distinctively progressive mold . . .": Russell Fridley and Dane Smith, "These Republicans Didn't Deny," *Growth & Justice*, August 12, 2008.

page 180 "Picture a Republican governor . . .": Fridley and Smith, "These Republicans."

pages 181–82 "It was not just his [Youngdahl's] name . . .": Esbjornson, *A Christian in Politics*, 134.

page 182   "oh, they were really Swedes": interview with Paul H. Anderson, July 28, 2014.

page 182   who conversed freely in Swedish: *Aftonbladet*, July 7, 1968.

page 183   The visit included a gala dinner with dance: *Aftonbladet*, January 13, 1948.

page 183   "this sense of obligation to a larger community": interview with Paul H. Anderson, July 28, 2014.

page 183   "honest, decent, kind, generous, civil": Andersen, *A Man's Reach*, 29.

page 183   "I see government as the people's partner . . .": Andersen, *A Man's Reach*, 184.

pages 183–84   "I saw him about a month or so before . . .": interview with Hyman Berman, March 14, 2013.

page 184   "it should never have happened": LeVander, *Call Me Pete*, 71.

page 185   "My parents spoke Norwegian . . .": interview with Al Quie, June 3, 2013.

page 185   "That's contrary to the Bible . . .": interview with Al Quie, June 3, 2013.

page 186   "A truly remarkable man": Pearlstein, *Riding into the Sunrise*, xxvi.

page 187   "I was very fond of him . . .": interview with Arne Carlson, June 12, 2013.

page 187   "Arne was a moderate Republican . . .": interview with Paul H. Anderson, July 28, 2014.

page 187   "I would say it . . .": interview with Arne Carlson, June 12, 2013.

page 188   He likes the phrase . . .: interview with Arne Carlson, June 12, 2013.

page 188   "I truly hope . . .": Arne Carlson's blog, http://govarnecarlson .blogspot.com.

page 189   "I don't think of myself . . .": interview with Paul Thissen, February 3, 2014.

page 189   "government is part of the solution . . .": interview with Tom Bakk, February 4, 2014.

page 190   "I feel so connected to Sweden . . .": interviews with Laurie Halverson, November 4, 2013, April 17, 2014.

page 192   "The fact is, I agree with Laurie . . .": interviews with George A. Nelson, May 9, 2014.

page 194   "the Republicans today are not . . .": interview with Martin Olav Sabo, March 13, 2013, June 3, 2013.

Chapter 9: "From Snoose Boulevard to Little Mogadishu"

page 195   "If you don't have political clout . . .": interview with Abdi Warsame, October 31, 2013.

page 195   "This is a very old American story . . .": Larry Jacobs, "With Rising Political Power, Somali Community May Get First City Council Representative," *MinnPost*, October 7, 2013.

pages 195–96   "In recent years, a couple of things . . .": interview with David Lebedoff, June 5, 2013.

page 196   "Swedish! I have been to Sweden": interview with Abdi Warsame, October 31, 2013.

page 197   "So the experience of the Africans right now is similar . . .": interview with Abdi Warsame, October 31, 2013.

pages 197–98   "The Somali involvement is a good . . .": interview with Robert Lilligren, October 31, 2013.

page 198   "The extent of ethnic concentration . . .": Byron Nordstrom, "The Swedes in Minneapolis."

pages 198–99   Scandinavian life in Minneapolis from Söderström, *Minneapolis Minnen,* and from Hansen, *My Minneapolis.*

page 199   "The saloons were the worst . . .": Rølvaag, *The Boat of Longing,* 97.

page 199   "even if they still are rubbing . . .": Söderström, *Minneapolis Minnen,* 213.

page 200   "a gentleman of the old school": Söderström, *Minneapolis Minnen,* 370.

page 201   "The fact that he misappropriated public money . . .": *Minneapolis Tribune,* January 25, 1898.

pages 201–2   "old-fashioned ward boss . . .": David Markle, "Dania Hall: At the Center of a Scandinavian American Community," in *Swedes in the Twin Cities,* ed. Anderson and Blanck, 176.

page 202   "it was like a political event of years long past . . .": *Minneapolis Tribune,* September 30, 1913.

page 202   "The barefoot boy is dead": Chrislock, "Profile of a Ward Boss," 35.

page 202   "That was me . . .": from *Minneapolis Tribune,* September 28, 1913, quoted in Chrislock, "Profile of a Ward Boss," 35.

page 202   "The spectacle of an immigrant politician . . .": Chrislock, "Profile of a Ward Boss," 35.

page 203   "brings a deep blush to my cheek": Chrislock, "Profile of a Ward Boss," 35.

page 204   "En *folkets man*": *Svenska Amerikanska Posten,* October 23, 1894; "En *arbetarnes sanne vän*": *Svenska Amerikanska Posten,* October 30, 1894.

page 204   "shared an interest in maintaining . . .": Chrislock, "Profile of a Ward Boss," 35.

page 205   "an oily . . . unscrupulous ward boss": *Minneapolis Journal,* September 20, 1906, quoted by Chrislock, "Profile of a Ward Boss," 35.

page 205   "manifestly unfair": Chrislock, "Profile of a Ward Boss," 35.

page 206   "Father of . . .": *Minneapolis Tribune,* January 19, 1913.

page 206   When David Markle moved to the Cedar-Riverside neighborhood in 1962: Markle, "Dania Hall," 173.

page 207   "We've gotten very good at change . . .": Home page of church website: www.trinitylutherancongregation.org.

page 207   "within whose walls . . .": Markle, "Dania Hall," 173.

pages 209–10   "You would think that . . .": interview with Jodi Harpstead, May 20, 2014.

page 210   "Minnesota has been a state . . .": interview with Joanne Negstad, June 3, 2013.

page 211   "pull factor": "As U.S. Considers Admitting More Syrian Refugees, Will Minnesota Be a Top Destination?" *MinnPost,* September 17, 2015.

page 211   "That is a good thing for our party": interview with Ken Martin, April 25, 2014.
page 212   "Now, anybody who was seeking work . . .": Yusuf, *Somalis in Minnesota*, 23.
page 213   "durable": Yusuf, *Somalis in Minnesota*, 65.
page 213   "their own Minnesota identity": Yusuf, *Somalis in Minnesota*, 65.
page 213   "inclusive political environment . . .": Yusuf, *Somalis in Minnesota*, 28.
page 213   "much more important . . .": interview with R.T. Rybak, April 25, 2014.
page 213   "I absolutely adhere this to the Scandinavian heritage": interview with R.T. Rybak, April 25, 2014.
page 213   "Samatar was the brightest light . . .": interview with R.T. Rybak, April 25, 2014.
page 214   "has concluded that the differences are stark": Carlson, *Somalier i Minneapolis*, 69.
page 215   "critical mass": Carlson, *Somalier i Minneapolis*, 68.
page 215   "virtually all the needs of an ethnic population could be met": Byron Nordstrom, "The Sixth Ward: A Minneapolis Swede Town in 1905," in *Perspectives on Swedish Immigration*, ed. Hasselmo, 153.
page 215   "My cultural worlds were joined": Rahma Dirie in *Somalier i Sverige*, ed. Carlson, 156.
page 216   "The people of the Ward were hard-working . . .": Nordstrom, "The Sixth Ward," 163.
page 217   "All of these things are local politics": interview with Abdi Warsame, October 31, 2013.
page 218   "I am running . . .": interview with Ilhan Omar, May 5, 2016.
page 218   "I was raised . . .": Ilhan Omar, "'Done Wishing': Ilhan Omar on Why She's Running for House District 60B," *MinnPost*, October 21, 2015.
page 218   "This is really about power": interview with Ilhan Omar, May 5, 2016.
page 219   "reaffirms what an amazing . . .": Abdi Warsame, "A Welcome Somali Voice at the Minnesota State Capitol," *Star Tribune*, August 12, 2016.
page 219   "The enduring contribution": interview with David Lebedoff, June 5, 2013.
page 220   "It is pretty deep in our DNA . . .": interview with Margaret Anderson Kelliher, February 6, 2014.
page 220   "It always takes a while with a new generation": interview with Walter Mondale, August 23, 2013.

Chapter 10: "On the Scandinavian Road"

page 221   "What a glorious new Scandinavia . . .": Bremer, *The Homes of the New World*.
page 221   "If only everyone could be . . .": President Obama quoted in "The Obama Doctrine," *The Atlantic*, April 2016.

page 221 "Any Swede visiting today . . .": Wendell Anderson, Swedish American of the Year, 1975.

page 221 "Nowhere during my trip . . .": Tage Erlander, *Dagböcker*, 65.

pages 221–22 "Minnesota sees itself as a Scandinavian state . . .": interview with Al Eisele, February 6, 2013.

page 222 "I don't think there is any doubt . . .": interview with David Lanegran, February 6, 2014.

page 222 "It's comfortable here as a Scandinavian . . .": interview with Kjell Bergh, February 4, 2014.

page 222 "People are so proud of their roots . . .": interview with Eivind Heiberg, October 29, 2014.

page 222 "values, quality, nature": interview with Lena Norrman, March 12, 2013.

page 222 "It's amazing how the Scandinavian legacy . . .": interview with David W. Preus, March 12, 2013.

pages 223–24 "In the interest of fjord-like clarity": Kim Ode, "Valkommen to the King and Queen," *Star Tribune*, October 4, 2012.

page 225 "Somalis are playing . . .": "First Somali Cultural Museum in North America Set to Open," kare11.com, October 18, 2013.

page 226 "convener, connector, and facilitator . . .": Norway House, Minneapolis, norwayhouse.org.

page 229 "It's been absolutely wonderful . . .": interview with George Latimer, February 5, 2014.

page 230 "We talk about immigration with a Swedish flavor . . .": interview with Lynne Blomstrand Moratzka, September 16, 2013.

page 231 "Is lutefisk food . . .": Holm, *The Heart Can Be Filled Anywhere on Earth*, 208.

page 234 "I told him, Alec Olson": interview with Dean Johnson, May 3, 2014.

pages 235–36 Holm, *The Heart Can Be Filled Anywhere on Earth*, 96–97.

page 236 "cultural icon": Williams, "The Kensington Runestone."

page 237 "State of Hockey": "Finns to the Left, Finns to the Right," *Star Tribune*, May 27, 2014.

page 238 "I sort of think that Minnesota is . . .": interview with Ryan Winkler, May 23, 2014.

page 238 "If Canada is halfway culturally . . . ": interview with Don Ostrom, March 31, 2014.

page 238 "Historically, we have been a state . . .": interviews with Martin Olav Sabo, March 13, 2013, June 3, 2013.

page 239 "has been extraordinarily important . . .": interview with David Lebedoff, June 5, 2013.

page 239 "shown signs of schizophrenia": Warner, "Prelude to Populism."

page 239 "capitol of anti-Semitism in the United States": McWilliams, "Minneapolis: The Curious Twin."

page 239 "To be honest, the picture has not . . .": interviews with Martin Olav Sabo, March 13, 2013, June 3, 2013.

page 239   "absence of corruption, honesty in government . . .": interview with Don Ostrom, March 31, 2014.

page 239   "It's a question of equity . . .": interview with Ken Martin, April 25, 2014.

page 240   "Scandinavian ethos": interview with David Lanegran, February 6, 2014.

page 240   "What I think Scandinavia is really doing well . . .": interview with Ryan Winkler, May 23, 2014.

pages 241–42   "since World War II this is a trend . . .": interview with Sören Holmberg, November 11, 2014.

page 242   "still unique in the United States . . .": interview with Marilyn Carlson Nelson, October 23, 2014.

page 243   "my father's friend": Marilyn Carlson Nelson speech as human rights award recipient, at The Advocates for Human Rights, Minneapolis, MN, June 25, 2014.

page 244   "communitarian approach to policy making": interview with Jan Malcolm, May 8, 2014.

page 244   "but I feel it is close to happening": interview with Susan Brower, December 12, 2013.

page 244   "sense of internationalism": Lori Sturdevant, "For Amy Klobuchar, If Immigration Then Were Like Immigration Now . . ." *Star Tribune*, August 25, 2015.

pages 244–45   #UnMinnesotan: ad in *Star Tribune*, February 1, 2016.

page 245   "soft socialist policies": interview with Eric Black, January 27, 2013.

page 245   Pioneer Press study: David Montgomery and Rachel E. Stassen-Berger, "The Numbers Tell the Tale: the Minnesota House Is Starkly Partisan," *Pioneer Press*, June 24, 2016.

page 246   "I leaned on my old Norwegian values . . .": interview with Steve Sviggum, March 24, 2014.

page 247   "sense of obligation . . .": interview with Paul H. Anderson, July 28, 2014.

page 247   "stemming from that, the political participation . . .": interview with David W. Preus, March 12, 2013.

page 248   "it was the sense of responsibility . . .": interview with Nils Hasselmo, September 11, 2013.

page 248   "Well, they are all very clannish, you know . . . ": interview with Warren Spannaus, April 10, 2014.

page 249   "Yes, I think so . . .": interview with Arne Carlson, June 12, 2013.

page 249   "What threatens us is this train-wreck brand . . . ": interview with Walter Mondale, August 23, 2013.

page 249   "affected by this national disease . . .": interview with Nils Hasselmo, September 11, 2013.

page 249   "I think Minnesota politics is in trouble": interview with Al Quie, June 3, 2013.

pages 249–50   "Minnesota is a wonderful state": interview with Arne Carlson, June 12, 2013.

page 250   Minnesota belongs to the moralistic tradition: Elazar, Gray, and Spano, *Minnesota Government and Politics*, xxvi, 19, 30.

page 250   "helps us understand why Minnesota's politics . . .": Steven Schier, "Where Minnesota's Political Culture Fits Among the States," *Politics in Minnesota*, December 29, 2014.

page 250   "very rational, very frugal": interview with Steven Schier, June 10, 2013.

page 251   "strong, lingering, entrenched northern European culture . . .": interview with Larry Jacobs, June 7, 2013.

Bibliography

DURING MY MANY VISITS to Minnesota for this book between 2013 and 2016, I discovered a rich history of Scandinavian immigration and politics through a large number of interviews as well as books, periodicals, newspapers, conference papers, dissertations, letters, and previously unpublished material.

I have tried to keep the endnotes as brief as possible. I have not cited general background information, but I have aimed to cite all people and material that I have quoted.

I found some works particularly valuable, such as *They Chose Minnesota*, the Minnesota Historical Society's 1981 study of the state's ethnic groups, as well as general history overviews by Annette Atkins, Theodore C. Blegen, William W. Folwell, Steven J. Keillor, and William E. Lass. The biographies by George M. Stephenson on John Lind, George H. Mayer on Floyd B. Olson, Millard L. Gieske and Steven J. Keillor on Knute Nelson, and Bruce L. Larson on Charles A. Lindbergh Sr. were essential reading.

There seems to have been a tradition to publish biographical information on leading figures in Minnesota, both politicians and non-politicians, in the early years of the state. Such works include Martin Ulvestad's on the Norwegians, A. E. Strand's on the Swedes, and O. N. Nelson on the Scandinavians as well as the publications by former governors Joseph A. A. Burnquist and Theodore Christianson.

On Norwegian immigration to Minnesota, the many works by Odd S. Lovoll are invaluable. Carl H. Chrislock, Lowell J. Soike, and Jon Wefald have dealt extensively with the Norwegians' role in Minnesota politics. On the Swedes, the works edited by Philip J. Anderson and Dag Blanck, Nils Hasselmo, Byron Nordstrom, Hans Norman, and Harald Runblom have been most helpful. The story of the Finns on the Iron Range has been richly told by both Finnish and Finnish American scholars, among them Arnold R. Alanen, Michael G. Karni, Peter Kivisto, and Auvo Kostiainen. And Henry Bengston, Walfrid Engdahl, Richard Hudelson, and Carl Ross have provided important insight into the radical Scandinavian immigrants and their particular role in Minnesota's political history.

Finally, I would also like to mention the importance of three periodicals for my research: the Minnesota Historical Society's *Minnesota History, The Swedish-American Historical Quarterly,* and the Norwegian-American Historical Association's *Norwegian-American Studies.*

Books

Aamot, Gregg. *The New Minnesotans: Stories of Immigrants and Refugees.* Minneapolis: Syren Book Company, 2006.

Aby, Anne J., ed. *The North Star State: A Minnesota History Reader.* St. Paul: Minnesota Historical Society Press, 2002.

Adams, John S., and VanDrasek, Barbara J. *Minneapolis–St. Paul: People, Place, and Public Life.* Minneapolis: University of Minnesota Press, 1993.

Alanen, Arnold R. *Finns in Minnesota.* St. Paul: Minnesota Historical Society Press, 2012.

Ander, O. Fritiof. *T. N. Hasselquist: The Career and Influence of a Swedish American Clergyman, Journalist and Educator.* Rock Island, IL: Augustana Library Publications, 1931.

Andersen, Elmer L. *A Man's Reach.* Edited by Lori Sturdevant. Minneapolis: University of Minnesota Press, 2000.

Anderson, Philip J., and Dag Blanck, eds. *Norwegians and Swedes in the United States: Friends and Neighbors.* St. Paul: Minnesota Historical Society Press, 2012.

———. *Swedes in the Twin Cities: Immigrant Life and Minnesota's Urban Frontier.* St. Paul: Minnesota Historical Society Press, 2001.

Anderson, Philip J., Dag Blanck, and Peter Kivisto, eds. *Scandinavian Immigrants and Education in North America.* Chicago: Swedish-American Historical Society, 1995.

Atkins, Annette. *Creating Minnesota: A History from the Inside Out.* St. Paul: Minnesota Historical Society Press, 2008.

Barton, Arnold. *Sweden and Visions of Norway: Politics and Culture, 1814–1905.* Carbondale: Southern Illinois University Press, 2003.

Bauer, Heidi, ed. *The Privilege for Which We Struggled: Leaders of the Woman Suffrage Movement in Minnesota.* St. Paul: Minnesota Historical Society Press, 1999.

Bengston, Henry. *On the Left in America: Memoir of the Scandinavian-American Labor Movement.* Carbondale: Southern Illinois University Press, 1999.

Benson, Adolph, and Naboth Hedin. *Swedes in America. 1638–1938.* New Haven, CT: Yale University Press, 1938.

Berg, Tom. *Minnesota's Miracle.* Minneapolis: University of Minnesota Press, 2012.

Berman, Hyman, and Linda Mack Schloff. *Jews in Minnesota.* St. Paul: Minnesota Historical Society Press, 2002.

Bessler, John D. *Legacy of Violence: Lynch Mobs and Executions in Minnesota.* Minneapolis: University of Minnesota Press, 2006.

Blanck, Dag. *Becoming Swedish American: The Construction of an Ethnic Identity in the Augustana Synod, 1860–1917.* Uppsala: Upsaliensis S. Academiae, 1997.

Blegen, Theodore C. *Minnesota: A History of the State.* Minneapolis: University of Minnesota Press, 1963.

Bremer, Fredrika. *The Homes of the New World: Impressions of America.* New York: Harper & Bros., 1853.

Brown, Aaron. *Overburden: Modern Life on the Iron Range.* Duluth, MN: Red Step Press, 2008.

Brunfelt, Pamela A. "Political Culture in Microcosm: Minnesota's Iron Range." In *Perspectives on Minnesota Government and Politics,* 6th ed., edited by Steven M. Hoffman, Angela High-Pippert, and Kay Walsborn. New York: Pearson Learning Solutions, 2007.

Brøndal, Jørn. *Ethnic Leadership and Midwestern Politics: Scandinavian-Americans and the Progressive Movement in Wisconsin, 1890–1914.* Northfield, MN: Norwegian-American Historical Association, 2004.

Burnquist, Joseph A. A. *Minnesota and Its People.* Chicago: S. J. Clarke Publishing Co., 1924.

Capps, F. H. *From Isolationism to Involvement: The Swedish Immigrant Press in America, 1914–1945.* Chicago: Swedish Pioneer Historical Society, 1966.

Carlson, Benny. *Somalier i Minneapolis: en dynamisk affär.* Lund, Sweden: Zufi, 2006.

Carlson, Benny, and Mohamed Abdi-Noor, eds. *Somalier i Sverige: Mellan förtvivlan & hopp.* Stockholm: Fores, 2013.

Carlsson, Sten. "Scandinavian Politicians in the United States." In *Scando-Americana, Papers on Scandinavian Emigration to the United States,* edited by Ingrid Semmingsen and Per Segerstad. Oslo: University of Oslo, American Institute, 1980.

———. "Skandinaviska politiker i Minnesota." In *Utvandring: Den svenska emigrationen till Amerika i historiskt perspektiv,* edited by Ann-Sofie Kälvemark. Stockholm: Wahlström & Widstrand, 1973.

———. *Skandinaviska politiker i Minnesota 1882–1890: En studie rörande den etniska faktorn i politiska val i en immigrantstat.* Uppsala: Almqvist & Wiksell, 1970.

———. *Swedes in North America, 1638–1988: Technical, Cultural, and Political Achievements.* Stockholm: Streiffert, 1988.

Chrislock, Carl H. *Ethnically Challenged: The Upper Midwest Norwegian American Experience in World War I.* Northfield, MN: Norwegian-American Historical Association, 1981.

———. "The Norwegian-American Impact on Minnesota Politics: How Far Left-of-Center?" In *Norwegian Influence on the Upper Midwest,* edited by Harald S. Naess. Duluth: Continuing Education and Extension, University of Minnesota, Duluth, 1976.

————. *The Progressive Era in Minnesota, 1899–1918.* St. Paul: Minnesota Historical Society Press, 1971.

————. *Watchdog of Loyalty: The Minnesota Commission of Public Safety during World War I.* St. Paul: Minnesota Historical Society Press, 1991.

Christianson, Theodore. *The Land of Sky-Tinted Waters: A History of the State and Its People.* Chicago: American Historical Society, 1935.

Clark, Clifford E. Jr., ed. *Minnesota in a Century of Change: The State and Its People since 1900.* St. Paul: Minnesota Historical Society Press, 1989.

Compendium of History and Biography of Central and Northern Minnesota. Chicago: Geo. A. Ogle & Co., 1904.

Conzen, Kathleen Neils. *Germans in Minnesota.* St. Paul: Minnesota Historical Society Press, 2003.

Day, Frank A., and Theodore M. Knappen. *Life of John Albert Johnson: Three Times Governor of Minnesota.* Chicago: Forbes & Co., 1910.

Delton, Jennifer A. *Making Minnesota Liberal: Civil Rights and the Transformation of the Democratic Party.* Minneapolis: University of Minnesota Press, 2002.

Dorsey Hatle, Elizabeth. *The Ku Klux Klan in Minnesota.* Charleston, SC: The History Press, 2013.

Dregni, Eric. *Vikings in the Attic: In Search of Nordic America.* Minneapolis: University of Minnesota Press, 2011.

Eberhart, Adolph Olson. "The American Way of Life." Unpublished memoir, 1943.

Eisele, Albert. *Almost to the Presidency: A Biography of Two American Politicians.* Blue Earth, MN: Piper Company, 1972.

Elazar, Daniel J., Virginia Gray, and Wyman Spano. *Minnesota Politics and Government.* Lincoln: University of Nebraska Press, 1999.

Engdahl, Walfrid. *My Life.* Unpublished and unfinished memoir, 1938.

Erlander, Sven. *Tage Erlander—Dagböcker 1952.* Möklinta: Gidlunds Förlag, 2002.

Erling, Maria, and Mark Granquist. *The Augustana Story: Shaping Lutheran Identity in North America.* Minneapolis: Augsburg Fortress, 2008.

Esbjornson, Robert. *A Christian in Politics: Luther W. Youngdahl: A Story of a Christian's Faith at Work in a Modern World.* Minneapolis: T. S. Denison & Company, 1955.

Fedo, Michael. *The Lynchings in Duluth.* St. Paul: Minnesota Historical Society Press, 2000.

————. *Zenith City: Stories from Duluth.* Minneapolis: University of Minnesota Press, 2014.

Fisher, David Hackett. *Albion's Seed: Four British Folkways in America.* New York: Oxford University Press, 1989.

Flanagan, John T. *Minnesota's Literary Visitors.* Lakeville, MN: Pogo Press, 1993.

Folwell, William W. *A History of Minnesota.* 4 vols. St. Paul: Minnesota Historical Society Press, 1956.

Friis, Erik J., ed. *The Scandinavian Presence in North America.* New York: Harper's Magazine Press, 1976.

Gieske, Millard L., and Steven J. Keillor. *Norwegian Yankee: Knute Nelson and the*

Failure of American Politics, 1860–1923. Northfield, MN: Norwegian-American Historical Association, 1995.

Gillespie Lewis, Anne. *Swedes in Minnesota*. St. Paul: Minnesota Historical Society Press, 2004.

Gjerde, Jon, and Carlton C. Qualey. *The Minds of the West: Ethnocultural Evolution in the Rural Midwest, 1830–1917*. Chapel Hill: University of North Carolina Press, 1997.

———. *Norwegians in Minnesota*. St. Paul: Minnesota Historical Society Press, 2002.

Graubard, Stephen R., ed. *Minnesota Real and Imagined: Essays on the State and Its Culture*. St. Paul: Minnesota Historical Society Press, 2000.

Grönberger, Robert. *Minnesota Historia*. Minneapolis: Svenska Folkets Tidnings Förlag, 1899.

Gustafson, Earl. *The Swedish Secret: What the US Can Learn from Sweden's History*. Minneapolis: Syren Book Company, 2006.

Haines, Lynn. *The Minnesota Legislature of 1909 and 1911: A History of the Session with an Inside View of Men and Measure*. Minneapolis, 1909 and 1911.

Haines, Lynn, and Dora B. Haines. *The Lindberghs*. New York: Vanguard Press, 1931.

Hansen, Carl G. O. *My Minneapolis: A Chronicle of What Has Been Learned about the Norwegians in Minneapolis through One Hundred Years*. Minneapolis: Privately printed, 1956.

Hansen, Marcus Lee. *The Problem of the Third Generation Immigrant*. Rock Island, IL: Augustana Historical Society, 1938.

Harpelle, Ronald N., Varpu Lindström, and Alexis Pogorelskin. *Karelian Exodus: Finnish Communities in North America and Soviet Karelia during the Depression Era*. Beaverton, ON: Aspasia Books, Inc., 2004.

Hasselmo, Nils. *Swedish America: An Introduction*. Minneapolis: Brings Press, 1976.

Hasselmo, Nils, ed. *Perspectives on Swedish Immigration*. Chicago: Swedish Pioneer Historical Society, 1978.

Hauser, Tom. *Inside the Ropes with Jesse Ventura*. Minneapolis: University of Minnesota Press, 2002.

Haynes, John E. *Dubious Alliance: The Making of Minnesota's DFL Party*. Minneapolis: University of Minnesota Press, 1986.

Helmes, Winifred G. *John A. Johnson: The People's Governor*. Minneapolis: University of Minnesota Press, 1949.

Hicks, John D. *The Populist Revolt: A History of the Farmers' Alliance and the Populist Party*. Minneapolis: University of Minnesota Press, 1931.

Hoerder, Dirk, ed. *Essays on the Scandinavian-American Radical Press, 1880s to 1930s*. Bremen, Germany: Labor Newspaper Preservation Project, Universität Bremen, 1984.

Hoglund, A. William. *Finnish Immigrants in America, 1880–1920*. Madison: University of Wisconsin Press, 1960.

Holm, Bill. *The Heart Can Be Filled Anywhere on Earth*. Minneapolis: Milkweed Editions, 2001.

Holmquist, June Drenning, ed., *They Chose Minnesota: A Survey of the State's Ethnic Groups*. St. Paul: Minnesota Historical Society Press, 1981.

Hudelson, Richard, and Carl Ross. *By the Ore Docks: A Working People's History of Duluth*. Minneapolis: University of Minnesota Press, 2006.

Humphrey, Hubert H. *The Education of a Public Man: My Life and Politics*. Minneapolis: University of Minnesota Press, 1991.

Johnson, Cecil M. *Minnesota's Ole O. Sageng, 1871–1963: The Man Behind the Plow*. Fergus Falls: Otter Tail County Historical Society, 2015.

Kälvemark, Ann-Sofie, ed. *Utvandring: Den svenska emigrationen till Amerika i historiskt perspektiv*. Stockholm: Wahlström & Widstrand, 1973.

Karni, Michael G., Matti E. Kaups, and Douglas J. Ollila Jr., eds. *The Finnish Experience in the Western Great Lakes Region*. Turku, Finland: Institute for Migration, 1975.

Karni, Michael G., and Douglas J. Ollila Jr. *For the Common Good: Finnish Immigrants and the Radical Response to Industrial America*. Superior, WI: Tyomies Society, 1977.

Keillor, Steven J. *Cooperative Commonwealth: Co-ops in Rural Minnesota, 1859–1939*. St. Paul: Minnesota Historical Society Press, 2000.

———. *Hjalmar Petersen of Minnesota: The Politics of Provincial Independence*. St. Paul: Minnesota Historical Society Press, 1987.

———. *Shaping Minnesota's Identity: 150 Years of State History*. Lakeville, MN: Pogo Press, 2007.

Kero, Reno. *Migration from Finland to North in the Years between the United States Civil War and the First World War*. Turku, Finland: Turun Yliopisto, 1974.

Kivisto, Peter. *Immigrant Socialists in the United States: The Case of Finns and the Left*. Cranbury, NJ: Associated University Presses, 1984.

Klobuchar, Amy. *The Senator Next Door: A Memoir from the Heartland*. New York: Henry Holt and Company, 2015.

Korth, Philip. *The Minneapolis Teamsters Strike of 1934*. East Lansing: Michigan State University Press, 1995.

Kostiainen, Auvo, ed. *Finns in the United States: A History of Settlement, Dissent, and Integration*. East Lansing: Michigan State University Press, 2014.

———. *The Forging of Finnish-American Communism, 1917–1924: A Study in Ethnic Radicalism*. Turku, Finland: Turun Yliopisto, 1978.

Lansing, Michael J. *Insurgent Democracy: The Nonpartisan League in North American Politics*. Chicago: University of Chicago Press, 2015.

Larson, Bruce L. *Lindbergh of Minnesota: A Political Biography*. New York: Harcourt Brace Jovanovich, Inc., 1971.

Lass, William E. *Minnesota: A History*. New York: W. W. Norton & Company, 1998.

Lebedoff, David. *The 21st Ballot: A Political Party Struggle in Minnesota*. Minneapolis: University of Minnesota Press, 1969.

———. *Ward Number Six*. New York: Charles Scribner's Sons, 1972.

Leiren, Terje I. *Marcus Thrane: A Norwegian Radical in America*. Northfield: Norwegian-American Historical Association, 1987.

LeVander, Bernhard. *Call Me Pete: Memoir of a Minnesota Man*. Reno, NV: A Dawson Creative, Ltd. Effort, 2006.

Lewis, Finlay. *Mondale: Portrait of an American Politician*. New York: Harper & Row, 1980.

Lewis, Sinclair. *Main Street*. New York: Barnes & Noble Classics, 2003.

Lindbergh, Charles A. Sr. *Why Is Your Country at War and What Happened to You After the War and Related Subjects*. Washington, DC: National Capital Press, 1917.

Lindmark, Sture. *Swedish America, 1914–1932: Studies in Ethnicity with Emphasis on Illinois and Minnesota*. Stockholm: Läromedelsförlaget, 1971.

Lintelman, Joy. *"I Go to America": Swedish American Women and the Life of Mina Anderson*. St. Paul: Minnesota Historical Society Press, 2009.

Ljungmark, Lars. *Swedish Exodus*. Carbondale: Southern Illinois University Press, 1996.

Lovoll, Odd S. *Nordics in America: The Future of Their Past*. Northfield, MN: Norwegian-American Historical Society Special Publications, 1993.

———. *Norwegian Newspapers in America: Connecting Norway and the New Land*. St. Paul: Minnesota Historical Society Press, 2010.

———. *Norwegians on the Prairie: Ethnicity and the Development of the Country Town*. St. Paul: Minnesota Historical Society Press, 2006.

———. *The Promise Fulfilled: A Portrait of Norwegian Americans Today*. Minneapolis: University of Minnesota Press, 1998.

———. *The Promise of America: A History of the Norwegian-American People*. Minneapolis: University of Minnesota Press, 1984.

Malmberg Johnson, Olive. *Kvinnan Och Den Socialistiska Rörelsen*. New York: Skandinaviska Arbetareförbundets förlag, New York Labor News Co., 1910.

———. *Woman and the Socialist Movement*. New York: Labor News Co., 1908.

Mattson, Hans. *Minnen*. Lund, Sweden: C. W. K. Gleerup, 1890.

Mayer, George H. *The Political Career of Floyd B. Olson*. St. Paul: Minnesota Historical Society Press, 1987.

McGrath, Dennis J., and Dane Smith. *Professor Wellstone Goes to Washington: The Inside Story of a Grassroots U.S. Senate Campaign*. Minneapolis: University of Minnesota Press, 1995.

McGrath, John S., and James J. Delmont. *Floyd Björnsterne Olson: Minnesota's Greatest Liberal Governor*. St. Paul, MN: McGrath & Delmont, 1937.

Mitau, G. Theodore. *Politics in Minnesota*. Minneapolis: University of Minnesota Press, 1960.

Moberg, Vilhelm. *Invandrarna (Unto a Good Land)*. Stockholm: Albert Bonniers Förlag, 1954.

———. *Nybyggarna (The Settlers)*. Stockholm: Albert Bonniers Förlag, 1956.

———. *Sista brevet till Sverige (The Last Letter Home)*. Stockholm: Albert Bonniers Förlag, 1959.

———. *Utvandrarna (The Emigrants)*. Stockholm: Albert Bonniers Förlag, 1949.

Mondale, Walter F., with Dave Hage. *The Good Fight: A Life in Liberal Politics*. New York: Scribner, 2010.

Morlan, Robert L. *Political Prairie Fire: The Nonpartisan League, 1915–1922.* St. Paul: Minnesota Historical Society Press, 1985.

Naess, Harald S., ed. *Norwegian Influence on the Upper Midwest.* Duluth: Continuing Education and Extension, University of Minnesota, Duluth, 1976.

Nathanson, Iric. *Minneapolis in the Twentieth Century: The Growth of an American City.* St. Paul: Minnesota Historical Society Press, 2009.

Nelson, O. N., ed. *History of the Scandinavians and Successful Scandinavians in the United States.* Minneapolis: O. N. Nelson & Co., 1893.

Nilsson, Fred. *Emigrationen från Stockholm till Nordamerika 1880–1893: En studie i urban utvandring.* Stockholm: Läromedelsförlaget, 1970.

Nordahl, Per. *De sålde sina penslar.* Stockholm: Svenska Målareförbundet, Tidens Förlag, 1987.

———. *Weaving the Ethnic Fabric: Social Networks among Swedish-American Radicals in Chicago, 1890–1940.* Umeå, Sweden: Almqvist & Wiksell International, 1994.

Nordstrom, Byron, ed. *The Swedes in Minnesota.* Minneapolis: T. S. Denison & Company, 1976.

Norlie, Olaf M. *History of the Norwegian People in America.* Minneapolis: Augsburg Publishing House, 1925.

Nye, Russel. *Midwestern Progressive Politics: A Historical Study of Its Origins and Development, 1870–1958.* New York: Harper & Row, 1959.

Parker, Florence E. *The First 125 Years: A History of Distributive and Service Cooperation in the United States, 1829–1954.* Superior, WI: Cooperative League of the U.S.A., 1956.

Pearlstein, Mitch. *Riding into the Sunrise: Al Quie, A Life of Faith, Service, and Civility.* Lakeville, MN: Pogo Press, 2008.

Pehrson, Lennart. *Den nya staden.* Stockholm: Albert Bonniers Förlag, 2014.

———. *Den nya tiden.* Stockholm: Albert Bonniers Förlag, 2015.

———. *Den nya världen.* Stockholm: Albert Bonniers Förlag, 2014.

Qualey, Carlton C. *Norwegian Settlement in the United States.* New York: Arno Press, 1970.

———. "Norwegians in the Upper Midwest: Immigration and Acculturation." In *Norwegian Influence on the Upper Midwest,* edited by Harald S. Naess. Duluth: Continuing Education and Extension, University of Minnesota, Duluth, 1976.

Rølvaag, Ole E. *The Boat of Longing (Laengselens Baat).* New York: Harper & Brothers, 1933.

———. *Giants in the Earth (Verdens Grøde).* New York: Harper & Brothers, 1927.

———. *Peder Victorious (Peder Seier).* New York: Harper & Brothers, 1929.

———. *Their Father's God (Den signede dag).* New York: Harper & Brothers, 1931.

Ross, Carl. *The Finn Factor in American Labor, Culture, and Society.* New York Mills, MN: Parta Printers, 1977.

Ross, Carl, and K. Marianne Wargelin Brown. *Women Who Dared: The History of Finnish-American Women.* Minneapolis: Immigration History Research Center, University of Minnesota, 1986.

Runblom, Harald, and Hans Norman, eds. *From Sweden to America: A History of the Migration.* Minneapolis and Uppsala: University of Minnesota Press and Acta University of Uppsala, 1976.

———. *Transatlantic Connections: Nordic Migration to the New World after 1800.* Oslo: Norwegian University Press, 1988.

Rybak, R. T. *Pothole Confidential: My Life as Mayor of Minneapolis.* Minneapolis: University of Minnesota Press, 2016.

Semmingsen, Ingrid. *Norway to America: A History of the Migration.* Minneapolis: University of Minnesota Press, 1991.

Semmingsen, Ingrid, and Per Segerstad, eds. *Scando-Americana: Papers on Scandinavian Emigration to the United States.* Oslo: America Institute, University of Oslo, 1980.

Sevander, Mayme, with Laurie Hertzel. *They Took My Father: A Story of Idealism and Betrayal.* Duluth, MN: Pfeifer-Hamilton, 1992.

Shields, James M. *Mr. Progressive: A Biography of Elmer A. Benson.* Minneapolis: T. S. Denison & Company, Inc., 1971.

Shutter, Marion Daniel. *History of Minneapolis: Gateway to the Northwest.* Chicago and Minneapolis: S. J. Clarke Publishing Co., 1923.

Skalstad, Doris E. *Minneapolis Ward Boundaries, 1855–1985.* Minneapolis: Minneapolis Public Library and Information Center, 1986.

Skarstedt, Ernst. *Svensk-Amerikanska folket i helg och söcken.* Stockholm: Björck & Börjesson, 1917.

Smalley, E. V. *A History of the Republican Party from Its Organization to the Present Time; To Which is Added a Political History of Minnesota from a Republican Point of View.* St. Paul: E. V. Smalley Publisher, 1896.

Söderström, Alfred. *Minneapolis Minnen: Kulturhistorisk axplockning från Qvarnstaden vid Mississippi.* Minneapolis, 1899.

Soike, Lowell. *Norwegian-Americans and the Politics of Dissent, 1880–1924.* Northfield, MN: Norwegian-American Historical Association, 1991.

Solberg, Carl. *Hubert Humphrey: A Biography.* St. Paul: Minnesota Historical Society Press, 2003.

Stassen, Harold. *Where I Stand!* Garden City, NY: Doubleday, 1947.

Stephenson, George M. *John Lind of Minnesota.* Port Washington, NY: Kennikat Press, 1935.

———. *The Religious Aspect of Swedish Immigration.* Minneapolis: University of Minnesota Press, 1932.

Strand, A. E. *A History of the Swedish-Americans of Minnesota.* Chicago: Lewis Publishing Co., 1910.

Stuhler, Barbara. *Gentle Warriors: Clara Ueland and the Minnesota Struggle for Woman Suffrage.* St. Paul: Minnesota Historical Society Press, 1995.

———. *No Regrets: Minnesota Women and the Joan Grow Senatorial Campaign.* St. Paul: Bramer Press, 1986.

———. *Ten Men of Minnesota and American Foreign Policy.* St. Paul: Minnesota Historical Society Press, 1973.

Sturdevant, Lori. *Her Honor: Rosalie Wahl and the Minnesota Women's Movement.* St. Paul: Minnesota Historical Society Press, 2014.

Ulvestad, Martin. *Nordmaende i Amerika, deras historie og rekord: Statistiske Oplysninger angaande Nordmaendene i Amerika.* Minneapolis: History Book Co.'s Forlag, 1907–13.

Valelly, Richard. *Radicalism in the States: The Minnesota Farmer-Labor Party and the American Political Economy.* Chicago: University of Chicago Press, 1989.

Wachtmeister, Wilhelm. *Som jag såg det.* Stockholm: Norstedts, 1996.

Wasastjerna, Hans R. *History of the Finns in Minnesota.* Duluth: Minnesota Finnish-American Historical Society, 1957.

Wefald, Jon. *A Voice of Protest: Norwegians in American Politics, 1890–1917.* Northfield, MN: Norwegian-American Historical Association, 1971.

Weiner, Jay. *This Is Not Florida: How Al Franken Won the Minnesota Senate Recount.* Minneapolis: University of Minnesota Press, 2010.

Werle, Steve. *Stassen Again.* St. Paul: Minnesota Historical Society Press, 2015.

Widén, Albin. *Emigrantpojken som blev governör: A. O. Eberhart.* Stockholm: O. Eklunds Bokförlag, 1954.

Wilson, Betty. *Rudy! The People's Governor.* Minneapolis: Nodin Press, 2005.

Woodard, Colin. *American Nations: A History of the Eleven Rival Regional Cultures of North America.* New York: Penguin Books, 2011.

Youngdale, James M. *Third Party Footprints: An Anthology from Writings and Speeches of Midwest Radicals.* Minneapolis: Ross and Haines, 1966.

Yusuf, Ahmed I. *Somalis in Minnesota.* St. Paul: Minnesota Historical Society Press, 2012.

Author Interviews

Gregg Aamot, John S. Adams, Paul H. Anderson, Philip J. Anderson, Wendell Anderson, Charles "Chuck" Arnason, Tom Bakk, Steve Berg, Kjell Bergh, Hyman Berman, William Beyer, Eric Black, Susan Brower, Jørn Brøndal, Pamela Brunfelt, Roger Buoen, Bill Buzenberg, Arne Carlson, Benny Carlson, John R. Christianson, Nick Coleman, Tor Dahl, Tove Dahl, Kirsten Delegard, Albert Eisele, Brad Engdahl, Michael Fedo, Arvonne and Don Fraser, Michael Freeman, Kris Garey, Mark Granquist, Joan Anderson Growe, Dave Hage, Gordon Hallstrom, Laurie Halverson, Jodi Harpstead, Nils Hasselmo, Eivind Heiberg, Richard Hudelson, Larry Jacobs, Dean Johnson, Bruce Karstadt, Margaret Anderson Kelliher, David A. Lanegran, Virginia Lanegran, Bruce L. Larson, George Latimer, David Lebedoff, Finlay Lewis, David Lillehaug, Robert Lilligren, John Lindstrom, Odd S. Lovoll, Jan Malcom, Ken Martin, Don Moe, Roger Moe, Walter F. Mondale, Lynne Blomstrand Moratzka, Joanne Negstad, George A. Nelson, Marilyn Carlson Nelson, Mohamud Noor, Byron Nordstrom, Lena Norrman, Alec G. Olson, Ilhan Omar, Don Ostrom, Jim Pederson, David W. Preus, Emily Pyenson, John Quam, Lois Quam, Albert Quie, Mark Ritchie, R. T. Rybak, Anders Rydåker, Martin Olav Sabo, Steven Schier, Larry Sillanpa, Dane Smith, Michael Steenson, Paul Stone, Lori Sturdevant, Steve Sviggum, Paul Thissen, Barbara VanDrasek, Marianne Wargelin, Abdi Warsame, Gregg White, Ryan Winkler.

Articles and Reports

Alanen, Arnold R. "Early Labor Strife on Minnesota's Mining Frontier, 1882–1906." *Minnesota History* 52, no. 7 (Fall 1991): 246–63.

Ander, Fritiof O. "Swedish American Newspapers and the Republican Party, 1855–1875." *Augustana Historical Society* 2 (1932).

———. "Swedish American Press and the Election of 1892." *Mississippi Valley Historical Review* 23, no. 4 (1937): 539.

Anderson, Anna Marie. "Adding 'A Little Suffrage Spice to the Melting Pot': Minnesota's Scandinavian Woman Suffrage Association." *Minnesota History* 62, no. 8 (2011): 288–97.

Anderson, Michael. "Minnesota's John Day Smith Law and the Death Penalty Debate." *Minnesota History* 58, no. 2 (2002): 84–91.

Atkins, Annette. "The State I'm In: Hubert Humphrey, Jesse Ventura, Bob Dylan, Garrison Keillor, and Me." *Western Historical Quarterly* 38, no. 4 (2007): 501–7.

Bengston, Henry. "Chicago's Swedish 'Book Cabin.'" *Swedish Pioneer Historical Quarterly* 15, no. 4 (October 1964): 159–66.

Benson, Elmer A. "Politics in My Lifetime." *Minnesota History* 47, no. 4 (1980): 154–60.

Berman, Hyman. "Political Antisemitism in Minnesota during the Great Depression." *Jewish Social Studies* 38 (1976): 247–64.

Bill, Ivan. "Floyd B Olson: Minnesota Governor with Blomskog Background." *The Bridge* 20, no. 4 (1988): 128–35.

———. "Magnus Johnson: The Swede from Liljedahl." *The Bridge* 21, no. 2 (1989): 39–42.

Blantz, Thomas E. "Father Haas and the Minneapolis Truckers' Strike of 1934." *Minnesota History* 42, no. 1 (1970): 5–15.

Brook, Michael. "Radical Literature in Swedish America: A Narrative Survey." *Swedish-American Historical Quarterly* 20, no. 3 (1969): 111–32.

Brunfelt, Pamela. "Karl Emil Nygard: Minnesota's Communist Mayor." *Minnesota History* 58, no. 3 (2002): 168–86.

Carlson, Benny. "Somalier i Minnesota och Sverige: Enade de stå, söndrade de falla." Jobbtorg Stockholm, Sweden, 2008.

Carlson, Benny, Karin Magnusson, and Sofia Rönnqvist. "Somalier på arbetsmarknaden: har Sverige något att lära?" Framtidskommissionen, Fritzes kundtjänst, Stockholm, Sweden, 2012.

Cederström, B. Marcus. "Don't Mourn, Educate: Signe Aurell and the Swedish-American Labor Press." *Swedish-American Historical Quarterly* 67, no. 2 (April 2016): 71–89.

Chrislock, Carl H. "Profile of a Ward Boss: The Political Career of Lars M. Rand." *Norwegian-American Studies* 31 (1986): 35–72.

Christensen, Thomas P. "Danish Settlement in Minnesota." *Minnesota History* 8, no. 4 (1927): 363–85.

Dornfeld, Steven. "The Minnesota Miracle: A Roundtable Discussion." *Minnesota History* 60, no. 8 (2007): 312–25.

Eighmey, Rae Katherine. "Andrew Volstead: Prohibition's Public Face." *Minnesota History* 63, no. 8 (winter 2013–14): 312–23.

Engdahl, Walfrid. "Charles Augustus Lindbergh Den Äldre (1859–1924)." *Kulturarvet*, Årg. 10, 1969.

———. "Magnus Johnson: Colorful Farmer-Labor Senator from Minnesota." *Swedish Pioneer Historical Quarterly* 16, no. 3 (1965): 122–36.

Fridley, Russell. "What Would Floyd B. Do?" *Minnesota Law and Politics* (1979).

Granhus, Odd-Stein. "Socialist Dissent among Norwegian Americans: Emil Lauritz Mengshoel, Newspaper Publisher and Author." *Norwegian-American Studies* 33 (1992): 27–71.

Hanson, Henry. "Dissent in Swedish America." *Swedish-American Historical Quarterly* 44, no. 3 (July 1993): 159–65.

Haynes, John E. "The New Times: A Frustrated Voice of Socialism, 1910–1919." *Minnesota History* 52, no. 5 (1991): 183–94.

Hildeman, Nils-Gustav. "Swedish Strikes and Emigration." *Swedish Pioneer Historical Quarterly* 8, no. 3 (1957): 87–93.

Hokanson, Nels. "Swedes and the I.W.W." *Swedish Pioneer Historical Quarterly* 23, no. 1 (1972): 25–35.

Hudelson, Richard. "Duluth's Scandinavian Left, 1880–1950." *Swedish-American Historical Quarterly* 53, no. 3 (July 2002): 179–96.

———. "The Scandinavian Local of the Duluth Socialist Party: 1910–1924." *Swedish-American Historical Quarterly* 44 (October 1993): 181–90.

Jenness, Doug. "Carl Skoglund: Example for Communist Workers." *International Socialist Review* (supplement to *The Militant*), August 3, 1984.

Jensen, Carol. "Loyalty as a Political Weapon: The 1918 Campaign in Minnesota." *Minnesota History* 43, no. 2 (1972): 42–57.

Keillor, Steven J. "A Country Editor in Politics: Hjalmar Petersen, Minnesota Governor." *Minnesota History* 48, no. 7 (1983): 283–94.

Kirby, Alec. "'A Major Contender': Harold Stassen and the Politics of American Presidential Nominations." *Minnesota History* 55, no. 4 (1996): 150–65.

Kolehmainen, John I. "The Finnish Pioneers in Minnesota." *Minnesota History* 25, no. 4 (1944): 317–28.

———. "Finnish Temperance Societies in Minnesota" *Minnesota History* 22, no. 4 (1941): 391–403.

Larson, Bruce L. "If Your Name is Anderson, You're Probably Governor." *Sweden and America* (Summer 1998).

———. "Scandinavian Americans and the American Liberal Political Heritage." *Scandinavian Review* 86, no. 3 (Winter 1998–99): 4–15.

Lindquist, Emory. "Reflections on the Life of Henry Bengston." *Swedish-American Historical Quarterly* 26, no. 4 (1975): 261–64.

Logue, John. "The Swedish Model: Visions of Sweden in American Politics and Political Science." *Swedish-American Historical Quarterly* 50, no. 3 (July 1999): 162–72.

Lovoll, Odd S. "*Gaa Paa*, A Scandinavian Voice of Dissent." *Minnesota History* 52, no. 3 (1990): 86–99.

———. "Going with the Leftward Tide or Finding the Middle Way: A Minnesota Scandinavian Dilemma." *Voices of Dissent: The Minnesota Radical Press, 1910–1920*, St. Paul, MN, May 20, 1989.

McWilliams, Carey. "Minneapolis: The Curious Twin." *Common Ground* (Autumn 1946): 61–65.

Millikan, William. "Defenders of Business: The Minneapolis Civic and Commerce Association versus Labor during W.W.I." *Minnesota History* 50, no. 1 (1986): 2–17.

Mitau, G. Theodore. "The Democratic-Farmer-Labor Party Schism of 1948." *Minnesota History* 34, no. 5 (1955): 187–94.

Morlan, Robert L. "The Nonpartisan League and the Minnesota Campaign of 1918." *Minnesota History* 34, no. 6 (1955): 221–32.

Naftalin, Arthur. "The Tradition of Protest and the Roots of the Farmer-Labor Party." *Minnesota History* 35, no. 2 (1956): 53–63.

Nathanson, Iric. "The Caucus that Changed History: 1948's Battle for Control of the DFL." *MinnPost*, February 26, 2016.

Nordstrom, Byron. "The Swedes in Minneapolis: A Complex Community." *Hennepin County History* 47, no. 4 (1988): 20–27.

Peterson, Anna Marie. "Minnesota's Scandinavian Women Suffrage Association." *Minnesota History* 62, no. 8 (2011): 288–97.

Riehle, David. "A Life We Can Learn From: Carl Skoglund (1884–1960)." Carl Skoglund Centenary Celebration, Labor Lyceum College, Minneapolis, MN, July 28, 1984.

Ross, Carl. "How Far We Have Come: A Report on the 20th Century Radicalism in Minnesota Project." *Minnesota History* 51, no. 4 (1988): 138–44.

Schmid, Calvin Fisher. "Social Saga of Two Cities: An Ecological and Statistical Study of Social Trends in Minneapolis and St. Paul." Minneapolis Council of Social Agencies, Bureau of Social Research, 1937.

Scott, George W. "Scandinavians in Washington Politics." *Swedish-American Historical Quarterly* 56, no. 4 (October 2005): 231–69.

Sirjamaki, John. "The People of the Mesabi Range." *Minnesota History* 27, no. 3 (1946): 203–15.

Smemo, Kristoffer. "A 'New Dealized' Grand Old Party: Labor and the Emergence of Liberal Republicanism in Minneapolis, 1937–1939." *Labor: Studies in Working-Class History of the Americas* 11, no. 2 (2014).

Stephenson, George, M. "Attitude of Swedish Americans Toward the World War." *Proceedings of the Mississippi Valley Historical Association* 10 (1918–19): 70–94.

———. "The John Lind Papers." *Minnesota History* 17, no. 2 (1936): 159–65.

———. "When America Was the Land of Canaan." *Minnesota History* 10, no. 3 (1929): 237–60.

Tedebrand, Lars-Göran. "Strikes and Political Radicalism in Sweden and Emigration to the United States." *Swedish-American Historical Quarterly* 34, no. 3 (July 1983): 194–210.

Thalin, Mikael. "Orsasonen som blev framgångsrik invandrare i USA." *Orsa Hembygdsförenings Årsskrift* (2011).

Wargelin, K. Marianne. "Finnish Americans." World Culture Encyclopedia, www.everyculture.com.

Warner, Donald F. "Prelude to Populism." *Minnesota History* 32, no. 3 (1951): 129–46.

Wefald, Jon M. "Congressman Knud Wefald, A Minnesota Voice for Farm Parity." *Minnesota History* 38, no. 4 (1962): 177–85.

William, Henrik. "The Kensington Runestone: Fact and Fiction." *Swedish-American Historical Quarterly* 63, no. 1 (2012): 3–22.

Wyman, Roger E. "Insurgency in Minnesota: The Defeat of James A. Tawney in 1910." *Minnesota History* 40, no. 7 (1967): 317–29.

PhD Dissertations

Barone, Michael. "The Social Bias for Urban Politics, Minneapolis and St. Paul." Harvard University, Cambridge, MA, 1965.

Berman, Hyman. "Education for Work and Labor Solidarity: The Immigrant Miners and Radicalism on the Mesabi Range." University of Minnesota, Minneapolis, 1964.

Engren, Jimmy. "Railroading and Labor Migration: Class and Ethnicity in Expanding Capitalism in Northern Minnesota, the 1880s to the mid-1920s." Växjö Universitet, Sweden, 2007.

Grepperud, Peter Johan Altena. "A Study of Three Norwegian Newspapers in Northwestern Minnesota: Ethnic Identity and the Motivations behind Political Debate 1890–1894." Oslo Universitet, Oslo, Norway, 2011.

Karni, Michael G. "For the Common Good: Finnish Radicalism in the Western Great Lakes Region, 1900–1940." University of Minnesota, Minneapolis, 1975.

Naftalin, Arthur. "A History of the Farmer-Labor Party of Minnesota." University of Minnesota, Minneapolis, 1948.

O'Connor, Thomas Gerald. "Toward the Cooperative Commonwealth: An Introduction History of the Farmer-Labor Movement in Minnesota, 1917–1948." The Union Institute, 1979.

Rondahl, Björn. "Emigration, folkomflyttning och säsongarbete i ett sågverksdistrikt i södra Hälsingland 1865–1910." Uppsala Universitet, Sweden, 1972.

MA Dissertations

Brunfelt, Pamela A. "An American Communist: Karl Emil Nygard." Minnesota State University, Mankato, 2000.

Grönberg, P. O. "Skandinaviska Socialistklubben Duluth, 1911–1920." Umeå Universitet, Sweden, 1994.

Nyberg, Janet. "Swedish Immigrant Press." University of Minnesota, Minneapolis, 1975.

Oral History

Vincent Raymond Dunne, interview. Twentieth Century Radicalism in Minnesota Oral History Project, April 27, 1969.
Walfrid Engdahl, interview by Steven Benson. Twentieth Century Radicalism in Minnesota Oral History Project, 1972.
Walfrid Engdahl, interview by Swedish oral historian Lennart Setterdahl, May 11, 1978.
Walter Malte Frank, interview by Lila M. Johnson, Minnesota Historical Society, and Professor Donald Sofchalle, Mankato State University, August 11, 1969.
Karl Emil Nygard, interview. Northwest Minnesota Historical Center, Moorhead, MN, September 13, 1973.
Carl Ross, interview by Professor Hyman Berman, University of Minnesota. Twentieth Century Radicalism in Minnesota Oral History Project, 1986, 1987, 1988.
Carl Skoglund, interview. Twentieth Century Radicalism in Minnesota Oral History Project, 1960.

News Media

Aftonbladet, Stockholm, Sweden
Bokstugan (The Book Cabin), Chicago
Budstikken, St. Paul, MN
Decorah [IA] Posten
Kulturarvet (Swedish Heritage), Chicago
Minneapolis Morning Tribune
Minneapolis Tidende
Minnesota Public Radio, St. Paul
Minnesota Stats Tidning, St. Paul
MinnPost, Minneapolis, MN
Pioneer Press, St. Paul, MN
Prärieblomman, Chicago
Star Tribune, Minneapolis, MN
Svenska Amerikanska Posten, Minneapolis, MN
Svenska Dagbladet, Stockholm, Sweden
Svenska Socialisten, Chicago
Truth, Duluth, MN
Two Harbors [MN] Socialist

Index

Page numbers in *italics* refer to illustrations.

Poirier, Joseph, 152
political involvement: and Americanization, 7, 40–42, 51–52, 220; current nature of, 246–47, 250; current quality of life issues, 240; effect of Scandinavian contribution, 219, 238–40, 250–52; effect of Yankee tradition, 250–52; ethnic solidarity, 58–59, 82–83, 103; founding fathers of modern, 167; of German immigrants, 23–25, 27; of Hmong immigrants, 211–12; and immigrant churches, 19; of Irish immigrants, 25–26; Minnesota as anomaly in Upper Midwest, 245–46; in Minnesota Territory, 6; as Scandinavian characteristic, 16, 19–20, 104, 191–92; secretary of state as gateway into Minnesota politics, 57, 58–59; Somali immigrants, 195–97, 212, 217–20; speed of Scandinavian immigrants, 50, 52–56; and temperance movement, 22; voting independent of party affiliation, 45; and ward bosses, 201–2, 203, 204–6; as way of serving religion, 19, 185, 248. *See also* progressivism
"Politics in My Lifetime" (Benson), 166
populism. *See* progressivism
Preus, David W., 222, 247–48
Preus, Jacob Aall Ottesen (J. A. O.), 57, 146, 147, 157
progressivism: and Dayton, 241; detours from, 239; in early twentieth century, 32, 44–45, 47; John Lind, 35–37; and nonpartisanship, 82, 83–84; as part of Scandinavian tradition, 81, 238–39, 247, 248; Progressive Party, 81, 83
—Republican Party: after World War II, 180, 183–84, 185–86, 192, 194; DFL as heir of, 192; and Lutheranism, 180; Progressive/Old Guard split, 6, 71, 81–83, 93–94, 98–102

Prohibition, 21–22, 68–69. *See also* temperance movement
Public Ownership Party, 89, 205
Puro, Henry, 132

Qualey, Carlton C., 54–55
Quie, Albert (Al): background, 185, 186; on effect of divisive national politics on Minnesota politics, 249; as governor, 29, 180, 186; on grandfather, Halvor Quie, 11; post-gubernatorial life, 186; and Republican Party, 185–86; in US House of Representatives, 186
Quie, Halvor, 11
Quist, Allen, 187

radicalism: allied press, 109, 110–12, 126, 129, 130, 133; Duluth community, 120–22, 143; Floyd B. Olson, 146, 152, 153–55; Frihetsförbundet, 109; as reason for immigration, 106–8, 114–15, 127, 128; recruitment by terrorist organizations, 216–17; and temperance movement, 107; women in, 68. *See also* communism and Communist Party of the United States of America (CPUSA)
—Iron Range Finnish immigrants/Americans, 123; background to, 127–28; causes, 124–25, 129; CPUSA, 126, 130–32, 136–37; leaders, 130–33, 137–41
Ramsey, Alexander, 26
Rand, Lars M.: background, 202–3; death, 202; and immigrant solidarity, 204; nicknames, 201; on opening of Dania Hall, 207; and temperance movement, 203; use of Scandinavian background, 204; as Ward Six City Council representative and political boss, 201, 202, 203, 204–6
Red Star label, 136–37
"Red stores," 135

About the Author

Klas Bergman is a Swedish American journalist and author. Born and raised in Stockholm, he is a graduate of Stanford University and has lived and worked in the United States for almost four decades. A veteran journalist and foreign correspondent, he has reported for both Swedish and American news organizations and has also held numerous positions in international/public affairs. Bergman is the  author of two previous books, one on the former Yugoslavia and Eastern Europe, and the second a personal and political retrospective on his years in the United States. Bergman lives with his wife in Silver Spring, Maryland.

Scandinavians in the State House has been typeset in Arno Pro, a typeface designed by Robert Slimbach and named for the Florentine river that runs through Florence, a center of the Italian Renaissance. Arno is an old-style serif font, drawing inspiration from a variety of 15th- and 16th-century typefaces.

Book design by Wendy Holdman.